World Perspectives
in the Sociology
of the Military

World Perspectives in the Sociology of the Military

Edited by
George A. Kourvetaris
and Betty A. Dobratz

Transaction Books
New Brunswick, New Jersey

Library of Congress Catalog Number: 76-45941.
ISBN: 0-87855-207-3.
Printed in the United States of America.

Library of Congress Cataloging in Publication Data
Main entry under title:

World perspectives in the sociology of the military.
    Includes index.
    1. Sociology, Military.   I. Kourvetaris,
George A.   II. Dobratz, Betty A.
U21.5.W65   301.5'93   76-45941
ISBN 0-87855-207-3

Contents

v

General Introduction

World Perspectives in the Sociology of the Military is an anthology of research articles and essays that explore a number of old and new issues pertaining to the sociology of military institutions and civil-military relations in the 1970's. The editors wanted to present a sociological/political science framework by including articles and essays dealing with major conceptual, research/empirical, and methodological issues in the field of sociology of the military.

Specifically, the book is designed with three goals in mind. *First,* it provides a concise overview of the field within a sociological/political science framework and world perspective for more advanced undergraduate and graduate students and academics in the social sciences and humanities (i.e., history, political science, and sociology) and for non-academics (professional soldiers, diplomats, government officials, etc.) who are interested in military institutions and civil-military relations. To accomplish this goal, a general introduction of about forty pages presents an analysis of the present state and development of sociology of the military. It attempts to give an overview of the entire field and provides a frame of reference from which one can further explore more specific issues. *Second,* the book examines certain major issues of the internal dynamics of the military organization as these are reflected in a changing military organization in a world perspective, and *third,* it considers the interrelationship between social and political change and the military and the way the armed forces responds to and internalizes these changes.

The major parts of the anthology focus upon the concepts of Professional and Organizational Perspectives and Civil-Military Relations. While the perimeters of the sociology of the military are not well defined, the editors believe that the organizational and professional aspects and civil-military relations are the major subdivisions in this area. The individual authors in this volume address themselves to a number of more specific questions in the sociology of the military including the following:

(1) What changes in recruitment patterns are taking place in western and non-western officer corps?

(2a) Are organizational/technological changes and modernization compatible with the culture and ideology of the nation? (2b) What are the political implications of such changes? (2c) Does broadening the base of recruitment make the military more liberal or conservative politically?

(3a) What role does socialization play in maintaining the military organization? (3b) What role does it play in transmitting military values to its young cadets and officers? (3c) To what extent are these values internalized?

(4) How are professional integrity and effectiveness maintained in a civilianized military?

(5) In what ways is Lasswell's conception of the role of the military as managers of organized violence expanding?

(6a) What is the rationale for the military intervening in emerging nations? (6b) What are some of the recent developments in measuring military intervention across nations? (6c) Are political and military roles of the armed forces incompatible in developing countries?

While one finds a number of readers on military institutions, there are very few texts or anthologies organized within a sociological frame of reference. For example, there are a number of books on sociology of politics, sociology of religion, sociology of education, and the like but little on the sociology of the military. Most of the books available on military institutions are based on certain themes from conferences on armed forces and society, edited by a small group of people, and often printed by the same publisher. Our volume is an independent effort, with most of the articles having been published in the *Journal of Political and Military Sociology* during the last three years. This means that each article has been evaluated by three anonymous referees as well as by the editors. As editor and assistant editor of the *Journal of Political and Military Sociology,* an independent professional social science publication (founded in 1972 and commenced in Spring, 1973), we believe that we are in a unique position which facilitates our understanding of the trends in the field and the relevance of the articles to the development of sociology of the military.

An additional significant feature of the book is its comparative world perspective with articles on African, European, Middle-Eastern, Latin American, and United States militaries. This includes a section devoted to the methodological aspects of the measurement of military intervention in developing nations. In Part I on "The State and Development of Sociology of the Military," we provide an integrated overview and sociological framework for analyzing and critically assessing the field. This covers both research and teaching aspects; the latter usually is not considered by sociologists of the military. Certain constraints on the field and some suggestions and propositions concerning its development are also presented.

The other two major parts of the anthology contain sixteen articles concerned with professional/organizational questions and civil-military relations. These reflect some of the theoretical, empirical, and methodological issues raised in the first part.

In Part II "Professional and Organizational Perspectives," we have included articles on the internal dynamics of the military organization with a focus upon professionalism, politics, recruitment, and socialization. First, Larson provides an excellent discussion of two major interpretations of military professionalism and civil control: Huntington's politically neutral profession and Janowitz's politically sensitive profession. Larson prefers Janowitz's pragmatic professionalism for handling civil-military relations in the post Vietnam War period but warns that the military's overemphasis on political sensitivity and integration with society could undermine the professional integrity of the officer corps and encourage political activism.

In discussing career patterns and occupational structure, Lang notes that technological and organizational developments in the U.S. military have led to a shift away from combat orientations to "resource management." Tactical operations are declining in importance as an area of military expertise and the subsidiary specialties are growing, resulting in increased bureaucratization. The occupational structure of each service is viewed as dependent on the technological base, which is in turn related to the basic military mission. Lang notes some political implications of these trends.

While technological change has had important effects on the American military, Garnier warns against generalizing about the effects of technology on other militaries. Although both the U.S. and the British military organizations have experienced an increasing technological complexity in military equipment, he argues that changes in the technology can be mediated by cultural and organizational factors. Using data from participant observations at the Royal Military Academy, Sandhurst, Garnier finds that, unlike the U.S. military, traditional patterns and criteria of recruitment still exist in the highly technological British Army while they are disappearing in the U.S. Army.

Based on secondary analysis of data, Kourvetaris and Dobratz also address themselves to the issues of social recruitment and political orientation of officer corps in fourteen countries. They argue that the broadening of the social base of recruitment has not been followed by a concomitant process of political democratization of the officers' political attitudes and/or behavior.

Lucas tries to determine the nature and content of the military images important in the professional socialization of Army ROTC cadets. Heroic, managerial, and technical images are distinguished. The heroic (combat) image is clearest, and the others are vague and fundamentally civilian oriented. Differences in cadet images are not associated with differences in the domestic political values or professional military opinions. Since the large majority of ROTC cadets have vague and inconsistent images, Lucas suggests that the ROTC experience had minimal influence on the average cadet.

Likewise Cockerham's research on airborne paratroopers argues against the importance of the socialization process. Using interview data, he analyzes the context of airborne socialization in the U.S. as a status passage. He concludes that there is little or no significant changes in the men's attitudes or values and that heroic action oriented men self-select into the airborne in response to such inducements as self-identification with an elite unit, higher status and pay, and availability of action and challenge.

The last part on "Civil-Military Relations" contains sections on explanations of military intervention, national studies of civil-military relations, and methodological issues in the study of intervention. In the first section Ben Dor, Thompson, and McKown examine various structural and behavioristic explanations of military intervention in civil-military politics. Ben-Dor outlines a behaviorally oriented theoretical approach to the study of military intervention in the Middle East. On the basis of his concept of threat as an independent and intervening variable, he suggests physical force, internal structure of the military, civilian institutions, and government activity as plausible explanatory variables of military intervention in the Middle East.

Likewise, Thompson advances a synthetic approach for explaining Arab military coups along systemic and sub-systemic dimensions of military and civilian structures and regimes, i.e., regime vulnerability, military grievances, and external conditions. Using event data from a number of Sub-Saharan African nations, McKown suggests analyzing elite political behavior in order to explain the causes of coups d'etat. In particular she recommends further examination of the variables of elite cohesion and coercive ability and potential.

In the second section four national studies examine different dimensions of the civil-military interface. Two of these authors attempt to analyze particular countries by using conceptual models of civil-military relations. Segal *et al's* article explores the thesis of convergence and suggests that the emerging pattern for industrial nations of the West may be one of divergence. Convergence can be seen as making the military functionally more independent of its host society and therefore insulated from it.

Using Moskos' developmental construct of convergent, divergent and segmented patterns of civil-military relations, Kourvetaris attempts to trace the linkages between armed forces and society in the context of military role in Greek politics both in diachronic and synchronic terms. He argues that Moskos' model might be appropriate for modern Greek socio-political history. It is during the periods of convergence, especially at the ideological level among political and military elites, that the military does not actively engage in politics.

In contrast to Kourvetaris, Drury assesses the effectiveness of military rule during 1964-1970. He argues that the success of military rule in Brazil may be enhanced by factors such as the following: (1) Weak interest groups and associations which tend to be subservient to the state and provide ineffective opposition to military rule; (2) Fragmented boundaries of military institutions which enable officers to acquire extensive political and administrative experience; (3) Institutional pride of the armed forces; and (4) A generally accepted political doctrine through which the officer may gain civilian confidence to assume an expanded political role.

Herspring provides background information on socialist countries while considering the effect that an increasing reliance on modern technology has had on civil-military relations in East Germany. He examines the ways the Communist Party developed various mechanisms of political control and indoctrination to insure both political reliability and technical qualifications of its officer corps. While the military's technical officers often lack enthusiasm for political affairs, Herspring concludes that there is little danger the officer corps will oppose Party policies.

The final subsection deals with the often neglected area of the measurement of military intervention, one of the crucial dependent variables in civil-military relations. The need for indices of military intervention is particularly important when one is dealing with various countries and historical periods. Sigelman begins with an examination of five indicators of the extent of military intervention in politics and derives his own Military Intervention Index (MII) from them. He then uses his MII to test Feit's proposition that smaller armies are more likely than larger ones to intervene in the domestic political order in nations of the third world. The final article by Tannahill discusses another new operationalization of military intervention. An application of this new variable in the context of military intervention in Latin America is given.

World Perspectives in the Sociology of the Military

PART I
AN OVERVIEW OF SOCIOLOGY OF THE MILITARY

1

THE PRESENT STATE AND DEVELOPMENT
OF SOCIOLOGY OF THE MILITARY*

GEORGE A. KOURVETARIS

Northern Illinois University

BETTY A. DOBRATZ

University of Wisconsin, Madison

The present analysis is an account and assessment of the state of the field of sociology of the military in the 1970's. It entails an examination of the recent major academic publications, i.e., books, monographs, and articles written by students of military institutions. Initially, we consider the emergence of sociology of the military by exploring the antecedents, boundaries, and landmarks in the last 30 years or so. The present state of sociology of the military in its teaching and research dimensions is examined. A number of major concepts for research — profession (stressing models and socialization), organization (emphasizing recruitment), social disorganization/problems, civil-military relations (including models and typologies, causes and consequences of military intervention, and military industrial complex) — are analyzed in terms of theoretical, empirical, and methodological issues in the area of sociology of the military. In particular, some criticisms of the dominant structuralist orientation of the sociology of the military are given. An open systems approach to the study of the organization of the military is suggested. Also an eclectic model of the causes of military intervention is presented to provide a more comprehensive and synthetic explanation of this phenomenon. Finally, limitations and suggestions for further development of sociology of the military are offered.

This article attempts to give an account of the present status and development of the sociology of the military and the constraints on it. Although the study of the military as an institution overlaps with other subfields of social organization — political sociology, complex organizations, professions, and sociology of conflict to mention the most salient — this paper will consider the sociology of the military as a distinct subfield of sociology proper. Despite the recent notable increase of social science publications, the appearance of two journals, and the efforts of the Inter-University Seminar on

*The authors wish to thank the following individuals for their comments on an earlier version of the paper: Charles Moskos, Northwestern University; David Segal, University of Maryland; Arthur Larson, University of Wisconsin, Parkside; Frank Trager, New York University; Scott McNall, Arizona State University, the director Maurice Zeitlin and the members of the fall 1975 social organization colloquium of the University of Wisconsin, Madison. However, the usual caveat that the authors alone are responsible for the interpretations and analysis is especially relevant here.

Armed Forces and Society, we believe the sociology of the military still occupies a marginal and ambivalent position within academic sociology.

Since sociology of the military has not been able to establish a broad base of academic legitimacy and institutionalization, it has not provided young sociologists in the field a "frame of reference" similar to those provided in other more accepted and developed areas of sociology. This may be due in part to the anti-military liberal academic environment and to the semi-closed nature of the military. The latter may tend to hinder critical sociological analysis.

We used both qualitative and quantitative sources of information to give an overall assessment of the field in the 1970's. While an attempt was made to cover the recent major sociological and political science publications, little or no effort was made to look into the in-house publications of the military (including military professional journals) or into the vast literature written by non-academics and fiction writers. To supplement the analysis, we used responses to an open-ended mailed questionnaire.[1]

Initially, we trace briefly the emergence of sociology of the military by noting its context, major landmarks, and protagonists. Secondly, we give an overview of the present academic status of the field. Thirdly, we examine the present research status and certain major works. This section constitutes the main thrust of the paper. Finally, we suggest some tentative propositions concerning the further development of the field and existing constraints.

EMERGENCE OF SOCIOLOGY OF THE MILITARY

While the study of military institutions and war has been the major pre-occupation of historians, philosophers, and poets for centuries, the sociological study of the military has been a rather recent phenomenon. The early literature tangentially related to the sociology of the military is the work of European proto-sociologists and social philosophers. However, as a field of study it commenced during World War II and initially it followed a more applied social science orientation. Due to the national mobilization during the war, draftees encountered serious problems of morale, motivation, and adjustment to the military way of life. The Troop Research Program of the U.S. army, which employed a number of outstanding sociologists and social psychologists during the war, tried to solve some of these social psychological problems. The proposed solutions helped to improve the efficiency of the military establishment (Roucek, 1962). Because of this early applied social psychological orientation, the broader theoretical, structural, and organizational issues were neglected (Walter, 1958; Janowitz, 1971b).

As in other subfields of social organization, the area of sociology of the military has not been clearly demarcated. However, two major perspectives have been identified: 1) Students use the insights and findings of sociology and other social sciences to increase the efficiency and effectiveness of the military

---

1. We mailed the open-ended questionnaires to a selective sample drawn from the following sources: 1) ASA Directory, 2) *Journal of Political and Military Sociology* subscribers, 3) Inter-University Seminar on Armed Forces and Society fellows. The responses from 65 completed questionnaires were used to provide some additional information for this analysis.

organization; 2) Others study the military as a major social institution having wide societal and political ramifications. These groups need not be mutually exclusive.

Illustrating the former view, Hutchinson (1957) argues that the ideological trait of the military sociologist is his commitment to the proposition that the application of sociological knowledge and research methods will increase the military effectiveness of the organization for which he works. Similarly, Bowers (1967) found an upward trend in the military's use of sociology although the slope of this trend depends on how many jobs are established for sociologists and whether they are willing and qualified to fill them.

While sociological research on the military has focused on organizational and institutional aspects of the armed forces rather than on war itself (Walter, 1958; Coates and Pellegrin, 1965), the sociology of the military is not limited to the study of military institutions, nor are military institutions studied only by sociologists (Millett, 1974). One can distinguish two broad types of analysis. First, a more universalistic approach in which common uniformities and patterns are stressed, and second, a more particularistic one in which military organizations are analyzed as national units reflecting political, cultural, and historical influences. Janowitz (1971b) refers to these as "organizational analysis" and "armed forces and society" respectively. Indeed, these approaches can be traced to the old European debate between nomothetic versus idiographic modes of analysis which in its more modern version has become the issue of structural vs. cultural and/or uniformity vs. diversity in sociological analysis.

Building on Lasswell's definition of the military institution as one dealing primarily with the management of the organized means of violence and warfare, Lang places the field of the sociology of the military within a more inclusive framework of the sociology of conflict within and across national societies and cultures. The fact that the military utilizes massive socio-political and economic resources to carry out national objectives makes it a major societal force requiring extensive sociological analysis. Lang sees the field of the sociology of the military as the study of the more permanent structural elements of the military system which are indispensable to the conduct of organized activities related to war and warfare. He identifies five major areas in this field: the profession of arms, military organizations, military system, civil-military relations, and war and warfare.

In general, the bulk of the recent studies deal with civil-military relations, organization and/or structure including bureaucratic aspects, and primary group relations (military roles, effectiveness, etc.). Studies of social origins and demographic character of armies and the officer corps as a profession have also been important (Stauss, 1971; Millett, 1974). The study of war tends more and more to be considered within the areas of conflict resolution and peace research (Millett, 1974).

Some Major Developments in Sociology of the Military. It seems to us that the first major work in sociology of the military was a result of the studies conducted in social psychology and sociology throughout WWII both in the U.S. and abroad. *The American Soldier* by Samuel Stouffer and associates analyzed many aspects of the adjustment to army life and the reaction to combat, job assignment and satisfaction, leadership, promotions, and Black troops. One of its major shortcomings was the emphasis on the attitudinal and behaviorial aspects of the soldiers rather than on the organizational aspects of the military system. *Continuities in Social Research: Studies in the Scope and Method of the American Soldier* edited by Merton and Lazarsfeld (1950) discussed the theoretical and methodological implications of the findings in *The American Soldier,* including those regarding primary groups, relative deprivation and reference group theory, and applied research. After the war, sociologists who served in the military or were involved in the research described their experiences and their views of military organization, including the bureaucratic aspects, stratification patterns, and authoritative methods of social control. In 1946 the *American Journal of Sociology* published a special issue entitled *Human Behavior in Military Society* which contained articles on these topics.

Although in the area of political science, Huntington's *The Soldier and the State* (1957) provided the first major treatment of civil-military relations as a separate and distinct category of political phenomena within a historical framework. In 1960 Janowitz contributed *The Professional Soldier* which provided a social and political profile and described the professional life, organizational setting, and the leadership of the American military as they developed during the first half of the century. Quite recently Moskos' *The American Enlisted Man* (1970) provided the first concise and comprehensive study of the rank and file in the American military since WWII. Moskos managed in a fairly compact volume to utilize a broader sociological analysis of the organizational and institutional aspects of armed forces and society than did the authors of *The American Soldier.* Other major works include Andreski's *Military Organization and Society* (1968) and Speier's *Social Order and the Risks of War* (1952). The former utilizes a comparative and macrosociological approach to the study of military and society while the latter contains a variety of articles related to the sociology of the military.

Under the chairmanship of Morris Janowitz the Inter-University Seminar on Armed Forces and Society (IUS) was founded in 1961 with the assistance of the Russell Sage Foundation. The IUS has served as a focal point for social scientists concerned with research on the armed forces, peace keeping, and arms control. In addition to various seminars and conferences, the IUS has sponsored various collections of essays in edited anthologies.[2] Slater (1972:6) has noted that many of the IUS sponsored essays, especially those dealing with organizational characteristics of the military, emphasize the improvement of efficiency, morale, attractiveness, and legitimacy of the military or a "blandly uncritical, problem-solving approach." Segal (1973:773) in his review of two of these edited volumes states that they show how far the field of sociology of the military has progressed since 1961, but more importantly they indicate how far the field must still go to develop the kind of

---

2. These include *The New Military* edited by Janowitz (1964), *Armed Forces and Society* and *Military Professions and Military Regimes* edited by Van Doorn (1968 and 1969), *The Handbook of Military Institutions* edited by Little (1971), *Public Opinion and the Military Establishment* edited by Moskos (1971), *The Military Industrial Complex* edited by Sarkesian (1972), *Military Rule in Latin America* edited by Schmitter (1973) and *Political Military Systems* edited by Kelleher (1974).

empirical base that characterizes more traditional areas of sociology. A number of writings have also appeared in various journals including recent special issues of the *Pacific Sociological Review* (April, 1973) and *Annals of American Academy of Political and Social Science* (March, 1973), and two new journals — *Journal of Political and Military Sociology* (Spring, 1973) and *Armed Forces and Society* (Fall, 1974) — have been initiated.

The results of our survey which asked what were the most important contributions to the advancement of sociology of the military tend to support our identification of the major works. Janowitz' book *The Professional Soldier* was mentioned most frequently followed by *The Soldier and the State. The American Enlisted Man* and *The American Soldier* were also cited with no other book appearing more than three times. The *Journal of Political and Military Sociology, Armed Forces and Society,* and Sage Publications (sponsored by IUS) were also listed.

While certain developments have been noted, there is also evidence to support our contention that sociology of the military has not as yet achieved academic respectability and recognition as a viable subfield of sociology. For example, according to ASA directories, 54 of 8,530 persons in 1970 named military sociology as one of their two major areas of competence while 61 of 7,590 in 1973-74 and 64 of 8,915 in 1975-76 listed it, making it one of the smallest subfields in sociology. However, since persons can list only two subfields, some of those interested in the study of the military may have selected other broader areas of competence, e.g., political sociology. A 1974 survey (Jones and Kronus, 1975) of a random sample of Full, Associate, and foreign members of the ASA asked them to indicate three fields of increasing and three of decreasing importance in sociology. One hundred twenty people (27%) were negative, only 3 (1%) were positive, and 322 (72%) were neutral toward sociology of the military. Of the 36 subfields, only rural sociology had a more negative rating.

TEACHING OF SOCIOLOGY OF THE MILITARY

More than a decade ago Roucek (1962) noted that sociology of the military was relatively unknown and ignored in terms of regular courses and textbooks in universities. The same is still true today.[3] While it is difficult to determine the exact number of sociology of the military courses, two surveys (1972 and 1974) of national security studies were conducted by the New York University National Security Education Program (1975).[4] The surveys found 9 undergraduate and 3 graduate courses in sociology of the military in 1972 and 13 undergraduate and 6 graduate courses in 1974. *The Guides to Graduate Departments of Sociology* published by the ASA indicate the limited number of schools where sociology of the military was an area of specialization for graduate students. In 1969 only one of the 169 departments listed sociology of the military, but in 1970 4 schools named it. The 1971-72 guide showed four schools claiming sociology of the military as an area of emphasis and 11 others

---

3. Jacobs (1972) found the mention of war infrequent and superficial in 31 widely used introductory tests.

4. In the first survey 473 of 728 questionnaires were returned while 776 of 1415 were analyzed in 1974. In 1972 there were 330 national security courses in 226 schools. In 1974 there were 479 courses in 335 schools.

said it was possible for a graduate student to specialize in it; in 1972-73 there was a slight decline with 3 and 9 departments respectively. In 1974 only 6 schools of 215 listed it and in 1975 9 of 216 did likewise.

The results from our survey suggest that sociology of the military may be taught more often than indicated in the graduate guide, but it is still quite limited. When asked if their department or university had offered a course in the last 3 years in sociology of the military, 20 of the 65 respondents said yes. Typically the courses were offered every other year but 5 were given every other semester. Fourteen persons indicated they themselves taught a sociology of the military course. When the universities were named, 3 appeared twice and 4 of the others were military academies or schools. Topics covered most often in the sociology of the military courses were the military as an organization/institution/system and its relation to and impact upon other institutions. Civil-military relations were often mentioned but specific reference to military-industrial complex was given only twice and to coups and revolution only once. Other major concepts were professionalism, career contingencies, and manpower recruitment.

At the military academies and colleges for advanced military officers the rubric sociology of the military is not officially utilized and sociology departments do not exist.[5] Thus sociology of the military is marginal within the military as well as in the universities.[6] The orientation at the U.S. Military Academy seems to be more psychological than sociological, but the latter portion of a Leadership course considers the interface between society and the military, stressing societal effects on the leadership process. The political science department of the U.S. Naval Academy offers a civil-military relations course, and others such as politics of developing areas have material related to sociology of the military. The Air Force Academy has an interdisciplinary seminar entitled The Military in Evolving Society which included such topics as the military mind, professionalism and the military ethos; war, politics and the professional soldier; and the military-industrial-congressional-academic complex. The National War College focuses on national security policy and area studies courses while the Naval War College has a Defense Decision-Making course. The more extensive curriculum catalogs received from the U.S. Army War College and Air University (Air Command and Staff College, Air War College, and Squadron Officer School) indicate a wide variety of courses related to sociology of the military. They consider such topics as command, management, organization, and strategy as well as regional studies including

5. We wish to thank Dr. G. Pope Atkins of the U.S. Naval Academy, Lt. Colonel John D. George, Jr. of the U.S. Military Academy, Captain E.C. Kenyon of the Naval War College, Colonel F. Loye, Jr. of the Air University, Lt. Colonel Franklin D. Margiotta of Air Command and Staff College, Colonel Donald T. Nelson, Jr. of the National War College, and Colonel John W. Williams of the U.S. Air Force Academy for taking time to reply to our requests concerning courses related to military sociology at the aforementioned schools.

6. According to Dr. David Segal, former chief, Social Processes Technical Area, U.S. Army Research Institute for the Behavioral and Social Sciences there are 10 sociologists in research positions in the US Army (9 more than 2 years ago), but only one in the Air Force and one in the Navy. The Army does seem to be sending more officers to graduate school for M.A.'s in sociology (personal correspondence, July 9, 1975).

the role of the military. Air Command and Staff College offered courses in The Military Institution in American Society and the New Military: Air Force Generals in the 1980's.

In our survey 35 persons who did *not* teach sociology of the military on a regular basis indicated that they did teach a course related to it. Most frequently noted courses dealt with leadership, organization of the military, national security, and civil-military relations; a number of references suggested an international focus (foreign policy, comparative politics) or the study of developing nations. Social control, military psychology, professionalism, military and economy were others mentioned more than twice. Twenty-three persons also indicated that their universities offered courses other than the ones they taught. The topics were similar to the above, but political sociology was named more frequently.

Thus while sociology of the military may not be offered, other courses related to it are taught relatively often. We might suggest that while broad and inter-disciplinary perspectives are quite valuable to sociology, the overall effect for the development of sociology of the military *per se* may be deleterious. Since military topics can be easily subsumed under other courses, the specific emphasis and specialization on sociology of the military is weakened.

STATE OF RESEARCH OF SOCIOLOGY OF THE MILITARY

While the state of research of sociology of the military is more advanced than its teaching aspects, it still lags behind other fields both in quantity and quality. A survey of 3 issues of *Sociological Abstracts* in the mid 1950's indicated that about 3% of the items included could be classified as military sociology (Walter, 1958). It was not until 1961 that military sociology appeared in the table of contents of the abstracts. Stauss (1971) found that nearly half of the abstracted articles were written by authors from foreign countries; this has reduced the number of articles available to American sociologists. The largest content category of military sociology that he identified was political. (This often included articles on policy, government relations, etc., and the articles there were difficult to distinguish from those under the topic of political sociology.) Organizational aspects, attitudes and technology within the military system were also frequent topics. In comparison with 5 other sub-areas Stauss randomly selected from the abstracts, military sociology was 2 to 5 times less represented than the other areas.

Regarding the general quality of articles, it might be pointed out that the two major sociology journals — *American Sociological Review (ASR)* and *American Journal of Sociology (AJS)* — have not devoted much space to sociology of the military. Table 1 shows the findings of our survey of the indices of these journals from their beginning to 1970. It reveals that the bulk of the writings on the military and on war occurred during and shortly after World War II. In 1946 *AJS* published a special issue entitled Human Behavior in Military Society. The *ASR* indices included military sociology, selective service, and veterans (21, 5, and 2 articles respectively). Our examination of ASR from 1971-74 revealed 3 more articles — one on the Greek military (Kourvetaris, 1971a), and two on veteran status and civilian incomes (Browning, et al., 1973; Cutright, 1974). *AJS* followed a somewhat related pattern but with a more dramatic increase during the 1970's. Through 1970 there were 39 different articles indexed under the topics military, military institution, militarism and soldiers. One encouraging sign is that 9 articles and several comments appeared in *AJS* from 1971 to 1974 including the topics of military-industrial complex, military organizations, black veterans, air-force socialization, women in the service, military spending, coup d'etats and authoritarian attitudes. As also shown in table 1, these journals have not recently published much on the topic of war.

A question concerning the present interests of the respondents and 2 other questions regarding contemporary and future topics/issues in the sociology of the military were asked in our survey. Civil-military relations as a broad category was considered most important with an emphasis on military-industrial-governmental complex and military spending, military in politics, and civilian control of the military. Professionalism ranked second in frequency but the enlisted man was seldom mentioned. Organizational topics (e.g., latent functions, impact of military on society, stratification, bureaucratization) occurred more than did socio-psychological ones (e.g., morale, cohesion, and combat motivation). Social disorganization or problem-oriented research was frequently mentioned with race relations most often included, but drugs, veterans, arms control, subversive activities, aggression, and conflict were also important. Methodological issues including the need for historical and broad comparative perspectives as well as the opening of the military to independent research were important future considerations. Recruitment was not considered important for future research although the all-volunteer force was mentioned a few times.

We realize that there are many ways to organize an analysis of a subfield of sociology. Since the boundaries and topics of the field of sociology of the military are still loosely defined, we believe that a comprehensive overview of

TABLE 1.   ARTICLES ON WAR AND MILITARY TOPICS IN ASR & AJS[*]

TOPICS	YEARS					
	1895–1935	1936–1945	1946–1955	1956–1965	1966–1970	1971–1974
War Related						
AJS	23	26	4	2	0	2
ASR	–	25	13	2	0	0
Military Related						
AJS	4	6	26	1	2	9
ASR	–	8	15	5	0	3

[*]Based on examination of journal indices through 1970 and authors' analysis of content from 1971–1974.

the entire field is not feasible within the scope of an article. Without attempting to make any premature closure on the topics that can be covered, we will be guided by the emphasis in the literature of the last decade and focus our discussion upon the specific concepts of profession, organization, disorganization, and civil-military relations.

Our classification is somewhat similar to that used in Lang's survey of military institutions and the sociology of war. We collapsed his topics of military systems and organization into the category of organization but added the category of social disorganization to our analysis. We do not consider the extensive literature on peace and war because we like Millett (1974) feel it is best analyzed under the rubrics of conflict resolution and peace research.

Some support for our classification can also be derived from the responses to our survey. In our query asking what the persons thought when they heard the term military sociology, the responses were grouped into similar categories with the most frequent being the establishment, systems, structure, institution set followed by civil-military, intervention, modernization; organization; profession, elite; small and primary group and socialization; peace and war; and military-industrial complex in that order. Most respondents perceive sociology of the military in rather itemized conventional terms or concepts which are often used in other areas of social organization as well.

A. PROFESSION

While the literature on the military as a profession covers many issues, we will concentrate upon some of the professional models that have been developed and the self-selection versus socialization debate. The role of the military profession in the post-Vietnam era has become an issue of debate between academics, professional officers, and policymakers. Although no major conceptual breakthroughs can be detected in the last 5 years or so, a new awareness and urgency to redefine the role expansion of the professional soldier is evident. Assuming the existence of the officer corps as a profession, one can identify 3 major conceptual models of the military profession somewhat analogous to civilian professions. These are the structuralist, the processual, and the pluralist.

The Structuralist Model. Huntington (1957) and Janowitz (1960) are the foremost representatives of this model which is also known as the attribute approach. The structuralists view professions in general and the military in particular as possessing certain "core attributes" that differentiate them from all other occupations. There is, however, no consensus among the structuralists as to what these attributes are. Huntington (1957) has noted 3 major characteristics of the military: expertise, responsibility, and corporateness. While Janowitz (1960, 1971) lists characteristics that make the military a profession — expertise, long period of education, group identity, ethics, standards of performance — he also tends to see the military as an organization changing over time.

While both scholars also accept the functional necessity of the military, they differ sharply as to its role in civilian politics. Huntington calls for a politically neutral military profession isolated from society and concerned with the efficient achievement of victory without regard to non-military issues.

This leads to an objective control of the military by civilian authority. Janowitz advocates a more pragmatic military professionalism which is responsive to civil control through law, tradition, and an acceptance of civil values and institutions; this results in a more subjective control of the military. Larson (1974) notes that Janowitz does not explicitly define the boundaries of military professionalism, explain how the military will retain its uniqueness under pressure to civilianize, or explain how it will maintain both expertise and detachment in the face of political pressures.

Both Huntington's and Janowitz's interpretations have influenced the thinking and role expansion of the military profession in the 1970's. While the structuralist model has achieved rather wide acceptance as in some other fields of sociology, it has been criticized as the least useful approach because its emphasis is on the product rather than on the process of professionalization (Vollmer and Mills, 1966).

The Processual Model. This is also known as the historical or developmental approach for it indicates how professions emerge, how they undergo a process of professionalization, and how they are legitimized in society. It stresses the process rather than the product. In its incipient stage this model for civilian professions was usually associated with the University of Chicago. More recently, however, a number of scholars (Wilensky, 1964; Vollmer and Mills, 1966; Abrahamsson, 1972; Van Doorn, 1965, Feld, 1975) have identified the civilian or military processes of professionalization. Abrahamsson (1972) distinguishes two subprocesses of military professionalization: on the one hand the term refers to the historical transformation, technological, economic, and social forces which determine internal organization and recruitment of the military, and on the other hand it refers to the processes of professional socialization of its officers.

Van Doorn (1965) also traces the processes of professionalization of the officer corps which he describes as a fusion of profession and organization. The author argues professionalization of the military followed a different sequence from that of most other professions: first commission, monopoly, a high social status and a code of ethics; then the establishment of training schools; finally the creation of professional associations which played only a minor role. The processual model is a more realistic approach to military professionalism because it depicts the military profession as both dynamic and reflecting societal change.

The Pluralistic Model. Known also as the segmented model, it has mainly been suggested by Moskos (1973) and a number of young professional officers (Hauser and Bradford, 1971; Hauser, 1973; Bradford and Brown, 1973; Jordan and Taylor, 1973; Deagle, 1973; Taylor and Bletz, 1974). Essentially the pluralistic model is a fusionist model reflecting both civilianized and traditional military professionalism. Larson (1974) sees the pluralistic model as an attempt to bridge the two positions represented by Huntington (1957) and Janowitz (1960). Larson is very critical of it because he feels it will destroy the unity and effectiveness of the military profession.

Furthermore, this model is a product of the post-Vietnam era. It calls for role expansion and redefinition of the military profession. It seems to us that the pluralists view the military profession as reflecting some of the conflicting views: specialist vs. generalist, ideal vs. actual, political vs. non-political, professional vs. bureaucratic, command vs. management, and heroic vs. managerial/technocratic. Some of these issues are also present in civilian professions. Hauser and Bradford (1971) and Hauser (1973) advocate a bifurcation of the U.S. army officer corps along heroic vs. managerial dimensions. They are critical of the "generalist" and "command" ideals and suggest that a new multiple and alternative system of career development be initiated by the services which identifies those who will become commanders, specialists, managers, or generalists early in their careers and rewards them equitably. Jordan and Taylor (1973) find the Lasswellian formulation of the military profession as the "managers of the organized means of violence" no longer adequate. The roles of deterrence, peacekeeping, and advisory roles of "civic action" and "pacification support" should also be added. (See, for example, Moskos, 1976 which deals with some of these issues especially the peace-keeping role of the United Nations in Cyprus.)

Taylor and Bletz (1974) argue for a new policy in which officer graduate education at civilian universities should be a prerequisite for promotion above the military middle management level. Margiotta (1974), commenting on Taylor and Bletz's article, questions the logic of this policy and the belief that a civilian graduate degree is a panacea to internal problems and effective leadership of the new military. Sarkesian (1972a) calls for an expansion of military professional roles to include political skills because of the changing political environment at home and abroad. While such political skills and orientations have already been present in a number of officer corps throughout the world, the increased political exposure of the military may compromise the professional standards and integrity of the professional officer.

We believe that the pluralistic model is simply a metaphor for social consensus and unity within diversity which is part of the more inclusive pluralist ideology in political sociology. We think that such a perspective may be more of a "minority utopia" position within the military profession, and it does not necessarily reflect the dominant thinking of the military establishment and the power structure in American society. While the pluralistic model is an effort to give the military profession more balance, it is still within the structuralist tradition in academic sociology.

A schematic representation of the 3 models of military professionalism and political perspectives is given in table 2. While the processual model considers change, we believe they all place a greater emphasis on social order and consensus than on conflict and change. There is a conspicuous absence of serious studies of consensus-projecting conflict of the armed forces and society where conflict transcends the existing institutional order and is viewed as disruptive and undesirable (e.g., Veterans Against the War).

One can speak of 2 continua of professions, *one,* an organizational-professional continuum (exemplified by the process of professionalization), and *two,* an individual professional continuum expressed through an ideology of professionalism. Most studies on military professionalism fail to identify and measure adequately both dimensions of the military professional model. Yet if individual officers strongly disagree with the formal policies of the military establishment, especially those aspects pertaining to their professional roles and values, the 2 continua will not be symmetrical possibly resulting in conflict within the profession as well as for the individual officer.

TABLE 2. PATTERNS OF PROFESSIONAL MILITARY CAREERS AND POLITICS

POLITICAL ORIENTATIONS FOR OFFICERS	STRUCTURALIST	PROCESSUAL	PLURALISTIC
A balanced view of civil-military issues (civilianized traditional, segmented)			Taylor & Bletz, 1974; Hauser & Bradford, 1971; Moskos, 1973; Jordon, 1971; Deagle, 1973
Politically Sensitive (The Citizen Soldier) Constabulary Concept	Janowitz, 1969 and 1971; Larson, 1974		
Politically Neutral (Socially Detached Soldier)	Huntington, 1957 & 1968		
Politically Independent & Powerful (Interest Group Theory)		Feld, 1975; Van Doorn, 1965 & 1970; Abrahamsson, 1972	

Since the military does not compete for clients in a civilian sense but is the client of the state, it has derived a sort of "ascriptive professionalism" and "surrogate authority" (Feld, 1968) from the state and thus is low on autonomy. The fact that the military is low on autonomy — the most important structural and attitudinal dimension of professions in general — has not been adequately considered. The issue of whether the military is more of a semi-profession than a profession should be seriously investigated. We believe that the military profession is more than a profession in the civilian sense of the term. It has both a military and civilian component.

Professional Socialization. The major debate in professional socialization concerns whether self-selection by the individual or the socialization process is more important in shaping the professional attitudes and behavior of the officer. In other words, which is more influential, the matrix of social experience and personality development prior to entering the military or the transmitting of technical knowledge and the inculcating of military values and outlooks during the training process? During the last 10 years self-selection has received more support than the socialization hypothesis, but the majority of the data are based on cross-sectional rather than longitudinal studies.

Lovell (1964) finds "relative" stability of professional orientations and strategic perspectives among the West Point cadets, but important changes occurred in certain specific attitudes requiring conformity and closely related to common experiences and career interests of the cadets. Radway (1971), looking at recent academy trends, concludes that young men who entered the academy had a special capacity to be undaunted by the prevailing surge of anti-militarism. Likewise Karsten (1971) favors the self-selection concept and refers to the socialization process as the impotence of militarization. In contrast, Galloway and Johnson (1973) and to some extent Ellis and Moore (1974) support the socialization hypothesis.

Some studies on the ROTC support Lovell's original contention of lack of change (Lucas, 1971, 1973; Malbin, 1971; Goertzel and Hengst, 1971). Lucas used the term *anticipatory* socialization to refer to the complex process in which individuals mediate social images and change their values to make them consistent with the norms of the group they anticipate joining (e.g. the military).

Wamsley (1972) suggests that much of the work on socialization has been limited because it singled out only a few values or attitudes believed to be associated with socialization. To him such fundamental traits as acceptance of all-pervasive hierarchy and deference patterns, emphasis on honor, integrity, etc. are introduced early in the career and are more fundamental than what Lucas and Lovell looked for. Using participant observation, he tests the *subculture hypothesis* which stresses the divergence of the military from civilian institutions. The teaching/training procedures of the Aviation cadet Pre-Flight Training School and the more recent Officer Training School are compared. While Wamsley feels that the socialization effects are apparent in the former which emphasized combat and heroic qualities, the low key and subtle socialization of the latter lead him to recommend a more powerful method (not specified) to evaluate such behavior and value change.

Using participant observation and interviewing, Cockerham (1973) finds *selective socialization* for airborne training although a number of values in the Parachutist's Creed corresponded to those mentioned by Wamsley. It was action-oriented individuals who select the airborne due to such inducements as self-identification with an elite unit, higher status and pay, and the presence of action and challenge. They indicated no significance changes in attitudes and values.

Overall the trend supports the hypothesis that there are no significant changes in major attitudes of the future officer during the socialization process. The findings are still inconclusive however because certain issues have not been resolved. Perhaps the fundamental one is the lack of longitudinal data. We need to go beyond comparing semantic differential scores of different classes of cadets or relying on recall of interviewees to evaluate change. Another question concerns the basic attitudes to be measured and the method of measuring the change. Lovell (1973) criticized Wamsley for failing to separate the surface manifestations of conformity that coincide with organizational demands from the internalization of organizational norms. Various methods and measurement techniques need to be used on different populations, though as Wamsley (1973) noted, it may be questionable to characterize the ROTC as a socialization institution in the same sense as the service academies and Pre-Flight. More rigorous sociological work in this area is needed.

B. ORGANIZATION

Initially the study of complex organizations can be traced back to the writings of the scientific management and human relations schools. In line with these traditions, the early literature on the military organization focused on primary group behavior and morale while trying to make the military more effective and efficient. More recently, the publications on complex organizations including the military have followed the structural approach.

On the issue of structural divergence/convergence of the military with civilian society the trend has been toward narrowing the differences between military and civilian organizations, although a total convergence cannot be achieved. To Janowitz (1971b) this convergence is partially due to continuous technological change leading to larger militaries, greater interdependence with society, and changes in the internal social structure. However, Segal, *et. al.* (1974) assert that convergence may make the military functionally independent of its host society and insulated from it, while the enforcement of military definitions of the armed services pressures them to maintain open boundaries and enter into exchange relationships with the society. More specifically, structural convergence is negatively correlated with the interdependence of these institutions. The importance of specifying which structures in society the military is supposed to be converging with is also noted.

While Moskos (1973c) sees the theme of convergence in the major studies of the military profession, he argues that work on the enlisted man stresses the divergence between military and civilian structures. Utilizing the topics of combat motivation, troop dissent, enlisted culture, race relations, and organizational change, he traces the divergent and convergent tendencies of the last 3 decades for the rank and file serviceman.

For reasons of parsimony and for the purpose of this analysis, first we look into the topic of recruitment which seems to be one of the major issues in the all-volunteer army. We examine the notion of the all-volunteer army and long term recruitment trends and other work related to social origins. Then we discuss additional studies related to the recruitment process and why men join the military. Finally we briefly consider other topics under the social-psychological and complex organization headings.

Recruitment. The recruitment process is of fundamental importance because it provides the means to replenish and revitalize the organization. The types of people recruited for the elite positions (officer corps) and those recruited for the enlisted ranks provide information on the social composition of the armed forces, including its internal ranking and its relationship to the societal stratification system at large.

While the American literature of the late 1960's and early 1970's focused on the draft or selective service system and its inequities (Kaufman, 1968; Reisner, 1968; Davis and Dolbeare, 1968; Evans, 1969; Tothe, 1971; Miller and Tollison, 1971; Blum, 1972), most recently the major issue has been the problematic nature of recruitment in the all-volunteer army in the U.S. Janowitz (1971a, 1972, 1973) argues that recruiting of such a force will make the military a more self-contained unit due to increased self-recruitment of officers and decline in ROTC, National Guard, and reserve enrollments. Revisions in rotation, tenure, discipline, and justice systems, consolidation of in-service schools, more emphasis on officer candidate schools, and more meaningful job assignments are recommended for a viable all-volunteer force. Another important issue is whether in the post-Vietnam military, resignations of younger officers will continue.

Women are increasingly admitted to the all-volunteer force — now even to the traditionally all male service academies, though they are still excluded by law from combat positions. Goldman (1973a and b) points out that while the ratio of women to men is low, the ratio of officers to enlisted is much higher for women than for men. She felt that women who volunteered for military service generally accepted the existing authority structure, the internal values of the military, and certain job inequalities although desiring a wider range of job assignments. More and more, however, women are striving for greater job equality.

At the enlisted level the goal is to recruit men with high school education, but the basic source will be from low and moderate income social classes including more blacks in all branches but especially in combat (Moskos, 1973b; Janowitz, 1973). At present blacks are overrepresented at the enlisted level but underrepresented among officers. Means for more balanced recruitment with less emphasis on "monetary" incentives and more emphasis on attracting people oriented toward post high school educations have been suggested (Johnston and Bachman, 1972; Janowitz and Moskos, 1974). While Moskos and Janowitz argued for a more balanced recruitment based on various kinds of incentives, they did not adequately consider the consequences of the high prevailing rates of unemployment for recruitment patterns.

While the long term trend has been toward broadening the social base in officer recruitment, a more recent reversal and narrowing of the base in the U.S. has been noted by Moskos (1971b) and Janowitz (1971a). Kourvetaris and Dobratz (1973a & b) suggested that this reversal may also be true in Western European officer corps. Van Doorn (1975) discusses the decline of the "mass army" which is related to the adoption of all-volunteer forces in Western nations. This may result in a decline in social representativeness and an increase in conservative outlook in the armed forces.

Social origins and recruitment patterns have often been used as explanatory variables in the study of military organizations. In their comparative study Kourvetaris and Dobratz (1973 a & b) find that the broadening of social base of recruitment is not associated with democratization of the officers' political attitudes and behaviors. Abrahamsson (1972) concludes that the prediction of military political behavior profits little from studies of social origins although he adds that the less the degree of professionalization of the officer corps, the more one would expect ascriptive criteria to provide clues to political behavior. Garnier (1972) finds that changes in British recruitment are not related to ideological changes in the academy. Kourvetaris' (1976) examination of the recruitment processes of Greek service academies shows it did not follow the Western European patterns. Shifts in military and national objectives and values precede changes in strategies and patterns of recruitment in the Greek academies.

The use of social origin variables to analyze recruitment and predict sociopolitical phenomena may be on the decline. More attention should be directed to the military's relation to the national and international system, the processes of political, military and ideological recruitment, and a broader examination of demographic, physical/mental, sociopsychological, historical, cultural, and structural influences upon the candidate's choice and upon the military's criteria for selection. While a limited number of such studies have been conducted in this area, more are needed. Johnson and Bachman (1972) use data from a nationwide panel study of youths to predict enlistment behavior. While it is the only longitudinal national study of American enlistment behavior, it is based on data collected prior to the all-volunteer forces, and it is therefore uncertain whether its findings apply to a non-draft situation.

White (1972) reports data on motivations for joining the British army, including lack of other suitable jobs, learning a trade, and interest in helping people. He also examines the restructuring of the military and the activities of the recruitment centers. Sperber (1970) discusses the U.S. military's use of "non-violent co-optation" to maintain the "corporate liberal welfare-capitalist state." His examination of military recruiting literature showed the different inducements for enlisting, including appeals to women, intellectuals, minorities, working class youth and their masculinity, patriotism, desire to travel, and professionalism. More thorough consideration of motivations for enlisting and of the socialization/indoctrination processes of the enlisted man is required for a better understanding of the processes of recruitment and reward.

Socio-psychological Studies. One of the major concepts analyzed under this rubric has been authoritariansim. Studying a sample of 128 officers at the Naval War College, Brewer (1975) finds that authoritarianism was negatively related to arms control support but positively related to development of strategic weapons, conflict and aggressive images of international politics, and anti-communist objectives. He calls for more research on the sources of authoritarianism and on the explanatory potential of non-rational personality variables in the analysis of officers' orientations and behavior. At the enlisted level, Roghmann and Sodeur (1972) conducted a panel study of 12 companies of the West German army from basic training to just before discharge. The prolonged military experience was found to reduce authoritarianism of draftees. (See Campbell and McCormick, 1957 for similar U.S findings.) This decline in authoritarianism was attributed to "relative deprivation" and "situational factors" rather than the long term influences of childhood experience, social class, aging, or education. The deprivation increases the sensitivity of soldiers and leads to increased respect and tolerance for fellow citizens. Alternatively Stinchcombe (1973) suggests that the somewhat forced solidarity of an originally diverse group of conscripts resulted in increased tolerance of differences. More research is needed in order to integrate the findings on authoritarianism into broader sociological and socio-psychological theories.

Moskos' (1970) analysis of the American enlisted man finds the primary group concept inadequate for explaining combat motivation of soldiers in Vietnam. Instead he proposes the concepts of "latent ideology," "anti-ideology," and the "life chances" or "situational" approach stressing pragmatic responses of soldiers fighting for their own survival. The soldier's individualistic view of the war according to Moskos is manifested in his skepticism of ideological appeals and his underlying belief in the sociocultural/materialistic superiority of the U.S.

Complex Organization Studies. Often the military is regarded as the prototype of bureaucratic organization with an emphasis on stratification and centralization of authority. Yet Miewald (1970) criticizes Weber's analysis of the modern military and calls for further investigation of the relationship between Weberian bureaucracy and the military model. Segal and Segal (1971) propose a tripartite typology of social and military structures: 1) the pre-bureaucratic model stressing traditional, affective, and non-rational criteria of recruitment and promotion; 2) the bureaucratic organized along a broader base of recruitment and career mobility and emphasizing combat expertise; and 3) the post-bureaucratic stressing organizational and administrative skills.

Results from a recent study of 450 officers (cited in Deagle, 1973) have suggested that bureaucratic managerial skills may be at cross-purposes with military professional standards of competence and integrity. It tends to support Segal's post-bureaucratic model since the system no longer rewards competence in combat but rather favors the bureaucratic managerial type including political skills. Palen (1972) finds a preponderance of managerial self-images among senior officers at the Industrial College of the Armed Forces while Kourvetaris (1971a) emphasizes the mixed (combined heroic and managerial) self-images of the Greek army officer.

Lang (1973) links technological change to the occupational structure of the U.S. military and notes a shift from combat orientation to "resource management." The development of the tertiary sector (service and management) represents a functionally autonomous growth of an organizational culture. The occupational structure of each service is viewed as dependent on the technological base which is in turn related to the basic military mission. Using data from 37 units of the U.S. Coast Guard, Childers, Mayhew, and Gray (1971) find size positively related to number of occupations but negatively related to internal specialization. Later Mayhew, James, and Childers (1972) apply Zipf's harmonic series model of the division of labor to the data and find that a variety of predictions about the "structure" of formal organizations (e.g., interdependence and stability of parts and anticipated changes) can be derived from it.

Overall this literature strongly supports a structuralist perspective stressing the stability, continuity, and homogeneity of values in the organization while disregarding conflict or viewing it as dysfunctional. This is not to say that changes such as in convergence patterns and future trends aren't discussed or that certain potential problems (e.g., all-volunteer army) aren't considered and even some recommendations or policy implications given. But what one misses is an in-depth explanation (not just prediction or association) of these phenomena and an analysis that includes both its internal dynamics and the processes of change between armed forces and society. Technology and various structural variables should not be viewed as determinants but rather as constraints which can be modified by other organizational and cultural features. For example, Garnier (1975) questions whether the organizational changes related to technology and noted by Janowitz for the U.S. are also present in other nations (e.g., broadening of recruitment). Traditional patterns and criteria of recruitment still prevail in the British military which is highly technological. Garnier thus argues that specific cultural and organizational factors can alter the effects of technological innovation.

While certain constraints exist, concepts such as decision-making, organizational choice, leadership, and the implementation of the decisions are important for future analysis. Head (1973) explores the basic determinants of military decision-making in the purchase of the A-7 Aircraft and develops a professional organization model which stresses the importance of situational factors and professional socialization (including service roles, interservice competition, and the mission of the organization). Power, one of the dimensions of stratification, (how it is obtained and used as well as who has it) should also be of major concern if one views the military as a system of actors with rule-making authority unequally distributed.

To obtain a fuller perspective of the organization which includes human beings with varying needs and values working in a military structure, an open systems approach (see Katz and Kahn, 1966; Segal et al., 1974; Garnier, 1975) is needed which considers both formal and informal elements and suggests that the military organization belongs to a larger system and is in continual interaction with other parts. Such an approach allows one to look at the influence of the environment and of social and historical factors on the organization, the workings of the organization itself, and the impact of the organization on the environment including other organizations. Civil-military relations may be considered part of an open systems perspective but it has been basically limited to one aspect, the role of the military in politics. Figure 1 shows some of the possible lines of analysis and variables that could be studied in such an approach. However such an analysis needs to integrate a wide variety of variables to provide a comprehensive and dynamic picture of the military and should consider indirect effects, interaction, and feedback processes.

C. SOCIAL DISORGANIZATION

In contrast to the organizational aspects of the military and in view of the lack of a more refined term in sociology, the concept of disorganization will be used interchangeably with that of internal problems of the military organization. Since 1950's until recently, studies of internal problems of the military were often de-emphasized. In a sense the military has not publicized its problems although they have conducted in-house research. However, many publications, both journalistic and social science, are now oriented to problem-solving or at least problem identifying in the U.S. military. Indeed it may be suggested that just as sociology of the military emerged as an applied science in World War II, an interest in the applied aspects of the sociology of the military has been stimulated by the Vietnam War, its aftermath, and the shift to the all volunteer military.

As previously noted, problems of under- and over-representation of various groups in the all-volunteer military, problems of race relations (Bogart, 1969; Moskos, 1970 and 1973) and equality of the sexes (Coye, 1971; Goldman, 1973a & b) have been important issues. Hauser (1973) analyzed problems of drugs, racial conflict, dissent, discipline and justice confronting the U.S. army and the steps taken or being taken to deal with them. Although he is critical of the military organization/profession, he argues that the present crisis is in part a spillover of society's social ills upon the military.

The federal government has increasingly charged the military with social and welfare roles. These roles are reflected in "Project 100,000" and "Project Transition" where the military has tried to prepare disadvantaged youth for the larger society (Moskos, 1970). Beck (1971) maintains that the military has

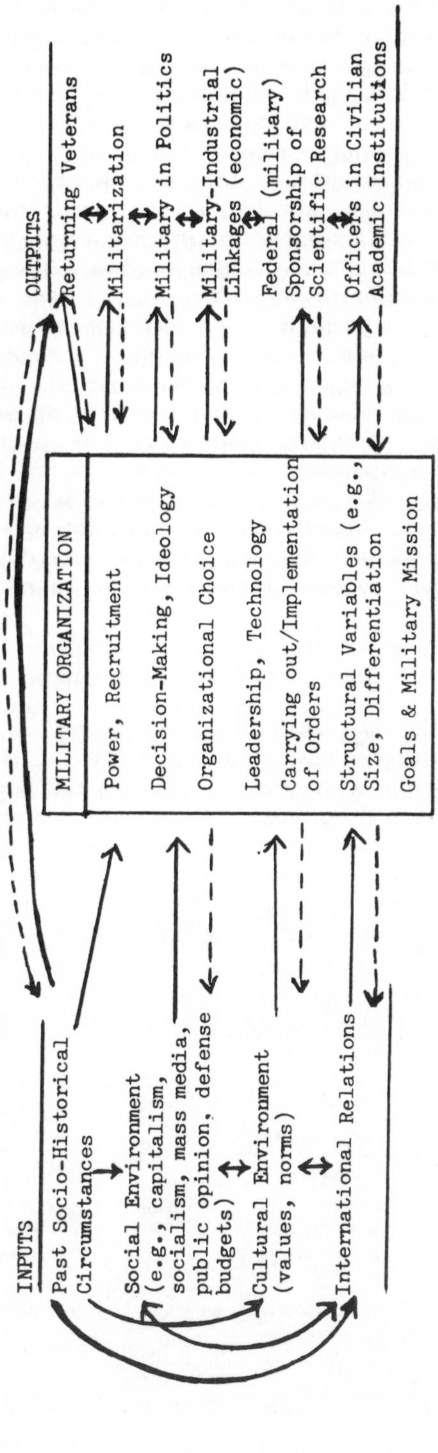

FIGURE 1. SOME SUGGESTED LINES OF ANALYSIS OF THE MILITARY AS AN OPEN-SYSTEM

INPUTS

Past Socio-Historical Circumstances

Social Environment (e.g., capitalism, socialism, mass media, public opinion, defense budgets)

Cultural Environment (values, norms)

International Relations

MILITARY ORGANIZATION

Power, Recruitment

Decision-Making, Ideology

Organizational Choice

Leadership, Technology

Carrying out/Implementation of Orders

Structural Variables (e.g., Size, Differentiation)

Goals & Military Mission

OUTPUTS

Returning Veterans

Militarization

Military in Politics

Military-Industrial Linkages (economic)

Federal (military) Sponsorship of Scientific Research

Officers in Civilian Academic Institutions

been successful in its welfare role because of the sense of legitimacy it has derived from its national defense role and emphasis on manly honor and esprit de corps. While Browning et al., (1973) find evidence to support the idea that military service provided a "bridging environment" to facilitate post-service economic achievement for minority men in the southwest, Cutright (1974) does not find similar confirmation from a national probability sample.

The relationship between veteran status and socioeconomic and attitudinal variable has become a major topic. Lifton (1973) presents a psychohistorical investigation of the attitudes of returning veterans based on taped "rap group" sessions with anti-war veterans. Helmer's (1974) *Bringing the War Home* discusses the combat experiences, impact of the Vietnam war, and adjustment and alienation after return home for working class veterans. Three types of veterans — the "straights," the "radicals" (e.g., Vietnam Veterans Against the War"), and the "addicts" are analyzed. Fendrich and Axelson's (1971) analysis of black veterans in Florida finds that single veterans and those with children were more politically alienated than married veterans without children.

Some work has emerged on the military system of justice, including Brodsky and Eggleston's (1970) description of the military correctional institutions, drawing material from a variety of disciplines. They examine patterns of military correction, restoration to duty, and research strategies. In a study of AWOL prisoners in a military stockade, Hartnagel (1974) conceptualizes going AWOL as a form of innovative deviance occurring largely because of the men's inability or disinclination to adapt to army life rather than as a protest against the Vietnam War. (They were often volunteers with less than a high school education and low IQs.) How much sociological research can contribute to explaining various aspects of disorganization may be an indicator of the viability of sociology of the military (especially to those interested in the applied aspects).

D. CIVIL-MILITARY RELATIONS

In this analysis the concepts of civil-military relations and armed forces and society are used interchangeably. Both concepts indicate the linkages between the military and the rest of the societal institutions. Political scientists are more interested in the relationship between the military and the state while sociologists are interested primarily in the linkages between the military and social institutions.

While the literature on civil-military relations is voluminous, it consists principally of case studies which are qualitative, descriptive, and essay type rather than comparative, quantitative, analytical and empirical. In the present analysis only selective aspects of civil-military relations are briefly examined: civil-military models, the causes and consequences of coercive intervention (including modernization and change), the role of the military in politics, and the thesis of military industrial complex (MIC).

Models and Typologies. A number of social scientists (Janowitz, 1971b; Lang, 1973; Huntington, 1957, 1968; Abrahamsson, 1972; Moskos, 1973; Lovell, 1974; Luckham, 1971) have suggested a broad range of conceptual models of civil-military relations. Most of these frameworks stress the "structural" and "symmetrical" dimensions rather than the "cultural" and "idiographic" aspects of civil-military relationships. Often they are extrapolations from the Western European political/military experience and are historical typologies with limited utility in explaining the contemporary complexity of civil-military and international political and military systems.

Janowitz (1971b) identifies 4 major historical models of civil-military relations of American and Western European societies: aristocratic-feudal, democratic, totalitarian, and the garrison model. Regarding the emerging nations of the third world, he offers a typology of 5 different forms of civil-military relations based on the degree of militarism and/or civil control of the military. However, it may be that terms such as democracy, oligarchy, etc., some of which have been known since the writings of Plato and Aristotle, are not sufficient for understanding contemporary civil-military phenomena in Western and non-Western polities alike.

According to Luckham (1971), the main weakness of the existing typologies of civil-military relations is that they stress the characteristics of civil politics and their influence on military intervention and civil-military relations to the exclusion of the organizational/professional qualities of the military itself or they stress the latter to the exclusion of the social and political environment. He attempts to show how a number of existing models of civil-military relationships — Huntington's distinction between objective and subjective control of the military, Lasswell's garrison state, Rapoport's typifications of the praetorian state and the nation in arms, and Janowitz's constabulary concept — fit into a more general schema along dimensions of civil and military power and the boundaries between armed forces and society.

A more recent typology of civil-military relations has been suggested by Moskos (1973a) who attempts to monitor the trends and changes in both the internal organization of the military and its relationship to the broader American society. It consists of 3 developmental constructs: the convergent or civilianized military which is becoming similar to civilian structures; the divergent or traditional military that emphasizes the increasing differentiation between military and civilian structures; and the segmented or pluralistic model which posits the internal bifurcation of the military along civilianized and traditional lines simultaneously.

Lovell (1974) discusses the inadequacies and limitations of traditional and modern approaches and offers a critique and alternative framework of contemporary civil-military relations. He suggests that civil-military relations can be studied by using the "national security" policy framework — in Lasswell's terms "Who gets what, when, and how." Processes of bargaining and trade offs among competing values in the arena of national security and politics are then identified. The problem of such a formulation is the ideological and problematic nature of the concept of "national security." What constitutes national security may not be the same for the legislative branch of government and the executive branch. The recent use of national security rationale and executive privilege for not testifying before legislative committees may indicate failure, deception, and ineptness in our foreign policy rather than risks to national security (e.g., Vietnam, Cyprus, Chile, Angola).

Military Intervention. The concept of intervention implies that the military is not an integral part of the national society. It is more of a descriptive than an analytical concept. For this analysis the concept of intervention will be used to mean the covert and overt roles of the military in domestic politics (e.g. coup d'etat).

Most studies on military intervention examine the active role of the military in national politics and probe into the causes and/or consequences of military intervention. Most often the authors (Bienen, 1968 and 1971; Feit 1973; Janowitz and Van Doorn, eds., 1971; Finer, 1968 and 1974) analyze the causes rather than the consequences of intervention. Lang (1972) distinguishes between limited intervention, occult intervention, and military takeover while Bienen (1968) describes the initial act of intervention (i.e., coups, rebellions revolts), the period after the seizure of power, and the institutionalization of power. Similarly Feit (1973) proposes a cyclical model through which military regimes pass: the military take-over, the military-civilian administrative alliance — cohesion without consensus (the praetorian regime), and finally the downfall and replacement.

Causes of Military Intervention: An Eclectic Model. Intervention of the military into politics is a multi-dimensional, persistent, and recurrent phenomenon. Many of the efforts to explain the underlying causes that predispose the military to take over the government are inadequate and lack persuasiveness. One reason for this is that most case and comparative studies of military intervention are post-facto analyses and are instances of overt armed intervention. Most analysts ignore or are unable to penetrate into the covert ways and processes in which military managers learn to become coupmakers, rationalizers, and usurpers of legal authority.

For reasons of parsimony the authors present an eclectic model of intervention in figure 2. The purpose of this model is to carefully select and arrange those variables that possess greater explanatory value for intervention. An eclectic model is based on a comprehensive, comparative, and interdisciplinary level of analysis with the choice of variables subject to change depending on their explanatory value. This model of intervention can best be depicted and analyzed in terms of both subsystemic and systemic variables. The subsystemic consists of three middle range explanations: the middle class and modernization, social psychological, and professional/organizational hypotheses. The systemic contains more general explanations including cultural/historical, social structural, ideological, international/geopolitical, and contagious/reinforcement aspects. Both sets of explanations interact with each other in explaining military intervention. The latter depends also on the regime's ability to diffuse and prevent the carrying out of the act of intervention.

Subsystemic Factors: Empirical Referents. (1) *The middle class and modernization theses* were put forth by students of development and stratification in the early 1960's as reasons for military intervention (Pye 1962; Halpern, 1962; Johnson, 1962; Lieuwen, 1961; Shils, 1962). However more recently these theses have been criticized by many students of civil-military relations (Moskos and Bell, 1967; Horowitz, 1967; Bienen, 1968; Ben Dor, 1973 Fidel, 1975) who contend that there is no empirical evidence to substantiate the claim that the military more than civilian elites are the carriers of middle class aspirations and modernization in their respective societies.

(2) *Social Psychological.* Under this general rubric a number of themes and hypotheses have been advanced as explanations of intervention including

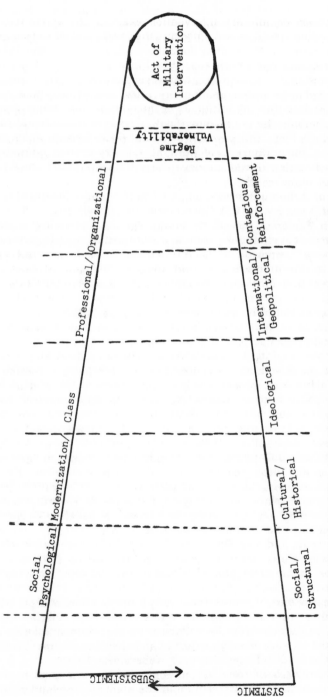

FIGURE 2. EXPLANATIONS OF MILITARY INTERVENTION: AN ECLECTIC MODEL OF INTERVENTION

socialization and subcultural hypotheses, reference group theory, personality and leadership correlates of interveners, associational criminological hypotheses, and attitudinal/behavioral theories in general (Ben Dor, 1973; Perlumutter, 1969; Thompson 1973; Eckhart and Newcombe, 1969; Ba-Yunus, 1975).

(3) *Professional/Organizational.* A number of scholars have developed hypotheses linking professionalization and organization of the officer corps (i.e., career mobility, promotion, specialization, organizational complexity, size, grievances) with politicization and/or intervention of the military in politics. Huntington (1957) advanced the thesis that the more professionalized the military, the less the propensity for military intervention. In a later publication (1968), however, he changed his position and sought the cause of military intervention in the external/systemic factors, i.e., political decay. Professionalization of the officer corps also meant increased military politicization, including intervention, especially in the countries of the third world (Finer, 1962; Fidel, 1970; Kourvetaris, 1971a; Feit, 1973).

Systemic Factors: (1) Social Structural. The social structural approach is the most frequent explanation of military intervention and includes a number of explanatory propositions dealing with socio-economic and political variables, i.e., the higher/greater industrialization, political participation, social differentiation, social complexity, mobilization, civic culture, economic and political stability, middle class, mobility, the less the likelihood for military intervention. The social structural approach, however, undermines the conscious, purposeful and deliberate social action of military protagonists and their civilian supporters. The social-psychological and human input is obfuscated by structural-functional variables (Baaklini, 1975; Stegenga, 1973).

(2) *Cultural/Historical.* In contrast to structuralist explanation is the culturalist/historical approach which emphasizes the unique and idiographic aspects of civil-military relations. According to this approach, the past behavior and habituation of the military to intervene increases the probability for military intervention (Finer, 1962 and 1974; Janowitz and Van Doorn, 1971a; Kourvetaris, 1971 b, c; Beltran, 1970; Beeri, 1969; Despradel, 1969).

(3) *Ideological.* Military coups and interventions in general are conspiratorial and ideological in nature. They are predicated on what Pareto termed "residues" and "derivations" such as national salvation, morality, nationalism, motherland, honor, myths, folkish and primordial notions of community, symbolism, and puritanism. These are usually associated with military rationale and ideology of intervention. With the exceptions of a few studies (Janowitz and Van Doorn, 1971b; Feit, 1973; Horowitz, 1972; Wells, 1974; Kourvetaris, 1971a) this approach is rather neglected.

(4) *International/Geopolitical.* Factors and concepts such as power politics, foreign missions, spheres of influence, and balance of power, especially in geopolitically and strategically located nations of the third world, play an important role in military intervention. The external inputs of superpowers to their client states in terms of political, economic, and technical military assistance are usually politically and ideologically linked (see Wells, 1974; Terreberry, 1968; Despradel, 1969; Kourvetaris, 1971c).

(5) *Contagion/Reinforcement.* The contagion hypothesis postulates that the occurrence of military intervention in one country (especially in countries

in geographic proximity) increases the frequency of intervention in another country. Simply put, coups are contagious and have a snowball effect. The occurrence of one reinforces the occurrence of another. Among others, Li and Thompson (1975), Midlarksy (1970), Wells (1974), Putnam (1967), and Mazrui (1969) support the contagion hypothesis.

Consequences of Intervention and the Role of the Military in Politics. Just as one can observe a shift from the causes to the consequences of prejudice in the study of intergroup relations, a similar trend has been noted by students of civil-military relations concerning intervention. Among others, Nordlinger (1970), Bienen (1971), Schmitter (1973), and Kelleher (1974) underline the redirection of the research on military intervention. One of the major debates about the consequences of intervention concerns the ability of the military regimes to serve as effective agents and brokers of social change and modernization in their respective societies. While social scientists are interested in issues of civil-military relations, structural convergence, recruitment, and organization of armed forces in industrialized societies, they often focus on the role of the military as a modernizing force when studying developing nations.

Regarding the latter two general but opposing views have been offered, one which sees the military as an energizing and modernizing force and the other which stresses the inability and limitations of the military in creating a viable political institution for economic and social development. Put somewhat differently, the military can be looked upon as champions of middle class aspirations and effective agents of change or as ineffective and divisive forces. In the early 1960's a number of social scientists (Shils, 1962; Halpern,1962; Pye, 1962) eulogized and exalted the modernizing ability of the military in non-western nations, but by the early 1970's this view has lost its appeal. It appears that much of the debate over the role of the military as effective agents of modernization and change in the third world countries has been conducted in an empirical vacuum (Bienen, 1971; Moskos and Bell, 1967).

Sharma (1971) and Perlmutter (1969) argue that military regimes have not helped in developing viable political institutions in Africa and Arab states respectively. Rather mixed evidence is offered by Mehden (1970) on Thailand who argues that while the military contributed to economic and social development, it did so within an atmosphere of uneasy cooperation between civilian and military elites. Similarly Huntington (1968) sees the military acting as a modernizing force when the issue is one of middle class entry into the political system but becoming a repressive force when the question revolves around lower-class demands. Budgley (1969) underscores the polarization of military and political leaders that characterizes much of Southeast Asia. While Thailand and Burma are moving toward a cooperative civil-military ruling coalition, they pursue sharply different public policies. Kourvetaris (1971c) views the role of the military in Greece as a cultural, national, and societal preserving institution which has also often played an active role in national politics. Using seven modernization indicators, Nordlinger (1970) found negative relationships between political strength of the military and economic change in Latin America, Middle East and N. Africa, and Asia but positive relations in tropical African countries. Overall he concludes the military has not been much of a modernizing force.

While the aforementioned studies consider the military as a governing force, it may also be involved in politics without actually ruling. The following studies are examples of this latter type. Bopegamage (1971) sees the role of the Indian military as modernizing and a vehicle for mobility, but he lacks empirical data to substantiate his thesis. Kolkowicz (1970) analyzes the Soviet military as an interest group with limited concern for liberalizing reforms. As long as its basic interests are satisfied by the Communist party, the military poses no challenge to the ruling elites. What their interests are and the extent to which the military yields power in national and international decision making are not specified by the author. Al-Qazzaz (1973) describes Israel as a garrison state and argues that the Israeli army is the most important channel for social integration, economic and social modernization, and nation building. It also helps integrate Israel into the international political system. There is a need to develop indices of modernization and militarization and relate them to other existing studies. Beltran (1970), in his comparative study of the U.S., Egypt, and Argentina, concludes that the lower the socio-political development of the society, the greater the political participation of the armed forces (similar to Finer's civic culture). Stepan (1971) examines the role of the military in Brazil and argues that it plays a moderating role in national politics. Drury (1974) argues that the Brazilian military has been successful because of the lack of effective civilian leadership and the undifferentiated institutional boundaries between the military and society. The military has offered some form of institutional legitimacy and political doctrine.

Methodology. A concomitant problem of how to conceptualize intervention and the role of the military in politics in general is how to measure it. Three approaches have been used in the literature: The Index of Military Intervention (IMI), the case study, and the comparative historical approach. (a) The IMI is a useful technique especially for correlational analysis. It allows one to test hypotheses on military intervention by weighting and summarizing all evidence. Putnam (1967), for example, has devised an index of military intervention based on a scale from 0 to 3 for each year from least to most intervention. The IMI score for each country or a group of countries can be calculated and compared in both diachronic and synchronic levels of comparative analyses. (See also Sigelman, 1974, and Tannahill, 1975 for composite MI indices.)

b) *Case Study.* This approach is the most frequently used in the literature. Since it is more idiographic and qualitative rather than nomothetic and empirical, its main use is for generating hypotheses rather than testing them. c) *Comparative historical.* This is a diachronic qualitative approach in which two or more countries are compared regarding the degree of military intervention in a historical perspective. The major disadvantage of this approach is its reliance on past behavior of the military to explain present conditions leading to military intervention. One finds an increase in the use of this approach but the quality of studies is still very low.

Military-Industrial Complex. The military-industrial complex (MIC) focuses upon the linkages between military and civilian (corporate and government) institutions. The magnitude of the interlock and its causes are the major issues in the controversy (Lieberson, 1971). MIC can be traced back to the debate between the elitist and pluralist perspectives concerning the role of the military in national decision-making and policy formation in the U.S. and other advanced societies. C. Wright Mills' (1956) thesis of power elite provided an intellectual catalyst for the analysis of a tripartite national elite structure made up of the military, the corporate rich, and political leaders. Eisenhower's caution against the MIC in his farewell address became a focus for debate in the 1960's and early 1970's.

Moskos (1974) traced the theoretical antecedents of the MIC concept to the neo-Machiavellian and Weberian writings. He believes MIC followed a natural development within the mainstream of American political sociological (liberal) thought and identifies 3 analytically exclusive themes: the military hierarchy (Lens, 1970; Heilbroner, 1970; Donovon, 1970; Kaufman, 1972); the administrative bureaucracy (Melman, 1970; Horowitz, 1972); and the corporate wealth (Baran and Sweezy, 1966; Magdoff, 1969; Stevenson, 1973).

The debate on MIC has intensified during the 1970's with numerous books and articles emerging representing the different perspectives. For example, the MIC book edited by Pursell (1972) supports a strong linkage between military and industrial complexes while the book edited by Sarkesian (1972) tends to be more representative of the pluralist school. Lieberson (1971) employs regression and input-output analyses in support of the idea that the economy does not require extensive military outlays to sustain itself. He uses the idea of "compensating strategies" to suggest that diverse interest groups are trying to maximize their net gains. Similarly Gross (1971) believes the MIC can occur without any conspiracy or even community of interest. It is simply an alternative theory on decision-making.

Stevenson (1971, 1973) criticizes Lieberson for not stressing the long run maximization of profits and not presenting a holistic analysis of American capitalist economy vis-a-vis spending on the military. He maintains that military spending is quite profitable for America's largest businesses, crucial to the maintenance of aggregate demand at home, and a defense of American foreign interests abroad.

The relationship between "military spending and economic stagnation," which is an extension of the larger debate on MIC, is now a major topic. Szymanski (1973) challenges Baran and Sweezy's view that the greater the military spending in a monopoly capitalist economy, the lower the unemployment, and the greater the economic growth. Using GNP and GNP/capita on government military and non-military expenditures of 18 advanced capitalist countries, he concludes that 1) military spending does not prevent economic stagnation but it reduces unemployment; 2) non-military spending contributes to greater economic growth than military spending in monopoly capitalism; and 3) in the absence of non-military spending, military spending does prevent stagnation.

The criticisms of Syzmanski come most frequently from his fellow radical sociologists. Zeitlin (1974) notes that Szymanski inadequately interprets Baran and Sweezy's theory and thus does not consider major variables related to monopoly and time-series data. Zeitlin (1974), Stevenson (1973, 1974), Sweezy (1973) and Friedman (1974) criticize Szymanski's methodology, particularly the dichotomization of the 18 countries and their use as independent entities, use of zero order correlations, failure to include major variables, and the causal ordering of the model. Friedman (1974) suggests an alternative model based on the idea of international power relations and long-run tendencies toward stagnation. His model recognizes investment in underdeveloped areas and arms expenditure as offsetting forces although long term national growth is increased more by investing in the civilian sector.

It is perhaps here at the international or multi-national level that additional research should be conducted because the issues of arms race and selling of military technology and hardware have widespread implications for the political systems and balance of power between countries. It is also not only the U.S. which may have a military-industrial complex but other developed and emerging nations as well. While the sociology of the military literature on the third world nations focuses primarily on intervention, modernization, and the role of the military in domestic politics, the military-industrial linkages need further investigation there also. A thorough analysis would include an examination of the agrarian, bureaucratic, intellectual, and ethnic linkages as well.

Lowry (1970) develops a historical typology and an explanation of changing military roles in both democratic and nondemocratic societies. He views the militarization of modern society as resulting from evolutionary processes of change (as in warfare and political development) rather than from cabals, coups, etc. He suggests some tentative directions for future changes which could modify the power and influence of military complexes.

The ideological issues involved in MIC have led to some rather polemical debate, but the increasingly significant sociological and empirical analysis appears encouraging. However, it is obvious that extreme difficulties exist in obtaining relevant data to test the MIC hypothesis. Those persons who analyze the military using a pluralist framework are more likely to consider themselves military sociologists while those who subscribe to the elitist or class perspectives are more likely to think of themselves as political or radical sociologists.

SUMMARY AND CONCLUSION

We have briefly traced the development of sociology of the military and attempted to evaluate its current state of teaching and research. Overall, while the field has recently made some progress, we still believe that it is underdeveloped and has not achieved widespread acceptance in sociology and the larger academic community. The development of sociology of the military has been uneven with greater emphasis on the applied aspects of research.

Since the boundaries of the field are only loosely delineated, we decided to examine those areas which traditionally have been of interest to sociologists of the military. While these conventional topics are useful for understanding the internal nature of military organization, we suggest that a more comprehensive sociology of the military should include a political sociological framework by focusing on the relationship between the military, state, and society. One should ask how the political process affects the military and how the military influences politics and society? Where does the military fit in the national and international decision and rule-making process? Is the military really a client of the state or a member of the ruling elite? In addition, since the military is a source of major expenditures in the national budget, deals with the issues of war and peace, and specializes in the management of the organized means of violence, its actions have widespread ethical, ideological, and economic implications which should be included in an overall study of the military.

Since increasingly large scale conventional wars and mass armies become dysfunctional in an atomic age, we believe sociology of the military should study more extensively the non-conventional quasi-military and paramilitary social formations, movements, and types of warfare, i.e., guerrilla wars, civil wars, revolutionary wars, terrorist groups, intelligence, surveillance, and political assassinations.

From our analysis we can identify certain constraints and limitations on the field of sociology of the military. For purposes of parsimony we will confine ourselves to a brief discussion of some of the major ones. Most of these can be traced to the nature of the military institution itself, the nature of society and culture in general, and the development of the field of sociology as a whole. These constraints and limitations may provide a tentative and partial explanation of why the sociology of the military has not received full acceptance as a legitimate subfield of sociology. More evidence, however, is needed before this question can be answered in detail.

First, since its inception sociology of the military has had an applied and social orientation in much of the work done on the military. This has led to the lack of theoretical/conceptual sophistication; possible theoretical significance of the findings is subordinated to more immediate problem solving and social policy matters. With the exception of a few studies there is a lack of methodological rigor. The majority of articles, books, and readings tend to be qualitative and have a low level of abstraction. At present, sociological data, methods, and analyses are imprecise predictive tools and are likely to remain so until there is either a more unified body of theory on military institutional behavior or more comprehensive research strategies (Millett, 1974).

Second, the majority of the writings have had a structural/functionalist or consensus orientation while conflict aspects and an open systems approach have often received little attention. This is to say that sociology of the military has developed along the same contours of the structuralist perspective which has dominated sociology as a whole during the last 30 years or so. With the exception of the writings of the last few years, sociologists of the military have failed to adequately examine the political and power dimensions of the military both in the national and international environments and their ramifications in synchronic and diachronic frameworks (especially the linkages between the institutions of the military, war, and the state).

Third, ideally the military is a non-partisan institution, but it is normally associated with a conservative ideology and is often distrustful of social and political change. Due to the role of the military as managers of the legitimate means of violence, ideology (both conservative and liberal) has often taken precedence over theoretical considerations. Those who study the military within a framework of sociology of the military tend to be more conservative and thus less critical of the military. There is also a lack of consideration of the ethical and moral implications of military activities, e.g., bombings, espionage, invasions, military regimes and repression.

Fourth, the closed or semi-closed nature of the military institutions has created problems of access to data, especially that relevant to controversial issues regarding the roles and uses of the military. In addition, in the U.S. and other Anglo-Saxon countries there has been a traditional belief in civil supremacy and a distrust and suspicion of the role of the military in the social and political life of the nation. This coupled with the liberal orientation of the social sciences and sociology may not have helped sociology of the military gain academic legitimacy and acceptance.

Fifth, since sociology of the military has been dominated by a few individuals and groups, it has been difficult for younger sociologists with new or differing perspectives to develop their interests and gain acceptance.

Sixth, the interdisciplinary character of the study of the military has made it problematic and difficult to determine the scope and material of the field, often resulting in fragmented forms of research and publication instead of studies building on each other to advance sociological knowledge. Even within the field of sociology, certain topics of study of the military have been covered under other subfields of social organization, e.g., the military as a profession, as an organization, as an institution, and as a dimension of political sociology.

Seventh, when government funding is obtained, the scope of the study is largely determined by the interests of the government. In such projects team research is often used and sociologists may be given subordinate positions so that the focus of the study, the methodology, and the format of publication are little influenced by sociological considerations.

In conjunction with the delineation of the present state and the structural, ideological, and methodological limitations noted for the sociology of the military, some general propositions concerning the future development of the field may also be suggested.

1) Sociology of the military will continue to encounter resistance from the more liberal academic disciplines and subfields of sociology before it is accepted as a genuine intellectual and scientific subject. Whenever military sociology is hindered in its growth and development and is not allowed a formal place in the university teaching curriculum, it will be taught more diffusely under the rubrics of political sociology, social change, studies on various third world nations and regions, political science (e.g., civil-military relations), and military history in academia and under the titles of management, leadership, command, strategy, etc. with a more applied orientation in the military schools.

2) Although not a viable part of the university curriculum, social scientific research relevant to the military may be carried out in the university under the sponsorship of the federal government. A large portion of research relevant to sociologists of the military may be conducted outside the university under federal/military auspices and control. When this occurs, a) the major thrust will be toward applied social science research and b) many of the more promising young scholars will not be inclined to select sociology of the military as an area of specialization.

3) Sociology of the military as a field is likely to attract those people who have had previous experience and association with the military or have a conservative orientation.

In conclusion, some encouraging signs are also present for the development of sociology of the military. It originally made important contributions to small group research and influenced prevailing theories of social psychology and the development of reference group theory. The recent resurgence of publications in the area, initiation of two new journals and the work of various organizations have also contributed to the field and promoted some sense of respectability for the study of the military. But in spite of these efforts, one can only speak of a partial legitimation and institutionalization of sociology of the military vis-a-vis other areas of sociology which have enjoyed greater acceptance within academia.

REFERENCES

Abrahamsson, Bengt
  1972   Military Professionalization and Political Power. Beverly Hills: Sage Publications.
Al-Qazzaz, Ayad
  1973   "Army and Society in Israel." PSR 16 (Apr.):143-165.
Andreski, Stanislav
  1954   Military Organization and Society. London: Routledge & Kegan Paul Ltd. 2nd edition in 1968.
Baaklini, A.
  1975   "The Military-Civilian Relationship in Contemporary Societies: A Methodological Note." (an Unpublished paper)
Baran, Paul and Paul Sweezy
  1966   Monopoly Capital. New York: Monthly Review.
Ba-Yunus, Ilyas
  1975   "The Genesis of Military Coup d'etat: A Criminological Theory" Presented at the military session of the Annual Convention of the American Sociological Association, San Francisco, (Aug. 25-29).
Beck, Bernard
  1971   "The Military as a Welfare Institution." Pp. 137-148 in Moskos (ed.), (1971).
Beeri, Eliezer
  1969   Army Officers in Arab Politics and Society. New York: Praeger.
Beltran, Virgilio Rafael.
  1970   "The Degrees of Development and Political Participation of the Armed Forces." Revista Espanole de la Opinion Publica. 20 (Apr-Jun):57-72.
Ben-Dor, Gabriel
  1973   "The Politics of Threat: Military Intervention in the Middle East." JPMS 1 (Spring):57-69.
Biderman, Albert
  1963   March to Calumny: The Story of American POW's in the Korean War. New York: MacMillan.
Bienen, Henry (ed.)
  1968   The Military Intervenes. New York: The Russell Sage Foundation
  1971   The Military and Modernization. Chicago: Aldine.
Blum, Albert A.
  1972   "Soldier or Worker: A Reevaluation of the Selective Service System." Midwest Quarterly 13 (January):147-157.
Bogart, Leo (ed.)
  1969   Social Research and the Desegregation of the U.S. Army. Chicago: Markham Publishing Company.
Bopegamage, A.
  1971   "The Military as a Modernizing Agent in India." Economic Development and Cultural Change. 2 (Oct.):71-79.
Bowers, R. V.
  1967   "The Military Establishment." Pp. 234-274 in P.F. Lazarsfeld, W.H. Sewell, & H.L. Wilensky (eds.), The Uses of Sociology. New York: Basic Books.
Bradford, Z. and F. Brown
  1973   The United States Army in Transition. Beverly Hills: Sage Publications

Brewer, Thomas
  1975 "Military Officers and Arms Control: Personality Correlates of Attitudes. JPMS 3 (Spring):15-25.
Brodsky, Stanley L. and Norman E. Eggleston (eds.)
  1970 The Military Prisons: Theory, Research, and Practice. Carbondale, IL: Southern Illinois University Press.
Browning, Harley L., Sally C. Lopreato and Dudley Poston Jr.
  1973 "Income and Veteran Status: Variations Among Mexican Americans, Blacks and Anglos." ASR 38 (Feb.):74-85.
Budgley, J. H.
  1969 "Two Styles of Military Rule: Thailand and Burma." Gov't and Opposition. 4 (Winter):100-117.
Campbell, D. T., and T. H. McCormack
  1957 "Military Experience and Attitudes toward Authority." AJS 62:482-490.
Childers, Grant W., Bruce H. Mayhew, Jr. & Louis N. Gray
  1971 "System Size and Structural Differentiation in Military Organizations: Testing a Baseline Model of the Division of Labor." AJS 76 (March):813-829.
Coates, C.H. and R.J. Pellegrin
  1965 Military Sociology: A Study of American Institutions and Military Life. University Park, MD.: Social Science Press.
Cochran, Charles L. (ed.)
  1974 Civil-Military Relations. New York: The Free Press.
Cockerham, William
  1973 "Selective Socialization: Airborne Training as a Status Passage." JPMS 1 (Fall):215-229.
Coye, Beth
  1971 "The Woman Line Officer in the U.S. Navy: An Exploratory Study." Paper presented at Inter-University Seminar on Armed Forces and Society. University of Chicago.
Cutright, Phillips
  1974 "The Civilian Earning of White and Black Draftees and Nonveterans." ASR 39 (June):317-327.
Davis, Jr., James W. and Kenneth M. Dolbeare
  1968 Little Groups of Neighbors: The Selective Service System. Chicago: Markham.
Deagle, Edwin A., Jr.
  1973 "Contemporary Professionalism and Future Military Leadership." Annals 406 (March):162-170.
Despradel, Sasson
  1969 "The Functions of Armies in Latin America and the Causes of their Political Intervention." Revue de 1' Institut de Sociologie, 4 (Feb.):698-708.
Donovan, James A.
  1970 Militarism U.S.A. New York: Scribner's Sons.
Drury, Bruce R.
  1974 "Civil-Military Relations and Military Rule: Brazil Since 1964." JPMS 2 (Fall):191-203.
Eckhardt, W. and Newcombe, A.G.
  1969 "Militarism, Personality, and other Social Attitudes." J of CR 13 (June):210-219.
Ellis, Joseph and Robert Moore
  1974 School for Soldiers: West Point and the Profession of Arms. New York: Oxford University Press.
Evans, Robert Jr.
  1969 "The Military Draft as a Slave System: An Economic View." SSQ 50 (December):535-543.
Feld, M.D.
  1968 "Professionalism, Nationalism, and the Alienation of the Military." Pp. 55-70 in J. Van Doorn (Ed.), Armed Forces and Society. The Hague: Mouton.
  1975 "Military Professionalism and the Mass Army." AF & S 1 (Winter):191-214.

Feit, Edward
    1973   The Armed Bureaucrats. Boston: Houghton Mifflin.
Feldberg, Roslyn L.
    1970   "Political Systems and the Role of the Military." SQ 12 (Spring):206-218.
Fendrich, James and Leland J. Axelson
    1971   "Marital Status and Political Alienation Among Black Veterans. AJS
            (September):245-261
Fidel, Kenneth
    1970   "Military Organization and Conspiracy in Turkey." Studies in Comparative
            Development 6:19-43.
    1975   Militarism in Developing Countries. (Edited) New Brunswick, New Jersey:
            Transaction, Inc.
Finer, S.E.
    1962   The Man on Horseback: The Role of the Military in Politics. New York: Fred
            A. Praeger.
    1974   "The Man on Horseback — 1974: Military Regimes." AF & S 1 (November):5-
            27.
Friedman, Samuel
    1974   "An Alternative Model to Szymanski's." AJS 79 (May):1459-1462.
Friedson, Eliot
    1970   Profession of Medicine. New York: Dodd, Mead.
Galloway, K.B. and R.B. Johnson
    1973   West Point: America's Power Fraternity. New York: Simon and Schuster.
Garnier, Maurice A.
    1972   "Changing Recruitment Patterns & Organizational Ideology: The Case of a
            British Military Academy." ASQ 17 (Dec.):499-507.
    1973   "Some Implications of the British Experience With an All-Volunteer Army."
            PSR 16 (April):177-191.
    1975   "Technology, Organizational Culture and Recruitment in the British
            Military Academy." JPMS 3 (Fall):141-151.
Goertzel, Ted & Acco Hengst
    1971   "The Military Socialization of University Students." SP 19 (Fall):258-267.
Goldman, Nancy
    1973a   "The Changing Role of Women in the Armed Forces." AJS 78 (Jan):892-911.
    1973b   "The Utilization of Women in the Military." Annals 406 (March):107-116.
Gross, Edward
    1971   "On Lieberson's Study of Military-Industrial Linkages: A Fan Letter with
            Implications." AJS 77 (July):131-133.
Hall, R.L.
    1956   "Military Sociology." Pp. 59-62 in H.L. Zetterberg (ed.), Sociology in the
            United States of America; A Trend Report. Paris UNESCO pp. 59-62.
Halpern, Manfred
    1962   "Middle Eastern Armies and the New Middle Class." in John J. Johnson
            (ed.) (1962).
Hartnagel, Timothy
    1974   "Absent Without Leave: A Study of the Military Offender." JPMS 2 (Fall):
            205-220.
Hauser, William L.
    1973   America's Army in Crisis. Baltimore and London: The Johns Hopkins
            University Press.
Hauser, William M. and Zeb B. Bradford, Jr.
    1971   "Modernizing the Military Profession" Paper presented at the Inter-
            University Seminar On Armed Forces and Society in November.
Head, Richard G.
    1973   "The Sociology of Military Decision-Making: The A-7 Aircraft." PSR 16
            (Apr):209-227
Heilbroner, Robert
    1970   "Military America." New York Review of Books 15 (July 23):5-8.
Helmer, John
    1974   Bringing the War Home: The American Soldier in Vietnam and After. New
            York: The Free Press.

Horowitz, Irving L.
  1967   "The Military Elites." In Lipset and Solari (eds.) Elites in Latin America. N.Y.: Oxford University Press.
  1972   Three Worlds of Development. New York: Oxford University Press.
  1973   "Political Terrorism and State Power." JPMS 1 (Spring):147-157.
Huntington, Samuel P.
  1957   The Soldier and the State: The Theory and Politics of Civil-Military Relations. Cambridge: Harvard University Press.
  1968   Political Order in Changing Societies. New Haven: Yale University.
Hutchinson, Charles E.
  1957   "The Meaning Of Military Sociology." Sociology and Social Research 41:427-433.
Jacobs, Ruth Harriet
  1972   "American Sociology and the Ostrich Approach to War." Paper presented to the Eastern Sociological Society meetings (April) in Boston, Mass.
Janowitz, Morris
  1960   The Professional Solidier: A Social and Political Portrait. New York: The Free Press (A reprint edition with a prologue added was published in 1971)
  1964a   The New Military: Changing Patterns of Organization (ed.) New York: Russell Sage Foundation.
  1964b   The Military in the Political Development of New Nations. Chicago: University of Chicago Press.
  1971a   "The Emergent Military." Pp. 255-270 in Charles Moskos, Jr. (ed.) (1971a)
  1971b   "Military Organization." in Roger Little (ed.) (1971).
  1972   "Strategic Dimensions of an All-Volunteer Armed Force." Pp. 127-167 in Sarkesian (ed.) (1972b)
  1973   "The Social Demography of the All-Volunteer Armed Force." Annals 406 (March):86-93.
Janowitz, M. and R. Little
  1959   Sociology and the Military Establishment. New York: Russell Sage Foundation. (Revised in 1965).
Janowitz, Morris and Jacques Van Doorn (eds.)
  1971a   On Military Intervention. Rotterdam University Press.
  1971b   On Military Ideology. Rotterdam University Press.
Janowitz, Morris and Charles C. Moskos, Jr.
  1974   "Racial Composition in the All-Volunteer Force." AF & S 1 (Fall):109-123.
Johnson, John (ed.)
  1962   The Role of the Military in Underdeveloped Countries. Princeton: Princeton University Press.
Johnson, J. and J. Bachman
  1972   Youth in Transition: Young Men in Military Service (Volume V). Ann Arbor: Survey Research Center.
Jones, Robert A. and Sidney Kronus
  1975   "A Note on the Future Importance of Sub-Fields in Sociology: A Survey of Recent Opinion." Paper Presented at Midwest Sociological Association Meetings in Chicago, April.
Jordan, Amos A.
  1971   "Officer Education." in Roger W. Little, (ed.) (1971).
Jordan, Amos A. and Taylor, William J. Jr.
  1973   "The Military Man in Academia." Annals 406 (March):129-145.
Karpinos, Bernard
  1967   "Mental Test Failures." Pp. 35-53 in Sol Tax (ed.), The Draft. Chicago: University of Chicago.
Karsten,
  1971   "Professional and Citizen Officers: A Comparison of Academy and ROTC Officer Candidates." Pp. 37-62 in Charles Moskos, Jr. (ed.) (1971a).
Katz, Daniel and Robert Kahn
  1966   The Social Psychology of Organizations. New York: John Wiley & Sons, Inc.
Kaufman, Arnold S.
  1968   "Selective Objection to War." Dissent 15 (July-August):306-313.

Kaufman, Richard F.
    1972   The War Profiteers. Garden City, New York: Anchor Doubleday.
Kelleher, Catherine M. (ed.)
    1974   Political-Military Systems: Comparative Perspectives. Beverly Hills, Calif.:
            Sage Publications.
Kolkowicz, R.
    1970   "Interest Groups in Soviet Politics: The Case of the Military." CP 2
            (Apr.):445-472.
Kourvetaris, George A.
    1969   "The Contemporary Army Officer Corps in Greece: An Inquiry into its
            Professionalism and Interventionism." An unpublished Ph.D. thesis.
            Northwestern University Library. Evanston, Illinois.
    1971a   "Professional Self-Images and Political Perspectives in the Greek Military."
            ASR 36 (Dec.):1043-1057.
    1971b   "The Greek Army Officer Corps: Its Professionalism and Political
            Interventionism." In Morris Janowitz and Jacques Van Doorn (eds.) On
            Military Intervention. Rotterdam: Rotterdam University Press.
    1971c   "The Role of the Military in Greek Politics." International Review of History
            and Political Science 8 (Aug.):91-114.
    1976   "Greek Service Academies: Patterns of Recruitment and Organizational
            Change." In Gwyn Harries — Jenkins and Jacques van Doorn (eds.) The
            Military and the Problem of Legitimacy. Beverly Hills, Calif.: Sage
            Publications
Kourvetaris, George A. and Betty Dobratz
    1973a   "Social Recruitment and Political Orientations of the Officer Corps in a
            Comparative Perspective." PSR 16 (April):228-254.
    1973b   Social Origins and Political Orientations of Officer Corps in A World
            Perspective. Denver, Colorado: University of Denver.
Lang, Kurt
    1972   Military Institutions and the Sociology of War. Beverly Hills Cal.: Sage
            Publications.
    1973   "Trends in Military Occupational Structure and Their Political Im-
            plications." JPMS 1 (Spring):1-18.
Larson, Arthur D.
    1974   "Military Professionalism and Civil Control: A Comparative Analysis of
            Two Interpretations." JPMS 2 (Spring):57-72.
Leigh, Duanne E. and Robert E. Berney
    1971   "The Distribution of Hostile Casualties on Draft-Eligible Males with
            Differing Socio-economic Characteristics." SSQ 51 (March):932-940.
Lens, Sidney
    1970   The Military — Industrial Complex, Philadelphia: Pilgrim.
Li, Richard P. Y. and William R. Thompson
    1975   "The 'Coup Contagion' Hypothesis." J of CR 19 (March):63-88.
Lieberson, Stanley
    1971   "An Empirical Study of Military-Industrial Linkages." AJS (January):563-
            584.
Lieuwen, R.
    1961   Arms and Politics in Latin America. New York: Fred A. Praeger.
Lifton, Robert J.
    1973   Home From the War: Vietnam Veterans. New York: Simon and Schuster.
Little, Roger W. (ed.)
    1971   Handbook of Military Institutions. Beverly Hills: Sage Publications.
Lovell, J.P.
    1964   "The Professional Socialization of the West Point Cadet." Pp. 119-157 in M.
            Janowitz (ed.), The New Military: Changing Patterns of Organization. New
            York: Russell Sage Foundation.
    1973   A Comment on Wamsley's "Air Force Socialization" AJS 79
            (September):438-441.
    1974   "The Agonies of Adjustment to Post-Vietnam Realities." In Lovell and
            Kronenberg (eds.) New Civil-Military Relations. New Brunswick, New
            Jersey: Transaction books.

Lowry, Ritchie P.
    1970   "To Arms: Changing Military Roles and the Military-Industrial Complex."
            SP 18 (Summer):3-16.
Lucas, William
    1971   "Anticipatory Socialization and the ROTC." Pp. 99-134 in Charles Moskos,
            Jr. (ed.), (1971a).
    1973   "Military Images in the Army ROTC." JPMS 1 (Spring):71-90.
Luckham, A.R.
    1971   "A Comparative Typology of Civil-Military Relations." Gov't and Opposi-
            tion. 6 (Winter):5-35.
Magdoff, Harry
    1969   The Age of Imperialism: The Economics of U.S. Foreign Policy. New York:
            Modern Reader.
Malbin, Nona Glazer
    1971   "The ROTC: Military Service on the College Campus." Pp. 63-97 in Charles
            Moskos, Jr. (ed.), (1971a).
Margiotta, Franklin D.
    1974   A Comment on Taylor and Bletz's "A Case for Officer Graduate Education:
            How Much is Enough?" JPMS 2 (Fall):269-271.
Mayhew, Jr., Bruce H., Thomas F. James, & Grant W. Childers
    1972   "System Size and Structural Differentiation in Military Organizations:
            Testing a Harmonic Series Model of the Division of Labor." AJS 77
            (Jan):750-765.
Mazrui, A.E.
    1969   "Violent Contiguity and the Politics of Retribalization in Africa." J of SR 12
            (Sept.).
Mehden, R.F.
    1970   "The Military and Development in Thailand." Journal of Compar. Adm. 2
            (Nov.) 323-340.
Melman, Seymour
    1970   Pentagon Capitalism. New York: McGraw-Hill.
Merton, Robert K. & Paul Lazarsfeld
    1950   Continuities in Social Research: Studies in the Scope and Method of "The
            American Soldier." New York: Free Press.
Midlarsky, M.
    1970   "Mathematical Models Instability and a Theory of Diffusion." Inter-
            national Studies Quarterly. 14 (March).
Miewald, R.D.
    1970   "Weberian Bureaucracy and the Military Model." Public Administration 30
            (March-April):129-133.
Miller, James C. and Robert Tollison
    1971   "The Implicit Tax on Reluctant Military Recruits." SSQ 51 (March):924-931.
Millett, Alan R.
    1974   "Arms Control and Research on Military Institutions." AF & S 1 (Nov.):61-
            78.
Mills, C. Wright
    1956   The Power Elite. New York: Oxford University Press.
Moskos, Charles C. and Wendell Bell
    1967   "Emerging Nations and Ideologies of American Social Scientists. The
            American Sociologist. 2 (May):67-72
Moskos, Charles C.
    1970   The American Enlisted Man. New York: Russell Sage Foundation.
    1971a   Public Opinion and the Military Establishment (ed.) Beverly Hills: Sage
            Publications.
    1971b   "Armed Forces and American Society: Convergence or Divergence?" Pp.
            271-294 in Moskos (ed.), (1971a).
    1973a   "The Emergent Military. Civil, Traditional or Plural?" PSR 16 (April): 255-
            280.
    1973b   "The American Dilemma in Uniform: Race in the Armed Forces." Annals
            406 (March):94-106.

1973c   "Studies on the American Soldier: Continuities and Discontinuities in Social
         Research." Paper presented at the ASA meetings in New York.
1974   "The Concept of the Military-Industrial Complex: Radical Critique Liberal
         Bogey?" SP 21 (Spring): 498-512.
1976   Peace Soldiers. Chicago: University of Chicago Press.
New York University National Security Education Program
1975   Second National Security Studies Survey: A Summary of Results. New York
         University: National Security Education Program.
Nordlinger, E.A.
1970   "Soldiers in Mufti: The Impact of Military Rule upon Economic and Social
         Change in the Non-Western States." American Political Science Review. 64
         (Dec.):1131-1148.
Palen, J. John
1972   "The Education of the Senior Military Decision Maker." SQ 13 (Spring):147-
         160.
Perlmutter, Amos
1969   "The Praetorian State and the Praetorian Army: Toward a Taxonomy of
         Civil-Military Relations in Developing Polities." CP 1 (April):382-404.
Pursell, Carroll W. Jr. (ed.)
1972   The Military-Industrial Complex. New York: Harper & Row.
Putnam, Robert D.
1967   "Toward Explaining Military Intervention in Latin American Politics."
         World Politics 20 (October):83-110.
Pye, Lucien
1962   "Armies in the Process of Political Modernization." Pp. 69-90 in John J.
         Johnson (ed.), (1962).
Radway, Lawrence
1971   "Recent Trends in American Service Academies." Pp. 3-36 in Charles
         Moskos, (ed.), (1971a).
Reisner, Ralph
1968   "The Conscientious Objector Exemption: Administrative Procedures and
         Judicial Review." University of Chicago Law Review 35 (Summer):686-720.
Roghmann, Klaus and Wolfgang Sodeur
1972   "The Impact of Military Service on Authoritarian Attitudes: Evidence from
         West Germany." AJS 78 (Sept.):418-433.
Roucek, J.S.
1962   "The Trends in American Military Sociology and its Educational Im-
         plications." Duquesne R., 8:26-49.
Russett, Bruce M. and Alfred Stepan (eds.)
1973   Military Force and American Society. New York: Harper.
Sarkesian, Sam C.
1972a   "Political Soldiers: Perspectives on Professionalism in the U.S. Military."
         Midwest Journal of Political Science 16 (May):239-258.
1972b   The Military Industrial Complex: A Reassessment (ed.) Beverly Hills,
         California: Sage Publications.
Schmitter, Philippe (ed.)
1973   Military Rule in Latin America. Beverly Hills, Calif.: Sage Publications.
Segal, David and Mady Segal
1971   "Models of Civil-Military Relationships at the Elite Level." in M.R. Van Gils
         (ed.) The Perceived Role of the Military. Netherlands: The Rotterdam Univ.
         Press. Pp. 279-292.
Segal, David
1973   Book Reviews of "Handbook of Military Institutions" and "Public Opinion
         and the Military Establishment." AJS 79 (November):773-776.
Segal, David and J. Blair, F. Newport, and S. Stephens
1974   "Convergence, Isomorphism, and Interdependence at the Civil-Military
         Interface." JPMS 2 (Fall):157-172.
Sharma, B.S.
1971   "The Military and Politics in Africa." Indian Journal of Pol. Sci. 32 (Oct-
         Dec.):536-550.

Shils, Edward
    1962   "The Military in the Political Development of the New States." In John J.
            Johnson (ed.), (1962).
Sigelman, Lee
    1974   "Military Intervention: A Methodological Note." JPMS 2 (Fall):275-281.
Slater, Jerome
    1972   "Opinions and Commentary: A Critique and Response." Bulletin of the
            Inter-University Seminar 1 (July):5-7.
Sperber, Irwin
    1970   "The Sociological Dimensions of Military Co-optation in the U.S."
            Sociological Inquiry 40 (Winter):61-72.
Spier, Hans
    1952   Social Order and the Risk of War. New York: Stewart.
Stauss, Joseph
    1971   "Historical Trends of Military Sociology." Paper presented at the Pacific
            Sociological Association Meetings in April 8-10.
Stegenga, James
    1973   Book Reviews of "On Military Intervention," "The Military Industrial
            Complex," and "Peace, War, and Numbers." AJS 79 (Nov.): 767-776.
Stepan, Alfred
    1971   The Military in Politics: Changing Patterns in Brazil. Princeton: Princeton
            University Press.
Stevenson, Paul
    1971   "American Capitalism & Militarism: A Critique of Lieberson." AJS 77
            (July):134-138.
    1973   "The Military-Industrial Complex: An Examination of the Nature of
            Corporate Capitalism in America." JPMS 1 (Fall):247-259.
    1974   "A Defense of Baran and Sweezy." AJS 79 (May):1456-1459.
Stinchcombe, Arthur
    1973   Comments on "The Impact of Military Service on Authoritarian Attitudes."
            AJS 79 (July):157-159.
Stouffer, Samuel, et al.
    1949   The American Soldier. Princeton, N.J.: Princeton Unversity Press.
Sweezy, Paul
    1973   "Comments on Szymanski's Paper 'Military Spending and Economic
            Stagnation.' " AJS 79 (November):709-710.
Szymanski, Albert
    1973   "Military Spending and Economic Stagnation." AJS 79 (July):1-14.
Tannahill, R. Neal
    1975   "Military Intervention In Search of a Dependent Variable." Journal of
            Political and Military Sociology 3 (Fall):219-228.
Taylor, William J. and Bletz, Donald F.
    1974   "A Case For Officer Graduate Education." JPMS 2 (Fall):251-267.
Terreberry, S.
    1968   "The Evolution of Organizational Environments." ASQ 12 (March):590-613.
Thompson, William
    1973   The Grievances of Military Coup-Makers. Beverly Hills: Sage Publications.
    1974   "Toward Explaining Arab Military Coups." JPMS 2 (Fall):237-250.
Toth, Michael A.
    1971   "The New Draft Lottery: Some Research Implications." American
            Sociologist 6 (June):38-40.
Van Doorn, Jacques
    1965   "The Officer Corps: A Fusion of Profession and Organization." European
            Journal of Sociology 6 (August):262-282.
    1968   Armed Forces and Society (ed.) The Hague: Mouton.
    1969   Military Professions and Military Regimes (ed.) The Hague: Mouton
    1975   "The Decline of the Mass Army in the West: General Reflections." AF & S 1:
            (Winter):147-157.
Vollmer, Howard M. and Donald L. Mills
    1966   Professionalization. Englewood Cliffs: Prentice Hall.

Walter, P.
  1958 "Military Sociology" Pp. 665-672 in J.S. Roucek (ed.), Contemporary Sociology. New York: Philosophical Library.
Wamsley, Gary L.
  1972 "Contrasting Institutions of Air Force Socialization: Happenstance or Bellwether?" AJS 78 (September):399-417.
  1973 "Reply to Lovell." AJS 79 (Sept.):441-443.
Wells, Alan
  1974 "The Coup d'etat in Theory and Practice: Independent Black Africa in the 1960's." AJS 79:871-887.
White, David
  1972 "Why Join the Army?" New Society 20 (April):172-175.
Wilensky, Harold
  1964 "The Professionalization of Everyone?" AJS 70 (Sept.):137-158.
Zeitlin, Maurice
  1974 "On Military Spending and Economic Stagnation" AJS 79 (May):1452-1456.

*The following abbreviations of journals have been used in the references:

AJS — American Journal of Sociology; Annals — Annals of the American Academy of Political and Social Science; AF & S — Armed Forces and Society; ASQ — Administrative Science Quarterly; ASR — American Sociological Review; CP — Comparative Politics; J of CR — Journal of Conflict Resolution; JPMS — Journal of Political and Military Sociology; PSR — Pacific Sociological Review; SP — Social Problems; SQ — Sociological Quarterly; SSQ — Social Science Quarterly.

PART II
ORGANIZATIONAL AND
PROFESSIONAL PERSPECTIVES

In this introduction we briefly attempt to point out three of the major issues in the study of organizational/professional perspectives which are raised by the authors in this part. One major consideration is how to maintain civilian control of the armed forces while at the same time the military is able to retain sufficient professional and organizational autonomy. This problem is particularly accentuated when one considers recent technological and other societal changes that have led to greater convergence between military and civilian structures. Among those authors who consider factors leading to an apolitical or a politicized military, Larson reassesses two of the major interpretations of civilian control of the military, Lang considers the effect of occupational structure, Kourvetaris and Dobratz examine the influence of the social base of recruitment, and Lucas relates military images to political orientations.

Larson's article on professionalism and civil control examines the two prevailing interpretations of "subjective and objective" control of the military set forth by Janowitz and Huntington respectively. While Larson favors the "subjective" approach which he sees as a more effective way to control the military, he warns against an overemphasis on political sensitivity and integration with civilian society which could undermine the professional integrity of the officer corps and encourage political activism.

Lang's article on trends in military occupational structure and their political implications sees military professionalism as influenced by changes of primary, secondary, and tertiary specialties. As military technology advances, the primary sector declines (combat and operations) and the tertiary specialties increase (i.e., intelligence and technical management) while the scientific, engineering and maintenance specialties in the secondary sector remain about the same. Lang believes that the multiplicity of relationships in the officer corps and these occupational trends have blurred the boundary between military and civilian to the extent that no longer can one argue that a politically neutral military exists.

Kourvetaris and Dobratz consider the impact of the social base of officer recruitment upon the political attitudes and behavior of the officers in 14 different nations. The authors argue that broadening of the social base of recruitment of the officers did not result in a concomitant process of political democratization of the officers' political attitudes and/or behavior. In fact, in some cases broadening the social base of officer recruitment encourages rather than deters the extra-parliamentary and conspiratorial activities of the officers in national and international politics.

In his discussion of military images in the ROTC, Lucas does not find that different cadet images (combat, managerial, technical) consistently influence the cadets' political conservatism or professionalism.

Another major organizational/professional issue is diversity versus uniformity of military institutions in different parts of the world. While there has been a shift from ascriptive to achievement criteria in recruitment and from generalist to specialist in occupational patterns, these changes have not been uniform or isomorphic among various militaries. Garnier in his study of the British military academy finds that military technological complexity and change are mediated by cultural and organizational factors which influence the recruitment policies for British military cadets. Thus the universalistic criteria of recruitment may not be applicable to all militaries throughout the world. Kourvetaris and Dobratz also point out that cultural idiosyncrasies of national armies should be considered.

The final major issue centers around the socialization process. The major question of the debate has been whether or not self-selection by the individual of the military or the military socialization process is more important in determining the attitudes and outlook of officers and enlisted men. Two articles, one by Lucas and the other by Cockerham, address themselves to this question.

Lucas' study of ROTC cadets tends to suggest the limited influence of the ROTC experience on the average cadet. The only clear referent for the cadets that emerges is the combat type but few cadets actually hold such an image. The managerial and technical images are civilian-oriented and lack clear expectations for role occupancy. Lucas believes the lack of effective referents is an important factor in the general absence of professional military socialization in officer education.

Cockerham considers the socialization process in the airborne, where the training process may be much more rigorous and intensive than in the ROTC. Cockerham stresses the significance of self-selection rather than the importance of the overall training process. Rewards such as self-identification with an elite unit, higher status and pay, and the availability of action and challenge are significant factors for joining the airborne. During training, there are no major changes in attitudes and values. Thus, both authors fail to see the military socialization process as important in influencing the development of individual attitudes in the military.

Professionalism, Recruitment, and Politics

2

MILITARY PROFESSIONALISM
AND CIVIL CONTROL:
A COMPARATIVE ANALYSIS
OF TWO INTERPRETATIONS

ARTHUR D. LARSON

University of Wisconsin—Parkside

The steps taken to strengthen civil control after World War II emphasized external administrative and political arrangements. In contrast, Samuel Huntington and Morris Janowitz focused on the internal controls provided by military professionalism. Huntington proposed a politically neutral profession, isolated from society and concerned with the efficient achievement of victory without regard to nonmilitary considerations. Janowitz proposed a politically sensitive profession integrated with the society and concerned with the measured use of force to achieve viable international relations. Huntington's professionalism reflected the radical tradition of U.S. military professionalism, the result of the reaction of the officer corps against civil control, while Janowitz's professionalism reflected the dominant pragmatic tradition, the product of the adaptation of the officer corps to civil control. Janowitz's pragmatic professionalism is the more desirable form for meeting the difficult civil-military relations problems of the post-Viet Nam war period. Institutional changes to achieve pragmatic professionalism must be made with caution, however, for an overemphasis on political sensitivity and integration with the society would undermine the professional detachment of the officer corps and encourage political activism.

There is widespread recognition that the relationships between the armed forces and the larger society in the post-Viet Nam war period will be fundamentally different from those which prevailed earlier. As a matter of fact, the anticipated changes will continue — if not consummate — the transformation of U.S. civil-military relations which began after World War II, when the national security demands of the cold war posed unprecedented challenges to civil-military relations as traditionally practiced. In the present effort to re-evaluate civil-military relations, there is considerable interest in the role of military professionalism. The purpose of this paper is to examine the concept of military professionalism and its contribution to meeting the post-Viet Nam war civil-military relations problem.

Arthur D. Larson

THE TRADITION OF CIVIL SUPREMACY AND CONTROL

Civil supremacy and control, the American tradition of civil-military relations, was part of the political culture inherited by the colonies from England.[1] It played an important role in the coming, course, and results of the Revolution, and thereafter was so well suited to the military needs of the United States that it became an almost sacred feature of the political and social culture (Ekirch, 1956; Smith, 1951).

But through World War II, the United States met its peacetime civil-military relations problem rather more by eliminating than solving it, and its wartime problem by letting it solve itself. Because of its geographic and political isolation from the centers of world conflict up to World War II, there was little danger of immediate attack, and there was time to prepare shortly before or even after the outbreak of war. Military policy through World War II therefore consisted in the main of the mobilization of manpower and resources when war appeared imminent or broke out, immediate demobilization when war ended, and the maintenance of armed forces at minimal manpower and resource levels during peace. During peacetime, antimilitarism was strong, and the concern was mainly that of preserving liberal values because the threat to these values from the military was considered to be greater than the threat from any external enemy. The military was maintained by Congress at the lowest possible personnel and budgetary levels. It was allowed to stagnate internally and was politically and socially isolated from the rest of society. During war, antimilitarism was muted, and the concern shifted from responsiveness to effectiveness. The military was rapidly expanded from a basic peacetime cadre by conscription, volunteers, and callup of reserves, was given almost unlimited resources, and was allowed to exercise widespread authority and influence in the government and larger society, all with the consent of Congress and the public.

The conditions which made possible this peacetime neglect of military security preparations did not prevail after World War II, however.[2] After the war, the armed forces were rapidly demobilized and the nation turned back to peacetime pursuits in the traditional fashion. But the outbreak of the cold war necessitated remobilization on a massive scale under what were essentially peacetime circumstances. During the decade of the 1950's, the typical wartime pattern of civil-military relations prevailed: muted antimilitarism, large armed forces with considerable influence in the society, executive domination of national security affairs, and an emphasis on effectiveness. Indeed, the conditions which traditionally had

---

1. Civil control is a solution to the problem of achieving responsibility in the military bureaucracy. The problem of bureaucratic responsibility is not confined to the military, of course, but extends to the entire public bureaucracy, both civil and military. As Levitan (1946) has pointed out, it is the central problem of a democratic political order today.

2. There was recognition immediately after World War II that the nation would be faced with a different problem of civil-military relations in the postwar years. See, for example, Kerwin, 1948:156-172, and Smith, 1951:1-6. The post-World War II crisis in civil-military relations is not confined to the United States, however, but is worldwide. See Kelly, 1963, and Finer, 1962:205-243.

worked to prevent militarism were substantially weakened during this time. The security threat became massive and diffuse, while its legitimacy became less clearcut. The ideas of careerism and professionalism became stronger both in and out of the armed forces, while that of the citizen soldier serving for the duration of hostilities weakened. Increasingly, antimilitarism was muted not only because military preparations were necessary to meet a security threat, but also because they served the economic and political interests of many people and groups in the society. The military, formerly a distinctive if not an alien institution in the society, became similar in many ways to large civilian bureaucracies and was integrated into the social and economic life of the society. And finally, executive domination and the emphasis on effectiveness increased because the massiveness and complexity of the security threat made it difficult for Congress and the people to make meaningful judgements about the nature and scope of military preparations, and less willing to accept risks in preparing to meet the security threat.

But sentiments against these trends grew during these years and were provided with a focus during the early 1960's by President Eisenhower's military-industrial complex warning, cold war indoctrination attempts by the military and other civil-military relations incidents, the defense policy of the Kennedy Administration, and ultimately the Viet Nam war. By the end of the 1960's, important sectors of public and governmental opinion had become convinced that there was a serious threat of militarization of the society, and there occurred a resurgence of antimilitarism, a redefinition of the security interests of the nation and the contribution of military power to achieving them, and a renewed congressional interest in playing a meaningful role in national security affairs. These developments are part of a return to peacetime traditions of civil-military relations. They are accompanied by conditions which reinforce the tendency of these traditions to isolate and suppress the military: in the larger society, radical antimilitarism, voluntarism, and the decline of ROTC; and within the armed forces, alienation over Viet Nam, and an inclination to carry out a professional purification after the dissent, liberalization, scandals, and dishonors of recent years.

These emerging conditions in the society and armed forces, combined with the need to maintain large and effective armed forces, pose a new dilemma. It is not the earlier and simpler dilemma of whether to accept large armed forces and the inconveniences and dangers which may attend them, or not to do so and risk the dangers posed by external enemies, for the external dangers are great and there is no alternative to being prepared to meet them. The real dilemma is how to insure responsiveness in the military without sacrificing effectiveness, since the traditional impulse to suppress the military cannot be indulged.

The radically changed security situation and military policies of the post-World War II period served to emphasize both the importance and the inadequacies of the tradition of civil control. The steps taken to strengthen civil control, beginning with the National Security Act of 1947 and extending through the changes introduced by Secretary of Defense Robert S. McNamara, were consistent with the tradition in focusing on political and administrative arrangements for direction and control of the military by

Congress, the President, and the Secretary of Defense and other civilians in the defense establishment (Smith, 1951; Hammond, 1961). But a quite different approach was proposed by two scholars in the emerging academic field of national security affairs, Samuel P. Huntington (1957) and Morris Janowitz (1960). They argued that military officership is a profession and as such, possesses certain characteristics which would contribute to effectiveness and responsiveness in the military. Their approach, focusing as it did on military professionalism, represents a radical departure from the tradition of civil supremacy, which includes a negative stereotype of the military profession and emphasizes safeguards against the dangers it poses for the larger society.

Although the Huntington and Janowitz proposals share a common overall orientation, there are fundamental differences. Huntington advocates an autonomous, politically neutral military profession which is isolated from the larger society, and concerned only with the efficient achievement of victory without regard to nonmilitary considerations. Janowitz proposes a politically sensitive military profession which is integrated with the society and concerned with the measured use of force to achieve viable international relations. Between them, they cover both the significant theoretical aspects of military professionalism and the important dimensions of the historical development of U.S. military professionalism in the context of the tradition of civil control. Analysis of the Huntington and Janowitz studies therefore provides a useful avenue of approach to the purpose of this paper.

HUNTINGTON'S OBJECTIVE CIVILIAN CONTROL

Samuel P. Huntington's *The Soldier and the State* (1957) was the first important treatment of civil-military relations as a separate and distinct category of political phenomena, and its central themes have strongly influenced the thinking of scholars and the military on the subject. Huntington argues that "subjective civilian control," the traditional approach to civil-military relations, sacrifices military effectiveness to insure military responsiveness, and should be replaced by "objective civilian control," which maximizes both effectiveness and responsiveness.

Huntington approaches civil-military relations in terms of interest group politics: civil-military relations constitute a subsystem of the pluralistic political system, and the crux of the civil-military relations problem is the relative power of the military and civilian groups in that subsystem. Civil control and military security will be greatest when the political power of the officer corps, which is determined by its size, resources, and prestige, is the minimum necessary to fulfill its function of providing security for the state. But under "subjective civilian control," an antimilitary liberal ideology forces the military to incorporate liberal values as the price of its political power. Responsiveness of the military as reflected in its commitment to liberal values is achieved at the price of effectiveness, however, because those liberal values compromise its professionalism.

Under "objective civilian control," on the other hand, the power of the officer corps is minimized by fully professionalizing it, making it an efficient and politically neutral instrument of state policy. Huntington argues that military officership is a fully developed profession because it manifests to a significant degree three principal characteristics of the professional ideal-type: expertise, corporateness, and responsibility. It carries out its purpose within the confines of political policy laid down by the state without regard to political, moral, or other nonmilitary considerations. It is not directly involved in the formulation and advocacy of policy but limited to providing professional military advice to Congress and the executive.

Only officers involved in and dedicated to the central expertise of the management of violence are members of the military profession; commissioned specialists such as lawyers and doctors, reserve officers, and enlisted men are not. The characteristics of the professional officer derive from and are shaped by the content and function of his profession. Above all, he is obedient and loyal to the authority of the state, competent in the military expertise, dedicated to using his skill to provide for the security of the state, and politically and morally neutral. He is motivated by a military ethic made up of values and attitudes which "inhere in" and are "implied by" the professional military function. According to Huntington (1957:79) these constitute a unique professional outlook or a "military mind" which may be characterized as "pessimistic, collectivist, historically inclined, power-oriented, nationalistic, militaristic, pacifist, and instrumentalist . . . in brief, realistic and conservative." The level of professionalism of the officer corps is directly related to the degree to which its members adhere to this conservative professional ethic. Liberalism, fascism, and marxism are hostile to the military ethic, however, and in societies in which they prevail the officer corps is unable to adhere to its ethic and cannot be fully professional. A necessary condition for full military professionalism is therefore a promilitary conservative political ideology in the larger society.

JANOWITZ'S CONSTABULARY FORCE

Janowitz's *The Professional Soldier* (1960) was the first comprehensive sociological study of the military institution.[3] Janowitz seeks to understand the military as a whole through empirical analysis of major dimensions of its institutional life, and to use this understanding as a basis for suggesting changes which will enable the military to meet the demands of security and civil control. He proposes that the military be transformed into a "constabulary force" committed to the reasoned use of force in support of "viable international relations" in a situation in which there is no clear distinction between war and peace or between military and political action. While not a police force in the usual sense, the constabulary force would be committed to keeping the peace while at the same time being prepared to make war.

While Janowitz specifies the characteristics which make officership a profession — expertise, lengthy education, group identity, ethics, standards of performance — he approaches the profession not as a static model but as a dynamic bureaucratic organization which changes over time in

---

3. The discussion is also based on Janowitz, 1959.

response to changing conditions. He argues that the character of the American military profession today is the result of the impact of broad social transformations which have occurred since the turn of the century. Although he does not describe in so many words the original state of the profession, his discussion suggests that he considers it to have been traditionalist, authoritarian, caste-like seniority-bound, elitist, closed and inward looking. As a result of broad social changes, the basis of authority and discipline has shifted to manipulation, persuasion, and consensus; military skills have become similar to civilian skills; officer recruitment has become more socially representative; membership in the elite has become more accessible; and the profession's ideology has become explicitly political. As a consequence of these changes, the typical role of the professional officer has changed from the traditional "warrior" or "heroic" role to the managerial-technical role, and the military profession as a whole has become similar to large, bureaucratic, nonmilitary institutions. It has, in effect, become "civilianized."

The constabulary force concept would require fundamental changes in the military profession. The constabulary force would recognize that the threat or use of violence should be carefully adjusted to the political objective pursued. In this approach, political and military factors cannot be considered independently of one another at any level. The military professional would therefore become sensitive to nonmilitary considerations and share the formulation of policy with civilians. Such traditional principles and practices as the use of maximum force to achieve victory, concentration on military factors to the exclusion of political and other nonmilitary considerations, distinction between wartime and peacetime conditions, and political neutrality and social indifference would be abandoned. Civil control of the military would be concerned with guiding range of managerial, political, and technological functions. Civilians, with military advice, would formulate standards of performance for the profession and evaluate its effectiveness. The professional officer would be broadly recruited, educated in political as well as military affairs, possess managerial and technical skills yet retain the "warrior spirit," cultivate a broad perspective on civilian and military, as well as domestic and international affairs, and be motivated by professional considerations. Steps would be taken to prevent the development of frustrations over objectives, doctrine, conditions of employment, and public esteem, for such frustrations would obstruct the realization of a high level of professionalism. The professional officer would be responsive to civil control because of law, tradition, and professionalism, and because of his integration with civil values and institutions.

TWO TRADITIONS OF U.S. MILITARY PROFESSIONALISM

As suggested earlier, the Huntington and Janowitz interpretations military professionalism reflect the major trends in the historical development of professionalism in the U.S. military under the impact of civil supremacy and control. A major concern of that tradition is to provide safeguards against the negative consequences of military professionalism. According to the tradition, a professional or "standing army" is wasteful and immoral institution which leads to aggression and war, and threatens the liberties of the people and the constitution of the republic, and its officers and soldiers are corrupt, autocratic, ignorant, and bloodthirsty (Ekirch, 1956; Miller, 1946).[4] To the extent that it denigrates military professionalism the tradition extolls military amateurism, holding that citizen soldiers, deeply committed to and fighting for their homes and beliefs, are more responsive to the people and more militarily effective than professional soldiers. These views support the ancient principle that standing armies should not be maintained in peacetime, but should be raised only to meet and on the occasion of specific threats to the nation's security, and should be composed of nonprofessional citizen soldiers. This negative view of military professionalism and the naive faith in military amateurism did not result in the exclusion of professionalism from the American military, however, but contributed to the emergence of two different and uniquely American forms of military professionalism: "pragmatic professionalism," which resulted from the reconciliation of professionalism with the tradition of civil supremacy, and "radical professionalism," which emerged from the estrangement of professionalism from that tradition.[5]

The faith in the superiority of nonprofessionals was nourished by the myth that it was the amateur citizen soldier who had defeated the professional soldiery of the British army during the Revolution. But contrary to the popular belief, the British regulars were defeated, not by untrained and undisciplined citizen soldiers carried to victory by their natural abilities and enthusiasm, but by troops which Washington and his officers had painstakingly raised to the same level of skill as the enemy (Weigley, 1962; Bernardo and Bacon, 1961). It was the early realization, driven home by repeated failures of untrained citizen forces in the face of regular troops, that whatever the natural virtues of the citizen soldier might be, he was almost useless until trained and seasoned — in a word, "professionalized" — which determined the general task of the military policy of the United States from the beginning: the reconciliation of military amateurism with military professionalism to create a military force sufficient to meet threats to the nation's security. The melding of amateurism and professionalism resulted in "pragmatic professionalism:" military professionalism shaped by the concrete needs and demands of an immediate objective and by what is suitable to and tolerated by a democratic society, with officers who are professionals not for professionalism's sake, but because it is an effective way to get a job accomplished. In pragmatic professionalism, the professional ideal is compromised by the incorporation

---

4. For a recent statement of the traditional theme of the incompatibility of a military institution and democracy, see Cohen, 1963.

5. This interpretation of the development of U.S. military professionalism, while the author's own, is based on discussions in Huntington, 1957, and Janowitz, 1960; on the analysis of professional military thought since the Revolution in Weigley, 1962, in which the idea of two traditions of military professionalism is suggested; and on other historical treatments of the American military, including, Weigley, 1967. Huntington emphasizes the level or degree of professionalism, and Janowitz the evolution of professionalism, but neither identifies different and coexisting professional traditions.

of such features of the tradition of civil control as military amateurism and a sensitivity to domestic considerations.

Pragmatic professionalism reflects a recognition on the part of the society that it needs effective armed forces, at least in time of crisis. But the basic antipathy between the tradition and military professionalism was not thereby extinguished, and when the military were not needed they were rejected. During the years between the Civil War and the Spanish-American War, the military were more suppressed and isolated by civilian society than during any earlier time; these years were the "dark ages" for both the Army and Navy. During this period, the services underwent professionalization on the model of European — particularly German — military professionalism. The reaction of the military to the rejection and hostility of civilian society affected in subtle ways the professionalization of the military, giving rise to "radical professionalism:" military professionalism shaped by abstract theories and absolute ideals of military purpose and efficiency, unrelated to the social and political realities of the larger society, and emphasizing such characteristics as functional specificity, political neutrality, and efficiency.

Neither the officer corps as a whole nor individual officers have, of course, been entirely pragmatic or radical in their professionalism. Officers of both persuasions have held positions of leadership in both the wartime and peacetime military, including Jackson, Grant, Wood, Palmer, Marshall, and Eisenhower in the pragmatic tradition, and Taylor, McClellan, Pershing, March, Patton, and MacArthur in the radical tradition. Generally speaking, however, the officer corps has always been characterized by pragmatic professionalism, although radical professionalism gained in prominence in the small peacetime regular forces. By keeping alive the study and practice of military art and science, and training military leadership, these professional traditions have helped to maintain a minimum level of military effectiveness essential to the military policy dictated by the tradition of civil control. At the same time, they have contributed to the institutional survival of the military by making it acceptable to the larger society and preserving its internal cohesion, pragmatic professionalism by making the military useful when it was needed and radical professionalism by reconciling it to rejection when it was not needed.

Huntington and Janowitz are the historians and theoreticians of these two traditions of American military professionalism, Huntington of the radical professionalism tradition, and Janowitz of the pragmatic professionalism tradition. In terms of the question at issue here, Huntington's position is that civil supremacy and control can be strengthened only by abandoning pragmatic professionalism, which is the result of subjective control, and embracing radical professionalism which would make objective civilian control possible. Janowitz, on the other hand, proposes not that pragmatic professionalism be abandoned, but that it be adapted to the new conditions of national security and civil control in the form of the constabulary force.

MILITARY PROFESSIONALISM
AND INTERNAL OBJECTIVE CONTROL

Accepting the desirability — indeed, the necessity — of placing greater emphasis on professionalism as a means of strengthening civil control, and setting aside for the moment the question of acceptability to the larger society, which form of professionalism — radical or pragmatic — would be more suitable for this purpose? The following theoretical distinctions provide a useful way of approaching this question. The controls by which effectiveness and responsiveness are achieved in any public bureaucracy may be divided into those which are "external" to it in that they are imposed and enforced by the legislature, executive, and courts, and by interest groups; and those which are "internal" in that they are based on values and standards held by individuals within the bureaucracy and enforced, at least in the first instance, by their sense of what is right, proper, and feasible (Gilbert, 1959; Dotson, 1957). Internal controls may be further divided into "subjective" controls, based on social, political, and moral values, and "objective" controls, based on scientific, technical, and professional values and standards.[6] Under the tradition of civil control, the emphasis has always been on rather rigorous external controls imposed by civilians, and more implicit subjective internal controls based on the values brought into the military by citizen soldiers and accommodated by pragmatic professionalism. It was recognized by some after World War II, however, that external controls designed to secure responsiveness in a large and complex military bureaucracy whose members fill roles characterized by considerable discretion, influence, and external pressures, would inevitably become so cumbersome as to introduce a degree of inflexibility fatal to effectiveness, and that greater emphasis should therefore be placed on internal controls which are general, flexible, ever-present, and self-enforcing (Levitan, 1946).

In terms of these theoretical distinctions, what Huntington and Janowitz are proposing is that, as an alternative to further elaboration of external controls over the military, civil control should be strengthened through greater recognition of and emphasis on internal objective control based on professionalism. The effectiveness of military professionalism as a basis of internal objective control would depend on the degree or level of professional development of the military. An occupation is a profession to the extent that it possesses certain structural characteristics displayed by the established professions of medicine and law (Cogan, 1953; Goode, 1960; Greenwood, 1957). Most important among these are a central set of skills which are difficult to master and of considerable social importance, organization, autonomy or self-government, extensive education, a code of ethics and a system of enforcement, social responsibility, and sense of community. With these characteristics, a profession efficiently and responsibly generates a socially essential and intellectually skilled service in the form of advice, action, or both. There are, however, certain negative tendencies or "pathologies" of profes-

---

6. On the nature and operation of internal controls, see Simon *et al.*, 1962: 541-56.

sionalism which can seriously impede the performance of this function
Included are "trained incapacity" or a lack of skill and understanding
outside of a field of professional expertise; "goal displacement" or the
transformation of professional means into ends; syndicalism, or the
tendency to become closed, inbred, and monopolistic; elitism, or the
tendency to become isolated and alienated from the larger society; and
opportunism, or the tendency to be readily available to the highest bid
der.[7]

Military officership displays to a considerable degree many of the
central characteristics of professionalism, but lacks one of the most
important ones — autonomy or self-government. Autonomy is the right
of an occupation to make decisions regarding recruitment, education,
performance, remuneration, expulsion, and other key matters within a
broad framework provided by law and its own code of ethics. Society
grants autonomy to an occupation if it is persuaded that the occupation
can and will control its members, and that it must be autonomous to do
its work (Goode, 1969). But in the course of the development of civil
military relations in the U.S. and other western societies, it has been
found that responsiveness and effectiveness in the military were best
insured by restricting its autonomy through nationalization and bureau
cratization.[8] The military therefore possesses little real autonomy, and
decisions regarding key professional matters are made by civilians or
within the military only under outside control (Smith, 1966:202).[9] Indeed
even the final judgement regarding the suitability of military advice and
action within its field of expertise is reserved to civilians (Abrahamsson
1972:66). With only limited autonomy, military officership, although
possessing many of the other necessary characteristics, could not be a
fully developed profession. Rather it is a "semi-profession," ranking
with such occupations as engineering, nursing, and public school teach
ing in degree of professionalization (Toren, 1969; Goode, 1969).[10] This
theoretical conclusion is consistent with information on the public's
evaluation of military officership. In surveys from 1925 to 1963, mili
tary officership, while ranked high among occupations generally, has
been consistently ranked below the established professions (Coates and
Pellegrin, 1965:43-47; Janowitz, 1971a:xli).

How do the Huntington and Janowitz conceptions of military profes
sionalism compare to this analysis? Huntington attempts to demonstrate

7. A deficiency of the academic literature on professionalism is an almost
complete lack of discussion of the negative consequences of professionalism, al
though these have long been recognized in nonacademic writing on the professions
See, for example, Laski, 1930. The undesirable results of professionalism sug
gested here are similar to the "unanticipated consequences" of bureaucratization
suggested in Merton, 1952.

8. Bureaucratization in itself does not preclude autonomy, the crucial test
being whether the members of a profession, rather than outsiders, control their own
affairs. Medicine, law, and the clergy are autonomous, while other professions are
granted lesser degrees of autonomy and are therefore less professional.

9. Van Doorn (1965) discusses the dual bureaucratic and professional charac
ter of the military.

10. For an argument that the degree of professionalism of the military is
declining, see Abrams, 1965.

that military officership is a highly developed profession, but his conclusion that it is almost as fully professionalized as medicine and law is not tenable in view of its status as a semi-profession. It should also be noted that in an effort to show that military officership is, indeed, a highly developed profession, Huntington distorts the process of professionalization. The professionalization of occupations is an aspect of social differentiation resulting from technological and other large-scale social changes. But Huntington does not provide for the impact of external factors, despite his assertion that he recognizes that the military profession is shaped by "functional imperatives" and "societal imperatives." He emphasizes that the development of the profession up to 1914 took place largely in isolation from political and social factors in the larger society and, in effect, argues that changes in the profession due to these factors after that time should be nullified and that the profession should not respond to them in the future. In fact, his proposal that the political orientation of the larger society should change from antimilitary liberalism to promilitary conservatism to accommodate the value commitments of radical military professionalism would mean that the profession would shape the society, reversing the dominant thrust of the interaction of profession and society.

While he notes that military officership possesses many of the traditional characteristics of professionalism, Janowitz does not employ the static ideal-type analysis on which Huntington bases his analysis. Rather he treats the military as a social system in which the professional characteristics are variables which interact with each other and with external conditions so that the system adapts internally and externally. He does not propose to insulate the profession from external conditions, but rather to have the profession respond to those conditions in ways which will preserve those unique qualities essential to responsiveness and effectiveness, while at the same time, creating external conditions which will nourish military professionalism. Finally, he does not propose that the military have professional autonomy, but that civilians, with the participation of the military, establish standards and evaluate the performance of the profession. While Janowitz avoids the pitfalls of Huntington's rigorous approach, he fails to define the boundaries of military professionalism, nor does he discuss how the profession is to retain its uniqueness under the pressures toward civilianization, or its members their expertise and detachment, with the heavy emphasis on political sensitivity and indoctrination which he proposes. But these deficiencies aside, the Janowitz conception of military professionalism would be the more suitable as the basis of internal objective control.

In addition to reflecting the limitations of military officership as a semi-profession, the Janowitz approach would maintain strong internal *subjective* control. Both Huntington and Janowitz recognize the need to accommodate military professionalism to the social and political values of subjective control, but their approaches to achieving this differ substantially. Huntington argues that these traditional values have prevented full military professionalism, and should be replaced by political and social values which are functionally supportive of professionalism. But the effect of subsuming the social and political values held

by the military within their professionalism would be to emasculate traditional internal subjective controls as an independent source of control
over the military.[11] While Janowitz would also systematically incorporate political and social values into the profession, the effectiveness of
internal subjective control would not be impaired because these values
would continue to originate in the larger society and would not be shaped
by the functional requirements of military professionalism.

In summary, then, it seems clear that the "objective civilian control" proposed by Huntington would not enhance civil control, and might
very well endanger it (Finer, 1962:23-30). The model of autonomous military professionalism which he proposes would not provide a dependable
foundation for internal objective control because of the underdeveloped
character of military professionalism and the pathologies which are
present in any profession, and which might be exacerbated in a semi-
profession. The effectiveness of subjective control would also be substantially diminished if the values on which it was based were only those
functionally relevant to or supportive of military professionalism. Further,
the idea that there is a real distinction between the ends and means of
war, and that the purpose of the military is to prepare for and win wars
in the most efficient manner possible without regard to nonmilitary considerations, became irrelevant with the technological, political, and military developments of World War II and the postwar period. The purpose
of military power now is not victory but deterrence, not to make war but
to preserve the peace. There has been a fusion of "political considerations" and "military considerations" and of policymaking and policy
implementation, and the military are now extensively involved in political
policy matters and civilians in military matters (Huntington, 1961:123-196;
Sapin and Snyder, 1954). Finally, the historical relationship between military professionalism and civil control suggests that the radical professionalism proposed by Huntington would not be acceptable to the larger
society. There is no evidence that the transformation of the political
orientation of the society from liberalism to conservatism, which he
argues would make his radical professionalism possible and acceptable,
is occurring or will occur. In fact, the evidence points in the opposite
direction in that the promilitary sentiments of the post-World War II
years are waning while antimilitarism is increasing.

The Janowitz "constabulary force" proposal, on the other hand, holds
considerable promise as a means of strengthening civil control. The model
of military professionalism Janowitz proposes would provide a substantial basis for internal objective control because it advocates participation
of responsible civilian officials in the formulation of standards and the
evaluation of performance, and the systematic incorporation of political
and social values from the larger society into the profession. Since these
values would be independent of the functional requirements of military
professionalism, the effectiveness of internal subjective control would not

---

11. Janowitz (1960:233-256) notes that while military officers overwhelmingly
identify themselves as conservative rather than liberal in political orientation,
their actual political beliefs are a reflection of those prevailing in civilian society.
For an argument that the military generally share the liberal outlook of American
society, see Guttman, 1965.

be reduced. Finally, the pragmatic professionalism proposed by Janowitz is consistent with the historical relationship of military professionalism and civil control, and should therefore be acceptable to the larger society.

CONCLUSIONS

Changes in civil supremacy to achieve the high levels of effectiveness and responsiveness which will be required in the post-Viet Nam period should, of course, involve both external and internal controls. But insofar as internal controls are concerned, the implication of the preceding analysis is that only the pragmatic professionalism proposed by Janowitz would provide a suitable basis for objective control without impairing subjective control. There will, however, be strong forces pulling the military away from pragmatic professionalism in the post-Viet Nam era. Janowitz (1971 a:x-lvi) has recently pointed out that a series of technological strategic, and political developments since World War II, culminating with the termination of conscription, have brought about the end of the traditional mass army. Concurrently, many of the long term changes within the military responsible for the convergence of the military institution with civilian institutions — "civilianization" — have reached their limits. As a result of these changes, and of the reassertion of professional identity by the officer corps, the military will be smaller, more self-contained, and more "military." When combined with a resurgent anti-militarism in the larger society, these developments raise the possibility of a new turn toward radical professionalism in the officer corps.

Some scholars and officers have suggested that these divergent institutional trends be accommodated by "military pluralism." Charles Moskos (1971, 1972) proposes that the process of institutional transformation in the military should be understood as a dialectical one, in which the "institutional persistencies" of the military react against the pressures toward civilianization arising in the larger society. As a result of this process, the military has passed through several successive phases of convergence which began after World War II. He argues that although there is now a movement toward greater divergence in the military, tendencies toward convergence will continue. The result will not be a "homogenous military somewhere between the civilianized and traditional poles," but a "pluralistic" military in which some parts are divergent and others convergent with respect to civilian society. Divergence would be most marked in combat units, certain support forces, and at higher command levels, and here the traditional ideals and practices of military professionalism would be cultivated. Convergence would be emphasized in these sectors and units concerned with administrative, educational, medical, logistical, technical and other areas which are not uniquely military, and these areas would be allowed to become "civilianized." Moskos suggests that a pluralistic military might be better suited for meeting the requirements of effectiveness and responsiveness because a heavily civilianized military would lack the élan necessary to effectiveness, while a highly traditional military would be incapable of maintaining a complex organization and might not be responsive.

The suggestion of a dialectic between the pressures toward professionalism and those toward civilianization is, of course, a reasonable interpretation of the dynamics of institutional development of the military. But the proposal that this dialectic should manifest itself by a division of the military into "professionalized" and "civilianized" sectors is a *reductio ad absurdum*. Effectiveness cannot be separated from responsiveness, for they are two sides of the coin. The meaning of each and the balance between the two must be continuously redefined as internal and external conditions change. But in a pluralistic military, units in which the emphasis was on effectiveness would neglect responsiveness, while those in which responsiveness was emphasized would neglect effectiveness. Great functional difficulties and unbridgeable ideological differences would develop very quickly between the two parts of the institution. Two military institutions in the place of one would soon emerge — one elitist and militaristic, the other popular and politicized. They would inevitably become locked in political struggle, and would ultimately use their military power against each other and the larger society.

Thus, a pluralistic military would not be responsive and effective for long, and would soon destroy itself and the larger society through the internal tensions it would generate. A pluralistic military is precisely what should be avoided, and a relatively homogenous military should be the objective. While some sectors, units, and individuals in the constabulary force may be more "civilianized" or more "militarized," or more "pragmatic" or more "radical" than others, it would constitute a cohesive whole organizationally and ideologically. But if the constabulary force is to be realized, those aspects of the current trend in the military toward divergence which are not necessary or useful must be contained. This may require what Janowitz (1971b) terms "institution building" in many areas of the military. In the officer corps, for example, he suggests lateral entry to insure its representative character and vitality, elimination of the practice of periodic rotation of officer personnel to achieve depth of knowledge, experience, and commitment, reform of officer education, particularly with respect to educating officers in the limits on and consequences of the use of force, and rationalization of the system of authority and discipline to insure that it is necessary to and serves the functions of the military institution.

A word of caution is in order regarding the extent of such "institutional building" innovations, however. Military pluralism is an attempt to bridge the gap between the position (represented by Huntington) that military professionalism is incompatible with traditional civilian values and that the military must therefore be isolated from civilian society to be effective, and the contrasting position (represented by Janowitz) that there is no incompatibility and that the military can and must be integrated with the larger society to insure responsiveness. While pluralism itself is unacceptable, the dilemma it addresses is a real one and must be recognized by any institutional changes intended to realize the constabulary force model. An overemphasis on integration with civilian society, and on political sensitivity, social awareness, and politico-military factors, would undermine professional objectivity and engender a spirit of political activism in the officer corps, lowering both its effectiveness and responsiveness.

REFERENCES

Abrahamsson, Bengt
1972 Military Professionalization and Political Power. Beverly Hills: Sage.
Abrams, Philip
1965 "The Late Profession of Arms: Ambiguous Goals and Deteriorating Means in Britain." European Journal of Sociology 6 (No. 2):238-261.
Bernardo, C. Joseph and Eugene H. Bacon
1961 American Military Policy; Its Development Since 1775. Harrisburg: Stackpole.
Coates, Charles H. and Roland J. Pellegrin
1965 Military Sociology: A Study of American Military Institutions and Military Life. University Park: Social Science Press.
Cogan, Morris L.
1953 "Toward a Definition of a Profession." Harvard Educational Review 23 (Winter):33-50.
Cohen, Carl
1963 "The Military in a Democracy." Centennial Review 7 (Winter):75-94.
Dotson, Arch
1957 "Fundamental Approaches to Administrative Responsibility." Western Political Quarterly 10 (September):701-727.
Ekirch, Arthur A., Jr.
1956 The Civilian and the Military. New York: Oxford University Press.
Finer, S. E.
1962 The Man on Horseback; The Role of the Military in Politics. New York: Praeger.
Gilbert, Charles E.
1959 "The Framework of Administrative Responsibility." Journal of Politics 21 (August):373-407.
Goode, William J.
1960 "Encroachment, Charlatanism, and the Emerging Profession: Psychology, Sociology and Medicine." American Sociological Review 25 (December):902-914.
1969 "The Theoretical Limits of Professionalization." Pp. 266-313 in Amitai Etzioni (ed.), The Semi-Professions and Their Organization: Teachers, Nurses, Social Workers. New York: Free Press.
Greenwood, Ernest
1957 "Attributes of a Profession." Social Work 2 (July):44-55.
Guttman, Allen
1965 "Political Ideals and the Military Ethic." American Scholar 34 (Spring): 221-237.
Hammond, Paul Y.
1961 Organizing for Defense; The American Military Establishment in the Twentieth Century. Princeton: Princeton University Press.
Huntington, Samuel P.
1957 The Soldier and the State: The Theory and Practice of Civil-Military Relations. Cambridge: Harvard University Press.
1961 The Common Defense; Strategic Programs in National Politics. New York: Columbia University Press.
Janowitz, Morris
1959 Sociology and the Military Establishment. New York: Russell Sage Foundation.
1960 The Professional Soldier: A Social and Political Portrait. Glencoe: Free Press.
1971a The Professional Soldier: A Social and Political Portrait. Glencoe: Free Press. (A reprint of the 1960 edition with a "Prologue" added.)
1971b "The Emergent Military." Pp. 255-270 in Charles C. Moskos, Jr. (ed.), Public Opinion and the Military Establishment. Beverly Hills: Sage.

Kerwin, Jerome G. (ed.)
  1948   Civil-Military Relations in American Life. Chicago: University of Chicago
         Press.
Kelly, George G.
  1963   "The Global Civil-Military Relations Dilemma." Review of Politics 25
         (July):291-308.
Laski, Harold
  1930   "The Limitations of the Expert." Harper's 162 (December):101-110.
Levitan, David M.
  1946   "The Responsibility of Administrative Officials in a Democratic Society."
         Political Science Quarterly 61 (December):562-598.
Lyons, Gene
  1961   "The New Civil-Military Relations." American Political Science Review
         60 (March):53-63.
Miller, E. Arnold
  1946   "Some Arguments Used by English Pamphleteers, 1697-1700, Concern-
         ing a Standing Army." Journal of Modern History 18 (December):306-
         313.
Merton, Robert K.
  1952   "Bureaucratic Structure and Personality." Pp. 361-371 in Robert K.
         Merton, Ailsa P. Gray, Barbara Hockey, and Hanan C. Selvin (eds.),
         Reader in Bureaucracy. Glencoe: Free Press.
Moskos, Charles C., Jr.
  1971   "Armed Forces and American Society: Convergence or Divergence?"
         Pp. 271-294 in Charles C. Moskos, Jr. (ed.), Public Opinion and the
         Military Establishment. Beverly Hills: Sage.
  1972   "The Emergent Military: Civilianized, Traditional, or Pluralistic?"
         Paper presented at the Second Annual Midwest Workshop on National
         Security Education, Inter-University Seminar on Armed Forces and
         Society, Chicago, May, 1972.
Sapin, Burton M. and Richard C. Snyder
  1954   The Role of the Military in American Foreign Policy. Garden City:
         Doubleday.
Simon, Herbert A., Donald W. Smithburg, and Victor A. Thompson
  1962   Public Administration. New York: Knopf.
Smith, Dale O.
  1966   The Eagle's Talons; A Military View of Civil Control of the Military.
         Washington: Spartan.
Smith, Louis
  1951   American Democracy and Military Power: A Study of Civil Control of
         the Military Power in the United States. Chicago: University of Chicago
         Press.
Toren, Nina
  1969   "Semi-Professionalism and Social Work: A Theoretical Perspective."
         Pp. 141-195 in Amitai Etzioni (ed.). The Semi-Professions and Their
         Organization: Teachers, Nurses, Social Workers. New York: Free Press.
Van Doorn, Charles
  1965   "The Officer Corps: A Fusion of Profession and Organization." Euro-
         pean Journal of Sociology 6 (No. 2):262-282.
Weigley, Russell F.
  1962   Towards an American Army; Military Thought From Washington to
         Marshall. New York: Columbia University Press.
  1967   History of the United States Army. New York: Macmillan.

3

TRENDS IN MILITARY OCCUPATIONAL STRUCTURE AND THEIR POLITICAL IMPLICATIONS*

KURT LANG

State University of New York at Stony Brook

Technological and organizational developments in the U.S. military have resulted in an occupational structure where tactical operations, though still the single largest category of officer assignments, nevertheless accounts for only a minority of all such positions. While junior officers, especially in the more technological services like the Air Force and the Navy, are disproportionately associated with combat and combat operations, even compared to the enlisted men, the progressive transfer of "fighters" to desk jobs as they advance in rank contributes to an inflation of assignments to "tertiary" sector activities (intelligence and technical management) as opposed to "primary" (operations) and "secondary" (scientific, engineering, and maintenance) activities among middle-level officers. The size of this group is partly a cause and partly a consequence of increasing bureaucratization. Some implications of these trends for civil-military relations are suggested.

The military, like many other traditional professions, is being affected by a far-reaching technological and organizational revolution. The revolution is closely linked, on the technological side, to progressive improvements in the power, range, and accuracy of weapons and to dramatic gains in troop mobility. These lines of development came to a head in World War II. That war not only saw the rise of strategic air power and the advent of nuclear arms but also opened a new chapter in the history of combined operations. And in the quarter century following V-J day there has been no significant slowdown in the rate of technological change. Whole generations of weapons valued primarily for their deterrent effect have passed through the entire cycle from the drawing board to the junkyard, their effectiveness having been tested only under simulated conditions.

In organizational terms, the predominant orientation has been shifting away from combat and toward resource management. The shift is partial and one of degree. Its manifestations can be found (1) in a force structure basically geared to the requirements of deterrence; (2) in the

---

* This article is a revision of my paper "Military Career Structure: Emerging Trends and Alternatives," presented at the Inter-University Seminar on Armed Forces and Society, Chicago, November 18-20, 1971, an earlier version of which appeared in the *Administrative Science Quarterly*.

increasingly complex arrangements to assure "conventional" ground combat forces, wherever they may be committed, adequate material and logistic support; (3) in a concept of efficiency that forces concentration on the development of a relatively few systems and components where the highest payoffs are anticipated; and (4) in a constant monitoring of the external social and political conditions which may affect the flow of manpower and resources into the military, including changes in public attitudes towards war and pressure to arrive at negotiated arms control measures.

The net effect of these changes has been to decrease the importance of tactical operations as the primary area of military expertise on top of which subsidiary specialties could then be developed. The officer career structure has traditionally been predicated on a conception of the military as a "primitive" organization as Feld (1964) uses that term. Professional and organizational imperatives were more or less fused (Van Doorn, 1965), with an officer's rank and the arm, branch, and service in which he was commissioned the only officially recognized differences among officers. Professional officers were subject to forced rotation. A progression of assignments, including study at schools, was to assure that those advanced would acquire the broadened competence and specific knowledge necessary to coordinate the increasingly diverse components to fall within their command. To be sure, there had always been a few exceptions: some officer specialists—like those in medicine, ordnance, or military history—were not subject to rotation but they also stood, for that reason, outside the common line of promotion.

The thesis that this paper will document is that the traditional career structure, which subordinates the need for specialized expertise to the development from within the organization of the military managers, is undergoing modification because it has ceased to be adequate to the variety of roles officers nowadays are required to perform. Some of the implications of present trends for civil-military relations are then sketched out.

OCCUPATIONAL STRUCTURE

Table 1 paints a picture—in admittedly broad strokes—of the current officer occupational structure in the U.S. military. The classification of positions is based on similarities of duties as described in service manuals. Therefore, some differences between services may only reflect what each service chooses to emphasize in writing the specifications for any particular job; others arise from special arrangements (for example, the Marine Corps has no medical corps of its own but relies on Navy medical personnel). To some extent, the occupational structure of each service is also subject to fluctuating demands, such as the requirement for certain types of personnel in Vietnam.

TABLE 1. U.S. OFFICER DISTRIBUTION BY OCCUPATIONAL
GROUPS: 1970 (IN PERCENTAGES)

	Army	Navy	Marine Corps	Air Force	Dept. of Def.
1. General Officers and Executives	1	4	4	*	1
2. Tactical Operations	49	23	63	38	41
3. Intelligence	5	3	1	4	4
4. Engineering and Maintenance	11	19	8	18	14
5. Scientific and Professional	4	6	1	6	5
6. Medical	11	11	—	8	9
7. Administrative	12	16	6	10	12
8. Supply, Procurement, and Allied	5	7	8	6	6
9. Others	4	11	10	9	8
Total**	100	100	100	100	100

* .5%
** Some percentages do not add up exactly to 100 because of rounding.
   Source: Statistics provided by U.S. Department of Defense.

Attention is drawn to the close correspondence of the rank order of
frequency but not of the actual proportions of the major occupational
groupings within each of the services. Officers in all four are more often
engaged in tactical operations than in any other occupational activity,
but only in the Marine Corps does the proportion so occupied constitute
a majority. In tactical operations are included officers in the basic
ground combat arms (such as, infantry and artillery), in close ground
combat support, pilots and their crews, those with sea commands or in
charge of missile or similar units, and those on the various operations
staffs. There is no doubt some shading off at the higher ranks of the
operations into the military manager category, consisting of general
officers and other executives not elsewhere classified, but this latter
category accounts for only diminutive fractions of all officers. Next in
size is the engineering and maintenance grouping, which together with
those in the scientific and professional fields accounts for about one fifth
of all officer positions—somewhat more in the Air Force and Navy,
somewhat less in the Marine Corps. Finally, significant proportions of
officers are allocated to administrative and support functions, such as
supply and procurement.

The occupational structure of each service derives from its technological base, which is related in turn to its basic military mission. As
long as ground combat remains in its fundamentals unchanged, the

greater preponderance of tactical operations assignments in the Army and especially in the Marine Corps reflects their continued reliance on manpower to do the fighting. To the extent that "fighter" roles are significant, one can expect the heroic type (Janowitz, 1960) to continue to prevail.

There is another way to look at these changes, namely to apply to the military sub-system a distinction analogous to that between sectors of economic activity: primary, secondary, and tertiary. The relative importance of the sectors shifts in the several stages of economic growth. Insofar as it is in the operational units that the base of military power ultimately resides, tactical operations are considered to make up the primary sector of military activity, even though operations have become highly mechanized—just as agriculture makes up the primary sector of civil society. The counterpart more or less of industrial activity is the production and maintenance of military equipment. Officers involved in such activities represent the secondary sector. Those who perform the various service and management functions, including intelligence and organizational planning, constitute the analogous tertiary sector. Officers here are occupied with information processing and resources management, activities which, although they may be essential to maintain organizational effectiveness, are only indirectly related to the primary military function. These services are nonspecific and equally essential in other organizational contexts.

The specific indicator for sector activity, like all such indicators, is less than perfect. For example, officers whose occupational duties fall into the "scientific and professional" category might be considered performing tertiary functions. Some uniformed personnel so classified undoubtedly are, but most such officers, as opposed to enlisted men, are charged with overseeing and participating in the development and maintenance of military hardware.

In Table 2 the categories used in the occupational classification by the Department of Defense (Table 1) have been regrouped to correspond to the three sectors. This table includes also general officers and executives performing managerial functions as a separate category but omits medical and other types of officer personnel having special, more narrowly circumscribed career lines. It affirms that the Air Force and Navy have proportionately more officer positions in the engineering, scientific, and related professional fields than the Army and Marine Corps. Insofar as this difference signifies the replacement of men by machines, the number of officers in the secondary sector should be inversely related to the number in the primary operations area, as is indeed the case. However, the relationship between the growth of the technological base and of the organizational superstructure, as indexed by the tertiary sector categories, is less clear. The Army has a large primary operations sector as well as a large number of officers in administrative, support, intelligence, and other information processing functions; the Air Force is the only service in which the number of officers engaged in secondary sector activities exceeds those in tertiary activity.

TABLE 2. U.S. OFFICER DISTRIBUTION BY SECTOR
ACTIVITY: 1970 (IN PERCENTAGES)

	Army	Navy	Marine Corps	Air Force
General Milit. Mgt.	1	4	4	1
Primary: Operations	57	30	69	45
Secondary: Sci. & Eng.	16	33	10	28
Tertiary: Adm., Logistic, & Intell.	26	33	14	26
Total*	100	100	100	100

* Exclusive of general officers, medical, and officer personnel classified as "other." Some percentages do not add exactly to 100 because of rounding.
Source: See Table 1.

Part of the expansion of the tertiary sector, which seems to have gone farthest in the Navy, represents a functionally autonomous growth of an organizational culture. Parkinson (1957), it will be remembered, founded the famous law that bears his name on the observation that the number of employees in the British Admiralty rose sharply in the very period the number of capital ships in the Royal Navy suffered a serious decline. Moreover, the rate of growth among Admiralty officials was higher by far than that among the designers, draftsmen, scientists, and technicians. If something like Parkinson's law is also at work in the American military, this would account for the growth of tertiary sector activity.

CAREER LINES

The growing significance of activities outside the primary military specialty influences the pattern of assignments that officers follow in the course of a typical military career. Studies that focus on the relatively few officers who achieve high rank or otherwise gain entry into the inner nucleus of the decisionmakers tend to miss this development (Janowitz, 1960; Van Riper and Umwalla, 1965; Segal, 1967), because the elements around which unusually successful careers are built are less significant for the careers of the overwhelming majority of officers. Opportunity within the military is largely defined by the rank structure, and outside the cohorts that benefit from wartime mobilization, the chances for regular and career officers to attain general or flag rank are really quite small.

Despite some accommodation of the military rank structure to the new skill structure, present grade distributions are unduly depressed by the continuing excessively large exodus of junior officers. This situation has been a boon for officers with specialties in areas of acute shortages. Selection to the rank of colonel has indeed come somewhat more rapidly for officers in some Air Force scientific and engineering fields and in some of the Army specialist programs than for those whose primary specialty remains in operations.[1] But, again, exceptions do not necessarily add up to a rule. We must therefore examine how occupational roles and specialties are typically related to length of service and rank attained. The examination will be confined to the Air Force and Navy, the two services most affected by the new technology, drawing on data describing existing distributions such as are used by the services themselves in monitoring their personnel systems.

Air Force. The personnel system of the Air Force incorporates a clearcut division between the "operational rated-pilot career" and a career in the technical and support area. After the rank of major, there is practically no crossover from one career to the other and nearly all of what there is is away from operations rather than the other way around. This accords well with Air Force officer requirements as these are defined through a computerized model designed by the Air Force. As shown in Table 3, the basic division is between the operations area, the various scientific and engineering specialties, and technical management fields (which include assignments in security, intelligence, and public information as well as the various aspects of material, financial, and personnel management—more or less what we have called the tertiary sector). As before, some categories—like medicine, law, the chaplaincy, band leaders—have been excluded from these tabulations.

TABLE 3. U.S. AIR FORCE OFFICER REQUIREMENTS BY GRADE AND MAJOR OCCUPATIONAL CATEGORY: 1966 (IN PERCENTAGES)

	Colonel	Lt. Colonel	Major	Capt./Lt.
Primary: Operations	37	43	43	55
Secondary: Sci. & Eng.	26	25	27	21
Tertiary: Adm., Logistic, & Intell.	37	32	30	24
Total	100	100	100	100

Source: U.S. Air Force, AFPDP.

---

1. Based on an examination of officer inventory print-outs and statements by informants.

If we apply to this grouping of occupational designators our earlier distinction among the three sectors of military activity, it becomes clear that more of the higher ranking officers, proportionately, are required for the technical management positions and fewer for tactical operations, with the proportion required in the scientific and engineering categories least tied to rank.

The actual pattern of distribution in 1970, shown in Table 4, has only a loose resemblance to the requirements set forth by the model. Thus, the proportion in operations does not progressively decline towards the higher ranks, as it should, but is highest at the rank of major, disproportionately large even above that rank, and with a deficit in the two longest ranks. On the other hand, the number of lieutenants and captains in the scientific and engineering as well as in the administrative, logistic support, and intelligence category exceeds authorization, with corresponding shortages at the higher ranks. Overall strength in such specialized career fields as research and development, communication and electronics, civil engineering, and cartography, where grade allocations are generally advantageous, can be kept close to actual au-

TABLE 4   U.S. AIR FORCE OFFICER OCCUPATIONAL ASSIGNMENTS BY GRADE AND YEARS OF PRIOR SERVICE: 1970 (IN PERCENTAGES)

| | GRADE | | | | | |
	General	Colonel	Lt. Colonel	Major	Captain	Lieutenant
General Mgt.	100	16	4	*	*	0
Operations		29	47	62	50	39
Science & Eng.		21	22	19	24	30
Admin., Logistic, & Intell.		34	27	18	25	31
Total**		100	100	100	100	100

| | YEARS OF PRIOR SERVICE | | | | |
	23 + above	18-22	12-17	4-11	0-3
General Mgt.	18	3	1	*	0
Operations	31	46	63	50	39
Science & Eng.	18	24	19	24	30
Admin., Logistic, & Intell.	33	25	18	26	31
Total**	100	100	100	100	100

* .5%

**Some percentages do not add up exactly to 100 because of rounding.

Source: Statistics provided by Headquarters of the U.S. Air Force.

thorization only by the overassignment of junior officers, usually without aeronautical ratings, many of whom have no strong career commitment and cannot therefore be expected to remain. In other words, the discrepancy between actual and authorized distribution is the result of either (a) selective attrition among officers with qualifications in given areas and sufficient years of service to be eligible for promotion, (b) deliberate avoidance of these very assignments by those qualified to fill them, or (c) failure on the part of those in these career fields to qualify for the higher positions with a resulting exodus to other areas. Length of service data accord with all these explanations but do not allow us to compare the relative importance of each factor.

To advance in the Air Force demands some change in outlook and accommodation to new roles. This affects particularly those in operations, for only a diminutive percentage of pilots, navigators, and bombardiers hold a rank higher than major. Above that rank, Air Force officers assigned to operations are likely to be on staffs, often as directors of operations, while those who become directors of an Air Force organization appear in our table as military managers. The largest number, however, move into the various aspects of management rather than into operational planning. The command most saturated with high-ranking officers is, perhaps not surprisingly, the U.S. Air Force Headquarters Command, but relatively favorable rank distributions can also be found in commands where the scientific and intellectual functions are strongly represented, namely in the Air Force Systems Command, the Office of Scientific Research, and the Air University. The latter, especially the last two, are too small to become havens for more than a small minority of those with field-grade rank. This means a significant movement into the areas of technical management.

The academic degrees of Air Force officers supply another clue to qualifications of officers at different ranks. Since the B.A. degree has for some time been a requirement for a commission, and the relatively few without degrees have been under pressure to obtain one, differences in undergraduate major of officers with different number of years of service probably reflect mostly the effects of attrition among persons with different entering qualifications; whereas the field of an officer's graduate degree is the better indicator of the kind of knowledge useful for an officer's professional advancement.

Table 5 shows that the higher an officer's rank, the more likely it is that he will have earned an advance degree—most often in the field of administration, management, or military science. Above the rank of lieutenant colonel the distribution changes toward a preponderance of advanced study in one of the social sciences, subjects considered relevant and broadening but without the direct applicability of such fields as administration and engineering. There is also a marked decline between the rank of lieutenant and the rank of colonel in the proportion

TABLE 5. ACADEMIC MAJORS OF U.S. AIR FORCE OFFICERS
BY GRADE: 1970 (IN PERCENTAGES)

	General	Colonel	Lt. Col.	Major	Captain	Lieutenant
Undergraduate						
Admin., Mgt., & Mil. Sci.	47	43	33	30	28	25
Engineering	18	14	17	18	14	18
Biol., Phys., & Math.	10	8	13	17	19	19
Soc. Sci.	15	19	18	16	22	23
Other, No Inf.	10	16	19	20	17	14
Total**	100	100	100	100	100	100
Graduate						
Admin., Mgt., & Mil. Sci.	35	33	40	36	28	27
Engineering	19	18	20	32	31	35
Biol., Phys., & Math.	8	7	9	10	13	17
Soc. Sci.	37	33	14	9	11	17
Other, No Inf.	2	10	16	14	16	5
Total**	100	100	100	100	100	100
Proportion with Grad. Degrees	.31	.29	.30	.19	.12	.06

* Excludes officers with degrees in medicine and law.
** Some percentages do not add up exactly to 100 because of rounding.
Source: Statistics provided by Headquarters of the U.S. Air Force.

with degrees, graduate as well as undergraduate, in the natural sciences and in mathematics and a correspondingly sharp drop in the proportion with graduate degrees in engineering between the rank of major and lieutenant colonel. All of these reflect in one way or another the low retention rates in many technical and scientific specialties. However, some background in a technical field as evidenced, for example, by an undergraduate degree in engineering, is no doubt a good springboard from which to move into other career areas. This probably accounts for the fact that the proportion with undergraduate degrees in this field is more or less constant through the ranks. Nor is there any decline above the rank of lieutenant colonel in the proportion of officers with graduate engineering degrees, which reinforces our previous contention that men with the right technical specialty have, if they choose to remain, an excellent chance to achieve general rank. (See also the evidence in Van Riper and Umwalla, 1965.)

The Navy. The Navy observes a basic distinction between unrestricted line officers and individuals designated for either restricted or special duties, including those serving in the several staff corps, a distinction that parallels in some ways the one between rated and nonrated officer personnel in the Air Force. All unrestricted line officers are considered to have the same primary specialty: naval warfare. Hence the Navy, unlike the Air Force, provides no specially designated career paths linking successive assignments within some pre-defined occupational area for its unrestricted line officers. These latter comprise well over 75 per cent of the officers when those in the medical, chaplain, and judge advocate corps are excluded.

Navy tradition mandates rotation between tours at sea and various shore assignments, though with the shortage of sea commands the sea-tour tradition is being modified. Partly exempt from rotation requirements are those not in the unrestricted line category, who serve as engineering or aeronautical engineering officers, or as special duty officers in such fields as cryptology, public affairs, hydrography, and the like. Distinct career lines are clearly foreseen for officers in the several staff corps. The specializations in the Supply Corps include the various aspects of financial and personnel management; those in the Civil Engineering Corps cover all the engineering specialties as well as architecture. Officers in the Civil Engineering Corps are normally sent to various civilian schools for two years of study leading to the Master of Science degree. The experience of the unrestricted line officers is far more varied by comparison. Despite a de-emphasis on specialization, a study of professional manpower situations in the Navy found that, as of 1969, a large number of the billets in some twenty different utilization fields were still being written for officers of the unrestricted line rather than specialists.

The structure of the Navy's personnel system permits filling requirements for professional manpower in specialties outside the primary operations career area either (1) by designating more officers for the restricted line and special duty categories and enlarging the staff corps or (2) by directing unrestricted line officers into specific paths of education and assignments corresponding to the career fields difficult to fill. The first alternative means the removal of a large number of line officers from unrestricted line duty, which the Navy has always resisted. Hence, the Navy took a half-step toward the second by inventing the concept of a "subspecialty," which combines the elements of a traditional career with formal education, training, and practical experience focused on some specific career field. Many positions are now defined by both rank and some particular subspecialty requirement, ranging from the natural sciences and operations analysis, through the various engineering and technical management disciplines, to public and international affairs. Except for those in ship-engineering, which has its own tradition, and those in financial and material management, the billets in the subspecialty areas have been dominated by officers of the unrestricted line.

The subspecialty requirements of the billet structure for officers in different ranks help define the changing duties and responsibilities that naval officers assume in their careers. To arrive at a categorization identical to that of the Air Force, not only did the subspecialties have to be allocated between the scientific and engineering fields on the one hand and the technical management fields on the other, but unrestricted line officer billets without subspecialty specifications had to be assumed to be in the operations area and a subspecialty requirement in political/strategic/military planning to identify a military management position. These assumptions are probably justified, even though the level of specialized competence indicated by a subspecialty requirement or qualification may not be at exactly the same level as the identical occupational designation in the Air Force.

Table 6 shows a sharp jump in the proportion of billets with subspecialty requirements between the rank of lieutenant and that of lieutenant commander. Until the latter rank is reached, most unrestricted line officers are employed in billets which, it seems, do not call for any significant degree of specialized expertise beyond the primary military specialty in operations. This continues to be the case as well for nearly eighty per cent of the billets for lieutenant commanders and above.

TABLE 6   U.S. NAVY OFFICER REQUIREMENTS BY GRADE AND MAJOR SUBSPECIALTY CATEGORY: 1966 (IN PERCENTAGES)

	Captain	Commander	Lt. Cmdr.	Lieutenant
General Milit. Mgt.	3	1	*	*
Primary: Operations	79	77	80	90
Secondary: Sci. & Eng.	13	16	17	7
Tertiary: Adm., Logistic, & Intell.	5	5	3	3
Total**	100	100	100	100
Proportion with subspecialty	.21	.23	.20	.10

* .5%

** Some percentages do not add up exactly to 100 due to rounding.

Source: Secretary of the Navy, Study of Career Management, Washington, D.C., August, 1967. (Appendices).

The majority of subspecialty positions at every rank are in the secondary sector, which is to say in science and engineering, although the balance is more nearly equal at the rank of captain. Subspecialty requirements in the tertiary sector gradually gain ground at the higher levels, just as they do in the Air Force, and what the Navy calls the political/strategic/military planning subspecialty gains even more. In interpreting these figures, one must remember that a significant number of positions in both the scientific and engineering and the technical management categories are filled with officers outside the unrestricted line. Some of the incumbents, as officer inventories show, are non-selectees passed over for promotion but retained in jobs for which they had been specifically trained though not necessarily demanding a sub-specialty qualification.

The actual qualifications, not billet requirements, of officers by rank are shown in Table 7. The proportion of unrestricted line officers with subspecialties in some technical management field is far greater, at every rank, than the proportion with scientific and engineering sub-specialties. In other words, more officers have developed expertise ap-plicable to the running of an organization than to the development and maintenance of naval technology. In this respect the Navy resembles the Air Force. More of its higher ranking officers qualify in technical man-agement—i.e., the tertiary sector—than in science and engineering fields.

Some special competence beyond operations is an obvious advan-tage, though not apparently a necessity, for an officer's advancement

TABLE 7. SUBSPECIALITIES OF U.S. NAVY OFFICERS BY GRADE: 1966 (IN PERCENTAGES)

	Total	Unrestricted Line Officers Only				
	Flag	Flag	Capt.	Cmdr.	Lt. Cmdr.	Lieut.
Political/Strategic/ Military Planning	39	48	7	4	*	0
Primary: Operations	30	9	55	56	70	89
Secondary: Sci. & Eng.	30	16	15	14	8	4
Tertiary: Adm., Logistic, & Intell.	40	38	23	26	22	7
Total	100**	100**	100	100	100	100

* .5%

** 70 Flag Officers and 55 Flag officers of the unrestricted line have more than one subspecialty qualification.

Source: Secretary of the Navy, Study of Career Management, Washington, D. C., August, 1967. (Appendices).

into the higher ranks. A large number of flag officers have more than one subspecialty qualification, but what more than anything else sets this group apart from the rest is the number whose subspecialty lies in the area of general military management, as indicated by a qualification in political/strategic/military planning. Nearly half of the unrestricted line admirals (but only one of five captains) have this subspecialty. This does not preclude officers with primarily technological expertise from advancing to high rank, but these officers, if they should achieve flag rank, are more likely to have been moved by that time into either the restricted line or the special duty category.

CONCLUSION AND IMPLICATIONS

What we have shown so far is that military occupational structure has become highly diversified; the number of officers who function in tactical operations, the primary sector of military activity, has declined to the degree that military technology has advanced. That fire power now depends on technical instruments rather than masses of men is mirrored in the increase in the number of officers in secondary sector occupations. Data on both assignments and qualifications point to shortages of experienced officers in many civilian-type specialties, particularly those involving technical skill, shortages which apparently go together with a significant movement among middle-level officers away from operations and into technical management, information processing, and other service functions.

The increasing convergence of military and civilian skill requirements as a consequence of changes in the technology of warfare has already been noted by Janowitz and Little (1965) but is documented only by reference to the enlisted job structure, with the impact on officer occupations left entirely out of the picture. Thus, the introduction of new arms, which has brought about a drastic reduction in the proportion of enlisted men in military-type occupations with no civilian counterparts, also provides an impetus to build a more highly professionalized force to replace the conventional mass army. The technological complexity of the new weapons requires more expertise from those charged to operate them, and because of their destructive potential they must be deployed under responsible direction. The result is that direct involvement in operations is increasingly concentrated at higher levels within the military hierarchy. In other words, the rank of those directing operations and/or in combat assignments will reflect the responsibilities they shoulder and the risks demanded of them.

A comparison of officer occupational distribution with that of enlisted men furthermore suggests that officers are at least in some respects more military than the men they command. (See also Biderman, 1967.) According to U.S. Department of Defense statistics for 1970, the number of enlisted men in combat assignments was 24 per cent for the Army, 9 per cent for the Navy, 28 per cent for the Marine Corps, and only 1 per cent (in 1969) for the Air Force. Though everyone of these percentages is higher than the percentage of officers in the same service in tactical operations assignments (see Table 1), enlisted men, except in the Air Force, still predominate among the fighters simply by force of their greater number. The actual ratio of enlisted to officer strength (operations and combat assignments only) is 3.2 for the Army, 3.0 for the Navy, 4.3 for the Marine Corps, and .2 for the Air Force. All these statistics seem to suggest that large numbers of officers in tactical operations are associated with proportionately even larger numbers of enlisted combat personnel, which is to say with a high enlisted-officer ratio. Thus, the large primary sector within the Marine Corps reflects the requirements of troop leadership, whereas in the Air Force, which has the highest officer allocations in relation to total strength, most of the actual fighting is done by officers themselves, with airmen relegated to civilian-type subsidiary tasks. The Navy, with its complex technological base, represents a clear deviation from the overall pattern. In contrast to the flying of sorties and other missions, the exercise of a ship command is still kept separate from the operation of its guns, and the crews of ships, unlike those of aircraft, usually function as a combat team only when under direct enemy fire.

Professionalism in the officer corps, insofar as it is built around the primary military specialty, implies an emphasis on civil-military differences but is not by any means synonymous with conflictual relationships. Certainly the Marine Corps, whose officer occupational structure is unique in the extent of its divergence from civilian bureaucracies, has been no more restive under civilian control than the more "civilianized" services, like the Air Force. In fact, plotting to circumvent or neutralize the political authorities is far more likely to originate among staff officers with political connections and centrally located within the military communications network, as for example in the intelligence branch. Yet the attitudes and commitments of those in tactical operations are also significant. They still most directly represent the mission that pervades the entire organizational culture, and it is on their performance that the effectiveness of the military establishment as a cold-war and limited-war instrument rests to a large degree.

The lack of professionalism among some unit leaders has been used to explain certain wartime acts of atrocity, like the civilian massacres in Vietnam, but lack of professionalism cannot account for the wholesale coverup of the episode or for the falsification, allegedly on orders from above, of reports of missions flown. For this one must invoke the fraternity that readily forms whenever a group feels unduly exposed to a common risk. In these circumstances, both loyalty to the service and loyalty to fellow officers command that the burden of responsibility be shifted either outside the organization or to a scapegoat within it.

No systematic data are available on how such experiences as a full tour of duty in Vietnam affect the political outlook of officers. One nevertheless suspects that operations at great distance from the home country itself and carried by a small and unrepresentative proportion of the age cohort will produce some divergence from civilian perspectives—all the more so when, with fewer troops to command, regular officers will be sheltered even from the limited countervailing influence of short-term draftees. The question is of course to what extent the attitudes so formed persist and then diffuse through other parts of the organization to officers who have no contact with tactical operations in combat.

Ideology is far less important, it seems, for those in secondary sector occupations. Here effectiveness is most directly contingent, not on "shaping up" new manpower, but on getting new weapons and improving existing ones. But the more technology a weapon contains, as Zuckerman (1962) points out, the more likely is it to have been the result of civilian rather than military thinking. The growth of the secondary sector notwithstanding, there is less reliance by the military on its own arsenals in favor of contracting out to industry all kinds of development work. The Air Force, which is the newest, least tradition-bound, and most technological of the services, has understandably led the way in this trend.

Civilian expertise is also highly useful, if not indispensable, in assessing the probable effects of the new weapons and of their most effective deployment to achieve certain goals. Thus, the military has been forced not only to pay its tribute to the scientist and engineer working on weapons development but also to cede some ground to the civilian-military specialists in the area of strategy, its proper professional domain (Ginsburgh, 1964). They have been dispossessed from their monopolistic position as the only qualified technical advisors to governments on all matters pertaining to the use of force in foreign affairs.

As a result, the representatives of the military become involved in a multiplicity of relationships. The boundary between what is properly military and what is properly civilian, once so clear, has been blurred to a point where it hardly exists any longer. Resources the military still commands are used to attain goals with only a very loose relation to the primary mission. Such a situation affords many opportunities for asserting influence—through industry, through Congressional representatives, through other public agencies.

Corresponding to the widening of the circle of military influence is an increase in internal organizational complexity especially evident in the growth of the tertiary sector. Part of this growth reflects the logistic requirements of modern weapons, the need for coordination among diverse components, and the effort to maintain control; another part seems less dictated by the organizational mission than a response to the emerging pattern of military-civil relations. For one thing, in its effort to meet the challenge of other groups, the military seeks to project an image of itself that is designed to rival in its up-to-dateness and modernism the other institutional sectors.

Certain programs and activities in the tertiary sector gain further impetus from the ambitions of officers, ambitions which, unless they receive some measure of satisfaction, could only produce discontent. For example, one "latent" but widely acknowledged function of much advanced academic training which middle-level officers receive at service institutions or at service expense is to prepare for a possible second career those who have no future in the military or no inclination to remain. Moreover, those whom age or obsolescent skills have made unsuitable for tactical operations without their having developed other significant skills are moved into administration or into some other subsidiary function. The transition is eased, no doubt, by the fact that administration already constitutes a significant component of many tactical operations jobs and that in many cases the administrative tasks with which they are charged in the new jobs will actually be done by civilians acting as their counterparts.

Although there is a clear trend toward civilianization, the above considerations suggest that it would be futile to rely on it to control the potential political power that naturally goes with the huge resources under the military control. The expansion of secondary sector activity has indirectly cemented the partnership between the military and some sectors of industry and the scientific community, and even while the demand for economies constantly pares away certain "non-essential" functions by assigning them to civilian personnel, pressure from within builds up anew to inflate the number of uniformed officers in all kinds of tertiary activity.

REFERENCES

Biderman, A.D.
    1967   "What is Military?" Pp. 122-137 in S. Tax (ed.), The Draft: Facts and
           Alternatives. Chicago: University of Chicago Press.
Feld, Maury D.
    1964   "The Military Self-Image in a Technological Environment." Pp. 159-187 in
           M. Janowitz (ed.), The New Military. New York: Russell Sage Foundation
Future Professional Manpower Requirements Study (FPMRS)
    1969   Report to the Chief of Naval Operations.
Ginsburgh, R.N.
    1964   "The Challenge of Military Professionalism." Foreign Affairs 42:255-268.
Janowitz, M.
    1960   The Professional Soldier: A Social and Political Portrait. New York: The
           Free Press.

Janowitz, M., and R. Little
    1965   Sociology and the Military Establishment (rev. ed.). New York: Russell Sage Foundation.
Lang, Kurt
    1964   "Technology and Career Management in the Military Establishment." Pp. 39-81 in M. Janowitz (ed.), The New Military. New York: Russell Sage Foundation.
Parkinson, C. Northcote
    1957   Parkinson's Law and Other Studies in Administration. Boston: Houghton Mifflin.
Segal, D.R.
    1967   "Selective Promotion of Officer Cohorts." Sociological Quarterly 8:199-206.
Van Doorn, J.
    1965   "The Officer Corps: A Fusion of Profession and Organization." European Journal of Sociology 6:262-282.
Van Riper. P.P., and D.B. Unwalla
    1965   "Military Career at the Executive Level." Administrative Science Quarterly 9:421-436.
Zuckerman, S.
    1962   "Judgment and Control in Modern Warfare." Foreign Affairs 40:196-212.

4

TECHNOLOGY, ORGANIZATIONAL CULTURE, AND RECRUITMENT IN THE BRITISH MILITARY ACADEMY

MAURICE GARNIER

Indiana University

Many changes affecting the U.S. military have been traced to changes in the technological complexity of the equipment used (Janowitz, 1971). This paper argues that changes in the technological complexity of military equipment are mediated by cultural and organizational factors. Focusing on recruitment practices in the British Army, the paper demonstrates that the universalistic recruitment practices described by Janowitz for the U.S. military are not as readily apparent in the British Army, despite the sophistication of that organization's armament. The mechanisms which make this pattern possible are described.

Summarizing organizational changes within the U.S. armed forces over the last fifty years, Janowitz (1971) implied that a major cause of changes was the increasing technological complexity of military equipment, which compelled the organization to recruit and promote increasingly on technical competence. While some of the old patterns remained in certain units, in the last 20 years the new patterns have become dominant and have spread throughout the armed forces generally.

Since military organizations are generally designed to meet the threat of other military organizations, they usually produce or acquire the most advanced weapons available. Thus, substantial technological convergence between most of the world's armed forces can be assumed. However, the degree to which the organizational changes that Janowitz isolated for the U.S. military also take place in non-American military settings is unknown. This paper argues that such changes are unlikely to affect non-American military organizations because the changes are mediated by cultural and organizational factors whose effects are not uniform in all cultures.

Part of the culture context is a society's educational system. Changes depend partly on the availability of individuals with certain educational qualificiations. In the U.S., an increase in the number of young people completing high school was necessary before military academies could broaden their recruitment. Also, the greater reliance on formal postgraduate work by career officers required the existence of many such programs in universities. In a society with limited education opportunities, the military would find it difficult at best to broaden its recruitment base, but that failure would not necessarily mean that ascriptive criteria still predominated, or that the organization was not adapting to changing conditions. Other cultural factors could also be cited — for example, subcultural segmentation in a given society. One group might define a military career as extremely desirable while another considered it undesirable, thus causing overrepresentation of members from one group and underrepresentation of members from the other.

The cultural definition of authority relations might favor the military's accepting members from certain groups but not from others.

Traditions, beliefs about desirable relations between officers and men, and allegiance to certain doctrines are only a few of the factors that may affect technological adoptions. At this stage, little is known about the interaction between technology and organizational change. It can be postulated that adopting new technology will not similarly affect all military organizations, although some similarities will exist. This paper shows how the British Army's need to recruit technically qualified officers interacts with the need to maintain the army's organizational identity. The British Army was selected for study because it has advanced weaponry (e.g., tanks, computer-guided missiles). At the same time that organization has a long history that, unlike several other European military organizations, has not been marked by a serious disruption (such as defeat, in the case of France and Germany). The only important change, the importance of which cannot be readily assessed, is the change (in 1961) from a conscription to an all-volunteer method of recruitment.

Necessarily, the increasing technological sophistication of the weapons has caused many changes. For example, a central selection agency for army officers was created after World War II, and an increasing proportion of officers have been sent to civilian universities after completing the military academy's curriculum. Such changes have obviously implied increasing reliance on universalistic criteria of selection and promotion. This paper therefore focuses on whether a shift from particularistic to universalistic criteria of recruitment has taken place in the British Army. Janowitz would argue for such a shift, whereas Britain's social and cultural differences would suggest changes unique to Britain.

METHOD

Data for this study were gathered during a stay at the Royal Military Academy, Sandhurst, between April and December, 1967. The data are of three types. Some come from questionnaires (designed after approximately six months of participant observation) administered to all cadets in October, 1967. Some derive from participant observation. (As a civilian instructor, I lived in the officers' mess; this arrangement provided numerous opportunities for lengthy conversations on the British Army, the training program at the Academy, the progress of various cadets, and so forth.)[1] Finally, some come from staff interviews conducted toward the end of my stay (only three civilians refused to be interviewed, and all military personnel cooperated).

SELECTION

To Sandhurst. Potential Sandhurst cadets (usually about 18 years old) are first checked for basic requirements and then given educational and psychological tests and an interview. The tests are used largely to confirm the selecting officers' opinions, but the interviews are crucial. The interviewing officers may ask about the candidate's family background, reasons for wanting to become an officer, the type of work he prefers, recreational activities, and so forth. Each officer both observes and talks to each candidate and then ranks him on established criteria.

---

1. For more details on participant-observation, see Garnier 1972 and 1973.

The criteria used during the interviews are clearly reflected in an incident that I witnessed. A candidate who seemed particularly qualified on intelligence and recommendations (by two relatively senior officers) was turned down because his speech, demeanor, and "attitude" identified him as an enlisted man rather than as an officer. More generally, sons of military families and candidates who have attended tuition-charging schools are far more successful in achieving entry into Sandhurst than are others (Garnier, 1972).

Once a cadet has entered the Academy, he is assigned to a company and his training begins (for details on assignment and socialization, see Garnier, 1973). The first quarter is devoted exclusively to military training, which is arduous but with little of the hazing usually associated with military academies. The following quarters include a combination of academic and military training. Toward the end of the first year (i.e., midway through Sandhurst's two-year curriculum), regimental selection occurs.

To Regiments. Regiments are quite independent of one another, and each has its own traditions. An officer spends most of his career within the same regiment, and regimental affiliation is thus extremely important to his identity. The regimental system is based partly on simple tradition but also on an ideology that places high emphasis on the system's efficiency and, most importantly, the very high morale such a system seems to foster (a morale that can be seen in very high reenlistment rates). The regiments form a hierarchy in the British Army. The Guards and the Household Cavalry have the most prestige, while the technical units have the least; few, if any, hold exactly the same prestige. The static nature of the British Army's prestige hierarchy is quite remarkable. Writing about the Army just prior to World War I, Baynes (1967) gave a ranking very similar to that shown in my data. Careful recruitment ensures a regiment of like-minded recruits and, therefore, maintenance of its distinctive life style.

Selection into a regiment begins after a cadet has expressed his preference for a certain regiment. Then his company commander expresses an opinion on that choice, usually after interviewing the cadet. Should a cadet from middle-class origins express a preference for, say, a cavalry regiment, his commander might well suggest "a more suitable unit," largely because the cadet is unlikely to have the private means necessary to participate in all the regiment's activities. If he "passes" the interview, the cadet is next interviewed by a Sandhurst staff member of the regiment the cadet seeks to enter. The staff member then makes informal inquiries about the cadet. Unfavorable responses virtually guarantee rejection; favorable ones usually result in an interview with the regiment's colonel.

Interviewers use different kinds of criteria. Often the interview is a simple formality because the colonel personally knows the cadet. Many cadets told me of "interviews" in which the interviewing officer and the cadet simply had lunch together and discussed, say, mutual friends and sports. One cadet, sponsored by a prominent member of the British Army elite (a family friend), told me that he had been "accepted" by his future regiment at the age of fifteen. Of course, selection interviews often follow a much different format. Interviews for technical regiments, for which competence is important, often use more contest-oriented criteria. For example, asked why a certain candidate had been turned down by a technical regiment, the representative of that regiment simply said that the applicant's math scores were too low. This mixture of interview criteria should not be surprising. Organizations often use both ascriptive and achievement criteria; only the relative importance of each varies from one organization to the next; in the British Army, as will be shown below, ascriptive criteria dominate.

ANALYSIS

The Relative Contribution of Ascription and Achievement. Ascription and achievement were tested using data from the questionnaires. For this analysis, schooling was chosen as the independent variable. Four categories were created. Public schools, because of their traditional association with elites, tend to socialize "gentlemen" (Kelsall, 1955). Grammar schools are state schools and differ among themselves.[2] Some resemble the public schools in their socialization process, but since no tuition is charged, they recruit more broadly. Welbeck, an army-run school, takes 16-year-old boys; its curriculum emphasizes mathematics and science, and its graduates may only enter technical regiments (but no fighting units). Upon completion of the Welbeck curriculum, these individuals enter Sandhurst without going through the selection procedure. Finally, an "other" category includes comprehensive and secondary modern schools, run basically along American lines. These have traditionally recruited from the lower-middle class. Knowledgeable respondents classified regiments into four categories: Guards and Cavalry, infantry, artillery-engineers (the old technical units), and other technical units. Table 1 shows a close association between the independent variable (school attended) and the regiment selected.

Of course, the prestige of the school attended by cadets prior to entering Sandhurst says nothing about their technical qualifications. Therefore, their educational qualifications must be examined. We would expect the cadets entering technical units to have a much higher level of skill in mathematics, science, etc., than cadets destined for the infantry and/or cavalry. Therefore, an association ought to exist between skill and the kind of regiment a cadet enters upon leaving the Academy. To test this expectation, several measures of educational attainment were isolated. First, cadets were asked how many "*A* levels*" (a measure of intellectual competence in various fields) they had obtained.[3] Despite the expectation of a correlation, Table 2 shows *no* relationship between the kind of regiment selected and the number of *A levels* achieved. Clearly, if intellectual ability was of primary importance to technical units, then 28.1 percent of the cadets destined for artillery-engineers units would not report a total lack of *A levels*.

The evidence above might rely too heavily on events occurring prior to the cadets' Sandhurst years. However, Table 1 showed a clear relationship between the type of pre-Sandhurst education and the type of regiment selected; hence the regiment choice cannot be validly dissociated from those experiences

---

2. Public schools are defined as members of the Headmaster's conference. Elite public schools are the 9 so-called Clarendon schools. Grammar schools have now virtually disappeared, but in 1967, the educational reforms that led to the virtual disappearance of grammar schools had not yet taken place.

3. *A* levels are taken at the end of a person's secondary schooling and each involves testing in a specific field. At the time the study was done, the official requirement was for 2 *A* levels (specific subject and grade obtained were unspecified). As the data later show, a substantial proportion of cadets did not even possess one.

TABLE 1.   SCHOOL ATTENDED AND REGIMENTAL SELECTION*

	Type of School					
	Elite****	Public	Grammar	Welbeck	Other	N
Aristocratic	30.8 (44.4)**	7.9 (51.8)	0	0	12.5 (3.7)	27
Non-Aristocratic	41.0 (14.8)	39.5 (64.8)	29.2 (17.5)	0	37.5 (2.7)	108
Artillery Engineer	28.2 (10.0)	32.8 (52.7)	43.1 (25.4)	18.9 (9.0)	37.5 (2.7)	110
Technical	0	19.8 (36.0)	27.7 (18.5)	81.1 (44.3)	12.5 (1.1)	97
	100.0%	100.0	100.0	100.0	100.0	
	N = 39*	N = 177	N = 65	N = 53	N = 8	342

Gamma = .588   Z = 4.69***   P<.001

*"No answers" were eliminated.

**Rows percentages in parentheses.

***Technically speaking, Z is unnecessary in this instance since the entire population is included in the analysis. However, some feel that such a statistic should be used.

****This category is a sub-division of "public" schools, sometimes called "clarendar" schools.   It includes, among others, Eton and Harrow.

occurring prior to entrance at Sandhurst. Furthermore, this initial evidence is supported by data that focus solely on events occurring at the Academy.

After one year at the Academy, cadets are ranked on a three-part order of merit: academic, military, and personal. The academic and military parts (e.g., mathematics and tactics, respectively) include performance on examinations. Each of these two elements constitutes one-third of a cadet's total score. The remaining one-third is given by the staff and is based on "officer qualities" criteria (a subjective evaluation of how well each cadet conforms to the ideal expectations of an officer). This ranking is virtually meaningless since it bears little relationship to the kind of regiment a cadet will enter and in no way predicts which cadets will be given positions of authority over other cadets when they are seniors (Garnier, 1969). The data actually show a very small, *negative* relationship between rank and type of regiment selected (see Table 3). The artillery and engineers recruit nearly 40% of their cadets from among those ranked high, but these same units also recruit cadets (28.6 percent) ranked low. Of cadets destined for high-status regiments, 61.5 percent ranked low and only 15 percent high. Performance and selection, then, seem only weakly associated.[4]

4.   This practice is in sharp contrast to West Point's, where a cadet's standing on the order of merit gives him priority for branch selection, much like a first-come, first-served system. The final order of merit is used in order to award a prize to the cadet who ranks first, but the purpose of the mid-curriculum order of merit is very unclear.

TABLE 2. EDUCATIONAL ATTAINMENT AND REGIMENTAL SELECTION

	Number of A Levels				
	0	1	2	3	4 or more
Aristocratic	10.9 (25.9)*	1.5 (3.7)	9.7 (40.7)	6.7 (22.2)	2 (7.4)	27
Non-Aristocratic	29.7 (16.6)	30.3 (17.5)	26.5 (26.3)	38.9 (30.7)	10 (8.7)	114
Artillery-Engineer	28.1 (15.5)	34.8 (19.8)	28.3 (27.5)	33.3 (25.8)	13 (11.2)	116
Technical	31.3 (18.5)	33.3 (20.3)	35.4 (37.0)	21.1 (17.5)	7 (6.4)	108
	N = 64	N = 66	N = 113	N = 90	N = 32	365
Gamma = -.076	Z = -.54	Not significant				

*Percentages along rows.

Perhaps more directly relevant is the academic curriculum to which a cadet is assigned upon entering Sandhurst. This is determined by the academic staff (who are civilian), and is based on the prior accomplishment of each cadet. There are five curricula: special mathematics (the most difficult course) and main mathematics (for those who want a scientific course but lack the

TABLE 3. ORDER OF MERIT RANKING AND REGIMENTAL SELECTION

	High (First 50)	Medium (51-100)	Low (101 & below)	
Aristocratic	2.4 (15.3)	2.6 (23.0)	9.3 (61.5)	13*
Non-Aristocratic	26.8 (24.7)	34.2 (44.9)	31.4 (30.3)	89
Artillery-Engineers	45.1 (39.7)	26.5 (33.3)	29.1 (26.8)	93
Technical	25.6 (23.3)	36.8 (47.7)	30.2 (28.8)	90
	N = 82	N = 117	N = 86	285
Gamma = -.062	Z = -.36	Not significant		

*Only 2 cohorts could respond since the 2 youngest had not been at the Academy long enough for a placement to be made. The numbers (first 50 etc.) refer to places, not to any score.

TABLE 4. CURRICULUM AND REGIMENTAL SELECTION

	Difficult	Easy	N
Aristocratic	7.3 (44.4)	7.5 (55.5)	27
Non-Aristocratic	21.2 (30.9)	39.2 (69.0)	113
Artillery Engineer	35.8 (50.8)	28.6 (49.1)	116
Technical	35.8 (54.6)	24.6 (45.3)	108
	N = 165	N = 199	

Gamma = -.26   Z = -1.51   P < .07

necessary preparation for the special curriculum), two similarly distinct "arts" curricula, and a fifth curriculum designed for cadets interested in learning one of several languages. The curricula can be classified as either difficult (the special) or easy (the main and the languages). Under a contest system one would expect technical units to recruit predominantly from among cadets enrolled in the special mathematics curriculum since these individuals would naturally have the kind of education most appropriate to such units.

In fact, the data show that a substantial portion of those enrolled in difficult curricula *are* destined for technical regiments; hence, the kind of training received is somewhat associated (although very imperfectly) with the eventual destination of cadets (see Table 4). This finding must be qualified, however, by noting that this association may represent an independent effect of secondary schooling.[5] Therefore, Table 5 presents the relationship between schooling, curriculum and regimental selection. First, Table 5 shows that for all regiments, curriculum plays either no role or an unimportant role. If

TABLE 5. SCHOOLING, DIFFICULTY OF CURRICULUM, AND REGIMENTAL SELECTION

Regiment	Public		Grammar		Welbeck		
	Difficult	Easy	Difficult	Easy	Difficult	Easy	
Aristocratic	14.3 (46.2)	10.7 (53.8)	0	0	0	0	N = 26
Non-Aristocratic	33.3 (26.9)	43.5 (54.8)	17.6 (5.7)	41.9 (12.5)	0	0	N = 104
Artillery-Engineer	34.5 (27.1)	30.5 (37.3)	55.9 (17.7)	29.0 (8.4)	19.5 (7.4)	16.7 (1.8)	N = 107
Technical	17.9 (15.6)	15.3 (20.8)	26.5 (9.3)	29.0 (9.3)	80.5 (34.3)	83.3 (10.4)	N = 96
	N = 84	N = 131	N = 34	N = 31	N = 41	N = 12	

Gamma public = -.058   Z = -.25

Gamma grammar = -.156   Z = -.45

Gamma Welbeck = .096   Z = .11

5. Traditionally, Sandhurst has performed as a remedial institution. There are a few cadets for whom Sandhurst represents an opportunity to prepare for *A* levels under the guidance of civilian instructors. These individuals claim, however, that the best they can do is to prevent cadets from forgetting what they already know.

anything, these regiments seem to prefer individuals enrolled in the easy curriculum (53.8 percent enrolled in easy curricula as opposed to 46.7 percent enrolled in difficult ones). Table 5 also shows that for those who have attended a public school, the kind of curriculum followed plays no role in regimental selection. However, for those who have attended either Welbeck or a grammar school, a more complex relationship prevails. Those who attended a grammar school and subsequently enrolled in a difficult curriculum tend to go into artillery-engineers units (i.e., the prestigious technical units), while grammar school graduates enrolled in the easy curriculum tend to go into fighting, low-status regiments. At the low end of the educational prestige continuum, curriculum difficulty makes no difference: most Welbeck students enter the technical units. Table 5, therefore, suggests that at the top and bottom of the prestige continuum, knowledge makes little difference. Only for the middle category can that factor make a difference.

The small contribution of skill to the association between type of school attended and regimental selection can be more closely examined by partialling the association between these variables. A tau of .29 obtains between school attended and regiment selected, a tau of .11 between school attended and curriculum, and a tau of -.02 between regiment and skill. The strength of association between school and regiment controlling for skill is .29.

In short, educational criteria per se are not of primary importance. Guards, cavalry and infantry units recruit largely along prestige lines. Artillery-engineers units recruit the largest percentage of technically qualified cadets insofar as technical qualification is measured by academic performance, although these units rely on other criteria as well. The technical units rely somewhat on a contest system but must be content to recruit the "leftovers" (who are not necessarily committed to the dominant ideology and/or who are not necessarily the best qualified individuals academically). The only exception is Welbeck cadets, who are required to enter technical units. It is interesting to note that the few Welbeck cadets selected by the artillery-engineers (their number is regulated) are enrolled in easy curricula. It may well be that these cadets exhibit a high degree of conformity to the dominant ideology and that fact makes them attractive to units that see themselves as fighting rather than as technical units (even though much of their work involves the manipulation of sophisticated equipment such as guns and missiles).

Technical competence aside, ideological conformity to the standards of the recruiting group is important to regimental recruitment. The data thus far have shown that with one exception, technical and educational qualifications did not predict which regiment a cadet would enter, despite the fact that these regiments have quite different functions. To test their degree of ideological conformity, cadets were asked whether "traditions should be respected" (tradition, obviously, is of an extremely salient value in the British Army). When the responses are classified as high conformist (agree strongly), medium conformist (agree), and low conformist (disagree and disagree strongly), we find an association between level of conformity and type of regiment selected (Table 6). The fighting regiments — aristocratic and nonaristocratic — recruit higher proportions of high conformists than do the artillery-engineers who, in turn, recruit more than the technical. Other items measuring cadets' ideological orientation also correlated with the type of regiment that had accepted them. Cadets destined for aristocratic regiments were far more likely

TABLE 6. CONFORMITY AND REGIMENTAL SELECTION

	High Conformist	Medium Conformist	Low Conformist	
Aristocratic	10.9 (53.8)	5.7 (46.2)	0	N = 26
Non-Aristocratic	36.7 (41.2)	30.5 (56.1)	15.0 (2.6)	N = 114
Artillery-Engineers	29.6 (33.0)	33.3 (60.9)	35.0 (6.1)	N = 115
Technical	22.6 (28.2)	30.5 (62.1)	50.0 (9.7)	N = 103
	N = 128	N = 210	N = 20	

Gamma = .253   Z = 1.51   P < .07

to give "conformist" responses (e.g., leadership is not an acquired trait; the regimental mess system ought to be continued) than were cadets who had been accepted by technical regiments; the latter seemed to exhibit a somewhat different definition of the officer's role. These differences were found despite the fact that as a whole, the cadets were conformists (i.e., the socialization process had been generally successful; Garnier, 1973).

DISCUSSION AND CONCLUSION

These data clearly indicate the juxtaposition of two systems, each representing a special organizational need. Prestigious regiments recruit individuals who have attended prestigious educational institutions and who are ideologically committed to maintaining traditional organizational practices. These regiments are also fighting units, in which organizational commitment and esprit de corps are crucial. Technical units emphasize educational qualifications, while the prestigious or old technical units rely on a subtle blend of skill and ascription, a practice that may well reflect their function (technical in contrast to fighting units). By creating and staffing units specifically designed to handle new technologies (those required by modern electronics and computers, for example), the British Army has been able to meet the demands of modern warfare while simultaneously avoiding the integration problems that including many different types of officers in the same units would create. This particular pattern of adaptation is an old one in the British Army. For example, the artillery and engineers were created when the services of trained individuals had become indispensible. However, engineers and gunners did not become part of the regular system, and they were the only ones who did not have to purchase their commissions. Likewise, their recruitment was totally different, both socially and educationally (they were trained at Woolwich, while all other officers were trained at Sandhurst).

The case study presented here suggests that changes resulting from technological innovations can be severely altered by the organizational context. This possibility was foreseen by Janowitz (1971—Preface). This convergence may apply to highly technical units, but it appears to have little relevance to fighting units. Turning back to a consideration of military organizations as a whole (armies, for example), a dynamic model of adaptation to change can be postulated and tested. Technological innovations tend to affect the percentage of the army actually engaged in combat. As the percentage decreases, the organization turns to new personnel sources and to new selection criteria. These new individuals tend to follow altered career patterns and to favor more managerial authority relations. As these new individuals reach elite positions, they tend to impose their standards upon the entire organization since career experiences tend to be powerful socializing influences. At that stage, fighting units may be expected to hold university degrees when, in fact, at the junior level particularly, such degrees are of no demonstrated advantage. Furthermore, solutions to problems may too often be approached technologically, thus maintaining the technically oriented elite in place.

It must be acknowledged that these are speculations whose testing should be undertaken. For such testing to be meaningful, greater use should be made of insights derived from organizational sociology. For example, Crozier's suggestions concerning the impact of social values on organizations should be examined, and then (as in this paper) the internal adaptations processes examined. Furthermore, as my discussion has implied, such analyses should be both historical and contemporary (many of the insights from systems theory could be employed also; Crozier, 1964; Katz and Kahn, 1966).

This case study demonstrates that traditional patterns and criteria of recruitment can prevail even in a highly technological army (recruitment was selected because of its salience, but the same case could be made for Janowitz's other four hypotheses). This paper has also argued that such organizational factors must be analyzed empirically, and not be assumed to derive inevitably from technological innovations. Similarly, such factors, when uncovered, should not be dismissed as anachronistic or the result of some "lag." To be a modern army can imply different things in different societal contexts.

Given that military organizations usually keep good records, the impact of technological change on organizational structure could be tested. This should be done on a broad multi-national scale so that the generalizations available to students of the military can be made on broader-based findings than those made available by case studies. Such multi-national investigations would make a substantial contribution to organizational sociology.

REFERENCES

Barnett, Corelli
    1967   "The Education of Military Elites." Journal of Contemporary History 2 (October):5-36.
Baynes, John
    1968   Morale: A Study of Men and Courage. London: Cassell.
Crozier, Michel
    1964   The Bureaucratic Phenomenon. University of Chicago Press.
Garnier, Maurice
    1969   "Social Class and Military Socialization: A Study of the Royal Military Academy, Sandhurst." Ph.D. dissertation. University of California.
    1972   "Changing Recruitment Patterns and Organizational Ideology." Administrative Science Quarterly (December):499-507.
    1973   "Power and Ideological Conformity." American Journal of Sociology (September):343-363.
Janowitz, Morris
    1971   The Professional Soldier (2nd edition). Free Press of Glencoe.
Kalton, Graham
    1967   The Public Schools: A Factual Survey. London: Longmans, Green.

Katz, Daniel and Robert L. Kahn
    1966   The Social Psychology of Organizations. New York: Wiley.
Kelsall, R.K.
    1955   Higher Civil Servants in Britain from 1870 to the Present Day. London: Routledge and
            Kegan Paul.
Smyth, Sir John
    1961   Sandhurst: the History of the Royal Military Academy, Woolwich, the Royal Military
            College, Sandhurst, and the Royal Military Academy Sandhurst, 1751-1961. London:
            Widenfeld and Nicolson.
Turner, E.S.
    1956   Gallant Gentlemen: A Portrait of the British Officer, 1600-1956. London: Michael
            Joseph.
Turner, Ralph
    1960   "Sponsored and Contest Mobility and the School System." American Sociological
            Review 25 (December):855-867.
    1966   "Acceptance of Irregular Mobility in Britain and the United States." Sociometry 29
            (December):334-352.
Wilkinson, Ralph
    1964   The Prefects. London: Oxford University Press.

5

SOCIAL RECRUITMENT AND POLITICAL ORIENTATIONS OF THE OFFICER CORPS IN A COMPARATIVE PERSPECTIVE*

GEORGE A. KOURVETARIS

Northern Illinois University

BETTY A. DOBRATZ

University of Wisconsin, Madison

This analysis examines the extent to which social democratization (as measured by the broadening of the social base of recruitment) has been followed by a concomitant process of attitudinal political transformation of the officer corps in a number of countries (from a basically conservative political outlook to one more liberal). It also considers whether the broadening of the social base of recruitment has hindered or facilitated the process of political democratization of the military profession. The examination was based on data from a selective number of countries for which qualitative and empirical studies on social recruitment and political perspectives of the officer corps had been conducted in the last two decades. A total of 14 nations were selected representing the three worlds of development and international stratification.

Using Janowitz' and Moskos' models of civil military relations as conceptual frameworks, certain tentative generalizations regarding the linkages between social and political structure of the officer corps were discerned: 1) Although the broadening of the social base in officer recruitment has taken

"Social Recruitment and Political Orientations of the Officer Corps in A Comparative Perspective," by G.A. Kourvetaris and B.A. Dobratz is reprinted from *Pacific Sociological Review* Vol. 16, No. 2 (April 1973) pp. 228-254 by permission of the Publisher, Sage Publications, Inc.

*The authors would like to thank Professors Panos Bardis, University of Toledo; Ruth Cavan, Northern Illinois University; David Eaton, Illinois State University; and Keith Legg, University of Florida for their comments on an earlier version of this project.

*place in all three worlds of development, this trend has begun
reversing itself for much of the First World of Development; 2)
Both the shift from a narrow base to a broader one in officer
recruitment and the reversal of this trend have not been uniform
in all officer corps examined; 3) The broadening of the social
base of recruitment has not been followed by a concomitant
process of political democratization of the officer's political
attitudes and/or behaviors; and 4) In some cases broadening the
social base of recruitment has encouraged rather than deterred
the active political involvement of the officers in the processes of
national and international politics.*

The sociological study of the military profession, as exhibited most fully by its officers, is a study of close to an
ideal-type of the managerial profession. When students of
organizations and professions analyze the development of
civilian or military occupational structures, it is conventional to
examine and discern patterns of social recruitment of professional elites. Janowitz (1960: 81), in his pioneer study of the
American professional officer, states, "The analysis of the social
origins of the military is a powerful key to the understanding of
its political logic although no elite behaves simply on the basis
of its social origins." On the other hand, Mills (1956: 192)
argues that "social origins and early background are less
important to the character of the professional military than any
other high social type."

Since the turn of the century, a steady long-term shift in
officer recruitment in the Western European and American
armies from a narrow, relatively high-social-status base to one
more representative of the population at large is noted by a
number of scholars (Janowitz, 1960, 1969; Halpern, 1962;
Shils, 1962; Van Doorn, 1965; Demeter, 1965; and von der
Mehden, 1969). In other words, an infusion of "middle-class"
patterns of social recruitment in the military profession has
occurred.

Moskos and Janowitz argue that, although the long-term
trend in the twentieth century in officer recruitment has been

more representative of the broader American population, more recent evidence shows that this trend has reversed itself in the late 1960s and early 1970s. Furthermore, both authors present somewhat similar indicators alluding to the trend of narrowness of the base of the American officer recruitment. Moskos (1971: 293), for example, lists three measures of the growing unrepresentativeness of the officer corps in the past decade: the overproportionate numbers of recent officers coming from rural and small-town backgrounds, the marked increase in the number of cadets at service academies who come from military families, and an increasing monopolization of military elite positions by academy graduates. Janowitz (1971), on the other hand, attributes this trend of divergence to the concept of an all-volunteer army, the limit in quality and number of ROTC units at prestige universities, and a decline in recruitment from the ranks because of the emphasis on college graduates.

One of the most spirited sociopolitical issues in Western Europe and elsewhere has been whether the broadening or narrowing social base of recruitment of the military elite has been accompanied by a concomitant process of political democratization of the officers' outlook and behavior (Janowitz, 1960: 10-11). According to Janowitz (1964: 118; 1969: 14), democratization of the military refers to both the extent to which the military profession is accessible to the sons of the working class and the extent to which the military elite is willing to accept and be accountable to civilian authority.

The purpose of the present analysis is twofold: *first*, to examine the extent to which social democratization (as measured by the broadening of the social base of recruitment) has indeed been followed by a concomitant process of attitudinal political transformation of the officer corps in a number of countries (from one basically conservative political outlook to one more liberal), and, *second*, to consider whether the broadening of the social base of recruitment has hindered or facilitated the process of political democratization of the military profession.

In this paper, the term social recruitment is used interchangeably with social origins and refers to various socioeconomic/ demographic indicators of the officers' background, particularly father's occupation or social class. The political orientations, on the other hand, refer to the officers' political beliefs, values, and attitudes toward national or international political issues. The latter will be determined by the officers' level of political participation and political efficacy—that is, voting patterns, party preference, political allegiance, covert/overt political involvement in national or international politics, coups, political indoctrination, and the like.

**TYPOLOGIES AND
MODELS OF CIVIL-MILITARY RELATIONS**

In an effort to analyze the linkage between social structure (that is, social recruitment, social class, and the like) and political structure (that is, political beliefs, attitudes, and the like) of the military organization and its officer corps on a cross-national level, a number of typologies and models of civil-military relations have been suggested.[1] Janowitz (1969) sees the present pattern of social recruitment and political orientations of the military in industrialized societies as evolving historically from the aristocratic/feudal model of Northwestern Europe. This model gave impetus to the emergence of the democratic, the Prussian/totalitarian, and the contingency model of the garrison state suggested by Harold D. Lasswell.

Although the Western and American democratic competitive model of military professionalism and organization had and still does have a profound effect on the nature of the military profession and organization of other nations, one can discern a more independent type of military institution in the nations of Latin America, Africa, and Asia. For, unlike the Western European professional armies, there was a marked absence of feudal domination in these armies. Officers emerged as powerful political groups following World War II, either in reaction to or in anticipation of the weakness of civilian political institutions and the breakdown of parliamentary forms of government.

Janowitz (1964) offers a range of five types of civil-military relations:

(1) authoritarian/personal, where national power is vested in the personal and authoritarian (charismatic-like) authority of one ruler;

---

1. Besides those discussed in the text, numerous other civil-military typologies have been developed in the area of military sociology. For an extensive discussion of certain of these, see McWilliams (1967), particularly the chapter by Germani and Silvert; Horowitz (1967), and von der Mehden (1969).

(2) civilian mass party where political power is lodged in a one-party state system under strong personal leadership with the military being controlled by the single civilian mass political party;

(3) democratic competitive/quasi-democratic system in which political power is exercised through a multiparty political and elective system, and the military is under the control of civilian political elites;

(4) civil-military coalition, in which the military expands its political activity and becomes a political bloc with the civilian leadership remaining in power only because of the military's active or passive support; and finally

(5) the military oligarchy, in which the military sets itself up as a ruling group, and civilian political activity is transformed and restricted.

Elsewhere in this issue, Moskos suggests three developmental models of civil-military relations of the U.S. military that provide a means for considering the dynamics of both social recruitment and political orientations: (1) the convergent or civilianized military, which emphasizes the increasing similarities between the military and civilian forms of social organization; (2) the divergent or traditional military, which stresses the growing differentiation between military and civilian social organization; and (3) the segmented or pluralistic military, which pictures a military that is internally segmented into areas which will be either convergent or more divergent than the present organization of the armed forces. In analyzing patterns of social recruitment and political perspectives of the officer corps on a cross-national level, an effort will be made to apply the aforementioned typologies.

THE THREE WORLDS OF DEVELOPMENT

This analysis is based on data from a selective number of countries in which qualitative and empirical studies in both social recruitment and political attitudes of the officers have been conducted in the last two decades. For the purpose of the present inquiry, fourteen nations have been selected representing the three worlds of development and international stratification.[2]

---

2. The countries included in this study were not randomly selected from a specified population, but were included because data on social origins and political

(1) *The first world of development* consists of the United States and its Western European allies of West Germany, England, France, Sweden, and Greece;

(2) *the second world of development* encompasses Russia and its Eastern European satellites of Poland, East Germany, and Czechoslovakia;

(3) *the third world of development* includes India, Pakistan, Argentina, and Egypt. Although the latter formally claim to be nonaligned, they nevertheless rely in varying degrees upon the first and second worlds of development for their political (including military), economic, and social modernization.

FIRST WORLD OF DEVELOPMENT

Of the six nations selected within this block, the four officer corps of West Germany, Great Britain, France, and Sweden evolved from the aristocratic/feudal model of recruitment. As Table 1 illustrates, each experienced a broadening in its social base of recruitment and a steady decline in the officers' noble origins. In comparing the elite officers with the total corps, one notices that aristocratic origins persisted longer in the upper ranks than in the total corps.

While Germany at one time fit the Prussian model of recruitment, West Germany, the United States, Great Britain, Greece, France, and Sweden presently have democratic bases of recruitment in the sense that over time they have become more representative of the society at large. Table 2 gives the social origins by class for the contemporary officer corps of the United States, Great Britain, Greece, and Sweden. Each of the militaries in these nations relies heavily upon recruitment from the middle class. Of the four nations, Great Britain has the highest percentage of elite officers from the upper- and

---

orientations were available. Also, an attempt was made to secure representatives from each of the worlds of development. For additional information on the three worlds of development, see Horowitz (1966). In this type of study, one encounters serious methodological and conceptual problems. Not only have the surveys been compiled from a wide variety of sources—i.e., directories of elite officer corps (*Who's Who* variety) or officer corps in general, military service academies vis-à-vis other sources of recruitment (that is, ROTC, general military versus elite military schools and the like, but different techniques of statistical interpretation and sampling have been employed by the authors. Yet, despite these limitations, one cannot dismiss the usefulness of secondary data in comparative sociological analysis.

TABLE 1

SOCIAL ORIGINS BY NOBLE BACKGROUND OF WESTERN EUROPEAN OFFICER CORPS, 1820-1962

(in percentages)

Social Origins	Germany		Great Britain		Sweden		France	
	Elite[a] Officer	Total Corps	Elite Officer	Total Corps	Elite Officer	Total Corps	Elite Officer	Total Corps
1820s–1830s	1824	1824	1830	1830	1823	1823		
Nobility	97	58	78	53	70	54		
Other	3	42	22	47	30	46		
n	(111)	(5,230)	(13)	(100)				
1860s–1970s	1872	1872	1870	1875	1865	1865		
Nobility	94	49	50	50	62	46		
Other	6	51	50	50	38	54		
n	(178)	(11,034)	(80)	(100)				
1890s	1898	1898	1897			1890	1895	
Nobility	81	40	40			40	25	
Other	19	60	60			60	75	
n	(254)	(14,778)	(63)					
1900s–1910s	1911	1911	1913	1912	1913	1913	1909	
Nobility	67	33	35	41	35	30	13	
Other	33	67	65	59	65	70	87	
n	(263)	(16,979)	(58)	(100)				

TABLE 1 (Continued)

Social Origins	Germany		Great Britain		Sweden		France	
	Elite[a] Officer	Total Corps	Elite Officer	Total Corps	Elite Officer	Total Corps	Elite Officer	Total Corps
1920s	1925	1925	1926		1923	1923		
Nobility	38	20	27		33	24		
Other	62	80	73		67	76		
n	(149)	(3,606)	(48)					
1930s	1932	1932	1939	1930			1939	
Nobility	33	20	22	11			7	
Other	67	80	78	89			93	
n	(149)	(3,766)	(45)	(100)				
1940s	1944				1943	1943		1949
Nobility	18				25	13		6
Other	82				75	87		94
n	(230)							
1950s– 1960s			1950	1952		1962 (Estimate)	1958	
Nobility			7	5		3	5	
Other			93	95		97	95	
n			(26)	(100)				

SOURCES: Janowitz (1960: 94); Otley (1968: 104); Razzell (1963: 253); Chapman (1959: 72); Ambler (1966: 151); Abrahamsson (1968: 80).
a. An elite officer refers to a top or an upper-echelon officer in the military hierarchy (e.g., generals, admirals).

TABLE 2
SOCIAL ORIGINS BY CLASS OF THE CONTEMPORARY MILITARY OFFICER CORPS IN THE UNITED STATES, GREAT BRITAIN, GREECE, AND SWEDEN (in percentages)

Class	U.S. Army Elite 1950	British Army Elite 1956-1960	Greek Army Officer Sample[a] 1968	Greek Total Army Corps 1968	Swedish Officer Sample 1962	Swedish Army College 1962
Upper	3	18	—	—	} 41	} 34
Upper-middle	47	39	34	29		
Other middle	45	43	32	22	46	54
Lower or working	5	—	34	49	13	12
n	(140)	(110)	(100)		(846)	

SOURCES: Janowitz (1960: 90); Abrams (1965: 251-252); Kourvetaris (1969: 85); Abrahamsson (1968: 80-81).
a. Greek Army Officer sample consists of officers of the rank of major or above.

TABLE 3
SOCIAL ORIGINS BY OCCUPATION OF OFFICER CORPS IN UNITED STATES, WEST GERMANY, AND GREECE (in percentages)

Occupation	United States NORC Study 1964	United States West Point Class 1960	West Germany Officers 1960-1961	West Germany Officer Candidates 1960-1961	Greece[a] Army Officer Sample 1968	Greece[a] Army Total Corps 1968
Military	5	—	12	11	18	11
Professional or managerial	—	50	21	28	16	18
Businessmen	50	15	10	17	24	11
White-collar	—	13	25	20	8	11
Farmers	9	—	7	7	32	39
Blue-collar or worker	29	19	23	16	2	10
Other	7	3	2	1	—	—
n	Approx. (7,000)	(765)	(137)	(329)	(100)	

SOURCES: Moskos (1970: 195); Janowitz (1960: 91); Waldman (1964: 210); Kourvetaris (1969: 85).
a. Greek professional or managerial social origins include professional and high-status white-collar classification. Army officer sample consists of officers of the rank of major or above.

upper-middle classes, while Greece recruited the smallest percentage of officers from the higher strata.

In terms of occupation, Table 3 shows that the U.S., West
German, and Greek Officer Corps have a majority of officers
with military, professional, managerial, business, or other
white-collar backgrounds. Great Britain has also recruited
heavily from these same classifications. On the basis of data
collected on the origin and recruitment of British Army elites
from 1870-1959, Otley (1968: 89) concluded that almost
ninety percent of the elite officers came from the propertied or
higher professional strata with only "slight signs of any process
of 'democratization' of recruitment." Although France has a
somewhat broader base of recruitment than Great Britain, a
1959 survey of French officer candidates at various military
academies revealed that only five percent of the candidates were
sons of workers, six percent sons of farmers, five percent sons
of clerks, and seven percent sons of employees or artisans
(Menard, 1967: 61).

That certain aspects of the base of officer recruitment may
be narrowing in the United States during the last decade has
been previously mentioned. With the exception perhaps of
officer recruitment in Greece, this trend has also been noted by
Waldman (1964: 210) for West Germany, Abrahamsson (1968:
61) for Sweden, Barnett (1970: 488) for England, and Ambler
(1966: 140) and Menard (1967: 61) for France.

Given the trends of social recruitment in the six officer corps
within the first world of development, what are the officers'
political orientations? Ideally, the officer corps in the Western
nations profess to be nonpartisan in national and international
issues; yet during the 1900s and particularly since 1940, the
militaries of the United States, France, and Greece have come
to play increasingly significant roles in politics. The German
military was particularly influential in governmental affairs
during World War I, and, during World War II, certain of its
officers unsuccessfully attempted to stage a putsch and assassi-
nate Hitler. Greek officers also staged coups and counter-coups
in 1909, 1922, 1926, 1933, 1935, and more recently in 1967.
During these times, the Greek nation experienced periods of
social and political turbulence and transition in her social
structure. The French officers also actively participated in
politics during 1958, when De Gaulle returned to power and in

the anti-De Gaulle movement of 1961. It would seem that only the Swedish and British Officer Corps have maintained a posture of nonactive political involvement throughout the century.

On the international level in the last quarter of a century, the tenor of the political orientations of all six officer corps has been conditioned by their anti-communist stance. Indeed, the raison d'être of the North Atlantic Treaty Organization, to which all of them except Sweden and France belong, was predicated on the assumption of communist threat in Europe and elsewhere. This supranational military organization has, since its inception in 1949, undoubtedly influenced and shaped the political beliefs and guided the professional military ethos of the officer corps. However, more recent developments such as Nixon's trips to China and Russia, current talks on strategic arms limitation, a possible future conference on mutual reductions of NATO and Warsaw Pact forces, and Brandt's *Ostpolitik* might lead to detente and rapprochement between East and West.

On the national level, recent studies indicate that officers tend to vote for more conservative parties. Data presented in Table 4 on the political orientations of the officer corps of the

TABLE 4

POLITICAL ORIENTATIONS OF OFFICERS IN UNITED STATES, WEST GERMANY, AND SWEDEN IN COMPARISON TO THEIR RESPECTIVE VOTING POPULATIONS (in percentages)

	United States		West Germany		Sweden	
Political Orientations	Army Officers 1954	Voters 1952	Officers 1962	Voters 1961	Officers 1962	Voters 1962
Liberal	26	44	5	36	4	54
Conservative	70	55	75	46	85	16
Other	4	1	20	18	11	30
n	(211)		(108)		(781)	

SOURCES: U.S.: Janowitz (1960: 237); Golenpaul (1957: 427). For Presidential election of 1952, Republicans were considered conservative and Democrats as liberal. West Germany: Waldman (1964: 216). Christian Democratic Union/Christian Social Union was regarded as conservative while Social Democratic Party was considered liberal. Free Democratic Party, other parties, and no information were listed as other (Europa Publications, 1964: 57). Election statistics are the results of the 1961 Bundestag election. Sweden: Abrahamsson (1968: 78). Social Democrats were classified as liberal while Conservatives were regarded as conservative. Liberals and Centre Party were classified as others. For the general election results, Communists (4%) were also classified as liberal, though no officer was a communist.

United States, West Germany, and Sweden show that officers are more likely to prefer a conservative party than the general voting population. However, the results, particularly for the United States, are not completely comparable. Political identification for the U.S. officers was based on responses to a close-ended question asking their position on domestic politics, while the results for the nation were taken from the 1952 presidential election, in which Republican preference was considered conservative and Democratic liberal. Swedish and West German officers were asked to identify their party preferences, and these were compared to the preferences of the overall population in elections during approximately the same time period. The French military also appears divergent in its political orientations vis-à-vis French civilian society, for the former has been described as anti-parliamentarian, authoritarian, and removed from the progressive elements of society (Ambler, 1966: 301, 303; Menard, 1967: 62, 63).

Within the Greek military a trend toward convergence seems to be occurring. The military views itself as the embodiment of national ideals and consciousness. According to certain officers interviewed by the senior author, one of the aims of the recent military intervention is to create the basis for a more equitable distribution of social wealth in that society. The military in Greece perceives itself as a cultural preserving institution with strong elements of nationalism and anti-communism. The model of conservatism that applies to Northwestern Europe and the United States is not particularly relevant in this case (Kourvetaris, 1969, 1971a, 1971b, 1971c).

Certain tentative generalizations of the linkages between social recruitment and political orientations can be discerned: (1) The broadening of social recruitment for Great Britain during wartime and Sweden from 1920-1960 did not mean a concomitant increase in political involvement. A narrow base of recruitment for Britain (other than wartime) and a narrowing base for Sweden in the 1960s (with respect to social class) have not meant greater or lesser involvement for their militaries, for they have simply remained apolitical. (2) In the United States and France, trends toward broadening of the social base of recruitment of the corps began in the early 1900s, but the role of the military in politics was not strongly increased until World War II. For France, military involvement has taken an overt form, while in the United States it has remained covert. Signs of narrowing the base in the 1960s and early 1970s for the United States do not seem to have altered the political involvement of the officers. (3) The Greek military has had a broadening of social origins of its officers at the same time that the military has been active in politics. (4) Germany represents an anomaly, for broadening occurred during World War I, when the military was very influential in politics, again during the 1930s, when Hitler controlled it, and during the 1950s, when it had little political activity. Thus, no general pattern of association between social origins and political activity emerged from these six Western nations.

SECOND WORLD OF DEVELOPMENT

As in the case of four of the nations in the first world of development, the selected East European countries originally had feudal, aristocratic backgrounds. Prior to communist takeover, social recruitment patterns of the four nations followed patterns similar to those of Northwestern Europe. More specifically, in Russia, the base of recruitment was becoming more middle-class-oriented, although aristocratic elements persisted prior to the Bolshevik Revolution. In Poland and Czechoslovakia, where communism was adopted much later than the USSR, more of their officers were recruited from the middle and upper classes, before the governments turned socialist. For example, the large majority of 58 Polish interwar generals for whom biographical data were available came from upper- or middle-class homes (Pool, 1955: 57). Also, the trend toward middle-class recruitment can be found in Germany, especially during the Hitler period. A virtually new East German Army had to be created after World War II, although some officers had formerly belonged to the Wehrmacht.

With the advent of communist control, the officer recruitment policies of all four nations favored those with working or peasant social origins in order to conform with the communist ideology of proletarian social recruitment in general. Table 5 shows the social background of the contemporary officer corps in Czechoslovakia, Poland, and East Germany. None of the sources from which the available data were obtained specifically defined criteria used for the classification in the table. For example, it is not clear who is a worker and how he differs from

TABLE 5

**RECENT ORIGINS BY OCCUPATION OF OFFICERS IN THE
SOCIALIST COUNTRIES OF CZECHOSLOVAKIA, POLAND,
AND EAST GERMANY (in percentages)**

Occupation	Czechoslovakia			Poland			East Germany	
	1957	1962	1967	1958	1962[b]	1964	1965	1966
Workers	63	64	61	51	49	48	82	83
Farmers/Peasants	13	12	13	34	33	33	3	
Craftsmen/Tradesmen	5	5	5	3	5	5	–	
Intelligentsia	12	13	16	10	11	12	–	17
Employees	7	6	5	–	–	–	–	
Industrialist/Businessmen	0[a]	0[a]	0[a]	–	–	–	–	–
Others	–	–	–	2	3	2	15	–

SOURCES: Cvrcek (1969: 97); Graczyk (1969: 88); Van Doorn, (1969: 17); Forster (1966: 184).
a. Less than 1%
b. Total of 101% according to source (Graczyk, 1969: 88).

an employee or a craftsman. The differences between employee and intelligentsia also need to be clarified. Despite the limitations of the data, Table 5 does indicate a strong recruitment of officers from the working class, with the higher percentages in the more industrialized countries of East Germany and Czechoslovakia.

In a similar pattern to that of the first world of development, where the nobility and upper classes tended to be concentrated in the more elite positions of the officer corps, the percentages of officers with nonproletariat backgrounds are greater in the elite corps of the militaries of the second world of development. In 1926, for example, 61.5% of the generals and higher command staff in the USSR had origins "other" than working-class or peasant, while they comprised only about 33% of the total corps (Garthoff, 1968: 247). More recently (in 1964), 29.7% of the Polish generals' fathers were intelligentsia, while officers with these origins accounted for only 12.2% of the total corps (Graczyk, 1969: 89).

From the data presented in Table 5, one might conclude that social origins of the contemporary officer corps in the second world of development are rather representative of their civilian population. Given the broad social base in these militaries, what are the political orientations of their officer corps?

In societies where pluralistic institutions and interest groups are lacking, the military elite as exemplified by its officer corps along with other social elites follows a model of convergence and behaves as an integral part of what Aron (1966) refers to as the "unified elite." The officer corps plays an important role in legitimizing the political elite which rules each country. Cvrcek (1969: 105) has cited three major ways in which the military has an elite or class character: (1) it usually supports the side of the ruling class in internal conflicts; (2) it functions as an instrument for carrying out the interest of the ruling class in foreign policy; and (3) it often serves as a police force to solve class conflicts.

Political indoctrination and training are emphasized in order to ensure the loyalty of the military to the government and the Communist Party. Allegiance to the state and formal membership in the Communist Party have often been viewed by the officers as necessary requisites for overall success or career advancement (Brzezinski, 1952: 584). Seventy-three percent of the officers in Poland (but almost 100% of the top commanders), 75% in Czechoslovakia, 93% in the USSR, and 96% in East Germany belonged to the Communist Party in the 1960s (Wiatr, 1968: 238; Garthoff, 1968: 253).

While the trend may be toward convergence in the four nations, it may be suggested that the Soviet military follows a segmented model of development due to its increasing role in international politics and its emphasis upon modern technology. Putting it another way, one segment of the officer corps may engage in political activities, another may act as an ambassador of good will, and a third may engage in technical and scientific research. However, this does not seem to be the case among the Soviet satellite countries. Since the demand for professional/technical expertise is not as great in these countries, and because the Russians are determined to maintain their spheres of influence and dominance over Eastern European armies (as illustrated by the invasion of Czechoslovakia), they may not be willing to allow a divergent or segmental model to develop in these officer corps.

All four nations belong to the Warsaw Pact, which serves as a counterpart to NATO and functions as an instrument binding the Eastern European nations to the USSR. In each of these countries, the social bases of recruitment have broadened since the communist takeover. Although the criteria for classification are not clear, recent data on East Germany, Czechoslovakia, and Poland tend to substantiate the claim that the corps are quite representative of their societies. At the same time, their militaries have been active in party politics in terms of supporting the communist regimes within and across societies.

THIRD WORLD OF DEVELOPMENT

Although these four nations may have recruited their officers from the upper classes at one time, recent policies of officer recruitment have tended to favor officers with middle-class backgrounds, particularly those from the new urban sectors. Specific statistical data on social class origins are available only for the Argentine and Egyptian Officer Corps. Table 6 shows the overwhelmingly middle-class backgrounds of the Argentine Air Force Brigadiers and Army Generals in 1960 and the junior and intermediate ranks of the Egyptian officers in 1948-1949. According to Beeri (1966: 35), this sample of junior and intermediate ranks of the late 1940s would be representative of intermediate and senior ranks of the Egyptian Corps during the 1960s. The more general data on India (Cohen, 1971: 184-185), and the formerly unified Pakistan (Sayeed, 1968: 279-280) also indicate an increasing reliance upon middle-class recruitment.

While the recruiting of officers from the middle class is indicative of the growing middle classes in these societies, the origins of the officer corps are far from approximating those of

TABLE 6

SOCIAL ORIGINS BY CLASS OF THE MILITARY IN ARGENTINA AND EGYPT (in percentages)

	Argentina	Egypt
Class	Elites Circa 1960	Jr. Ranks 1948-1949
Upper	—	16
Upper-middle	74	16
Other middle	24	65
Working or lower	2	3
n	(114)	(343)

SOURCES: Horowitz (1967: 162). Higher middle class became upper-middle class and dependent middle class became other middle class (Beeri, 1966: 38). Other middle class includes 36% middle-middle class and 29% lower-middle class.

the general population which still includes a substantial number of working or farming classes. In 1950, for example, Germani and Silvert (1967: 228) reported that only 36% of the Argentine population could be classified as middle class. Beeri (1966: 14,37), on the other hand, points out that the Egyptian aristocracy and nearly 80% of the population referred to as the masses are not represented in the social origins of the officers.

In Pakistan, diverse ethnic origins were partially responsible for the war between East and West Pakistan which resulted in independence for the eastern section now called Bangladesh. The composition of the officer corps itself reflected some of the deep-rooted inequalities in the society. In 1955, only 14 of 894 army officers (1.6%) above the rank of major were East Pakistanis (Jahan, 1970: 280), although 55% of the total population lived in East Pakistan. Military recruitment policy exhibited little sign of change, for in 1964 only 13 of 108 candidates admitted to the military academy were East Pakistanis (Sayeed, 1968: 280).

Political orientations of officers in these nations are normally measured on the basis of overt intervention in politics because the military's role in the government is often more apparent than in the Western and socialist nations. Also, more refined studies are not available concerning officers' attitudes. Recent overt military intervention in politics has taken place in Pakistan, Egypt, and Argentina, but not in India.

In 1958, Ayub Khan successfully staged a military coup and gained control of the Pakistani government. The generals who dominated the cabinet had upper-class origins like Ayub Khan himself. Few economic and political reforms were attempted (Sayeed, 1968: 285). Though social origins were not significant in explaining the reasons for intervening, it has been suggested that they may partially explain why no radical reform was undertaken (Hurewitz, 1969: 104). Ayub Khan was forced to resign in 1969, and General Yahya Khan then gained control. Only after the recent West Pakistan defeat in the fourteen-day war and the creation of Bangladesh has the government returned to civilian control for the first time in thirteen years (under Zulfikar Ali Bhutto).

The Egyptian military revolt occurred in 1952 and was led by men of middle-class origins, including Gamal Nasser and Anwar el-Sadat (Vatikiotis, 1961: 46; Mansfield, 1965: 3; Abdel-

Malek, 1968: 45; Hurewitz, 1969: 104). Much more liberal reform has been introduced, with many socialist programs being undertaken.

According to Springer (1968: 166), military intervention in political life has become institutionalized in Argentina. Often, middle-class army officers desire some reform, but at the same time are apprehensive about the demands and power of the more leftist working class (Lieuwen, 1962: 138-139). For example, the army supported Peron's takeover in the 1940s because he promised both modernization of the military and societal reforms. However, in 1955, they were instrumental in his overthrow because of economic crises, corruption, and fear that Peron would form a working-class militia. It would be of more than passing interest to watch what type of new relationship will emerge between the military and Peron, who recently returned to Argentina after seventeen years in exile. Altogether, Argentina has had 31 military revolts from 1900-1966 (Canton, 1969: 256).

Although the aforementioned militaries play vital roles in their governments, the Indian Officer Corps still remains aloof from politics. The linkage between political orientations and social origins of the four officer corps is again not well defined. While each officer corps has experienced democratization of social recruitment, only three overtly participated in politics with the middle-class officers being more favorable to reform programs. An increasingly middle-class military in India has not been involved in politics.

CIVIL-MILITARY MODELS: AN OVERALL COMPARISON AND APPLICATION

In this section, the comparative data will be synthesized along the dimensions of civil-military relations, social recruitment, and political orientations of the fourteen selected officer corps. In line with the discussion in the earlier part of the paper, the democratic-competitive model is appropriate for five nations of the first world (United States, West Germany, England, France and Sweden) and one in the third world (India), while civil-military coalition is appropriate for one nation of the first world (Greece) and three in the third world (Pakistan, Argentina and Egypt). The civilian mass party model is applicable to all the nations of the second world (Russia, East Germany, Czechoslovakia, and Poland).

As in the case of any typology, these models represent approximations of reality, for, realistically, each model contains rather diverse elements within it. For instance, in the demo-cratic-competitive type, the military should have little involve-ment in politics. While this appears true for the British and Swedish Officer Corps, the U.S. and French militaries have been increasing their roles in politics since 1940. Also, the USSR, with its greater power and need for skilled technical expertise in its military, differs from the others in the civilian mass party group.

Concerning the applicability of the developmental models to the fourteen contemporary officer corps, the traditional/ divergent model applies to those countries in which the military is and more than likely will be differentiated from the civilian society in terms of social recruitment patterns and political orientations. Both West Germany and Great Britain fit this model. Countries from each world of development are repre-sented in the civilianized convergent model, where similarities between the military and civilian forms of social organization are evident. The social base of officer recruitment is broadening in Greece, Egypt, and Argentina and tends to be quite broad in the socialist countries of East Germany, Czechoslovakia, and Poland. It must be noted that the militaries in each of these countries participate in politics.

Pluralistic/segmented models are also represented in nations from each bloc. The United States, which seems to be moving toward a voluntary military, is the prototype of the pluralistic/ segmented model (Moskos, 1973). The social recruitment patterns in France's Officer Corps are also illustrative of trends toward both convergence and divergence (broadening in social class but high rate of self-recruitment). Regarding political orientation, she seems to diverge from society presently. With respect to social-class representation, the Swedish military of the 1960s appears to be less representative of the society than previously; yet, at the same time, self-recruitment has been declining, which indicates a convergent tendency. The Soviet technocrats are diverging from the political participation and indoctrination that are still the norms for other officers. The Indian Officer Corps has increasing middle-class recruitment patterns which indicate a greater similarity to the class origins of their country, but it remains separate from society by maintaining political aloofness. The Pakistani military (prior to separation of East Pakistan) was converging with society in class patterns, but was very divergent from the population in terms of its ethnic composition.

Overall, it might be noted that no one model corresponds completely to any particular world of development. Rather, each world of development and the individual officer corps within it can more genuinely be explained in terms of balanced or synthetic developmental models or civil-military typologies.

To further determine whether or not broadening of the bases of recruitment has led to a concomitant willingness on the part of the officer corps to be accountable to civilian governments and to refrain from involvement in the political decision-making processes, a 3 x 3 figure has been constructed to show various alternatives that exist in the relationship between social recruitment patterns and political activities. Looking at Figure 1, it is possible for a combination ± to exist in social recruitment patterns because social-class origins, ethnicity, self-recruitment, and the like all influence the pattern and may affect it in different ways. A ± occurs in terms of political activities if one segment of the officer corps refrains from active politics while another remains politically involved.

Further, one sees that six of the fourteen countries belong to Box A, which has both a broad or broadening base of social recruitment and an increase in political activities. Countries from each world of development are present though three of the six are socialist countries. The broadening of social recruitment accompanied by a low degree of political involvement is characteristic of India as shown in Box B.

The USSR, like other socialist countries, has a broad base of recruitment but is placed in Box C because the technocrat/ specialist is becoming less involved in national political affairs; the remainder of the corps, however, is still politically active. Box E shows both narrow or narrowing social recruitment patterns and a low level of political participation, which characterize Great Britain and West Germany.

A trend toward increasing political involvement is concomitant with some elements of social recruitment broadening and some parts narrowing in the United States, French and Pakistani

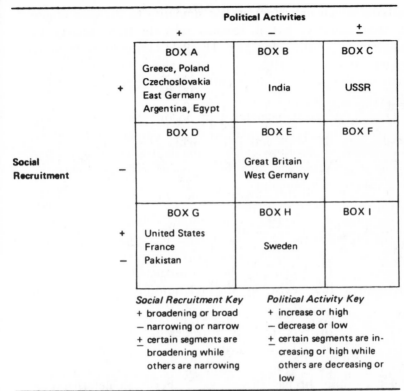

Figure 1: CONTEMPORARY RELATIONSHIP BETWEEN SOCIAL RECRUITMENT AND POLITICAL ACTIVITIES FOR THE FOURTEEN SELECTED NATIONS

militaries as represented by Box G. In Box H, the social recruitment patterns are similar to the ones in Box G, but there is low political participation. Sweden is the example of this trend. None of the fourteen countries presently belongs to Boxes D, F, or I.

Overall, the broadening of social recruitment patterns does not necessarily indicate an increased political democratization of the military. Indeed, the chart indicates that, more often, broadening of social base of recruitment is concomitant with increasing political activities by the officer corps. Yet this relationship certainly has not been constant or stable. The examples of present-day India, Sweden prior to the 1960s, Great Britain during and after World War II, and West Germany in the 1950s illustrate a lack of political involvement in spite of the broadening bases of recruitment in terms of social class.

SUMMARY AND CONCLUSION

This analysis, which focuses on the social recruitment and political orientations of 14 officer corps, indicates that, although the broadening of the social base in officer recruitment has taken place in the last 60 years, this trend began reversing itself for much of the first world of development in the decades of 1960s and 1970s. While this reversal is more evident in the U.S. Officer Corps, the information presented here indicates that it may be true in certain other officer corps (West German, British, Swedish, and French) as well. It is further noted that both the shift from a narrow base to a broader one in officer recruitment and the reversal of this trend have not been uniform in all 14 officer corps, nor have the officers' political orientations changed in any marked consistent pattern over the years. Putting it in a slightly different way, broadening the social base of recruitment has not been accompanied by a concomitant process of political democratization in the officers' political attitudes or political behavior. Indeed, this comparative analysis somewhat indicates the reverse to be the case. In some instances, broadening the base in officer recruitment has encouraged rather than deterred the propensity of the officer corps to actively participate or intervene in the processes of national and international socio-politics.

Thus, the social origins approach as a research strategy of political behavior does not provide a sufficient index for explaining the political perspectives of the officers. To understand fully the political orientations and activities of the officer corps, one has to analyze both the internal (military organization) and external (ecological) environment, including among others the national symbols, folk heroes, national ideologies, national history, the geostrategic position, and the economic resources of the country. Political orientations of the officer corps reflect not only the politics of the internal military subsociety but the broader national and international political environment. Often the officer corps serves as a barometer of national and international politics. Indeed, the military and political are intertwined, particularly in those issues affecting national security and international spheres of influence.

Though the scope and objectives of the present analysis are rather circumscribed, a more comprehensive future analysis of the sociopolitical dimensions of the military should also include an examination of the processes of political, military, and ideological recruitment, particularly the ways and conditions under which the professional soldier becomes politicized or ideologized. Also, such studies must consider not only what Janowitz (1970) refers to as stratification, institutional/organizational, and macro-sociological thrusts, but the psychological and social-psychological dimensions of the professional officers in politics as well.

REFERENCES

Abdel-Malek, Anouar
1968 Egypt: Military Society. New York: Random House.
Abrahamsson, Bengt
1968 "The ideology of an elite: conservatism and national insecurity." In J. Van Doorn (ed.) Armed Forces and Society: Sociological Essays. The Hague: Mouton.
Abrams, Philip
1965 "The late profession of arms: ambiguous goals and deteriorating means in Britain." European J. of Sociology 6: 238-261.
Ambler, John Steward
1966 Soldiers Against the State. Garden City, N.Y.: Doubleday.
Aron, Raymond
1966 "Social structure and the ruling class." In L. Coser (ed.) Political Sociology. New York: Harper.
Barnett, Correlli
1970 Britain and Her Army 1509-1970. New York: William Morrow.
Beeri, Eliezer
1966 "Social origins and family backgrounds of the Egyptian army officer class." Asian and African Studies 1: 1-40.
Brzezinski, Zbigniew
1952 "Party controls in the Soviet Army." J. of Politics 14: 565-591.
Canton, Dario
1969 "Military interventions in Argentina: 1900-1966." In J. Van Doorn (ed.) Military Profession and Military Regimes. The Hague: Mouton.
Chapman, Guy
1959 "The French army and politics." In M. Howard (ed.) Soldiers and Governments. Bloomington: Indiana Univ. Press.
Cohen, Stephen P.
1971 The Indian Army: its contribution to the development of a nation. Berkeley and Los Angeles: Univ. of California Press.
Cvrcek, Jaromir
1969 "Social changes in the officer corps of the Czechoslovak People's Army." In J. Van Doorn (ed.) Military Profession and Military Regimes. The Hague: Mouton.

Demeter, Karl
1965 The German Officer-Corps in Society and State 1650-1945. New York: Frederick A. Praeger.
Europa Publications
1964 The Europa Yearbook 1964. Volume I. London.
Forster, Thomas M.
1966 The East German Army. New York: A. S. Barnes.
Garthoff, Raymond L.
1968 "The military in Russia, 1861-1965." In J. Van Doorn (ed.) Armed Forces and Society: Sociological Essays. The Hague: Mouton.
Germani, Gino and Kalman Silvert
1967 "Politics, social structure and military intervention in Latin America." In W. C. McWilliams (ed.) Garrisons and Government: Politics and the Military in New States. San Francisco: Chandler.
Golenpaul, Dan (ed.)
1957 Information Please 1958 Almanac. New York: Macmillan.
Graczyk, Jozef
1969 "Social promotion in the Polish People's Army." In J. Van Doorn (ed.) Military Profession and Military Regimes. The Hague: Mouton.
Halpern, Manfred
1962 "Middle Eastern armies and the new middle class." In J. J. Johnson (ed.) The Role of the Military in Underdeveloped Countries. Princeton: Princeton Univ. Press.
Horowitz, Irving Louis
1966 Three Worlds of Development: The Theory and Practice of International Stratification. New York: Oxford Univ. Press.
1967 "Military elites." In S. M. Lipset and A. Solari (eds.) Elites in Latin America. New York: Oxford Univ. Press.
Hurewitz, J. C.
1969 Middle East Politics: The Military Dimension. New York: Frederick A. Praeger.
Jahan, Rounaq
1970 "Ten years of Ayub Khan and the problem of national integration." J. of Comparative Administration 2: 277-298.
Janowitz, Morris
1960 The Professional Soldier: A Social and Political Portrait. New York: Free Press.
1964 The Military in the Political Development of New Nations: A Comparative Approach. Chicago: Univ. of Chicago Press.
1969 "Military organization." In R. Little (ed.) A Survey of Military Institutions. Vol. 1. Chicago: Univ. of Chicago Press.
1970 Political Conflict. Chicago: Quadrangle.
1971 "The emergent military." In C. C. Moskos, Jr. (ed.) Public Opinion and the Military Establishment. Beverly Hills: Sage Pubns.
Kolkowicz, Roman
1967 The Soviet Military and the Communist Party. Princeton: Princeton Univ. Press.
Kourvetaris, George A.
1969 "The contemporary army officer corps in Greece: An inquiry into its professionalism and interventionism." Ph.D. dissertation. Northwestern University.
1971a "Professional self-images and political perspectives in the Greek military." Amer. Soc. Rev. 36 (December): 1043-1057.

1971b "The Greek army officer corps: its professionalism and political interventionism." In M. Janowitz and J. Van Doorn (eds.) On Military Intervention. Rotterdam: Rotterdam Univ. Press.

1971c "The role of the military in Greek politics." International Rev. of History and Pol. Sci. 8 (August): 91-114.

Lieuwen, Edwin
1962 "Militarism and politics in Latin America." In J. Johnson (ed.) The Role of the Military in Underdeveloped Countries. Princeton: Princeton Univ. Press.

Lipset, Seymour Martin and Aldo Solari (eds.)
1967 Elites in Latin America. New York: Oxford Univ. Press.

Mansfield, Peter
1965 Nasser's Egypt. Baltimore: Penguin.

McWilliams, Wilson C. (ed.)
1967 Garrisons and Government: Politics and the Military in New States. San Francisco: Chandler.

Menard, Orville D.
1967 The Army and the Fifth Republic. Lincoln: Univ. of Nebraska Press.

Mills, C. Wright
1956 The Power Elite. New York: Oxford Univ. Press.

Moskos, Charles C., Jr.
1970 The American Enlisted Man. New York: Russell Sage.
1971 Public Opinion and the Military Establishment. Beverly Hills: Sage Pubns.
1973 "The emergent military: civil, traditional, or plural." Pacific Soc. Rev. 16 (Spring).

Otley, C.C.
1968 "Militarism and the social affiliations of the British Army elite." In J. Van Doorn (ed.) Armed Forces and Society: Sociological Essays. The Hague: Mouton.

Pool, Ithiel de Sola
1955 Satellite Generals: A Study of Military Elites in the Soviet Sphere. Stanford: Stanford Univ. Press.

Razzell, P. E.
1963 "Social origins of officers in the Indian and British Home Army: 1758-1962." British J. of Sociology 14: 248-260.

Sayeed, Khalid B.
1968 "The role of the military in Pakistan." In J. Van Doorn (ed.) Armed Forces and Society: Sociological Essays. The Hague: Mouton.

Shils, Edward
1962 "The military in the political development of the new states." In J. J. Johnson (ed.) The Role of the Military in Underdeveloped Countries. Princeton: Princeton Univ. Press.

Springer, Philip B.
1968 "Disunity and disorder: factional politics in the Argentine military." In H. Bienen (ed.) The Military Intervenes. New York: Russell Sage.

Van Doorn, Jacques
1965 "The officer corps: a fusion of profession and organization." European J. of Sociology 6: 262-282.
1969 "Political change and the control of the military." In J. Van Doorn (ed.) Military Profession and Military Regimes. The Hague: Mouton.

Vatikiotis, P. J.
1961 The Egyptian Army in Politics. Bloomington: Indiana Univ. Press.

von der Mehden, Fred R.
1969 Politics of the Developing Nations. Englewood Cliffss, N.J.: Prentice-Hall.

Waldman, Eric
  1964 The Goose Step is Verboten: The German Army Today. New York: Free
         Press.
Wiatr, Jerzy J.
  1968 "Military professionalism and transformations of class structure in Po-
         land." In J. Van Doorn (ed.) Armed Forces and Society: Sociological
         Essays. The Hague: Mouton.

Socialization

6

MILITARY IMAGES IN THE ARMY ROTC*

WILLIAM A. LUCAS

Rand Corporation

This study seeks to determine the nature and content of the military images important in the professional socialization of Army ROTC cadets. The respondents are 458 cadets in their third and fourth years in the Army ROTC programs at UCLA and Ohio State. The research isolates combat (heroic), managerial, and technical images in terms of both the subjective identifications of the cadets and of their future expectations of their roles and assignments. The results suggest that there is a sharp dichotomy between the combat image, which is the clearest, and all others, which are vague and fundamentally civilian-oriented. Differences in cadet images are not associated with differences in the domestic political values or professional military opinions of the cadets. The clarity and the congruence of self-images and role expectations seem to be strongly related to increased cadet acceptance of professional military opinions and values. However, the overwhelming majority of ROTC cadets have vague and inconsistent images, and this absence of clear images is offered as an explanation for the minimal influence the ROTC experience has on the average cadet.

Just as war has overshadowed other events of history, the concept of the heroic leader in war has pervaded man's imagination. No one in modern society can escape some exposure to the image of the military hero. The stereotyped role is being played in games and fantasy by children before they enter school, and novels, television, movies, and history books elaborate on the image of the aggressive and successful leader in battle. This research is an effort to isolate what impact this social image has on those who intend to enter military service as officers through the Army ROTC.

The subjects of the research were 458 Army ROTC cadets in the Advanced Programs at the Ohio State University and at the University of California at Los Angeles. The data were collected in 1966, before the events in Vietnam and Kent State swept college campuses in this country with anti-ROTC sentiment. There was no indication that the respondents were either constrained or over-reacting in their answers. The methodology of the survey is discussed in an earlier report (Lucas, 1971).

---

* First presented to the November 1971 meeting of the Inter-University Seminar on Armed Forces and Society. The research is the responsibility of the author. It was not supported by and does not necessarily reflect the views of Rand Corporation.

MILITARY SELF-IMAGES AND ROLES

A key concept in any study of socialization or change in perception and attitude is the socializing agent or reference group of the individual, but the reference group for ROTC cadets is not at first evident. In all but a few military colleges, a cadet's formal contact with the military is at best limited. He is certainly not an active member of a military "group". Moreover, there are few identifiable groups within the military that the cadet might aspire to join. The variety of functional activities, the different military services, the transfer of officers across functional lines, and the fluctuating nature of military service in a period of rapid social and technological change suggest that internal groups would be too numerous, too ambiguous, and too unstable to serve as reference groups. Nor, when asked what they are joining, did cadets and midshipmen have distinct "groups" in mind. Thus, just as with any other broadly defined reference group which includes individuals and images (Merton, 1957:284;302-304), the army offers the cadet for identification the image of the officer he hopes he will encounter and whom he wants to emulate.

Given a lack of specific information about sub-groups within the military, society's perceptions of the military take on great importance. Except for that small proportion of ROTC cadets that has direct contact with military life as sons or close relatives of military men, the images of the military held by the cadets are determined by the prevailing view of the military held by society or some group within society.

For most individuals, the clearest military referent is the heroic, combat soldier. Every devotee of John Wayne as the U.S. cavalry officer and every American boy who has owned a BB-gun has some vision of what a combat officer does and what his style is like. This heroic type, as Janowitz suggests, may be associated with a personality factor, a "fighter spirit" (Janowitz, 1960:32), but regardless of the psychological forces that lead an individual to adopt this image, we feel that the image itself is at root the heroic figure that pervades the common view of the military in combat.

The salience of the combat image may be such that there is no other military style or image except its negation. That is, a cadet may recognize that he is either a combat "type" or he is not. In case of the latter, there are no other strong images to be sought as substitutes. However, other military types have been suggested in the literature and should be explored for their relevance to socialization during the ROTC experience.

Janowitz has suggested that there is a second, more pragmatic orientation within the military which he calls the "managerial" type. He contends that these pragmatists are associated with an operational military code that varies from that of the heroic. Writing in the late 1950's,

Janowitz argued that the pragmatist tends to believe in graduated deterrence, active alliance systems, and holds a more moderate view of the military goals of the Soviet Union. On the other hand, he identified the heroic type, as exemplified by General Douglas MacArthur, as being absolutist and associated with massive deterrence and a desire for total supremacy of American military power (Janowitz, 1960:273).

There is, however, an ambiguity in the concept of the military manager. The manager deals with budgets, bureaucracy and logistics. He could see himself as either simply an executive in a green flannel suit or he could be highly conscious of the military and unique qualities of his job. While responsibility falls on the commanding officer, a staff officer gives advice that could lead to death and destruction. Is the military manager aware of the special and lethal consequences of his function as military strategist and planner, or does he feel no different from an executive in a large organization?

Maury Feld advances a third type of possible military self-image for the ROTC cadet. He points to the increasing importance of military technology in three spheres—the military arsenal, industry, and the laboratory. Feld believes that the arsenal concept is compatible with a commitment to the military profession where work in industry and the laboratory may lead to commitments to values external to the military. Under the arsenal concept, Feld feels that an armed force can "allow some of its members to be *innovators* without running the risk that they may become *deviants*" (1964:162). Here again the question arises whether the image, if it does exist, is essentially non-military in content, or whether the technical image—like Feld's arsenal concept—includes commitment both to technical skills and to the military profession.

While this research was under way, John Lovell used a similar approach to study the professional socialization of West Point cadets. Following Janowitz's formulation of the heroic and managerial types, Lovell asked the cadets a question about what he believed to be the characteristics of different orientations to the military profession: "The most important aspects of a career, in terms of satisfaction, are that it is ——?" Answers such as "demands spiritual strength" and "demands a colorful, aggressive personality" were classified by Lovell (1964:151) as heroic type answers. Responses considered characteristics of a managerial orientation were "demands broad cultural interests" and "provides a full family life".

Lovell, thus, drew a distinction between those cadets who emphasized qualities central to the charismatic-combatant side of military life as opposed to those that were managerial and highly civilianized. He found that freshmen from civilian families were more likely to have "heroic" orientations, but that the difference between cadets from military and civilian backgrounds tended to decrease over time (1964:145). But professional orientation measured in this way was not an important explanatory variable, and did not seem related to the strategic military perspectives of the West Point cadets.

Rather than emphasizing the qualities the observer would consider appropriate to each type, this study relied upon the subjective identifications and role expectations of the Army ROTC cadets. ROTC socialization is thus defined as the learning of the attitudes and behavior associated with officer roles and self-images. Note that we distinguish between role and self-image. In this research the two concepts are separated analytically to avoid a conceptual confusion not uncommon in the literature. The role concept is generally associated with behavior, while self-image is linked to perceptual screens and attitudes. They do not necessarily coincide, as the data will show, although they may well have interacting influences on the beliefs, opinions, and behavior of future officers. Only by attempting independent measurement of both concepts can one begin to look for the effects of their interaction. But first one needs to isolate heroic, managerial, and technical Army self-images and roles, and to assess their independent impact.

The influence that self-image can have on political opinions is well documented. The literature on political party identification is particularly rich, showing that it shapes the individual's perceptions, his opinions, and his political behavior. It has been shown that a voter with opinions similar to the positions of the Republican candidate in his district does not necessarily vote Republican, nor does a voter with contrasting views necessarily support the Democrat. To explain the seeming inconsistency, one must understand the intervening effects of party identification. In their study of voters in Elmira, New York, Bernard Berelson and his associates found that voters would sometimes misperceive the political platforms of the candidates so as to vote in accord with their partisan self-images. Democrats and Republicans saw the positions of the candidates differently, with partisans of both parties skewing the issue positions of their own candidates so as to create greater perceived agreement with their own views. Particularly for those not exposed to much information about the campaign, the partisan was likely to support the candidate of his party despite objective differences between his views and those of his candidate on the issues (Berelson, *et al.*, 1954:213-233). These results have been supported by other literature that, while not focusing on the issue of correct perceptions specifically, has documented the pervasive influence of party identification in serving as a perceptual screen, influencing attitudes and behavior. If ROTC cadets and midshipmen have military self-images, it seems reasonable to presume that they could be analogous to party identification.

To operationalize this subjective identification, we used a self-administered questionnaire to ask the advanced Army ROTC cadets at the University of California at Los Angeles and the Ohio State University which of the three military types best fit them. The question focused on the respondent's future expectations. "On the basis of your expectations of your future military service which of the following tends to identify you best?" Because we felt that most individuals would pale at the prospect of calling themselves heroic, we gave the respondents the choice of picking "a combat officer," "a staff or managerial officer," "a scientific or technical officer," or "don't know." At Ohio State, 15.5% of the respondents identified themselves as combat officers; 43.2% gave staff officer as a response; 25.5% chose technical officer; and 15.8% didn't know. In the smaller program on the UCLA campus, 25.4% picked the combat image; 31.0% chose managerial or staff; 21.1% selected the technical image; and 22.5% said they didn't know. It remained to be seen if different responses were related to meaningful variation in values and opinions.

Subjective identification is not the only approach to the study of military images, however. Corresponding roles must also be identified. To do this, we put heroic, managerial, and technical factors in a form involving behavior expectations. We did not expect the cadet to be familiar with the behavior of a particular type of officer because he has not experienced the role position to which he aspires. In absence of face-to-face interaction, the detailed content of roles seemed too remote for the cadet to learn. It therefore seemed inappropriate to ask a cadet how he would behave in particular situations analogous to those facing different types of military officers or to ask how he would expect to behave in the future as an officer. Instead, we requested each cadet to identify career assignments that he would expect to perform, giving him a choice between combat, managerial, technical and other duties. A cadet's role expectations were thus approached through the jobs and functional position he expected to occupy. In the questionnaire, the Army ROTC cadets were asked: "Now suppose you decide to make a career in the Army. Reflect for a moment and try to visualize yourself some 10 or 15 years in the future. Which of the following best describe the Army career you see for yourself?" The cadets were then asked to pick not less than two nor more than five of the twenty roles that followed.

For the Army questionnaire, appropriate roles for each type of referent were developed. The combat or heroic cadet could choose to see himself as commander of an airborne unit, and the technical type could see himself as a technical advisor. To measure the degree to which the individual chose to apply non-military criteria, three civilianized roles were listed. The non-military content of the managerial image could thus be separated from the military staff choices, such as director of a budget team or member of a strategic planning board. A combat-staff role (at the command center of Strike Command) and a combat-technical role (commander of Nike unit) were added to test for specifically military content in the staff and technical self-images. Two non-traditional combat roles were included to see whether the combat identifier was a personality type picking dangerous jobs or someone with a realistic view of the combat role (officers with ten years of service are not customarily assigned to pilot armed helicopters). Finally, to absorb choices that might be forced by the format, three romantic items involving duty abroad were added that could be both attractive and compatible with the other roles.

The responses to this question allow us to ascertain whether there are consistent, generalized expectations to support the view that combat, managerial, technical or other career expectations have a part in Army socialization. If there is a distinct managerial role, for example, we would expect the individuals who chose being on a strategic planning board to select heading a team working on a fiscal budget for operations. Instead, we find that of the 95 cadets at Ohio State who picked one of these categories, only twelve (12.6%) picked both. Of a total of 458 advanced Army ROTC cadets at both universities, 113 cadets chose one or the other indicator of managerial behavior, and a mere 14 selected both.

Similarly, we provided two technical options on the questionnaire—being administrative director for an R & D team, and being a technical advisor to an evaluations group. At Ohio State, of those picking either of these two technical choices, 18.9% picked the two together. At UCLA, the percentage was 9.5%. Again, there was at best a weak demonstration of consistency. Only 25 cadets out of a total of 458 at both universities focused on both roles with technical content.

Different results were derived from the responses to the combat or heroic role expectations. While fewer cadets (77 of 458) chose the central career assignments of commander of an infantry battalion or of an airborne unit, those that did showed considerably more consistency than did those anticipating managerial and technical assignments. Of those who saw themselves as serving as at least one of these central combat types, 41.9% at Ohio State and 53.3% (of 15) at UCLA, envisaged themselves serving as both.

In the combat category, more than two tasks were provided as possible choices, allowing further study of the consistency of combat related task expectations. At Ohio State, selection of executive officer of a Special Forces group was not chosen consistently with the combat tasks above. The results at UCLA are inconclusive because of the small number of cadets there who had combat role expectations, but it is suggestive that five of the seven expecting to see themselves in the Special Forces also chose the airborne option. Very few of those choosing these three combat-oriented career tasks also saw themselves becoming an armor or artillery group commander. There is little evidence to suggest that this particular career assignment was perceived as part of the combat role, which indicates the prevalence of a "foot soldier's" view of the combat function.

A further test of military referents emerges, however, when we check our data on expectations of role occupancy against the self-images of the Army cadets. Role "does not stand alone but must be regarded as one of a set of conceptions—this set describable on a dimension of congruence of compatibility" (Sarbin, 1968:550). Just as the accuracy of an individual's role performance is thought to be affected by the congruence of his role and his self-image, we expected the degree of a cadet's professional socialization to be a function of, among other variables, the congruence of his self-image and career role expectations. Cross-tabulating these variables provided both a check on the meaningfulness of the cadet responses and, more importantly, a test of their congruence.

The results suggest that there is a dichotomy between those cadets with a combat officer self-image and all others. As shown in Table 1, the combat identifier was likely to choose the orthodox roles of commander of an infantry battalion and armor or artillery group commander. He was much more prone to select the charismatic and dangerous roles in airborne and Special Forces units. While he was no different in his tendency to fill out his choices with romantic assignments, he was inclined to avoid those selections that had a non-military orientation. He did not think of himself in a managerial job, such as working on a planning board or with a budget, and generally did not choose any of the technical roles.

Variation between Ohio State and UCLA suggests that the UCLA cadet had a clearer conception of career patterns and role sets. Assignment to Strike Command at Fort Bragg, N.C., with its quick troop deployment capability, was seen as consistent with other combat roles. Also, a realistic differentiation was made between flying and more likely career patterns for Army officers, for very few UCLA cadets picked the jobs associated with observation aircraft or helicopters. The Ohio State cadets did not choose Strike Command, in part because they were not sure what such an assignment would entail, and a fifth of those with a combat self-image chose the pilot role in an armed helicopter.

The non-combat self-images appear to fall into a broad civilian-equivalent category; cadets with these identifications were not very different from those without any self-image at all. Conspicuously, over 40% of all three of the non-combat groups selected a role that would be good preparation for a valuable job in civilian life. Being near home had little attraction for anyone, but the non-combat types were more likely to accept an office job with time for their families. In fact, an office assignment was remarkably attractive to those at both UCLA and Ohio State calling themselves managerial or staff officers. All non-combat type identifiers tended to avoid the combat roles.

Except for the combat/non-combat division, there was extremely weak differentiation. Evidence suggests a vague technical self-image. At

TABLE 1. CONGRUENCE BETWEEN SELECTED EXPECTATIONS OF ROLE OCCUPANCY AND SELF-IMAGE BY UNIVERSITY

Role Expectations	University	Percent of Identifiers				Sig. Level
		Combat	Managerial	Technical	Don't Know	
Commander of an Infantry Battalion	Ohio State	58.6	3.1	4.2	8.2	.001
	UCLA	50.0	0	6.7	12.5	.001
Armor or Artillery Group Commander	Ohio State	32.8	4.3	5.2	11.5	.001
	UCLA	44.4	9.1	20.0	12.5	.05
Commanding Officer of an Airborne Unit	Ohio State	41.4	2.5	7.3	4.9	.001
	UCLA	50.0	0	0	0	.001
Director of a Team Preparing a Fiscal Year Budget for Strategic Operations	Ohio State	0	26.5	3.1	11.5	.001
	UCLA		27.3	13.3	0.	.05
Assigned to a Position that Gives Good Preparation for a Valuable Job in a Civilian Life	Ohio State	12.1	59.3	42.7	41.0	.001
	UCLA	11.1	40.9	46.7	43.8	—
In an Office Job with Considerable Time for Your Family	Ohio State	5.6	57.6	25.0	11.8	.001
	UCLA	0	57.1	14.3	28.6	—
Administrative Director for a Research and Development Team	Ohio State	5.2	18.5	60.4	13.1	.001
	UCLA	0	22.7	53.3	25.0	.01
Total Number of Advanced Army ROTC Cadets	Ohio State	38	162	96	61	
	UCLA	18	22	15	16	

both universities over half of the technical type identifiers envisioned themselves as an administrative director of a research and development team. At Ohio State, these cadets were more likely to choose a role as a technical advisor. At both schools, they were the only cadets significantly attracted to the technical, but non-military, role of assistant director of a Corps of Engineers waterways project. This highly civilianized perspective needs to be qualified, however, by the responses of the UCLA cadets, who again seemed to have a more realistic conception of role sets. A larger percentage of technical identifiers in the small ROTC program at UCLA picked the tasks of the armor or artillery group commander and of a commander of a Nike-Hercules anti-aircraft missile battalion. While the technical self-image of ROTC cadets was basically non-combat, there did appear to be a possibility that the technical image could be strengthened and given military connotation by the technical tradition of the field artillery and the growing importance of missiles. After all, West Point has long produced engineers who could lay a transit as well as they could range in a howitzer. While the data suggest that the nascent ROTC technical image is basically civilianized, the artillery man and combat engineer may provide traditional military content of the technical self-image.

There may also be a budding managerial concept. A fourth of the staff type identifiers at both universities saw themselves as directors of a budget team, an almost classic conception of the military manager. Membership on a strategic planning board was chosen somewhat more by managerial types at Ohio State than by other groups. The UCLA cadets showed some awareness of the command and control implications of the staff concept. Of those choosing the managerial self-image on that campus, a fifth expected to see themselves attached to the command center of Strike Command and 45% were interested in the combined travel and staff aspects of a NATO staff officer. In general, particularly when we remember that half of the managerial type identifiers picked the office job with time for their families, the image seems to imply a civilian orientation. The managerial type identifiers in the ROTC saw the military as just another job.

Thus, while there is a suggestion of military roles involving the traditional and unique qualities of a military career, cadets with technical and managerial self-images were, like those not selecting a self-image, generally civilian-oriented. Of the non-combat types, the technical type identifiers with their link to the R & D role have a clearer conception of their probable career pattern. There are no differences between those with a managerial self-image and those with no military self-image that would suggest that the managerial image has any uniquely military content. In sum, we find a basic combat/civilian dichotomy in the military images held by the ROTC cadets. The combat image is not particularly strong, and the technical and managerial images are quite vague and without much professional military content.

ROTC PROFESSIONALISM, CONSERVATISM AND THE MILITARY REFERENTS

Having identified these weak military referents, it remained to ascertain whether they are related to differences in the opinions and values of the ROTC cadets. Two areas were of particular concern: the cadets' professionalism, and their conservatism. Members of most professions are more positive than outsiders about the value of their professional expertise and the social utility of increased influence for their profession. Military professionals are no different. In our survey, variation in the degree of acceptance of professional values and opinions was therefore used to reveal whether there were differences in the content and process of the professional socialization of ROTC cadets that could be linked to the influence of differences in their self-images.

The professional outlook of the ROTC cadets in this study was tapped by two questions regarding the place of the military in the United States. The first probed the cadets' views on the status of the military in terms of the respect "that the people of the United States generally give the armed forces." The second inquired about the attention given the "military point of view" by the national government on questions of national defense. At UCLA, the responses of the cadets did not vary with self-image. Just over half the UCLA cadets were satisfied both with the respect paid to the armed forces and with the attention given to the military point of view, regardless of which self-image they held.

At Ohio State, there was some variation in the attitudes of the cadets with different self-images. Of the cadets with combat self-images, 47.4% were more likely to feel the military point of view was occasionally, or even dangerously, neglected. The managerial and technical types at Ohio State were less likely (36.4% and 35.8% respectively) to feel the military did not receive adequate attention. Greater concern for the military cannot simply be associated with the combat image, however, because 44.8% of those with no self-image also wanted more attention for the military point of view. Three fourths of the combat identifiers felt the armed forces received less respect than deserved; 53.1% of the managerial group were similarly dissatisfied; and the technical and no self-image groups fell in between.

As a group, the Ohio State ROTC was more positive towards the military profession than was a random sample of non-ROTC juniors and seniors. Half the non-ROTC sample was dissatisfied with the respect being given, and only a fifth felt the military point of view was occasionally or dangerously neglected. The earlier emphasis on the civilian orien-

TABLE 2. AFFECT FOR MILITARY AND POLITICAL CONCEPTS* (MEAN SCORES)

Ohio State

ROTC by Military Self-Image

Concept	Combat	Managerial	Technical	Don't Know	Non-ROTC Sample
Military	+3.58	+3.09	+3.13	+3.05	+1.37
Professional Soldier	+3.58	+2.39	+2.85	+2.18	+0.47
Officer	+4.39	+3.72	+3.93	+3.53	+1.31
Supreme Court	+2.96	+3.73	+3.62	+3.72	+3.72
Segregation	−1.63	−2.65	−2.51	−2.05	−2.27
Socialism	−1.39	−1.10	−1.71	−2.03	−0.83
Medicare	+0.26	+0.82	−0.16	+0.22	+0.89
	N=57	N=159	N=96	N=60	N=49

UCLA

ROTC by Military Self-Image

Concept	Combat	Managerial	Technical	Don't Know
Military	+3.72	+3.57	+2.53	+4.00
Professional Soldier	+3.72	+3.33	+2.60	+3.67
Officer	+4.28	+4.81	+3.67	+4.60
Supreme Court	+3.16	+2.90	+2.80	+2.73
Segregation	−4.11	−3.62	−4.13	−4.67
Socialism	−0.78	−2.52	−1.73	−1.53
Medicare	+0.44	−0.24	+1.20	+1.13
	N=18	N=21	N=15	N=15

*The maximum possible range is from +6.0 to −6.0. A score of +4.0 is "moderately" positive, +2.0 is "slightly positive," and zero is neutral.

tation of the managerial type is thus further supported in that the views of the Ohio State cadets with managerial self-images were the closest to the views of the non-ROTC students.

Moving from opinions to values as measured by the semantic differential, we compared the attachment of the cadets to concepts central to military professionalism: the professional soldier, the military, and the officer. Because of the small number of UCLA cadets and the resulting unstable means, interpretation is difficult. The results support the opinion data, however, and suggest that there are no great differences among the categories of identifiers. As Table 2 shows, at Ohio State the cadets all differ from the non-ROTC group, the combat identifiers somewhat more so. On the key symbol of the "professional soldier," the combat type identifiers are distinctly the more positive, while the managerial group and those not picking a self-image were more like the non-ROTC sample.

Thus, while there is some variation, the professional opinions and the values of cadets with different self-images appear fairly similar. At Ohio State, the combat types are somewhat more enthusiastic about the profession, and the managerial types somewhat less so, but the differences are small and there is no such pattern in the UCLA data. We conclude then that differences in self-image alone are not important in the professionalism of these Army ROTC cadets.

On the other hand, variants of political conservatism, rather than degrees of professional loyalty, have been held traditionally important in distinguishing military styles. Janowitz and Lovell are concerned with how heroic versus managerial orientations are linked to military strategy. Huntington (1957:93, 94) sees conservatism as a key element in the "military mind," and he bases his recommendation for civil-military relations on what he judges to be the incompatibility between that conservatism and society's present liberal ideology. If the combat or heroic image is related to political conservatism, then it might well be an influence on the political ideology of ROTC cadets. In order to test this supposition, we chose to focus upon selected domestic political differences that might be related to military self-images. For that reason, the affective attachment the cadets have for the concepts "Supreme Court," "Medicare" (before its passage by Congress), "segregation," and "socialism" was measured. At Ohio State, the combat type identifiers were the only group not reflecting the same sentiment as that held by the non-ROTC sample for the Supreme Court, and they were more negative. At UCLA the combat types were more positive than the others. The least negative towards segregation at UCLA was the managerial group; at Ohio State it was the combat types. All the ROTC groups were less positive toward socialism and Medicare than the non-ROTC at Ohio State, suggesting a possible tendency among potential officers to be conservative on politico-economic issues. There were no

TABLE 3. CONSERVATIVE AND LIBERAL IDENTIFICATION BY MILITARY SELF-IMAGE (IN PERCENTAGES)

| | Ohio State | | | | |
	Combat	Managerial	Technical	Don't Know	Non-ROTC Sample
Conservative or Somewhat Conservative	58.6	46.9	53.7	55.0	44.0
Liberal or Somewhat Liberal	41.4	53.1	46.3	45.0	56.0
Total	100.0	100.0	100.0	100.0	100.0
	N=58	N=162	N=95	N=60	N=50

| | UCLA | | | |
	Combat	Managerial	Technical	Don't Know	
Conservative or Somewhat Conservative	70.6	57.1	40.0	40.0	
Liberal or Somewhat Liberal	29.4	42.9	60.0	60.0	
Total	100.0	100.0	100.0	100.0	
	N=17	N=21	N=15	N=15	

differences in the area of race relations. Within the ROTC groups, the military referents were unrelated to consistent differences in the cadet attachments to these political symbols.

As another test to determine whether or not there is a relationship between political conservatism and military self-image, we expressed the distinction between liberalism and conservatism in terms of self-identification. Following Janowitz (1960:237), we asked the cadets, "In domestic politics, do you regard yourself as: conservative, a little on the conservative side, a little on the liberal side, liberal." According to Table 3, the results at UCLA indicate that the combat type identifiers thought of themselves as more conservative. The comparable group at Ohio State was also more conservative vis-a-vis the other groups there, but did not really seem different from those not choosing a self-image. Again the Ohio State cadets with managerial images are most similar to the non-ROTC sample on that campus. In conclusion, the political self-images of potential officers appear to be more conservative than those of other students, and combat type identifiers have a stronger tendency toward conservative self-identification only at UCLA.

Summarizing the findings of the ROTC study, it seems fair to say that military self-identifications are not related in a systematic way to differences in professional or political values. The cadets with a managerial self-image were less conservative, less professional, and more like the non-ROTC at Ohio State, but that pattern is not found at UCLA. There are suggestions that combat type identifiers at Ohio State were more professionalized, and those at UCLA more conservative, but there is no strong consistent difference that can be attributed to a societal image serving as a socializing influence at both schools. Potential officers differ from other students, but the differences do not seem to be associated with variation in the military images. Attachment to one military referent rather than another is not related, in the aggregate, to differences in loyalty to the profession, or to political conservatism.

CLARITY, CONSISTENCY AND THE IMPACT OF THE COMBAT REFERENT

Several conclusions could be drawn. First, the different referents could have no impact upon opinions because they were not related in fact to functional and attitudinal divisions within the military, or because the self-concepts and role expectations considered in this study were inadequately operationalized. Second, the varying identifications within the military could have roughly the same professional and attitudinal content, and thus would have the same influence on cadet beliefs. Third, the position explored here, is that the combat type and perhaps the other referents may reflect differences in professional orientations within the Army that are potentially important in socialization. We believe that one cannot assess the impact of any functional division within a profession without taking into account the intervening or mediating effect of the clarity and consistency of the group's image as a referent for professionals in training.

With ROTC cadets, the military referent must be clearly perceived to have influence. An individual does not change his views lightly or easily, and the average ROTC cadet has little incentive to do so. He faces no direct sanctions or rewards for having inappropriate or appropriate beliefs, and only his desire to fit into a role sometime in the future motivates him to change. In this context, vague cues about professional opinions are likely to go unnoticed, and even if noticed, may be disregarded. In order to influence individuals with minimal incentive to conform it is necessary for the military referent to be clearly distinguishable, if change is to occur. Yet, the only impression that most Americans, including apparently these cadets, seem to have about the military is that, unlike other careers, it can involve direct participation in combat.

It is, therefore, not surprising that the only referent that yielded sufficient data to assess the effect of increasing clarity of role on the attitudes of Army ROTC cadets was the combat type. The role expectations of the technical and managerial career types were not consistent with each other nor were they particularly well related to the corresponding subjective self-images. For the combat type referent however, we have evidence that there were some cadets who indeed had a coherent referent.

At Ohio State, there were both a sufficient number of respondents for detailed analysis and the suggestion of a relationship between the combat referent and military professionalism. The responses of the cadets at that university were therefore used to explore the impact of role and self-image congruency and clarity on professional attitudes. To measure consistency of role expectations, the Ohio State cadets were arranged according to the number of combat roles they expected to occupy. We assumed that the choice of an increasing number of consistent function-related roles is an index both of commitment to that type and of the clarity of the type. In order to show attachment to a combat career pattern by choosing the "correct" assignments, the cadet had to have a minimal knowledge of what kinds of jobs go with a combat orientation. The cadets were grouped according to whether they had chosen none, one, two, three, or four of the heroic roles (airborne unit commander, armor or artillery group commander, Special Forces executive officer, commander of an infantry battalion).

As Table 4 demonstrates, when the cadets at Ohio State were separated in this fashion and their self-images examined, their perceived role was strongly related to the congruency of role and self-image. The separation between the combat type and all others became even more salient. Only 2.1% of those not picking a combat role thought of themselves as assuming a combat self-image. Of those picking one, 41.0% identified themselves as combat types. There were 72.0% of those picking two and 75.0% of those picking three or four roles who had combat self-images. As consistency of combat role expectations increased, a marked rise in the choice of combat self-image and an equally clear tendency not to pick the managerial or staff self-image emerged. Consistency of role choice and congruence of role and self-image in this instance were strongly associated.

TABLE 4. CONGRUENCE OF COMBAT SELF-IMAGE AND EXPECTATIONS OF COMBAT ROLE OCCUPANCY

	Ohio State ROTC			
	Number of Combat Roles Picked			
Military Self-Image	None	One	Two	Three or Four
Combat	2.1 (6)	40.9 (25)	72.0 (18)	75.0 (9)
Managerial	52.7 (147)	19.7 (12)	12.0 (3)	0 (0)
Technical	28.7 (80)	19.7 (12)	8.0 (2)	16.7 (2)
Don't Know	16.5 (46)	19.7 (12)	8.0 (2)	8.3 (1)
Total	100.0 (279)	100.0 (61)	100.0 (25)	100.0 (12)

The test of the importance of consistency and congruence, then, comes by determining whether they are related to attitudinal differences. Furthermore, the issue at stake is whether or not the combat image plays a part in the socialization of the ROTC cadet into the military profession. With increased consistency and congruency together at work, we find in Table 5 that professional socialization of those with clear combat identification is greater than those without such a referent. On the questions about the attention given the military point of view and the respect shown the armed forces, the greatest loyalty to the profession came from those with the clearest and most consistent attachments to the combat referent. Over half of those with two or more combat role expectations felt that the military point of view was occasionally or dangerously neglected, and three-fourths thought the United States armed forces received less, or much less, respect than they deserved. This concern both for the corporate military point of view and for the respect due to the military declined steadily with those choosing only one combat role and then those with no expectations at all of filling a standard combat role. Of the last group, 37.1% thought attention to the military point of view was less than adequate and 43.2% felt there was at least adequate respect for the military. This group does not conform totally to the views of juniors and seniors in the random sample of non-ROTC students at Ohio State, but considering the non-ROTC

TABLE 5. ATTENTION GIVEN THE MILITARY POINT OF VIEW AND RESPECT
PAID THE ARMED FORCES AS A FUNCTION OF CONSISTENCY OF
COMBAT ROLE EXPECTATIONS (IN PERCENTAGES)

| | Ohio State ROTC | | | |
| | Number of Combat Roles Picked | | | |
Attention Given the Military Viewpoint	None	One	Two, Three or Four	Non-ROTC Sample
Too Much or Adequate	62.9	59.4	45.9	80.0
Occasionally or Dangerously Neglected	37.1	40.6	54.1	20.0
	100.0	100.0	100.0	100.0
	N=278	N=64	N=37	N=49
Respect Paid the Armed Forces				
More or About That Deserved	43.2	36.5	24.3	50.0
Less or Much Less than Deserved	56.8	63.5	75.7	50.0
	100.0	100.0	100.0	100.0
	N=280	N=63	N=37	N=50

group as a base level suggests that a great deal of the variation in
concern over the status of the military is related to the consistency and
congruence of a cadet's attachment to his combat referent.

CONCLUSION

There appears to be only one clear military referent for Army ROTC
cadets. The respondents knew whether they were either combat types
or not. The managerial or staff image is largely the negation of the
combat image, and it, like the technical image, is civilian-oriented and
not associated with clear expectations for role occupancy. The data
suggest that professional military socialization is a process that involves
a cadet identifying with a military image. When that image is clearly
perceived and supported by congruent expectations of role occupancy
and self-image, it serves as the source of values.

In the Army ROTC units studied, however, very few cadets perceived the combat, or any other, referent very clearly. There were 386
advanced cadets at Ohio State. The seniors were on the brink of active
duty, and the juniors would soon be in ROTC summer camps. All had
had three and four years of exposure to the ROTC cadre and curriculum.
Yet only 98 picked *one* of the combat roles so central to the Army
profession, and a paltry 37 picked more than one. Very few cadets had
a congruent referent that was clearly and consistently held. This absence of effective referents must be an important factor in the general

absence of professional military socialization in officer education (Lovell, 1964, and Lucas, 1971).

Whatever impact the heroic and managerial types may have had in the 1950's we find no reflection of it in two ROTC programs in the 1960's. The managerial role as a military orientation does not exist in the ROTC, and there is no strong conservative content to a combat type identification. Whether the distinction would have appeared as a result of the experiences of active duty, or if they had been transferred to the Air Force, as Janowitz suggests (1960:296), or whether finally the distinction has simply become irrelevant (Huntington, 1963:802) cannot be ascertained. It remains for us to conclude that the choice of images and roles that will shape the military officers of the future was left open in the years 1965-1966.

Army images without military content do not seem likely to aid the cadet officer in preparing for the realities of military service. An emphasis on the heroic role in combat holds less than great appeal on college campuses in the aftermath of the Vietnam conflict. Yet these were the two styles that were weakly perceived by the cadets in this study, and there is evidence that the ambiguity of the referents for cadets in the ROTC, the academies, and elsewhere has continued to increase. To meet the corresponding growth in problems of officer recruitment, education, and retention, new and positive military referents appropriate to the 1970's must be found. The choice of images to guide the future military officer is too important to be left up to chance.

REFERENCES

Berelson, Bernard R.; Lazarfeld, Paul F.; and McPhee, William N.
    1954   Voting: A Study of Opinion Formation in a Presidential Campaign. Chicago: The University of Chicago Press.
Feld, Maury D.
    1964   "Military Self-Image in a Technological Environment." In Morris Janowitz (ed.), The New Military. New York: Russell Sage Foundation.
Huntington, Samuel P.
    1957   The Soldier and the State. Cambridge: Harvard University Press.
    1963   "Power Expertise and the Military Profession." Daedalus 92 (Fall):785-807.
Janowitz, Morris
    1960   The Professional Soldier. New York: the Free Press of Glencoe.
Lovell, John P.
    1964   "The Professional Socialization of the West Point Cadet." In Morris Janowitz (ed.), The New Military. New York: Russell Sage Foundation.
Lucas, William A.
    1971   "Anticipatory Professional Socialization and the ROTC." In Charles Moskos (ed.), Public Opinion and the Military Establishment. New York: Russell Sage Foundation.
Merton, Robert K.
    1957   Social Theory and Social Structure. New York: The Free Press of Glencoe.
Sarbin, Theodore
    1968   "Role: Sociological Aspects." In David Sills (ed.), International Encyclopedia of the Social Sciences. New York: Macmillan Company and Free Press.

7

SELECTIVE SOCIALIZATION:
AIRBORNE TRAINING AS STATUS PASSAGE*

WILLIAM COCKERHAM

University of Illinois

This article describes the social context of airborne socialization in the U.S.. Army as status passage, including the value system inculcated by that process. In accordance with the Davis and Moore (1945) theory of stratification, this study found that action–oriented individuals self–select into the airborne in response to such inducements as self–identification with an elite unit, the reward of higher status within the military and higher pay, and for the availability of action and challenge. Because of the self–selection of the individuals being socialized, there were no significant or dramatic changes of attitudes and values.

Among the socialization experiences associated with institutionalized education and training, there is in the United States Army a particular event of status passage which allows those individuals completing the passage to gain acceptance as members of an elite subgroup and to acquire role specific knowledge as a basis for organizing behavior. This elite subgroup is the airborne which exists not only as a formal organization but also as a social perspective based upon an elaborate construction of symbolic meanings representing a social experience unique to those involved.

The primary socializing experience inculcating the social perspective of the airborne is airborne training which is conducted at the U.S.. Army Airborne School at Fort Benning, Georgia. In airborne training the trainees acquire not only knowledge about military parachuting, but also those shared norms, values, sentiments, attitudes, and social traditions of the airborne soldier which are intended to develop a compatible community of like–mindedness and purpose. Airborne training thus serves as a rite of passage in that the airborne trainee is inducted into an area of specific social knowledge and into the particular human collectivity which ongoingly produces this knowledge as social reality. The successful trainee is able to assume the role and self–concept of the paratrooper upon the completion of his passage, a role which is enhanced by the fact that, as Just (1970:95) points out, the

---

*The author gratefully acknowledges the comments of Audie Blevins Jr., William Catton Jr., Norman Denzin, and Anselm Strauss on an earlier version of this paper. The author also wishes to thank Morris Janowitz for providing relevant material. In addition, JPMS referees Robert Krone and John Lovell, who were identified through their suggestions for revision, provided extremely helpful guidance.

paratrooper, a soldier trained to jump out of airplanes, is surrounded by "a very considerable mystique."

It is the intent of this article to examine the structure of airborne socialization as status passage, including the value system which accompanies that passage.

THEORETICAL PERSPECTIVE

With the exception of an anthropological description of the ritualistic aspects of airborne training (Weiss, 1967), the only published sources available on airborne socialization have been written by psychologists. These studies (Kepecs, 1944; Basowitz, et al, 1955; Farrell, 1967; Lopez–Reyes, 1971) have been essentially Freudian in theoretical orientation and concern themselves primarily with the effects of anxiety and stress in relation to group solidarity. Regression of the ego in favor of the group has been seen to decrease individual anxiety and increase group bonds. This focus, however, upon individual experience and the anxiety – group solidarity factor, while important, does not fully account for the social context within which airborne socialization occurs. It explains very little from a macro–sociological perspective. Since military subsocieties are complex organizations made up of a great variety of roles and positions that must be filled if the organization is to function effectively, the influential Davis and Moore (1945) theory on social stratification provides an important dimension for the analysis of airborne training.

Davis and Moore (1945) maintain that differential reward and prestige are necessary as a means of ensuring that essential jobs get done. All societies need some method for distributing their members along social positions, and people must be motivated to perform the duties these positions require. Positions serving important functions in a society must be filled by people who are both skilled and motivated. Thus, arrangements must be made to ensure that such people are available to fill these critical positions, and the authors argue that it is necessary to make such positions attractive so that people will compete for them. The Davis–Moore theory is that the greatest rewards are associated with those roles which (1) have the greatest importance for society and (2) require the greatest training or talent.

Having made a commitment to airborne warfare in the late 1930's, which was further influenced by German airborne operations in Norway, the Low Countries, and the island of Crete during the early (1940-41) stages of World War II, the U.S. military needed rewards as inducements to fill airborne positions. Such inducements were necessary because an airborne operation behind enemy lines, with its high risk of serious injury or death, was a hazardous mission. A special esprit was necessary for paratroop units. Airborne trainees were thus socialized to believe that they were elite, and they reflected their differential status with distinctive insignia and extra pay for their hazardous duty[1]. Fehrenbach (1963:553) notes that the swagger,

---

1. Extra pay for hazardous duty (parachute) in the U.S. Army is $ 55 per month for enlisted men and $ 110 per month for officers. It is a common joke among enlisted men that it takes twice as much money to get an officer to jump.

special insignia, and nurtured arrogance of paratroopers, "seemingly in conflict with most decent, democratic practices, make sense only when what
paratroopers must do is considered."

Stratification arises, according to Davis and Moore (1945), when a society must have rewards to use as inducements and a way to distribute these
rewards according to position. The U.S. Army has rewarded participation
in the airborne, not only psychologically and with extra pay, but also more
tangibly in the form of upward mobility for career–minded officers. Just
(1970) has observed that during the 1950's, the Army collectively was run
by General officers who served during World War II in airborne units, especially the U.S. 82nd and 101st Airborne Divisions. Just believes that the
airborne has become an institution within an institution and that it rests
atop the Army's social structure. Since the 1950's all new incoming Regular
Army officers have been required to be either airborne— or ranger-qualified.

Further support for this thesis can be found in Aran's (1972) paper on
Israeli paratroopers. Aran (1972:50) states, "In general the parachutist
corps enjoys a very glamorous, elitist image." Israeli paratroopers have symbolic rewards such as red berets and distinctive winged – insignia, but there
is also an overt policy of encouraging the best young people to volunteer
for the parachute corps, to assign the parachute corps more significant and
prestigious missions, and to recruit within the corps itself for personnel to
fill more important positions in the Israeli Army as a whole.

Although airborne training has been important to military society, its
function in the wider civilian society in the United States is less explicit.
Some status from an airborne experience may transfer to those areas of civilian society where action–oriented types who have served in leadership
positions requiring some managerial expertise are often recruited by business corporations. In present–day America such transfer of status would
most likely be psychological and not directly convertible into civilian benefits. Status, however, is often situational, and Israel provides a stronger
example of the importance of airborne training for the wider society. Aran
(1972:55) argues that military parachuting in Israel is seen as service to the
society and the state. Membership in the Israeli parachute corps, particularly for new immigrants, facilitates upward mobility also in the larger
civilian society because the parachute corps has a strong commitment to the
collective cause; airborne training can thus be conceived as "a ritual of
initiation into the center" of Israeli society.

The question arises, however, under what circumstances is the normative
and value system of the airborne functional in terms of the Army's missions
and under what circumstances is it dysfunctional? In the past, airborne socialization has been related to the effective task accomplishment of combat
missions requiring highly trained and motivated soldiers for delivery behind
enemy lines. Ironically, airborne warfare never proved itself as a concept
and is expensive in terms of personnel, equipment, and time needed for the
training of paratroopers and air crews. It has been phased out of the U.S.
Army in favor of the air-mobility (helicopter–borne) concept. Yet the Army
still trains 5,000 men annually as paratroopers. Why? Quoting Lieutenant
General Willard Pearson, Just (1970:97) reports, ". . . paratroopers are the

best men to command. But it has nothing to do with the fact they jump out of airplanes. It is that all paratroopers are volunteers and the training is exceedingly rigorous. The units are tougher, and the commanders magnetic."

The point is that although military parachuting per se may no longer be a highly relevant military skill, airborne socialization remains important because, as Aran (1972:50-53) explains, the military is one of society's organizations where the action–seeking individual is desirable as a personality type, particularly in certain units. Lucas (1973:72) has noted that the salience of the action–oriented, combat image may be such that there is no other military type except its negation. In the military an individual is an action type or he is not. There are no other strong personality images available as substitutes. Therefore, parachuting also serves the Army as (1) a means of selection for action–oriented individuals (non–action types can be identified and distributed into non–combat positions) and (2) a means of role–specific socialization for action–oriented individuals into units where such behavior types are desired. Although too much action–seeking can be dysfunctional for the entire military organization, parachuting serves as a controlled outlet for the expression of action.

The Davis and Moore (1945) theory of social stratification thus relates to airborne training in the following manner :

1. Differential reward and prestige are necessary as a means of ensuring that essential jobs get done (inducements of identification, status, pay, and action are used to attract soldiers to the airborne).

2. Greatest rewards are associated with those roles which

A. have the greatest importance for society (the importance of the airborne is that it provides a source of skilled and motivated action-oriented soldiers necessary for the goals of the military, which may or may not be important to the wider society);

B. require the greatest training or talent (as a demanding occupational specialty within the military, airborne training represents a technical skill beyond normal combat training).

In accordance with the Davis–Moore theory, it is the hypothesis of this study that action – oriented individuals self–selected into the airborne in response to such inducements as self–identification with an elite unit, the reward of higher status within the military and higher pay, and for the availability of action and challenge. Such inducements are necessary to ensure that the airborne is attractive to skilled and motivated soldiers.

VALUE CHANGE

A major concern in undertaking research on the airborne is that existing studies of the socialization experiences of officers and cadets within American military institutions are inconclusive in their treatment of the values associated with military training. In his comparison of the U.S. Air Force's Officer Training School and the now–defunct Aviation Cadet Pre–Flight Training School, Wamsley (1972) argues that the appropriate focus for studies of military socialization are those indicators which distinguish the military officer from the civilian. Wamsley (1972:401) singles out the following as being fundamental values of the military subculture: (1) acceptance of all–pervasive hierarchy and deference patterns; (2) extreme emphasis on dress, bearing and grooming; (3) specialized vocabulary; (4) emphasis on honor, integrity, and professional responsibility; (5) emphasis on brotherhood; (6) fighter spirit marked by aggressive enthusiasm; (7) special reverence for history and traditions; and (8) social proximity for dependents.

The fundamental values associated with airborne socialization can also be derived from a "Parachutist's Creed." This creed indicates that the paratrooper (1) is a volunteer, fully realizing the hazards of chosen service; (2) is an elite shock trooper; (3) is mentally and physically fit; (4) is loyal to superiors and comrades; (5) is courteous, neat, and attentive toward maintenance of weapons and equipment ; (6) reflects high standards of training and morale; (7) fights fairly and never surrenders; (8) shows a high degree of initiative and fights on to the objective; (9) has proven ability as a fighting man on the field of battle; (10) fights as a member of a team; and (11) always upholds the honor and the prestige of the finest unit in the army.

A comparison between the aforementioned values contained in the Parachutist's Creed and those mentioned by Wamsley shows that the great majority of airborne values are related to fighter spirit marked by aggressive enthusiasm (airborne values 1,2,3,7,8,9,10). Other appropriate comparisons are emphasis upon brotherhood (airborne values 4,10); extreme emphasis on dress, bearing, and grooming (airborne value 5); emphasis on honor, integrity, and professional responsibility (airborne value 11); and special reverence for history and traditions (airborne value 11). The point to be stressed is that the prototype for the paratrooper is the aggressive, masterful man of action (Farrell, 1967).

Wamsley (1972) insists, however, that to date the literature of military socialization fails to view the military as a subculture distinct from the larger general culture of our society. He maintains that military socialization must be viewed as a series of socialization experiences distinctive to the requirements of task–oriented military organizations. As a distinctive form of socialization, Wamsley (1972:415-416) claims that military socialization involves a significant change in the underlying attitudes and values of those socialized.

But Wamsley's (1972) thesis can be challenged by asking if impressions of changing surface behavior indicate a significant change of values and attitudes. Catton (1973) questions whether most human beings who have undergone any appreciable amount of socialization can submit to instant redefinition of self. Instead, when circumstances change and habitual or customary ways of behaving become obsolete, there is social and psychological tension and conflict until new adaptations are attained. However, these new adaptations usually include many elements carried over from the old. Obviously in the environment of military socialization there is an extreme demand to conform to the military's normative system, yet the bulk of existing studies (Lovell, 1962, 1964; Lebby, 1970; Lucas, 1971, 1973; Roghmann and Sodeur, 1972) tend to support the null hypothesis (no extreme change) rather than the hypothesis that socialization into the military is accompanied by dramatic changes of attitudes and values. Roghmann and Sodeur's (1972) survey of the formation of authoritarian attitudes among West German basic trainees found no permanent change of attitude. In the United States, both the Lovell (1962) study of West Point cadets and the Lebby (1970) study of Annapolis midshipmen failed to find significant attitude change, while the Lucas (1971) study concluded that anticipatory socialization among ROTC cadets provided a better explanation of observed attitudes and values than did the socialization process itself. More recently, Lucas (1973) has found that a majority of ROTC cadets favored the civilian–related managerial or technical role, despite the fact that the combat role is central to the Army's mission. Only those few cadets who identified with a combat officer self–image were likely to select a combat role.

Although little empirical research has been done on the theory that individuals have the tendency to seek out and establish social relationships with other individuals with similar opinions and values, it appears that an individual will be motivated to accept the outlook of a group to the extent that the group is attractive for the individual (Katz and Lazarsfeld, 1964). A possible explanation for the lack of significant attitude and value change during military socialization is the self–selection of the individuals being socialized. If individuals self–select into volunteer military organizations, such as the airborne, because they are attracted to the life–style, then presumably there would not be significant changes of attitudes and values during socialization. As will be demonstrated, this study supports the hypothesis of no significant value change because of the self–selection among those respondents experiencing airborne socialization.

RESEARCH PROCEDURES

Two research techniques were used for collecting data: (1) participant observation in 1964 (basic airborne) at Fort Benning, Georgia and 1969 (jumpmaster) at Fort Bragg, North Carolina as an airborne trainee; (2) interviews conducted in 1971 among a group of fifty–two airborne–qualified respondents belonging to a U.S. Army Reserve airborne unit (N=47) and to a Reserve non–airborne unit (N=5). Additional interviews were obtained from forty–eight respondents who were not airborne–qualified in the same airborne (N=3) and non–airborne (N=45) units. With the exception of the independent variable of airborne training, both units were essentially homogeneous in terms of demographic and related social characteristics, i.e., residence (Northern California), ethnic background (mixed, but with Anglo–Saxon majority), age (22-48 years), education (mostly college graduates), sex (all male), and religion (slight Protestant majority). The officer ranks of the airborne (N=18) and non-airborne (N=15) respondents were captains and lieutenants; enlisted ranks of the airborne (N=34) and non–airborne (N=33) ranged from sergeant–major (E–9) to private (E–1). Three of the airborne respondents completed airborne training during the course of the interviews; the remainder had completed the training prior to the study. The reader should be cautioned that interview data were collected from reservists, not career soldiers. However, it was the author's observation that the socializing process of airborne training does not distinguish experiences between the regular and the reservist trainee.

AIRBORNE TRAINING PROCEDURES

The U.S. Army Airborne School is a military institution with a well–defined singleness of purpose: to train military parachutists. The objective of this training is similar to that of other military institutions in that it is a two fold process of transmitting technical knowledge and instilling in the trainees an outlook considered appropriate for its members (Dornbush, 1955).

Airborne training qualifies as status passage because it represents not only transition of status within a social structure, but also possible change in personal identity in terms of prestige among those who accept the value system (Becker and Strauss, 1956; Glaser and Strauss, 1971). The strategic question about the desirability of status passage, as Glaser and Strauss (1971: 89) point out, is from whose viewpoint is the passage desirable or undesirable? In the case of airborne training the passage is viewed as mutually desirable by both the training cadre and trainees as they agree that to be a paratrooper is a rewarding experience. Both cooperate to achieve a desirable passage, but the cadre place demands upon the trainees during the actual condition of passage to ensure that the trainees are worthy of their future status. The desirability of such passage is evident because in order to become a paratrooper, the potential trainee must first volunteer for training.

Van Gennep's (1960) division of the process of passage into rites of separation, rites of transition, and rites of incorporation provide a framework for the discussion of airborne training procedures. First, the airborne trainee is separated from his non–airborne environment, next comes the stage of transition as the trainee begins to attend to the conditions of passage, and finally, upon completion, the former trainee is incorporated into his new group – the airborne.

Rite of Separation: Definition of the Situation. The definition of the situation in airborne school begins immediately upon reporting. This definition serves to temporarily separate the trainee from his former social world. The duration of passage is publicly known as three weeks. Territorial definitions of status are established: normal social relations common to the military prevail outside of airborne training areas, but inside those areas trainees are subordinate to the cadre. Officer trainees, however, are not subject to degrading harassment (Krone, 1963).[2] All trainees are expected to demonstrate the highest degree of military courtesy, bearing, and personal appearance; in addition, they are expected to reflect a high degree of enthusiasm for the training and the desired goal.

---

2. Senior (field-grade) officers represent an exception. They are given physical training apart from the other trainees and are treated with the full courtesy due their rank. Junior (company-grade) officers are trained entirely with the enlisted men and are occasionally subject to non-degrading harassment. For a discussion of airborne training from an Air Force officer's perspective, see the Krone (1963) article.

A distingushing characteristic of airborne training is the absolute control exercised over the passage by cadre. Trainees have no rights or privileges and are treated as inferior by the cadre in a repetitive and public fashion. They constantly are reminded that they are volunteers (Does your mother know you're here?) and that airborne troops are elite. Trainees are reminded also that they may quit at any time, an act defined publicly as deviance and personal weakness. The direction of the passage leads only toward one thing – airborne qualification – and neither the cadre nor the trainees have the authority to change the conditions of passage except that a trainee may quit, be injured or killed, or be removed for cause by the cadre. The trainees have no choice but to place great faith in the cadre and in the fairness of the tests and judgments. All tests are conducted openly so that the trainees can see for themselves how they and others are performing; in fact both failure and success are public. Despite the rigor of passage and inferior status, the trainees have an explicit promise that completion of the training will raise them to elite status.

Rites of Transition: Ground, Tower, and Jump Week. The first week of jump school is known as Ground Week and each day begins with an inspection in ranks in which penalty push–ups are awarded for the slightest infraction of the airborne's standards of appearance, deference and demeanor, and presentational conduct. Next comes a daily session of intense physical conditioning. It was the author's observation that most of the trainees who quit do so during Ground Week as a result of the morning run primarily, but also as a response to the general harshness of the social and physical environment. During the training, the cadre often tell the trainees to look about them and notice their thinning ranks, which aids in reinforcing an image of superiority and self–potency among those remaining. Exact figures citing the number of failures in airborne school were not available. However, the author's 1964 class began with 246 and finished with 197.

Training during Ground Week consists of properly fitting and wearing the parachute, learning the procedures and jump commands used inside an aircraft, practicing aircraft exits and parachute landing falls, and jumping from a 34-foot tower while attached to a cable. The 34–foot tower also allows the trainee to practice his body position while exiting the aircraft, to experience falling, to check his canopy after the opening shock, to activate his reserve chute in case of malfunction, to keep a sharp look–out during descent, and to prepare to land. This exercise is repeated almost endlessly until the trainee is able to demonstrate split–second response.

The second week of jump school is Tower Week, called that because the primary feature of this week of training is the 250 – foot tower from which every trainee is dropped by parachute at least twice. In addition to repeating the training routines of Ground Week, the trainee is introduced to the Swing Landing Trainer, the most difficult apparatus to master of the entire passage. Here the trainee is swung and slowly lowered until dropped on the ground where he is expected to execute a perfect parachute landing fall. At least half of the trainee's landings must be satisfactory or else he is held back to repeat the entire week's training.

During Jump Week the harshness of the cadre – trainee relationship is relaxed somewhat as the trainee devotes his time to making five parachute jumps from an aircraft flying in mass formation with several other troop – carrying planes. One of the jumps is made wearing a full load of combat equipment, including weapon. Completion of all five jumps is necessary to become airborne–qualified. Therefore, jump injuries are typically concealed, if possible, until after the fifth jump.

Military parachuting can be characterized as an abrupt confrontation with physical reality involving acute sensory stimulation. Aboard the air-craft the paratrooper is typically seated in bulk (loaded down with parachute and equipment) with several others, all awaiting the jumpmaster's commands. The jumper suspends his own judgment and places the control of his behav-ior fully in the hands of his group (the jumpmaster). This suspension of individual judgment and the turning over of one's fate to others appears, according to Lopez–Reyes (1971), as a state of egolessness or self–abandon-ment where death loses its dread. Aran (1972) describes this same state as a regression into a trance of non–selfhood where the jumper identifies totally with the group. Control by the group appears to make performance possible despite anxiety.[3] On the command to stand up all jumpers are directed through a standardized ritual of checking equipment which insures safety and alertness. The command to jump is a light changing color from red to green, sometimes accompanied by a verbal "go" or finger tap below the buttock. Once he has exited the aircraft, the jumper is buffeted by the engine's blast and surrounded by the visual stimuli of sky and earth. Following the shock of the parachute opening, the physical sensation of soft descent through space typically brings a strong feeling of exhilaration. While in the air, the jumper, for the first time in his airborne activity, is completely alone. On the ground the jumper reverts back to group control, but not before he experien-ces a personal feeling of accomplishment and self–worth.

Aran (1972) believes that parachuting is bipolaric in that it involves extremely intense psychological and social states of an opposite nature. First, during the pre-jump phase, particularly aboard the aircraft, there is an intense state of group control; next comes the jump and an extreme state of individualism during descent, which, in turn, is followed by post-jump return to group control as the paratrooper begins his ground mission. The intensity of both the group and individual experience, along with the poten-tial danger, no doubt exists to strengthen group solidarity and, as Lopez–Reyes (1971) observes, provides an illusion of omnipotence.

Rite of Incorporation: Self Potency. The focal point in the passage is the closure ceremony which signifies the end of passage and maximizes aware-ness of the new status. Glaser and Strauss (1971:91) state that these cere-monies are especially important when the passage has not been pleasant,

---

3. The expression of anxiety and stress in military parachuting appears to be related to group solidarity (Basowitz *et al.*, 1955; Farrell, 1967; Lopez-Reyes, 1971). Basowitz *et al.*, (1955) report as long as a group was cohesive, there was little expression of anxiety concerning physical danger during parachuting except for fear of not measuring up to per-sonal or group expectations. It has been the author's experience that anxiety was situational and decreases considerably when jumping on a regular basis with familiar others.

148   William Cockerham

yet the achieved goal is desirable. The ceremony thus symbolizes having traveled a rough road to success.

The airborne graduation ceremony is normally held on the drop zone following the fifth and final jump. The senior representative of the cadre, emphasizing the new status of the former trainee, personally pins a metal, winged parachute badge on each individual and welcomes him into the airborne. Not only is there a strong feeling of self–worth and accomplishment, but also the individual's passage into the ranks of the airborne is accompanied by feelings of pride and personal identification with the airborne and its values, norms, and traditions. The image of self – potency and superiority, both in relation to the individual and to his group, is pervasive.

Personal identification with the airborne is important because it increases one's concept of personal potency in the face of danger. The element of danger and mastery of anxiety, in turn, add to the image of superiority. Whenever an individual jumps from an aircraft he assumes a risk that his parachute may not open. The estimate of malfunctions is very low, yet risk is a factor which is always present. Farrell (1967) explains that joining such a group demands a certain degree of psychological regression because the individual partially suspends his critical judgment in favor of group control. Instead the jumper draws his strength from his identification with the group whose supports are idealized through the denial of objective danger. The danger of military parachuting tends to draw airborne soldiers together on the basis of shared experience. In comparing similarities between the police and the military, Janowitz (1960) notes that strong social solidarity is required in any profession that has to be preoccupied with the threat of danger.

In brief, the transmission of the airborne's value system, with its emphasis upon fighter spirit and aggressive enthusiasm as part of a pervasive sense of eliteness, is accomplished during airborne socialization in the following manner: (1) during the first stage of separation, the trainee is isolated from his former social world and forced to devote his time and energy to the passage; (2) during the second stage of transition, the trainee learns his new role, including both technical skills and the rationale for pride in self and unit. The mastery of danger encourages the trainee to adopt this rationale; and (3) during the third stage of incorporation, the trainee is inducted into the airborne after having completed its tests. Knowledge that other individuals have met the same challenge contributes to group cohesion and the social solidarity of the airborne.

SELF–SELECTION

According to interview data, all the airborne respondents in this study maintained that there had been little or no significant change in their attitudes and values as a result of airborne socialization. These subjects viewed themselves as already action–oriented individuals who stressed the personal values of being capable, courageous, and self–reliant. As Lucas (1973:77) has noted, it is the individual who identifies himself as being a combat type who is "much more prone to select the charismatic and dangerous roles in airborne and Special Forces units." This type of self–image was apparent in the responses of these airborne subjects in explaining their desire to become a paratrooper. One–half (50.6%) of the airborne respondents stated their primary motivation for volunteering for airborne training was their desire to meet a personal physical and psychological challenge; 22.8% stated they volunteered mainly for the excitement. Other primary reasons given for volunteering were self–identification with an elite military unit (22.8%) and extra pay for hazardous duty (3.8%).

The three airborne respondents who completed airborne training during the interview period likewise demonstrated no evidence of a dramatic change in attitudes and values. Prior to their training they revealed themselves as having followed an active and aggressive pattern of behavior since childhood. The effect of airborne training upon their self–concept was to enhance their already established self-image of personal potency and to reduce any anxiety about not being able to measure up to the paratrooper image. One respondent replied, "I think it helps a guy to keep his head straight to do something a little terrifying once-in-a-while to prove to himself that he's got some guts."

Besides self–selection, two other related themes appear in the interview data of the airborne respondents : (1) the expression of status (self–identification with an elite unit) and (2) the expression of self–potency. The status passage of airborne training provided the reward of self–identification with the elite of the U.S. Army along the lines suggested by Davis and Moore. These respondents, both officer and enlisted, believed very strongly that the airborne is elite and this attitude has been confirmed for them through experience. By comparing the functions and capabilities of others and their units, including the type of military personnel in other units, they saw themselves as the best according to their value system. And as the best, they believed the Army has rewarded them in terms of status, extra pay, interesting assignments and distinctive insignia. These are some typical comments from the airborne respondents supporting this point: "Because I am airborne I do not have to take a back seat to anybody in the Army." "I benefited greatly from the training and the association with people I consider to be among the best I have ever met." "The airborne is the best possible unit in the U.S. Army; it demands a high professional ability." "It is the best unit in the Army and I want to make the most of the military."

As for the expression of self–potency, these respondents insisted that airborne training provided them with a sense of accomplishment and made a positive contribution to their personality. They emphasized a strong faith in their own capabilities and the usefulness of aggressive behavior to deal with physical challenge. This is apparent in these typical interview comments: "Jump school instilled confidence in me. I realized after the training that I could do almost anything that I put my mind to." "I feel proud to reflect upon a past jump, knowing that I controlled my fear. It will be very difficult for me ever to be brow–beaten by anyone after having been through jump school." "Airborne school either makes you or breaks you." "Airborne school shows a man himself, what he is and what kind of unit he is in–the best." "The training can be harmful to one's personality if he takes it seriously. He might think he is indestructible, becomes brutish, hard, maybe unruly. It can foster anti–social behavior. But it is worthwhile for the same reason it can be harmful. It tests a man. He can see how it feels to be scared, he can feel pride, self–esteem and a sense of accomplishment." "In the case of airborne training, it was a real challenge to me because of bruised ribs and pneumonia. I spent three weeks in Ground Week and one-and-a-half weeks in Tower Week, but nothing stopped me. I got through."

A comparison of interview data between the airborne and non–airborne respondents demonstrated a significant difference in regard to attitudes toward military service. All of the non–airborne respondents either joined the Army to satisfy their military obligation or were drafted. The primary reason given by the airborne for joining the Army, however, was enjoyment (50.6%) followed by draft/military obligation (26.6%), and patriotism (22.8%). Respondents were asked if they felt their time spent in the Army was worthwhile. As shown in Table 1, 92.4% of the airborne replie positively; only 4.2% of the non–airborne replied in the affirmative. Thed airborne respondents expressed positive feelings about their military service because they believed that the airborne provided them with a life–style in which, by exposing themselves to challenge and coping with it successfully, they could reaffirm faith in themselves as capable individuals. The non–airborne respondents felt no such challenge.

TABLE 1. PERCENTAGE OF RESPONSES TO QUESTION: "DO YOU FEEL WHAT YOU ARE DOING IN THE ARMY IS WORTHWHILE?"

Response	Airborne Subjects (N=52)	Non-Airborne Subjects (N=48)
I usually feel it is *not* worthwhile	7.6	95.8
I usually feel it is worthwhile	92.4	4.2
T O T A L	100.0	100.0

To emphasize how important the airborne was to them, 60.8% of the airborne–qualified respondents stated they would never serve in a non–airborne unit. The remainder of the airborne group indicated they would be very reluctant about accepting a non–airborne assignment, but would do so if there were no other alternative. Only 6.4 % of the non–airborne group indicated any interest in an airborne assignment.

As an important indicator of the involvement of self in the military role, these respondents were asked how important it was to them personally to make good as a soldier. Table 2 indicates that the great majority of the airborne (77.0%) stated it was very important compared to only 6.4% of the non–airborne. These data are indicative of the airborne's requirement for highly motivated soldiers who will demonstrate a strong desire to succeed in hazardous missions. Those airborne candidates who are not motivated are not likely to pass the airborne's test of airborne training.

TABLE 2. PERCENTAGE OF RESPONSES TO QUESTION: "HOW IMPORTANT IS IT TO YOU PERSONALLY TO MAKE GOOD AS A SOLDIER?"

Response	Airborne Subjects (N=52)	Non-Airborne Subjects (N=48)
It is very important	77.0	6.4
It is pretty important	17.3	20.8
It is not so important	3.8	52.0
It is not important at all	1.9	20.8
T O T A L	100.0	100.0

In comparing the attitudes of the airborne respondents in the airborne and non–airborne units, the airborne–qualified respondents in the non–airborne unit expressed positive feelings about themselves and their training, but they did not geneially demonstrate the same high degree of enthusiasm toward parachuting as did members of the airborne unit. Perhaps the subsequent reinforcement of close interaction with other airborne–qualified individuals is necessary as a locus for the airborne "perspective" or perhaps the effects of airborne socialization are modified by later situational factors. More investigation is needed on this point.

It appears, however, that in general the completion of airborne tiaining led to increasingly positive feelings about self which, in turn, is related to the selection of the men themselves and their belief in this kind of calculus before they volunteer for the training. Airborne training did not produce a dramatic change in attitudes and values among the airborne respondents, but served instead to enhance pre–existing attitudes and values which guided their selection of a desired military role.

CONCLUSION

It is clear that more empirical research of longitudinal nature is needed not only to determine the effects of airborne socialization, but also to investigate the question of self-selection and whether or not there is significant attitude and value change during different types of military socialization. However, this study supports the Davis–Moore (1945) theory of stratification which states that the greatest rewards are associated with those roles which have the greatest importance for society and require the greatest training or talent. In the example of airborne training, action–oriented individuals self–select into the airborne in response to such inducements as self–identification with an elite unit, the reward of higher status within the military and higher pay, and for the availability of action and challenge. Although the

Army insists that all branches have equal status, they in fact do not (Stouffer, et al., 1949). Despite professing equality, the Army faces the dilemma common to American society, as pointed out by Myrdal (1944), where explicit equalitarian standards are circumvented in social reality. In the Army's case it has been functionally necessary to fill important positions by people who are both skilled and motivated; inducements in the form of status and pay have served to attract people to these positions.

As for airborne training, it appears erroneous to suggest that airborne socialization brings about a significant change in individual values and attitudes. Obviously one must self-select for this type of socialization since airborne training is available only to volunteers. As a recent Special Forces recruiting poster, featuring a parachute jump, states: "Men join us not because we are different, but because they are."

REFERENCES

Aran, Gideon.
1972 "The Sociologist as a Young Parachutist." Unpublished manuscript, University of Chicago.
Basowitz, Harold, Harold Persky, Sheldon J. Korchin and Roy R. Grinker.
1955 Anxiety and Stress. New York: McGraw - Hill.
Becker, Howard and Anselm Strauss.
1956 "Careers, Personality, and Adult Socialization." American Journal of Sociology 62 (November): 253 - 263.
Catton, William Jr.
1973 "Social Inertia and the Shape of Things to Come." Unpublished manuscript, University of Wyoming.
Davis, Kingsley and Wilbert Moore.
1945 "Some Principles of Stratification." American Sociological Review 10 (April): 242-249.
Dornbusch, Sanford.
1955 "The Military Academy as an Assimilating Institution." Social Forces 33 (May): 316-321.
Farrell, D.
1967 "The Psychology of Parachuting." Pp. 657-674 in R. Slovenko and J. A. Knight (eds.), Motivation in Play, Games, and Sports. Springfield, Ill: Thomas.
Fehrenbach, T. R.
1963 This Kind of War. New York: Macmillan.
Glaser, Barney and Anselm Strauss.
1971 Status Passage. Chicago: Aldine.
Janowitz, Morris.
1960 The Professional Soldier. New York: Free Press.
Just, Ward.
1970 "Soldiers." The Atlantic 226 (October): 59-98.
Katz, Elihu, and Paul Lazarsfeld.
1964 Personal Influence. New York: Free Press.
Kepecs, Joseph.
1944 "Neurotic Reactions in Parachutists." Psychoanalytic Quarterly 13: 273-299.
Krone, Robert.
1963 "Drop for 22, Sir." TAC Attack 3 (April): 14-16.
Lebby, David.
1970 "Professional Socialization of the Naval Officer: The Effect of Plebe Year at the U.S. Naval Academy." Ph.D. dissertation. University of Pennsylvania.
Lopez-Reyes, Ramon.
1971 Power and Immortality. New York: Exposition Press.

Lovell, John.
  1962 "The Cadet Phase of Professional Socialization of the West Pointer: Description, Analysis, and Theoretical Refinement." Ph. D. dissertation. University of Wisconsin.
  1964 "The Professional Socialization of the West Point Cadet." Pp. 115-117 in Morris Janowitz (ed.), The New Military. New York: Russell Sage.
Lucas, William.
  1971 "Anticipatory Socialization and the ROTC." Pp. 99-134 in Charles Moskos (ed.), Public Opinion and the Military Establishment. New York: Russell Sage.
  1973 "Military Images in the Army ROTC." Journal of Political and Military Sociology 1 (Spring): 71-90.
Myrdal, Gunnar.
  1944 An American Dilemma: The Negro Problem and Modern Democracy. New York: Harper.
Roghmann, Klaus and Wolfgang Sodeur.
  1972 "The Impact of Military Service on Authoritarian Attitudes: Evidence from West Germany." American Journal of Sociology 78 (September): 418-433.
Stouffer, Samuel A., Edward A. Suchman, Leland C. DeVinney, Shirley A. Star, and Robin M. Williams, Jr.
  1949 The American Soldier. Vol. I. Princeton: Princeton University Press.
Van Gennep, Arnold.
  1960 The Rites of Passage. Chicago: University of Chicago Press.
Wamsley, Gary.
  1972 "Contrasting Institutions of Air Force Socialization: Happenstance or Bellwether?'' American Journal of Sociology 78 (September): 399-417.
Weiss, Melford.
  1967 "Rebirth in the Airborne." Transaction 3 (May): 23-26.

PART III
CIVIL-MILITARY RELATIONS

While the second part of the anthology deals primarily with the internal dimensions of the military profession and organization, the issues raised there may have some bearing on this third part which deals with the external environment or the interface between armed forces and society.

The first major consideration of this part is a discussion of the factors that prompt the military to actively participate in the social and political processes of their respective societies. Ben-Dor suggests three interrelated propositions based on a behavioristic model of threat. Active military intervention in the Middle East is related to the concepts of physical force, the military's internal characteristics, and the impact of the external sociopolitical environment on the military.

In contrast to Ben-Dor, Thompson advances a more structural or systemic approach to explain the Arab coup. He suggests push of the military sub-system (i.e., access to and control of the instruments of organized violence), pull factors (i.e., regime vulnerability, legacies, fillers of the void, middle class spear carriers, etc.), military grievances and push-pull of external politics as factors.

While Ben-Dor and Thompson look at the behavioristic and structural factors, McKown focuses upon the behavior of one particular group in society, the elites. In her analysis of domestic correlates of intervention in various sub-Saharan African nations, she argues that the sources of the coup d'etat can only be explained by analyzing the behavior and motivations of elites and aspiring elites.

The next important issue concerns how similar or distinct the military is from civilian society. This is also known as the convergence vs. divergence debate in civil-military relations. Segal *et al.* attempt to address themselves to both the conceptual and empirical (U.S. data) aspects of the question. They

155

suggest that in an era of all volunteer militaries, the emerging pattern in Western societies may be one of divergence.

Three more national studies explore the same issue. Kourvetaris attempts an analysis of civil-military relations of Modern Greece by using Moskos' framework of convergent, divergent, and segmented patterns of armed forces and society. He argues that the present trend is toward a more segmented pattern of civil-military relations.

On a different level of analysis of civil-military relations, Drury questions the prevailing contention that militaries are ineffective as political rulers. In his study of military rule in Brazil, he notes that the military has brought about some short-run political stability and economic development, although at the expense of progressive political and social change.

While the three previous authors analyze civil-military relations in Western societies, Herspring considers the interrelationships among communist ideology and Party politics, technology, and the officer corps in East Germany. Although noting an increase in the military's reliance upon modern technology, Herspring maintains that the Communist Party has developed sufficient control structures to ensure that the officers will follow the directives of the Party regardless of the institutional loyalties they may have.

The final issue focuses upon the methodological problems encountered when quantifying military intervention across nations. Initially Sigelman finds various previous indices of intervention lacking in sensitivity and validity. He attempts to improve the measurement of military intervention by combining five other indicators to form his own Military Intervention Index (MII). Then he uses his MII to test Feit's hypothesis that small armies are more likely than larger ones to actively intervene in politics in third world countries. Sigelman's findings do not support this inverse relationship between size of military and propensity to intervene. Tannahill presents another alternative to the measurement of intervention. His composite index considers both the event of the military coup and the process of intervention. He illustrates the operationalization of his approach with data for Brazil and Uruguay.

Explanations of Military Intervention

8

THE POLITICS OF THREAT: MILITARY
INTERVENTION IN THE MIDDLE EAST

GABRIEL BEN-DOR

University of Haifa, Israel

This article outlines a parsimonious, behaviorally oriented theoretical approach to the study of military intervention in the Middle East. First, the author critically reviews the major prevailing explanations of military intervention and finds them inadequate. Second, he offers an explanation based on the concept of threat which is used as both an independent and intervening variable. Finally, on the basis of threat, he suggests three hypotheses dealing with physical force, internal characteristics of the military, and civilian institutions and governmental activity as plausible etiology of military intervention in the Middle East.

The study of military intervention in Middle Eastern politics[1] has attracted considerable attention, both among scholars of military politics in general and among specialists in Middle Eastern politics. (See Perlmutter, 1970; Beeri, 1969; for surveys of the most significant works.) Nevertheless, the theoretically significant results have not been very impressive. In this paper it will be argued that the prevailing theories based on structural variables are inadequate, and that it is much more promising to attempt to look for behavioral variables. Moreover, the paper will argue that what we need most is not just more variables, but a variable that can help explain the connections between variables already known. It is held that the behavioral concept of threat is such a key explanatory variable.

One problem is that some of the empirically most sound studies exhibit a lack of willingness to generalize (Dann, 1969; Khadduri, 1960 and 1969), even to the extent of formulating the findings of the particular case in the form of limited hypotheses. Although this is very unfortunate, an analysis of such works does help in finding many clues of general interest and perhaps applicability. Much more serious—and illuminating—are the problems with the literature that does attempt to deal with the issue in general terms.

One trend in the literature concentrates on patterns. Here we have some interesting contributions, the most extensive among these by Rus-

---

1. In seven Arab countries alone between 1939 and 1969, 41 coups were attempted by the military, 23 of which proved to be successful. See Perlmutter, 1970:291. This article reviews a number of prevailing views on the military in Middle Eastern politics.

tow (1966). Such contributions tell us a good deal about the possible combinations of circumstances in which intervention takes place, the characteristics of regimes following the coup, and above all, the different models of relationships between civilians and soldiers at various stages of military activity (see Luckham, 1971).

Many of the points raised in this literature (the most impressive example of which is Rustow, 1966) reveal a high degree of insight, but on the whole they do not explain the phenomenon of military intervention adequately. Furthermore, several of the patterns perceived originally have proven to be incorrect, at least in part. The point regarding the timing of the first coup ("4-5 years after de facto independence," Rustow, 1966:390) no longer seems convincing, if we bear in mind the examples of the Yemen and Lybia, among others. In general we may safely say that the trend has been toward expanding the Rustow patterns: the military now seem to intervene in a much larger variety of cases than one would anticipate from the earlier patterns. Armies seize power not only after defeat on the battlefield, but also after long periods of inactivity as far as combat is concerned; they stage coups at all stages of the postindependence era following periods of obvious unrest as well as periods of seeming calmness; and above all, they continue to stage coups after the success or failure of the first attempt (Perlmutter, 1969; Seale, 1965), a fact of major importance at which Rustow hints.

While Rustow's patterns do not attempt to put forth a comprehensive explanation, "the theory of 'the natural course'" does have this ambition. This theory (which, of course, tends to overgeneralize), widely prevalent among Middle Eastern intellectuals who support military regimes, is based on the assumption (Beeri, 1969; Nasser, 1955) that only the army officers have the ability to effect the changes necessary to overcome the deep crisis of underdevelopment and transition in the Arab world. The corollary of this theory is that the officers move to fill a political "vacuum" or "to break a stalemate," a "natural" development in the perspective of Islamic history.

Such explanations are not particularly helpful and are often conspicuously false. Military coups occur in a variety of situations, and more frequently in countries where sophisticated alternatives to the officers such as political activists (political parties, trade unions, intellectuals, professionals, bureaucrats etc.) have definitely existed, as in Syria, Turkey or even Egypt. The idea of a political vacuum there does not appear to be valid at all. Similarly, as far as the idea of the stalemate is concerned, the Yemen, Iraq and other cases indicate nothing of the sort, even if the notion itself could be made less vague. Perhaps even more important is the fact that this class of explanations has nothing to contribute to the study of continuing military intervention once the supposed vacuum has been filled and the alleged stalemate has been broken. It says nothing about second, third and consecutive coups; it does not deal with the factionalism so obviously crucial in Middle Eastern armies; and it cannot handle the question of ethnicity in the ranks of the military.

The third school attempts to explain intervention on the basis of class: the point has been made (Halpern, 1962) that the military represent the vanguard of the salaried, new middle class, which —unlike the old, ruling classes—has a stake in the transformation of society. (See Nordlinger, 1970 for the controversy over the middle class thesis.) Whatever the merit of the argument in regard to the potential for "modernization," the explanatory value of these theories is low, as is their general validity: again the point being that the military intervene in cases where they do seem to come from the middle class (old or new, as in Egypt or Turkey), where they come from the lower classes (as is the case with the rural, minority-oriented group in Syria), and where they seem to conflict at times openly with the middle classes (e.g., in the Sudan.) Just as important, the explanatory power of the middle class hypothesis is weak in that it fails to demonstrate the direct, empirically verifiable connection between the class to which the officers belong, on the one hand, and their motives, methods and behavior at the time of intervention (and often their policies once they do capture power), on the other. And as was the case with the "natural course" theory, there is nothing very helpful said about ethnicity, factionalism, and continuing coups.

Among the earlier general (i.e., not specifically Middle Eastern) theories, the one by Finer (1962) seems the most explicit and systematic. On the basis of legitimacy and the existence and strength of civilian institutions (which define the order of the political culture), Finer (1962:168) presents a typology of resistance to military intervention, its mode and characteristic level, and the resultant type of regime. Although in principle legitimacy and strength of institutions could be measured through independent indicators, in Finer's book they border on tautology. How can one find out the degree to which legitimacy is accepted, except at times when it is threatened by challenges such as military intervention? How can one measure the strength of civilian institutions except by observing them in times of resistance to threats such as military coups? And how can one refute the hypotheses derivable from the typology when every successful coup means *ipso facto* weakness of legitimacy and civilian institutions?

Institutionalization also plays a key role in the elegant, appealing, and presently widely prevalent theory of praetorianism, most extensively articulated by Huntington (1968). No longer content with (frequently tautological) efforts to explain intervention by "military variables," the theorists of praetorianism specify the type of society in which military intervention is likely. In such praetorian societies, the ratio of institutionalization to participation is low, power is fragmented; there is a general politicization of social forces, without the corresponding development of institutions capable of absorbing and mediating such conflict. In such a society, military intervention is likely, not because of any intrinsic attributes of the praetorian armies, but because the military follow the pattern of general politicization: "Countries which have political armies also have political clergies, political universities, political bureaucracies. . . ." (Huntington, 1968: 194).

Even if we accept the praetorian model as applicable to the Middle East, the theory neglects crucial variables that differentiate between the various Middle Eastern countries. It seems highly unlikely that we can derive from the praetorian model hypotheses accounting for the prevalence of seemingly never-ending series of coups in Syria, for one, while Egypt, on the other hand, seems to enjoy a relatively stable period following the initial coup—although Perlmutter (forthcoming) labels Egypt "the praetorian state"! Neither can the praetorian model give us much help in attempting to account for the timing of the coups, or perhaps in attempting to predict them, apart from the general proposition that praetorian society as such is vulnerable to likely military intervention. While not necessarily disputing the general proposition, we may well state that we need a more dynamic, more specifically oriented, and more discriminating explanation for military intervention in the Middle East.

THE NOTION OF THREAT

In attempting to find more fruitful theoretical avenues, it seems more promising to explore behavioral rather than structural variables. The case for such a re-orientation in the study of "internal war" was made crystal clear by Eckstein (1971). The main problem with structural theories (of which there has been an abundance) has been their inadequacy when used to explain cases, since a large number of structural variables ("objective" social conditions such as economic factors, stratification and mobility) have been found consistent with cases of internal war—including military coups. For this reason, it seems more promising to explore behavioral variables, i.e., factors emphasizing attitudes and their formation and orientations (such as strain, anomie, and socialization,) particularly since, as Eckstein (1971:31) argues, "Patterns of attitudes while responsive to the settings in which men are placed, seem also to be, to an extent, autonomous of objective conditions, able to survive changes in these conditions or to change without clearly corresponding objective changes."

Practically all theoretically oriented explanations of military intervention in the Middle East have been structural in nature. They specify general social conditions, which may or may not be accepted as valid; still, we have found that indeed several of these structural explanations are at least partially plausible, factually fairly sound, and certainly insightful. Precisely on this account, we may state that a variety of structural conditions in the Middle East have been found compatible with military intervention, without explaining why intervention in fact occurs at a certain point in space and time. Differential origins of the officer corps and the civilian politicians or the weakness of institutions may well be important accompanying features of many coup-stricken countries, but they definitely do not explain violent takeovers by the military or a faction of it.

Utilizing the insights of the theories already mentioned, and attempting to use also the fruits of research in other areas of the world, I now would like to argue for a behaviorally oriented approach, based on the notion of threat. Threat will be used in this theoretical approach not only as the fundamental variable, but also as an intervening variable if grafted onto an existing theory. The argument is centered around the basic proposition that in the Middle East the military is motivated to intervene as a result of perceived threats to itself.

For the purposes of the argument here advanced, military intervention is defined only as outright takeover, i.e., supplantation of governmental personnel (not merely change of policy) by the military for purposes of control, and through the use or threat of force. We may accept the praetorian theory (Huntington, 1968) to the extent of taking for granted a political situation in the Middle East in which the military are already involved in the political process, even fairly heavily so. The notion of threat is intended to help clarify when and why such involvement leads to the supplantation of incumbents.

Threat is defined as a drastic (rapid, or dramatically unexpected) reduction of the previously available political resources (in this case, to the military). As Dahl (1963:15) put it, "A political resource is a means by which one person can influence the behavior of other persons; political resources therefore include money, information, food, the threat of force, jobs, friendship, social standing, the right to make laws, votes, and a great variety of other things . . . Control over political resources is unevenly distributed in virtually all societies."

Clearly, the proposition of threat is intended in a probabilistic, not a deterministic sense. One must always be on guard against the teleological fallacy of such statements as "the military had to intervene in order to protect itself." There is a good deal of variation in the ways in which threat may be perceived by different armies or factions within them. All the proposition does claim is that in the vast majority of cases the motivation of supplanting the incumbents is the perception of threat.

Another important point to bear in mind is that such factors as the international constellation are not necessarily held constant. This means that while there is no intention to deny that coups may and do occur as a result of external encouragement, example and even outright agitation, armies and factions (about which more will be said later) are most likely to respond to these external stimuli to the point of a coup when they perceive threats to themselves.

It is not claimed that this approach will remedy all the deficiencies of the existing, mostly structural theories. Since it is based on motivation, it neglects opportunity, resistance by incumbents, and similar factors of obvious importance in explaining the timing and circumstances of military coups. One may well argue that the entire notion is one-dimensional in its over-simplicity. Is not threat present in every conflict situation?

In order to overcome this objection, we must recall that by definition threat is treated here as a drastic or sudden reduction of political resources. In other words, what is at stake is not just changes in the costs and benefits of a conflict relationship, but such a change for the worse in the possession of the means of conducting conflict by the military as to call their ability to continue the structured relationship in the future into question. There is a certain threshold of tolerance in a conflict, beyond which potential changes are perceived to be qualitative rather than quantitative. While it is difficult to establish this threshold precisely, it seems that armies tend to react drastically when they fear danger to their monopoly of organized armed force, prestige, and whatever degree of unity they possess.

A similar objection could be made in regard to the need for more behavioral variables. Is threat really new? Is it that much more important than traditions, socialization, cognitive dissonance, attitudes toward government, alienation, strains, or orientation toward violence? The choice to neglect all these behavioral variables in the present paper is dictated by a number of crucially important considerations. First, while threat may not be a completely new variable, it has not been used in the double capacity here suggested: on the one hand, as a variable linking motivation to action with structural conditions, thus supplying a missing link between general processes and specific acts, and on the other, as an explanatory variable in its own right. Also, it seems that adding a number of further variables would only increase confusion and disorder, while the notion of threat is held capable of fulfilling an important function of parsimonious organization. Finally, threat as a variable appears promising for generating hypotheses on a useful level of generality. It is in terms of such a comprehensive usage that threat may be regarded as a new variable.

THE USEFULNESS OF THE NOTION OF THREAT

The explanation of military intervention on the basis of threat seems to be congruent with the findings of recent empirical research,

while at the same time it appears to encompass and re-interpret some
of the most striking points made in earlier theoretical efforts. For instance a recent, detailed comparative study of the military in West
Africa concludes that: "Although the military intervene in politics for a
variety of manifest and concealed reasons, the single strongest motivation for intervention, at least in this sample, has been the protection of
narrow corporate and personal security interests and of the "legal"
claim on the share of scarce national resources so far unjustified by the
countries' defense requirements. . . .Military intervention helped the
Armies of the four countries to achieve the objectives of improved corporate security and welfare, but invariably at the expense of internal
cohesion" (Bebler, 1971:329).

Time and again one is struck by examples of military groups planning a variety of long-range actions, and then suddenly carrying out a
coup when they feel the threat of being discovered, transferred, arrested,
or purged. Just as frequently one may notice cases in which coalitions
between military and civilian groups or between various military factions lead to a coup by one of the factions when it feels itself being
threatened, particularly in terms of being phased out of control on the
central level. (This was the case in Syria in the March and September
coups of 1966.) Particularly is this so when the military feel that perhaps
their most important political resource—the monopoly or the lion's
share of organized, large-scale physical force—is in danger. The unhap-
piness of the military with the establishment of militias not subject
directly to the army's control is notorious, and has led to several coups
(for instance, the November 1963 coup in Iraq; or as an African example,
the 1966 coup in Ghana).

The notion of threat makes it understandable that military coups
should occur following a "period of internal unrest in which civilian
authorities have come increasingly to rely on armed forces to maintain
themselves in power" (Rustow, 1966:391). Such a situation involves
either discrediting the military by engaging it in unpopular action to
remedy a series of political mistakes not of its own making, or else the
military's fear of excessive civilian interference leading to the destruction of its ability to act in the future.

Similarly, the fact that armies tend to seize power after defeats on
the battlefield (although by no means is the case always so) can be explained by the fear of drastic decline in the status, prestige, or allocations of the military in the wake of defeat. Certainly the conviction of
the Syrian military that the civilian politicians were trying to destroy
the standing of the army after the defeat in the 1948-1949 war with Israel
was the key precipitant to the original coup in that country, although
many more were to follow (Seale, 1965; Torrey, 1958; Beeri, 1969; Carleton, 1950; Shimoni, 1949). The key variable here is not the question of

defeat or victory on the battlefield, but rather the issue of whether the defeat can be absorbed without leading the military to believe that their standing inside the country will be drastically threatened in the wake of losing to an external foe. This may explain the limited applicability of one of Rustow's patterns.

Another key pattern observed by Rustow tells us that although most military leaders promise to return power to the civilians rather quickly, very few actually do so. One may accuse the aforementioned leaders of simple craving for and infatuation with power, but the issue is more complicated. The evidence (Dekmejian, 1969) indicated that even those military leaders who otherwise appear quite sincere and dedicated to ideals and ideologies fail to relinquish power to the civilians. We may hypothesize that this general reluctance has to do with the difficulty of extricating the army or the faction from direct involvement in controlling the governmental apparatus without exposing it to serious threats by those groups (civilian or military) antagonized, alienated, or potentially vengeful as a result of previous action taken in the course of capturing or maintaining power.

It is also understandable that the military should be more willing to turn power back to civilians when the initial coup was relatively free of violence or bloodshed. Our understanding of cases in which the military do relinquish power—the most conspicuous among these are in the Middle East, Turkey, and elsewhere, Burma and Ghana—is rather imperfect (and interestingly, in all three cases mentioned the military have eventually taken over control for the second and third time).

Therefore, military intervention may pick up and sustain momentum of its own, apart from the original alignment, but with the motivation of threat strongly operative. It is doubly important, as a consequence, to attempt to analyze the units of behavior—in this case, the units of threat—within the general, and often quite misleading, framework of the "army." As Rustow indicates, rifts in military juntas after their coming to power are quite common. The empirical evidence also indicates that the countries suffering most from military coups are those where factionalism in the military is most prevalent, i.e., Syria and Iraq (of the 41 Middle Eastern coups in 1939-69, 13 took place in Syria and 17 in Iraq). Rather than specifying the military as yet another social force in a praetorian society, it seems more promising to look upon the military as a complex network of relationships within which other forces (religious, familial, and ethnic as well as personal, factional) operate, compete for control, and if the fundamental proposition advocated here is correct, act drastically when threatened.

One may well argue that not only is corporate professionalism a highly ambiguous factor in relation to military intervention (Luckham, 1971), but also that the professional army in the Middle East is clearly less frequent and far less important for explaining intervention than the factional or ethnic army. Certainly the interaction of ethnic and factional interests in Syria (where the officers corps is vastly overrepresentative of relatively small minorities) and in Iraq (where it is vastly overrepresentative of the majority while the minorities also hold considerable armed might apart from the official military framework) seems to be an infinitely more important factor than corporate professionalism, which may be somewhat (but not much) more important elsewhere in the region. It is predominantly important to attempt to determine what group within the military feels threatened by action taken against groups inside as well as outside the army.

AVENUES FOR FUTURE RESEARCH

If the proof of the pudding is in the eating then the real payoff of a theoretical proposition is surely in the hypotheses it may help generate, in addition to its function in drawing attention to significant phenomena and in bolstering the explanatory power of other theoretical propositions. The notion of threat here outlined appears to point to three major series of hypotheses derivable from it, which will be spelled out along with one possible example for each series—exclusively for illustrative purposes—in order to demonstrate the potential inherent in the detailed analysis of the notion here given in a preliminary form.

1. *Hypotheses relating the likelihood of military intervention to the distribution of physical force in a given society.*

E.g.: widespread distribution of force (i.e., the capacity to utilize organized violence and the possession of arms) among groups other than the military will increase the likelihood of intervention, since it is likely to increase the number of instances in which threat may become operative, as well as aggravate the feelings of uncertainty, and intensify them. Iraq, Sudan, and Syria throughout most of their independent statehood are cases in point.

2. *Hypotheses relating the likelihood of intervention to the internal characteristics of the military.*

E.g.: if the military are united at the top, but factionalized[2] at the middle levels of the officer corps, the likelihood of intervention increases, as the officers on top may feel obliged to intervene in order to establish a certain degree of unity, while the various factions may feel

---

2.   It is desirable of course, to attempt to relate such factionalism—and the distribution of force mentioned in the preceding paragraph—to general societal forces. For one such point—the analysis of the crucially important ethnic dimension of coups—see Luttwak, 1968:68-73.

threatened by purges from the top as well as by action from opposing factions on the middle levels. The Turkish Army in 1960-1961, the Sudanese Army at the time of the 1971 coup, and the Syrian Army on a number of occasions seem to demonstrate this point.

3. *Hypotheses relating intervention to civilian institutions and governmental activity.*

E.g.: rapid increase in governmental penetration in a society characterized by a small number of civilian institutions is likely to trigger military intervention, as such a development may intensify existing feelings of threat and cause significant new feelings of threat as a result of impinging on areas previously monopolized by the military relying on their domination of force and the virtual lack of organized competition in such areas. Algeria in 1962-1965, Turkey in the late 1950's and 1960, and to a certain extent Yemen before 1962 would be examples of such a state of affairs. This hypothesis obviously contains many structural qualifications reducing the *independent* weight of threat. On the other hand, it demonstrates the usefulness of threat in organizing structural variables and linking them with motivation to action.

Needless to say, the three series of hypotheses and the accompanying examples are at a preliminary stage and in need of much more careful development and refinement. Furthermore, it should always be borne in mind that they are based above all on the cases known from the Middle East, i.e., no universal claim of validity is in order. They could, however, be placed in a comparative perspective. In order to accomplish this in the most potentially fruitful manner, and in order to make much-needed distinctions within the Middle East, one further subject mentioned seems promising in terms of generating possible hypotheses: that of political resources. It seems that a thorough comparative study of the political resources held and used by the military in various cases, their legitimacy, relative importance, and distribution in the hands of various groups and factions inside the military as well as outside should contribute a good deal to our understanding of the operation of the threat factor in terms of timing and intensity. This could be done in a variety of ways, whether as a dimension of political culture or in the manner of refined studies of elites and community power. Perhaps this could also help further our understanding of the differences in vulnerability to military intervention in various areas.

CONCLUSION

Complex phenomena such as military intervention can rarely be explained by a single variable. The notion of threat here outlined attempts no such reductionism, but it offers a key variable for purposes of organizing and developing other known variables, for making relevant connections with the mass of data accumulated, and above all for generating hypotheses on a reasonable level of specificity making possible much-needed distinctions between various groups of cases.

Clearly, the theoretical direction thereby taken is limited, in that it neglects the question of opportunity, the resistance of the incumbents, and a host of other obviously relevant factors in internal wars. It is "one-dimensional" in that it concentrates on motivation. Nevertheless, the notion of threat appears to be more promising for future research—particularly once further work brings about refinements, development, and the definition of more precisely determined empirical indicators—than the prevailing school of structural theories, which, while obviously contributing a good deal to our understanding of the general background to the events leading to military intervention, has by and large failed to explain the timing of intervention, its circumstances, and other such crucially important differences between armies and cases of intervention. Although explanations based on threat do not now seem to fill all these lucunae, they seem to promise to fill some of them— certainly more than the prevailing structural theories.

While the notion of threat is a behavioral one, it has impressive potential for generating hypotheses in a manner linking motivation with societal-structural variables (and thus, possibly with clusters of variables characterizing what scholars usually label stages of political development). Although the present analysis merely hints at this possibility (when demonstrating Class 3 of possible hypotheses), the potential definitely exists. Perlmutter (1970:276) and others seem to be entirely correct in insisting that rather than listing more and more conditions and variables that seem to accompany military intervention "what we must explain is the connections among these variables." The argument of this paper is that the notion of threat, however imperfect at this stage, helps us advance in the right direction by contributing to the explanation of such crucial connections.

REFERENCES

Bebler, Anton A.
    1971   Military Rule in Africa. Princeton: Center of International Studies.
Beeri, Eliezer
    1969   Army Officers in Arab Politics and Society. New York: Praeger.
Carleton, Alfred
    1950   "The Syrian Coups d'Etat of 1949." Middle East Journal 4 (January):1-11.
Dahl, Robert A.
    1963   Modern Political Analysis. Englewood Cliffs: Prentice Hall.
Dann, Uriel
    1969   Iraq Under Quassem. New York: Praeger.
Dekmejian, Richard H.
    1969   "The Egyptian Power Elite." Paper delivered at the annual meeting of the Middle East Studies Association of North America, Toronto.

Eckstein, Harry
    1971   "On the Etiology of Internal Wars." In Bruce Mazlish et al. (editors),
            Revolution. New York: MacMillan.
Finer, S.E.
    1962   The Man on Horseback: The Role of the Military in Politics. New York:
            Praeger.
Halpern, Manfred
    1962   "Middle Eastern Armies and the New Middle Class." In John J. Johnson
            (editor), The Role of the Military in Underdeveloped Countries. Princeton:
            Princeton University Press.
Huntington, Samuel P.
    1968   Political Order in Changing Societies. New Haven: Yale University Press.
Khadduri, Majid
    1960   Independent Iraq. London: Oxford University Press.
    1969   Republican Iraq. London: Oxford University Press.
Luckham, A.R.
    1971   "A Comparative Typology of Civil-Military Relations." Government and
            Opposition 6 (Winter):5-35.
Luttwak, Edward
    1968   Coup D'Etat: A Practical Handbook. New York: Knopf.
Nasser, Gamal Abdul
    1955   Egypt's Liberation: The Philosophy of the Revolution. Washington: Public
            Affairs Press.
Nordlinger, Eric
    1970   "Soldiers in Mufti." American Political Science Review 64 (September):1131-
            1149.
Perlmutter, Amos
    1969   "From Obscurity to Rule: the Syrian Army and the Ba'th Party." Western
            Political Quarterly 12 (December):827-845.
    1970   "The Arab Military Elite." World Politics 22 (January):269-300.
    forthcoming Egypt, the Praetorian State.
Rustow, Dankwart A.
    1966   "The Military in Middle Eastern Society and Politics" in Jason L. Finkle
            and Richard W. Gable (eds.), Political Development and Social Change. New
            York: Wiley.
Seale, Patrick
    1965   The Struggle for Syria. London: Oxford University Press.
Shimoni, Yaacov
    1959   "Syria and her Revolutions." Hamizrah Hehadash (October):7-20.
Springer, P.B.
    1968   "Disunity and Disorder: Factional Politics in the Argentine Military." In
            Henry Bienen (editor), The Military Intervenes. New York: Russell Sage
            Foundation.
Torrey, Gordon
    1958   Syrian Politics and the Military. Columbus: Ohio State University Press.

9

TOWARD EXPLAINING
ARAB MILITARY COUPS*

WILLIAM R. THOMPSON

Florida State University

*As Arab military coups have become more common, their impor-
tance to an understanding of Arab political behavior has increased
accordingly. This paper surveys a number of approaches to explaining
Arab military coups and discusses four major clusters: the push of the
military subsystem, the pull of regime vulnerability, the pulling and
hauling of coup-maker grievances, and the push/pull of external actors
and conditions. Relative emphasis is placed on discussing the five
sub-themes discovered within the regime vulnerability group in contrast with some of the available findings related to reputed Arab coup-
maker grievances. In conclusion, a synthetic interpretation is advanced
in order to place the four approaches in generalized perspective and to
underline the fact that they need not be utilized in a mutually exclusive
manner.*

In the past twenty-five years, military coups (which occur whenever
members of the regular armed forces remove or attempt to remove a
state's chief executive through the threat or use of force) have become
fairly central to Arab politics. Successful coups have taken place in Algeria,
Egypt, Iraq, Libya, Oman, Sudan, Syria, and Yemen. Unsuccessful
efforts have been attempted in Jordan, Lebanon, Morocco, and Southern
Yemen. To date, Saudi Arabia and Tunisia have experienced only alleged
military plots. Thus there can be little doubt that a better appreciation
of the military coup can only enhance the quality of our understanding of
Arab political behavior. Toward such an end, this paper will critically
survey the several explanatory themes currently available in the literature
on Arab military coup-makers. Most of the analyses fall roughly into
four groups: the push of the military subsystem, the pull of regime vulnerability, the pulling and hauling of coup-maker grievances, and the
push/pull of external actors and conditions. Each group will be described
and discussed prior to the presentation of a more synthetic interpretation.

THE PUSH OF THE MILITARY SUBSYSTEM

Perhaps the most obvious characteristic exhibited by military coups
is that military elites possess clear advantages in the access to and control of the instruments of organized coercion. Civilian regimes have not

*An earlier version of this paper was read at the 1973 meeting of the Middle
East Studies Association of North America. A number of people have provided
valuable criticism and encouragement including: Fouad Ajami, Jere Bacharach,
George Lenczowski, George Modelski, Amos Perlmutter, and Manfred Wenner.
Much of the research was made possible by a U.S. A.C.D.A./National Academy
of Sciences dissertation grant (1971-1972).

been spectacularly successful in regulating this essential resource base. The present political resources of the military were initially improved by the gradual intrusion of the members of the European state system into the Middle East in the seventeenth through nineteenth centuries. Recognizing their relative weakness, local rulers responded to the European threat by attempting to rebuild and modernize their armies. In the early and mid-twentieth century, the newly sovereign Arab states responded to the prevailing status values of the international system by strengthening their armed forces as symbols of their sovereignty and as sources of increased security. In the main, then the military have been chosen to be a prime beneficiary of the resources available to the Arab state. This is a trend, as Hurewitz (1969:103) has noted, which has been facilitated by such factors as cold war rivalries and regional arms competitions, not to mention the pre- and post-world war Arab officer movements and the Arab-Israeli impasse. The result has been partially modernized/technically-conscious military organizations which at the same time variably retain certain traditional characteristics in the way of symbols, uniforms, customs, perspectives, and allegiances.

The military's effective capacity to act in the political system is derived from its advanced training and communication networks, its access to hierarchically disciplined manpower, and its near monopoly of heavier arms. It matters not that Arab armies look better on paper than they do on the battlefield. Few soldiers are required to execute a coup and the resources of the military are rarely rivaled by other politically competing groups. The military commander who has access to troops has access to important and convertible political resources and therefore has potential political capability. On occasion, the troops need not even be told that they are being used in a coup d'etat.

Once in power, the extent of the military's capabilities for ruling remains a fairly open research question. In lieu of rigorous studies of military regime performance, stereotypes of the politician in uniform prevail (see Pye, 1962:68-70: Janowitz, 1965:43).[1] Wherever the truth may lie, two serious and closely related weaknesses of military regime are fairly evident. First, military regimes are no more secure from military coups than their civilian counterparts. Slightly more than half of all Arab coups (1948-1970) were directed against chief executives who were or who had been military officers. Second, little evidence has been forthcoming that military regimes are able to overcome or improve the socioeconomic and political conditions which are so frequently held responsible for their intervention in the first place.[2] Consequently, military

---

[1]Too frequently the Egyptian experience is taken as a standard for evaluation. It is likely, however, that the Egyptian case, a civilianized exception, will prove to be a deviant case for any future generalizations about military rule in the Arab world.

[2]Some quantitative evidence for this position is offered by Nordlinger's (1970: 1146-1147) finding of a mean correlation of -.14 between the "political strength" of the military and seven indicators of economic change for the 1957-1962 period in the Middle East and North Africa. Nordlinger argues that "officer politicians either fail to contribute to economic change or oppose modernizing demands and efforts where these exist."

personnel may have access to the sword, but it is a two-edged sword. Both edges help bring about military coups.

REGIME VULNERABILITY: THE PULL OF THE SYSTEM

A number of analysts stress that governmental institutions subject to coups are weak and therefore vulnerable to the coup. The appearance of circular reasoning notwithstanding, analysts then customarily address the question of why the governmental institutions are weak. Occasionally, attempts are made to clarify why the stronger military sometimes attack the weaker governments. Too often this linkage problem either is assumed or ignored. In any event, these writers have taken several almost sequential paths to date: (1) legacies, (2) the failure of democracy, (3) the filling of the void, (4) the middle-class spear carriers, and (5) the disjointed system. Each sub-theme will be briefly outlined with an almost exclusive emphasis on representative writers on the politics of the Arab military.

Legacies. Most Middle Eastern specialists choose the seventh century as their initial benchmark.[3] In that century, Islam arose as a major belief system and a guiding and "glueing" force for imperial expansion. In order to spread the faith, as well as for acquiring spoils of war, armed force was required. *Jihad* (holy war) was given religious sanction, and the establishment of the Arab empires as world powers can be partially attributed to military superiority. The theory of the caliphate system recognized no distinction between ultimate civilian, military, and religious leadership. In addition, Islamic political theory enhanced the status of the military by entrusting it with the enforcement of God's laws. Glubb (1966a:56) has, as a result, suggested that this theory very early led to the Islamic military identifying themselves as the guardians of community morality. Be that as it may, the general implication is that the military obtained early theological support. Partially as a consequence, the renown of some of the earlier Islamic military figures is greater in the twentieth century than that of several of the Caliphs.

Early Islamic political theory was rarely in accord with practice and by the ninth century, the caliphate system was virtually a system in name only. The failure to institutionalize any acceptable formula for succession, combined with the practice of recruiting military forces from slaves and mercenaries, led to the loss of control by the Abassid Caliphs to their military commanders. The lack of a succession formula resulted in a zero-sum environment for power competition. Successful candidates required strong military backing. What the military had lost in terms of religious sanction was compensated by the gains in actual control, a pattern which seems to have characterized much of the political history of the Islamic world.

The essential argument of this sub-theme is that for the twelve to thirteen centuries prior to contemporary developments, the military have been either closely associated with or have in fact dominated and supplied

---

[3]Representative legacy discussions can be found in the works of Halpern 1963:19-20;251-252); Be'eri (1970:275-285); Glubb (1966a,1966b); and Haddad 1965:11-39).

Muslim rulers. Therefore, it is argued that Arab politics has ample historical precedent for what is regarded as the "modern", but hardly novel, variety of military intervention. Hence, the conditioning and survivals of the past account for contemporary governmental weakness and the lack of tradition for the division of civil-military powers and functions.

The Failure of Democracy. Khadduri's (1953) requiem for Middle Eastern democracy argued that the westernization process had been artificially accelerated in the post-World War I era among a population unprepared for the abstractions of democracy. Western powers were blamed for their ignorance of local conditions and their subsequent haste. Local elites who cooperated with the foreign powers were accused of failing to reconcile their existing institutions with the newly introduced ones. The result was a general lack of respect for the novel ideas, and when it was realized that few reforms were to be forthcoming, democracy shouldered the major blame. When all the various opposition groups had failed to win power, Khadduri concluded that "the army intervened to carry out a moderate program of reform by force." Thus, the army also conveniently satisfied the nostalgic longing for strong regimes inspired by democracy's poor showing. In a similar vein, Glubb (1966a:11, 17 and 1966b:59) has pushed the argument to what this writer considers an extreme by claiming not only that western institutions, particularly the occidental concept of the democratic party, had failed, but that their failure was preordained by the nature of Arab tradition, climate, and national character.[4] Still, if one ignores the nebulous concept of national character, readers are left with the impression that military coups occurred to correct the frustrations and the ineffectiveness of what might be conceived of as a noble institutional experiment.

The Fillers of the Void. In the third theme, the locus of blame was shifted from the shortcomings of democracy to the more concrete failures of institutions and politicians. According to one Middle Eastern analyst (Badeau, 1959:149) the target of repudiation was not necessarily democracy but rather the ineffective organizations, institutions, and politicians of the era.[5] Pre-coup Arab regimes were said to be characterized by traditional elite intransigence, disaffected and educated youths, ineffective parties, abuse of theoretically representative processes, and a fundamental lack of adherence to the rules of the political game. Constitutional rulers imposed by external forces lacked traditional foundations. With the withdrawal of those external forces and the advent of a myriad of political problems, local politicians misunderstood and/or corrupted the new political game rules. Non-politicians, including the army, had no traditional loyalty to either the rules or the politicians. The strength of political parties atrophied, elections were rigged, and the press was controlled. Governmental structures became weak and intra-elite struggles for control intensified. Whatever initial agreement on the rules had existed

---

[4]Apparently, Glubb regards the "Arab character" as one of intense jealousy and quick emotions which lead to frequent intrigues and outbreaks of violence. A more cautious treatment of this problem is offered by al-Qazzaz (1969:45-47).

[5]Other writers on this sub-theme are Rustow (1963:4-5); Campbell (1963: 105-107); Vatikiotis (1961:250); and Sharabi (1966:56-57).

soon evaporated. What was left constituted a "political vacuum," a political system highly susceptible to crisis and stalemate. The situation was summarized by the often invoked Hobbesian phrase: clubs become trump when no rule of trump is established. The armed forces, having remained outside the political system, avoided the stigma of political failure. Lacking any constitutional alternatives, the military entered the vacuum in order to force a popularly desired change of government or in order to save a crisis-ridden political system.

The Middle-Class Spear Carriers. Theorists of political develop-ment (Pye, 1962:75-80) have asserted that in the attempt to establish modern organizations, the creation of modern armies has been the most successful effort and the easiest to achieve. Officers were forced to stand some distance from their own societies and to look abroad for suitable models and standards of behavior and attitudes. Asked to perform roles more commonly found in industrial societies, the officers became more sensitive to the weaknesses of their own systems. In the early sixties Halpern (1963:253-260) advanced the thesis that the more Middle Eastern armies were modernized, the more their very existence constituted a radical criticism of their respective political systems. The frustrations of civilian occupations in the late 1940's, it was argued, prompted educated young men to join the army since it was one of the few expanding and modern bureaucratic organizations. In the process, the new officers were transformed into representatives of a salaried "new middle class." This, in turn, made the military the most powerful instrument of the middle class in its struggle for social reform and nationalism. Thus, one could hardly expect the military to resist the overwhelming temptation to re-move a recalcitrant and traditional ruling elite.

The Disjointed System. For Perlmutter (1969), a modern praetorian state is one in which the military tends to intervene and potentially could dominate the political system.[6] A number of socio-political conditions are viewed as conducive to the development of such system-states: (1) a low degree of social cohesion, (2) the existence of fratricidal classes, (3) a high level of social polarity and a nonconsolidated middle class, (4) a low level of recruitment for group action and for the mobilization of material resources, (5) the development of a gap between center and periphery, (6) a low level of political institutionalization and lack of sustained support for political structures, (7) the presence of weak and ineffective political parties, and (8) frequent civilian intervention in mili-tary affairs. These conditions often appear in the early and middle stages of modernization and political mobilization. Civilian groups faced with these structural conditions, the existence of corruption, the failure to bring about material improvements, and the traditional orientations of most of the population, find themselves incapable of establishing political institutions and structures capable of sustaining the momentum of modern-ization. When the civilian groups fail to legitimize themselves and civi-lian government comes to a standstill in its pursuit of nationalist and

---

[6]A different and in some respects broader view is presented in Perlmutter (1970).

modernist goals, professional soldiers are "propelled into political action."

On Pulls and a Missing Link. Each of the five sub-themes gives the appearance of having been incrementally modified from previously prevailing perspectives. Still, none of the sub-themes really promotes extreme departures from any of its predecessors. The pulls of the past gave way to the failure of liberal democracy. The democratic "experiment" failed because, for reasons of cultural and historical experience, the area was not prepared for the new way of politics. This perspective was shortly altered by emphasizing that the new institutions were too weak to withstand the pressures encountered in the transition from the old to the new. The resulting "vacuum" had to be filled by someone. The army was available and undiscredited. In the late 1950's and early 1960's the availability of the army came to be seen as a potential blessing. The military were believed to possess an organization of advanced development and an officer corps which was predominantly middle class. Therefore it was only logical that the military would become the champions of the middle classes' hopes. The praetorian thesis further advanced the image of regime vulnerability by offering a much more sophisticated version of the "institutional vacuum" and a more complete evaluation of the socio-political factors associated with the praetorian phenomenon.

Despite the modifications, all of the themes share a common explanation of the military coup: weak institutions pull the military into political action. It is difficult to take exception to the notion that governments which are overthrown by coups tend to be vulnerable. But by continually focusing on this point, the precise linkage between regime vulnerability and the military coup is given short shrift. Instead, the overly-pervasive vacuum imagery seemingly dictates the rather weak conclusion that the military are teleologically pulled into the situation to save the day.

There are a number of ways in which to surmount this problem. One might choose to raise questions about the very dubious conceptualization inherent in the terms "vacuum," "stalemate," and "intervention." One might request more specific evidence about the reforms coup-makers are supposed to be pursuing or about the assumed connection between a "new middle class" and the coup-makers. One might ask how much the legacy argument really explains and how unique the legacies really are. Or, one might examine quantitative data on background factors to test the strength of the pulls of the system.[7] But the most informative and direct approach should be to collect data on why the coup-makers apparently attempt to overthrow governments. It is to a consideration of this sort of data that the paper now turns its attention.

---

[7]This last avenue is explored in Thompson (1973a). Regime vulnerability situations, at the global level, are variously but not overwhelmingly associated with (a) a previous history of regime vulnerability, (b) a number of systemic indicators (e.g., levels of economic development, social mobilization, and cultural heterogeneity) which measure background conditions related to the development of alternative regime support relationships, and (c) processes of deterioration in terms of economic welfare, public order, and regime performance.

MILITARY COUP-MAKERS' GRIEVANCES

Since coup-making involves some risks, it appears that coup partici-pants have motives and goals for which they are willing to assume costs ranging from death to demotion. Ideally, one might wish to interview a random sample of the by now large and scattered population of relevant subjects to determine their grievances. Unfortunately, restrictions of time and money and the dubious receptiveness of the prospective interviewees tend to rule out the ideal approach. On the other hand, there are a number of descriptive accounts available for each coup event. While the available information is certainly never complete for any single case, systematically mining these traditionally favored reports for reputed grievance data does provide an alternative course.

In exploring this avenue, Thompson (1973b) viewed military coups as small-scale internal wars fought over scarce positions and resources (see Mack and Snyder, 1957:218). But whose positions and resources? The answer to this question provides a basic handle for categorizing coup-maker grievances. Since military coup-makers are socialized members of a more or less professionalized organization with interests and needs of its "own," corporate grievances are concerned with the position and resource standing of the military organization. But within any organization there are elites, factions, and minority groups with their own positions and resources to protect and advance. Thus, a second category, not-so-corporate grievances, refers to conflicts which are sometimes linked to corporate loyalties but which more acutely reflect the elementary behavior of elites and suborganizational groups engaged in political competition. Finally, military coup-makers are occasionally concerned with the societal distribution of positions and resources. They may seek to preserve or to alter the prevailing distribution. Or they may choose to require other actors to attempt their alterations in an orderly manner. This creates a need for a third category, labelled the "societal residual" for, in fact, few coups tend to fall into this analytical cell.[8]

Corporate Grievances. At least one in every two Arab military coups (1948-1970) involved perceived failures on the part of the regime in satisfying or respecting the military's needs. A military organization tends to surround its established position within the socio-political system with myths and traditions. Perceived infringements of these organizational boundaries are likely to be interpreted as threats to the military's turf. The most common Arab corporate positional grievance deals with the defense of the military's political position. On a continuum ranging from as little direct political participation as possible to the opposite extreme where the armed forces choose to dominate the political system, Arab armies have tended to approach the latter extreme. Civilian attempts to

---

[8]Frequently, coup-makers are only temporarily united in quite often diverse coalitions. Hence, grievance packages can be expected to contain multiple and sometimes conflicting components. Consequently, none of the three major categories need be considered mutually exclusive. Regrettably, space does not permit a detailed consideration of either the methodology or the content of coup-maker grievances. Instead, only the more important features of the 1948-1970 data can be highlighted.

regain some level of political control can bring about protective reactions on the part of the military, particularly if rival military/paramilitary units are created to act as countervailing forces and/or if purges of military personnel are utilized to remove potential sources of opposition. In addition to attacks on such corporate values as autonomy and functional monopoly maintenance, stab-in-the-back syndromes may also develop if the military's sense of honor and prestige is impugned as when non-military groups seek to place the blame for war defeats at the doorstep of the army.

Positional conflicts are frequently intermingled with corporate grie-vances involving three sub-types of resource conflicts: (1) dissatisfaction over pay, promotions, appointments, assignments, and/or retirement policies; (2) dissatisfaction over budget allocations, training facilities, and/or interservice favoritism; and (3) dissatisfaction over general military policy and/or support for military operations such as war and insurgency suppression. Promotions, assignments, and retirement policies are parti-cularly prone to politicization by regimes seeking ways to guarantee military loyalties. Loyal officers may receive the quickest promotions and key assignments. Those of dubious allegiance are apt to be assigned to remote areas, given desk jobs to remove them from effective control of troops, or retired early. Less political and more professional per-sonnel are affronted by these policies. Those men most directly affected by the personnel policies may realize that they must remove the incum-bents before their own political capabilities are stripped.

Not-So-Corporate Grievances. Equally if not more important to an understanding of the Arab military coup is the not-so-corporate dimen-sion which is applicable to about two out of every three Arab coups (1948-1970). Coup-makers have a number of suborganizational — personal, factional, and sectional — interests to pursue as well. Personal interests refer to specific pre-coup events and regime actions which are evidently interpreted by the coup-maker as personal threats to their own political resources and positions. Military organizations, not unlike other bureau-cratic agencies, are also prone to internal "patron-client" sub-sets. Some officers, distinguished by rank, professional distinctions, political connections, ideology, or personal charisma attract the personal loyalties of other officers. In military organizations more directly involved in politics, these cliques are vital to the intra-military political system, especially in terms of career advancement, as well as to the larger political system. In Arab armies, these military factions tend to overlap with ethno-regional or sectional groupings based on the cement of pri-mordial loyalties. Elements of the armed forces may also seek and be sought for alliances with small opposition parties or with the disgruntled wings of a ruling party. Most of the alliances are made with the same few parties. Frequently, the military allies do not share the motivations of their civilian partners, and hence the military-party coalitions are often marriages of convenience. The few parties which do gain power via a coup alliance appear to become dominated eventually by their mili-tary partners either in the name of the party or in the name of the military.

Finally, military coups are particulary good examples of wars fought over the occupancy of political positions. Of course, the removal of regime incumbents is definitionally intrinsic to the coup but there is structurally more to these personnel wars than simply a negative focus on regime incumbents. In the Arab world, the most common "personnel adjustment" process is the coalition reduction type. In this process, coup-makers apparently are attempting to reduce the size of a previously successful coup coalition or to anticipate or to counter the possibility of a reductionist effort. Once the coalition has served its initial purpose, the intra-coalitional struggle for primacy is apt to become acute.

The Societal Residual. In approximately one out of every six Arab coups (1948-1970), the military coup-makers gave the appearance of being strikingly reformist. That is, they seemed to be primarily interested in attempting to correct societal injustices and abuses rather than simply disguising corporate and not-so-corporate grievances with the umbrella of social reform. To some extent, this is a reflection of the regional preeminence of Arab socialism and the associated struggles of Nasirite and anti-Nasirite factions. But while the one in six ratio indicates that "strikingly reformist" coups are proportionately twice as common in the Arab world as they are in the world at large, the relative frequency still does not seem to justify the numerous references to reformist coups in the regime vulnerability literature.[9] The fact remains that in a world which endows reform with great legitimacy, it should not be surprising that coup-makers make the obligatory appeals in their post-coup propaganda. It never hurts to differentiate the winners from the losers by portraying the new regime as a fresh and clean force laboring on behalf of the entire community. To be sure, some reformers may be found in any coup-making group but it is still the earthier corporate/not-so-corporate grievances which provide the missing link between regime vulnerability and the military coup.

THE PUSH/PULL OF EXTERNAL POLITICS

Symbolically, the military are concrete manifestations of the nation-state's independent status. Instrumentally, the military have a special interest in the state's relative capabilities with accompanying interests in the military standing of other states. Furthermore, Arab military elites interact fairly regularly with their counterparts in other Arab states. It is equally significant that nearly one of every two Arab coups involved disputes over the direction of regime foreign policy orientations. An

---

[9]It should be noted that the grievance generalizations discussed in this paper are based on regional aggregations. Several qualifications are worth considering. Iraq and Syria provided roughly half of the number of Arab military coups. Since the grievances of Iraqi and Syrian coups have tended to be more corporate oriented (78% vs. 39%) and less societal oriented (8% vs. 29%) than the coups of other Arab states, some distortion is caused by relying on Arab world generalizations. However, the not-so-corporate dimension is roughly equivalent in the same comparison. It is particularly worth observing that "first coups" demonstrate grievance profiles which are remarkably similar to the grievances of subsequent coups, with one important exception. "First coups" have tended to be much more societal oriented (55% vs. 8%). In this respect, then, Arab "first coups" are significantly different from those which follow.

early preoccupation with Hashemite designs was gradually superseded by conflicts with groups variously seeking the severance of ties, rapprochements, and/or union with Abd al-Nasir's country. All of these considerations would suggest that military elites occupy important positions in regional and global communication networks.

One of the functions of such networks is to transmit and receive various types of political signals. Assured of wide press coverage, military coups are likely message sources. Several consequences are conceivable. Midlarsky's (1970:74-77) "coup diffusion" theory suggests that through a modeling effect, observers copy the behavior exhibited by a prototype in an earlier coup and possibly in another state. Gamal Abd al-Nasir is an obvious candidate for the role of model. It is no exaggeration to state that he was a reference individual for a number of Arab military elites. The Iraqi Free Officer movement, for example, is said to have been inspired and encouraged by the 1952 actions of the Egyptian Free Officers despite the lapse of six years. Libya's Qaddafi and Sudan's Numeiri are only two of a number of younger officers who appear to have been more recently influenced. A reference group or individual may thus tend to pull domestic and regional subsystems in certain directions, in this case for more than a decade and a half.

Even though the modeling effect is probably restricted to especially charismatic individuals, a successful military coup may at least have a basic disinhibitory effect in that it demonstrates the relative ease with which military force can remove an incumbent with little fear of internal or external opposition. Although regime incumbents also receive the same message and presumably seek to de-emphasize its impact, what is important is that the officers who are pre-disposed for whatever reason to intervene are a far more receptive audience for such messages. In line with their own predispositions, the decision to coup may be reinforced by the experience and history of neighboring military coup-makers.

There are other external factors which play roles in the coup calculus. Regime support is not limited to domestic sources. Foreign powers may possess a veto power over military actions in political affairs. Just as regimes claim external support, so do the military coup-makers. The literature is fairly abundant with often oblique references to direct subversion.[10] It is highly probable that outside actors participate in coups by at least facilitating their occurrence in order to further their own goals and interests. While encouraging and fostering coups is less costly than engaging in war, the role of external powers is easily inflated. There is no more need to invent international plots than there is a need for foreign agents to invent military officers interested in seizing power. Foreign military training of Arab officers is another little-studied topic of interest for the analysis of this cluster. Such training may contribute to the incidence of military coups in that it strengthens the military sector and not necessarily the regime, thereby intensifying a civil-military im-

---

[10]For representative treatments, see Copeland (1969) for American involvement in Syria and Egypt, Dann (1969:130-131,169) for Syrian and Egyptian involvement in Iraq, Seale (1965:72) for Iraqi involvement in Syria, and Schmidt (1969:22-28) for Egyptian involvement in Yemen.

balance. Training and aid missions may also be a means for foreign penetration and influence. Trainees may also widen the scope of their reference groups.[11] A final type of exogenous factor is suggested by economic
reliance upon world price fluctuations. Subsequent economic deterioration may diminish the political credit of a regime thus contributing to
its vulnerability. While none of the factors discussed in this section are
necessarily of primary causal importance, they can only be ignored at
the risk of accepting an incomplete explanation. Unfortunately, they have
received little systematic attention to date.

SUMMARY AND SYNTHESIS

Many of our efforts to account for political phenomena are characterized by uncomfortable similarities with the hoary fable of the blind men
groping at different parts of an elephant's anatomy — each man eventually
arriving at different conclusions as to the beast's identity. Explanations of
the military coup have been no exception and not without reason. Ideological and ethnocentric biases as well as the limited availability and reliability of empirical data all conspire to derail the effort. Coup-makers
themselves cannot be expected to fully understand their own actions. And
those actors who know the most are the least likely to publicize their real
intentions. Those very few who do record their sentiments must be read
discriminately. Losers are still fighting old battles and winners have new
battles to avoid. Furthermore, there are a wide range of potential factors and approaches — several of which have been admittedly ignored in
this essay — which scholars can exploit for their explanatory products.
Any generalizations, certainly including those made in this paper, should
then be treated as tentative hypotheses of military behavior in politics
and naturally subject to additional research and confirmation.

Yet, since this paper has examined the coup "elephant" from several
angles, it is appropriate to attempt a synthetic over-view. Figure 1
outlines this paper's perspective on approaches to explaining the military
coup.

At the root of the problem are the military coup-makers striving, like
other political actors, to advance or protect position and resource stand-
ings. The level of perception may be either individual, group/faction,
corporate, societal, or, more likely, some combination of the four levels.
But the focus on grievances does not require the scrapping of the idea of
regime vulnerability. Military coup-makers do not exist in vacuums but
rather in political systems at least nominally regulated by a regime. Where
the demand for the services of the military is great and where the regime
is without or is in the process of losing alternative (to the military) support, the regime will increase its dependency on the military and the
occupancy of the regime's leadership positions will become more tenuous.
Regime vulnerability is further increased and the likelihood that the
positions and resources of military elites will be threatened by regime
leaders struggling for survival will also be enhanced. Regime vulnera-

---

[11]On this subject, Wenner (1967:58) offers an intriguing note on the later political activities of the first Yemeni cadets sent to Baghdad in 1934.

FIGURE 1.   A SYNTHETIC REVIEW

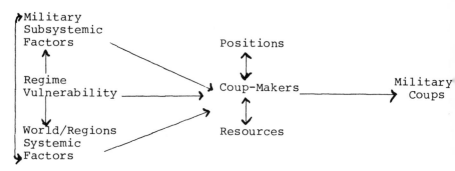

bility, of course, is relative to the organizational strength and cohesion of the military sub-system. At the same time, it is not unusual for intra-military disputes to spill over and escalate into control of the political system. Finally, political systems are neither isolated nor closed. Coup activity in one system may reinforce coup predispositions as well as perceptions of regime vulnerability in other systems. In addition, both the attacks of the coup-makers and the defenses of the regime leadership may be facilitated to varying degrees by interested "external" actors. However, in the Arab world, it is frequently difficult to make firm distinctions between internal and external issues and actors.

The interpretation advanced in this paper provides only the rough tools for the examination of any specific coup case. A focus on general patterns necessarily precludes any attempts to encompass all the nuances and idiosyncracies which have been exhibited in Arab military coup behavior. And while this is assuredly not the last word on the Arab military coup, it is hoped that the perspective outlined here will contribute to the development of more sophisticated explanations, both at the more general level and in terms of single country/coup case studies.

REFERENCES

Badeau, John S.
    1959 "The Revolt Against Democracy." Journal of International Affairs
          13:149-156.
Be'eri, Eleizer
    1970 Army Officers in Arab Politics and Society. New York: Praeger.
Campbell, John C.
    1963 "The Role of the Military in the Middle East: Past Patterns and New
          Directions." Pp. 105-116 in S.N. Fisher (ed.), The Military in the Middle
          East. Columbus: Ohio State University Press.
Copeland, Miles
    1969 The Game of Nations: The Amorality of Power Politics. London: Weiden-
          feld and Nicolson.

Dann, Uriel
    1969   Uraq Under Qassem: A Political History, 1958-1963. New York: Praeger.
Glubb, John B.
    1966a "The Role of the Army in the Traditional Arab State." Pp. 52-60 in
           J.H. Thompson and R.D. Reischauer (eds.), Modernization of the Arab World.
           Princeton: D. Van Nostrand.
    1966b "The Conflict Between Tradition and Modernism in the Role of Muslim
           Armies." Pp. 9-21 in Carl Leiden (ed.), The Conflict of Traditionalism and
           Modernism in the Muslim Middle East. Austin: University of Texas Press.
Haddad, George M.
    1965   Revolutions and Military Rule in the Middle East: The Northern Tier.
           New York: Robert Speller and Sons.
Halpern, Manfred
    1963   The Politics of Social Change in the Middle East and North Africa.
           Princeton: Princeton University Press.
Hurewitz, Jacob B.
    1969   Middle East Politics: The Military Dimension. New York: Praeger.
Janowitz, Morris
    1964   The Military in the Political Development of New Nations: An Essay in
           Comparative Analysis. Chicago: University of Chicago Press.
Khadduri, Majid
    1953   "The Role of the Military in Middle East Politics." American Political
           Science Review 47:511-524.
Mack, Raymond W. and Richard C. Snyder
    1957   "The Analysis of Social Conflict: Toward an Overview and Synthesis."
           Journal of Conflict Resolution 1 (June): 212-248.
Midlarsky, Manus
    1970   "Mathematical Models of Instability and a Theory of Diffusion." Inter-
           national Studies Quarterly 14:60-84.
Nordlinger, Eric A.
    1970   "Soldiers in Mufti: The Impact of Military Rule Upon Economic and Social
           Change in the Non-Western States." American Political Science Review
           64:1131-1148.
Perlmutter, Amos
    1969   "The Praetorian State and the Praetorian Army." Comparative Politics
           3 (April):382-404.
    1970   "The Arab Military Elite." World Politics 22 (January):269-300.
Pye, Lucian W.
    1962   "Armies in the Process of Political Modernization." Pp. 69-89 in J.J.
           Johnson (ed.), The Role of the Military in Under-developed Countries. Prince-
           ton: Princeton University Press.
Al-Qazzaz, Ayad
    1969   "Political Order, Stability and Officers: A Comparative Study of Iraq,
           Syria and Egypt from Independence till June 1967." Middle East Forum
           45:31-50.
Rustow, Dankwart A.
    1963   "The Military in Middle Eastern Society and Politics." Pp. 1-20 in S.N.
           Fisher (ed.), The Military in the Middle East. Columbus: Ohio State University
           Press.
Schmidt, Dana A.
    1968   Yemen, The Unknown War. New York: Holt, Rinehart and Winston.
Seale, Patrick
    1965   The Struggle for Syria: A Study of Post-War Politics, 1945-1958. London:
           Oxford University Press.
Sharabi, Hisham B.
    1966   Nationalism and Revolution in the Arab World. Princeton: D. Van Nostrand.
Thompson, William R.
    1973a Regime Vulnerability and the Military Coup. Unpublished manuscript.

1973b The Grievances of Military Coup-Makers. Beverly Hills: Sage Publications.
Vatikiotis, P.J.
    1961 The Egyptian Army in Politics: Pattern for New Nations? Bloomington:
           Indiana University Press.
Wenner, Manfred W.
    1967 Modern Yemen, 1918-1966. Baltimore: The John Hopkins University Press.

10

DOMESTIC CORRELATES OF MILITARY INTERVENTION IN AFRICAN POLITICS*

ROBERTA E. McKOWN

University of Alberta

The military coup is examined because of its prevalence, its potential international implications, and the possible insights such an examination might provide for developing a comprehensive theoretical framework. The political process in most African states suggests that, a focus on elite political behavior will prove more fruitful than viewing the coup d'état merely as a reaction to economic or other societal conditions. Three dimensions of elite political behavior were analyzed: the ability to govern effectively, intra-elite cohesion, and the position of the military vis-a-vis other coercive forces and the state. Event data collected for elite and "mass" instability and coercion in fourteen countries provided strong evidence for the usefulness of examining elite cohesion per se.

A primary reason for focusing on the military coup d'état is its pervasiveness throughout Africa. Of thirty-two sub-Saharan states, over half have experienced military take-overs and another quarter have had unsuccessful attempts. Only Sierra Leone has seen the military voluntarily return power to civilian politicians and remain on the sidelines. We do not suggest that military take-over and rule is the most common form of political activity but do emphasize its importance and the need for greater understanding of the military coup d'état as a political event.

A second reason is the potential impact on international politics. As yet, the definitive theoretical links between domestic and international instability have not been constructed, certainly not in operational terms. The work in this area was critically appraised in a recent article by Scolnick (1974), although he dealt mainly with the quantitative efforts and did not evaluate Rosenau's (1964; 1969) theoretical work.

Slighted in the early "global" data banks, Africa began to emerge as a quantifiable continent in the 2nd edition of the *World Handbook* (Taylor and Hudson, 1972) and particularly in the work of the Northwestern University *Black Africa* project (Morrison, et al., 1972) and the *Africa* project at Syracuse (McGowan, 1973; McGowan et al., 1972). The earlier (immediate post independence day) tendency of scholars to view the African political scene somewhat uncritically[1] has been replaced by a perhaps equally pessimistic

*The research assistance of Robert E. Kauffman is gratefully acknowledged. Donald G. Morrison, Robert C. Mitchell, Hugh M. Stevenson and John N. Paden of the Northwestern University "African Instability Integration Project" generously allowed the use of their background data.

1. An earlier dissenter from this view was Huntington (1965). Much of this literature is reviewed in my earlier article (McKown and Kauffman, 1973:48-54) and need not be repeated.

appraisal of the prospects for democracy and non-violent politics (see O'Connell, 1965; Zolberg, 1968a).

A comprehensive model or theory of the political process in the Third World generally or Black Africa specifically has not yet been developed although promising work has been done on specific aspects of the process: Nellis (1970) on ideology, Stallings (1972), Green and Seidman (1968), among many others, on economics, Melson and Wolpe (1970) and Bates (1974) on ethnic competition, Morrison and Stevenson (1972a), Ake (1967) and Mazrui (1972) on integration, and Morrison and Stevenson (1972b) on instability.

A final reason for examining the coup d'état, then, is for the insights it can provide for a theoretical framework for the study of Sub-Saharan African politics. The focus on Africa minimizes the potentially obscuring differences in cultural and historical background, gross disparities of size, level of industrialization, or the like, that too often emerge as the major results of factor analysis of the characteristics of *all* nations. This is intended not as a blanket criticism of that research technique but as agreement with those who suggest that progress in comparative theory is more likely to result from attacks on the famous "middle-range" problem rather than from more grand theorizing. A brief summary of the political process in African states is a necessary preface to the theoretical and statistical analysis of the coup d'état.

THE POLITICAL PROCESS IN AFRICA

If we exclude the remaining white-dominated regimes and colonial dependencies, Sub-Saharan Africa is a relatively homogeneous set of political systems. All have experienced about fifteen years of independence following something like three-quarters of a century of imposed colonial administrative–bureaucratic systems with some continuation of traditional systems. Some have singled out this "administrative-traditional" political process during the colonial era, and what seems to be an attempt to return to some version of it by reversing the populist-oriented participatory politics of the independence period, as a primary reason for the high incidence of coups (Feit, 1968). Kautsky (1964) suggested that military rule was the modal form rather than the exception in pre-colonial societies. This is a tempting answer, the historic political culture reviving and reasserting its sway, but it is at once too "mechanistic" and it ignores the important experience of the colonial period. This did have an impact on styles of life and ways of thinking for those who now provide the leadership, civilian or military, in these states. The colonels and generals who seized power today or last year are not the warrior-chiefs of a century ago. Some (Janowitz, 1964; Pye, 1966) have argued persuasively for the essentially modern (i.e. technical, achievement-oriented) outlook of the military. The politicians they replace used the rediscovered 'glorious past' only as a temporary societal cement for the present and future; the general in office is similarly uninterested in actually reviving the past.

The nature of present society, with its mix of "bush" and modern, seems more important for an understanding of contemporary politics than does the form or substance of pre-colonial political structures. Although the latter may still be important to a few, these are neither the men who hold political power nor those who try to take it from them, particularly as publics in these states largely remain on the fringes of the political process[2] because of low levels of

---

2. *Black Africa* reported, for the "number of voters voting in the election prior to independence, as a percentage of population" in the fourteen countries in the event sample, an average figure of 24 percent. This reflected a variation from 1 percent for Tanzania to 51 percent for Cameroon.

literacy, heavy reliance upon subsistence agriculture, and underdevelopment of transport and communications systems. The penetration of the government into daily lives, particularly in rural areas, whether to extract, regulate, mediate, or benefit is often superficial. Loyalties frequently remain at subnational levels with little awareness of politicians and public issues. The apparent indifference which greets the overthrow of supposedly charismatic leaders is one indicator of this lack of national awareness and loyalty. It is not that attentive publics see no difference between the various elites who may wield power, or feel no impact upon their lives and fortunes from various policies; the important thing is that politics in Africa is most usefully viewed as an elite activity, despite facades of mass party organizations, rallies, and high turn-outs at the occasional election (Zolberg, 1966; Bretton, 1973).

The uniformity of the justifications advanced by successful military usurpers of political power — saving the country from corruption, potential tyranny, economic and social chaos, and/or stagnation — also suggests the utility of broad generalizations concerning the nature of political and social problems. On the other hand, the lack of uniformity in societal, economic or general political conditions in countries which have experienced a coup d'état versus those which have not cautions against a too ready acceptance of "preconditions" models. Decalo (1973), in an excellent review of current theorizing and research on this topic, calls into question the conventional wisdom regarding the coup phenomenon as a reactive one (to social conditions) and directs our thinking and theorizing toward a view of the military as an active element in the political equation. Zolberg (1968a; 1968b) and Welch (1970) have suggested much the same focus.

POLITICAL ELITE BEHAVIOR

A major reason for the continuing importance of elites is the recentness of independence and their role in attaining it. The independence movements were the work of a select few—the emerging middle class and/or the intellectuals (Shils, 1960). Many of these first-generation elites are still in positions of leadership or have been replaced by others from the same small group. Those designated as "national elites" form a minuscule percentage of the total population, compared not only to western nations but to other non-western areas (Lloyd, 1966; Raser, 1966). The private economic sector is largely nascent. The contrast with the developed world is summed up in the observation that in the West one enters politics because of one's social and economic status; in the developing world, one enters politics in order to attain economic and social status. This was the understanding behind Nkrumah's famous dictum to "Seek ye first the political kingdom".

The military in these countries (the officers, not the foot-soldiers) is part of the elite. In education and training, in modern versus traditional attitudes, even in pay, but certainly in terms of present or potential political roles, they belong with the prime ministers, the intellectuals and the civil service. Their role in the political process prior to active intervention on their own behalf is also important. Zolberg notes the decline in political power and legitimacy as problems go unsolved and self-imposed goals unmet. This is not only in terms of publics vis-a-vis elites but within the elite itself. This decline is followed by what Chalmers Johnson has called a "power inflation", the necessary application of more and more force in order to obtain the same amount of compliance (Zolberg, 1968a:77).

There are difficulties in operationalizing an elite approach to politics, since elites are generally reluctant to provide extensive attitudinal data. However, used with caution, one may employ selected aggregate indicators to test possible hypotheses related to elite interactions.

There are three dimensions of political elite behavior that are important in our analysis. The first is, broadly, their ability to govern effectively. This involves not only the capability to extract resources from the political system but also the ability to maintain oneself in power. The second dimension is that of intra-elite cohesion. We hypothesize some probable behavioral manifestations of intra-elite conflict, as well as indicators of the particular governing elite's ability to discipline its dissident members, to prevent a "breaking of the ranks".

The final dimension is the role of the military and its position vis-a-vis other force institutions. This is actually only an analytically distinct factor, for if a civilian political elite can keep its military either under adequate control, counter-balanced to prevent a bid for power, or sufficiently "happy" with modern equipment, it has demonstrated an important ability to maintain itself in office. Each of these dimensions will be examined in greater detail below and hypotheses made explicit.

The sample of twenty-five countries was categorized, as of the end of 1969, as follows.[3] No coup d'état: Cameroon, Chad, Gambia, Guinea, Kenya, Malawi, Mauritania, Niger, Tanzania (mainland only), Uganda and Zambia. Although some may question the inclusion of the three East African states in this category, the analysis of Bienen (1968) makes it difficult to see the 1964 mutinies as other than strikes by uniformed personnel. The Ugandan intervention on behalf of the regime in 1966 similarly does not qualify as a coup, although on different grounds. Unsuccessful coup d'état: Ethiopia, Gabon, Ivory Coast, Liberia, Senegal. (Again, it is admitted that Senegal and Ivory Coast are contentious inclusions.) Successful coup d'état: Central African Republic, Congo (Brazzaville), Dahomey, Ghana, Mali, Sierra Leone, Somali, Togo, Upper Volta. While the categorization of Uganda, Ethiopia and Niger has changed since the research was carried out, both that data and the *Black Africa* figures are current only to the end of the sixties and it did not seem wise to try to 'stretch' them to the present. The drought in Ethiopia, an important catalyst of that coup, would not show up in the national account figures of 1969.

Elite Capability. The ability of political authorities to meet societal needs, cope with new and continuing problems arising from the domestic and international environment, or maintain sufficient domestic order is too often in the literature assessed using negative and *ex post facto* measures. That is, it is assumed that a set of governing officials who are turned out of office by means of force and violence have in some sense demonstrated a high level of incompetence and hence those who retain office are competent. This is conceptually inadequate but is implicit in statistical analyses that use only instability as a measure of system performance. Few research efforts attempt

---

3. The use of the Northwestern variables is indicated as derived from "Black Africa". Their sample of 32 countries was reduced to 25 by excluding those which had suffered severe internal war, thus putting them beyond the relevant point on our instability continuum, and the two former high commission territories in their sample, which were deemed too dependent upon South Africa to be considered truly independent. The coercion and instability data presented in the figures was collected by an advanced undergraduate and graduate student class in the fall of 1969.

to devise measures of elite capability that can be applied before the coup d'etat occurs.

Our first concern is with the performance of the economy, with the provision of essential educational services by government, and similar considerations. Grouped under "structural correlates" are three types of measures.[4] Some are frequently utilized as measures of societal welfare or of social mobilization and have, in other studies, emerged as the most important determinants of societal instability. This may reflect better the relegation of politics to the status of dependent variable than the theoretical power of these available independent variables.

Stepwise regression, using only variables with the highest simple correlations, produced mixed results. The best economic variable, "number of industrial types possible by 1980", had a moderately strong negative correlation with the Black African military intervention variable, suggesting it was inversely related to economic development potential. This was reinforced by the correlation with "percentage of labor force in subsistence agriculture" but contradicted by a positive correlation with per capita GNP in 1966. The three best educational measures also had negative correlations, reinforcing the finding that military intervention was associated with lower rather than higher levels of socio-economic development. Two of the social mobilization measures, urbanization and rates of change in newspaper circulation during 1960-64, resisted this general trend with positive correlations. When all the "best" structural variables were entered in a single regression equation, the results were as in Table 1. The combined variables still suggest divergent theses concerning development and instability, and account for not quite half of the variation in the dependent variable.

TABLE 1:   STRUCTURAL CORRELATES

OF MILITARY INTERVENTION *

	Multiple r
Percent of population in cities of 20,000	.38071
Change in newspaper circulation, 1960-64	.50516
Change in primary enrollment, pre to post independence	.62834
% labor in subsistence agriculture	.69056
	$r^2 =$ .47688

Data Source: Northwestern University "Black Africa" project
* All variables run from less to more, unless otherwise indicated. The military intervention variable was coded 1= no interventions, 2= unsuccessful attempt, 3= successful military coup d'etat.

4. The 112 variables with their Kendall Tau β correlation with the composite military intervention variable (no intervention, unsuccessful attempt, successful military coup d'état) is available from the author on request. Only those variables that "worked" the best are included in the stepwise multiple regressions reported in subsequent tables.

Further explanatory factors were sought in the actual operation of political systems in their extractive and disbursement functions. Failure in this area is a common rationale advanced by the military for intervention. Measures of several aspects of fiscal performance are shown in Table 2. Again, the results are mixed. The relationship between military intervention and increasing direct taxes, government revenue and spending relative to GNP (or per capita or rate of change) is clear; so, unfortunately, is the contrary relationship between lower levels of government revenue or per capita budget and higher levels of military intervention.

TABLE 2:   GOVERNMENTAL PERFORMANCE

AND MILITARY INTERVENTION

	Multiple r
Direct taxes as a percent of total governmental revenue, 1966	0.29758
*Central Government revenue, 1966	0.49940
Government spending as a percent of GNP, 1961	0.59118
*Per capita central government budget, 1961	0.62422
Government spending, per capita, 1966	0.64767
Government revenue, percent rate of growth, 1963 to 1966	0.65461
Government revenue as a percent of GNP, 1966	0.65982
	$r^2 =$ .43536

Data Source: Northwestern University "Black Africa" project.
*Simple correlation with dependent variable was negative.

Finally, there is the ability of a governing elite to cope with its citizens. This can be done either by satisfying all reasonable demands (measurable by societal welfare indices) or by applying sufficient coercive force to contain unreasonable demands, or both, as is normal.

Elite Cohesion. There are a number of questions involved for which the data collected for fourteen states provides provisional answers.[5] Both coercive events (actions taken by the government and directed against individuals or groups) and instability events (actions by people or groups against the

5. Sources used included *The Times* (London), *West Africa, Africa Report, Africa Diary,* and *Africa Confidential* as well as extensive reading in monograph and periodical literature.

government), were subdivided into those which could easily be attributed to or directed at elites and those which did not as readily fall into this category.[6]

Figure 1 presents profiles for three of the four countries in the smaller event sample which had successful military coups during the period to 1969. (Mali is excluded because of the paucity of data, particularly on coercive events.) The first question is whether the activity of "publics" (as opposed to elites) really matters. Figure 1 suggests an answer: "probably not". Elite-public profiles for the first three non-intervention states in Figure 2, Uganda, Chad, and Tanzania, indicate that the situation was fairly similar in those states.[7] In both categories of countries, it does not appear to be terribly important whether "mass" instability is or is not being contained by prompt and effective governmental coercion. The major difference between the two sets of profiles (only elite events are presented for the remaining seven countries) is that in the countries with military intervention, elite instability tended to be greater than coercion by government whereas the opposite was more likely in those countries with no intervention. Gabon is the major exception to this rule and in that country a temporarily successful coup d'état in 1964 was nullified by French military intervention. We thus have some evidence that political elites are directing their attention to their own group, as posing the more serious threat, rather than being overly concerned with manifestations of discontent among the public at large. We may also conclude that there is a generally low level of political activity in any and all of these countries.

This analysis indicates the importance of examining elite behavior. The theses regarding the relationship of elites to military intervention may be restated more explicitly: the tendency of the military elite to intervene in politics will be a negative function of the incumbent elite's ability to build and maintain an adequate political coalition. The earlier discussion of the African political process emphasized the smallness of that part of the population that could be designated as elite. The literature further emphasizes the similarities in educational backgrounds of these individuals and we would emphasize the point that the underdeveloped state of the private industrial or business sector precludes much employment opportunity outside of government for the well-educated. An educated and modern (or development-oriented) individual cannot escape from continual awareness of the political system even though he might wish to. For many the confrontation between the real and the idealized political process is easily accepted and adjusted to; others, however, never quite

---

6. Elite Instability events: resignations or appointments of politically significant people, fall of a cabinet, organization of a new or reshuffle of an old government, organization of an opposition party, suicide, assassination, and attempted coup d'état. Elite Coercive events: dissolution of the legislature, dismissal, exile or arrest of politically significant persons. Public Instability events: elections or plebiscites, significant change of laws, severe trouble within a non-governmental organization, strikes, demonstrations, boycotts, riots, terrorism, sabotage. Public Coercive events: governmental action against specific groups, arrest of non-significant persons, imposition of martial law and executions. The graphed data represent not numbers of events per year but the additive intensity of violence score for all events of each class (see Feierabend and Feierabend, 1966). An assumption is made that all events may be ranked according to a zero-to-six scale (least to most), depending upon the degree of violence of each. Since low-key events (such as minor cabinet shuffles or peaceful elections) were usually rated as "0", the use of the F-F-N scale helps to eliminate distortions in profiles that might result in only raw numbers of events were used.

7. The F-F-N scale score for a successful coup d'état was, in each instance, deducted from the instability score for the year in which it occurred; unsuccessful coups, however, are included as part of the appropriate yearly score.

Figure I

Coercive & Instability Events, Countries with Coup D'États, 1961-1969

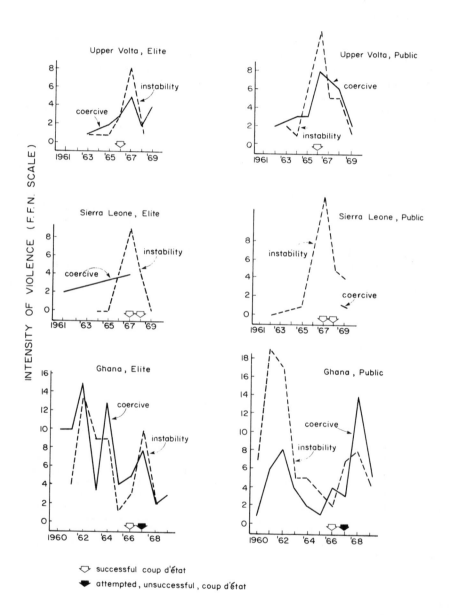

⬓ successful coup d'état

⬧ attempted, unsuccessful, coup d'état

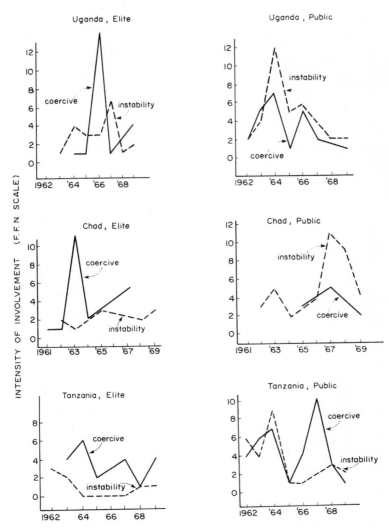

Figure 2

Coercion & Instability Events, Selected
Without Military Intervention, 1961-'69

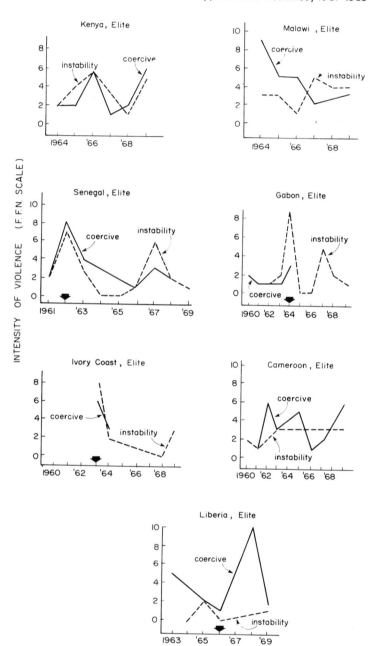

Figure 2 (continued)

Elite Coercion & Instability, Selected Countries, 1961-1969

manage it. A "return to the bush" is generally out of the question; they must remain either in active physical involvement in the political system or in acute awareness of it, and, most usually, both (Schwartz, 1973).

That political leadership in some of these states has been less inept than in others at maintaining control of dissenting cohorts, and in buying off brash young idealists with good jobs and the perquisites thereof is obvious. Rather more interesting is an examination of some of the ways in which this is accomplished. Huntington's discussion (1968) of the need to create "political order" is as easily operationalized as any competing hypothesis, particularly as we wish to focus upon elites. He suggests institutionalization of political structures as the necessary first step. I have elsewhere considered the role of party systems in African politics and found it was "not necessarily useful (as an analytic concept) in the attempt to understand political, social or economic change" (McKown and Kauffman, 1973:68). Other "institutionalization" variables gave mixed results although perhaps, on balance, supporting Huntington's thesis. There were negative correlations with the number of voters in an election prior to independence as a percentage of population with the ratio of civil servants to the number of wage earners, and with the number of party splits and mergers from 1957 to 1967; there were positive correlations with the percentage of votes cast for the ruling party prior to independence and the years from the founding of the first political party to 1967. The total variance accounted for by all these variables was, however, only 36%. (See also Hakes, 1973.)

The Military as Political Elites. This final dimension concerns variables reflecting the position of the armed forces within the political structure. The literature is replete with hypotheses linking military intervention to a variety of factors (see Decalo, 1973:108-115). The provisional hypothesis taken here is Zolberg's thesis that those who must apply force to maintain(inflated) power in office are likely to question the legitimacy of that power. There are some problems with this, however. It must be noted that the military itself does little of the actual applying of force in the course of domestic politics; arrests are generally made by the police or by internal security forces. Urban instability such as strikes or demonstrations tend also to be in the sphere of police action yet police forces do not usually initiate coups d'état (Ghana in 1966 and Zanzibar in 1964 are exceptions). The army may be involved in domestic politics when demonstrations turn into riots, when secessionist movements threaten to escalate into guerrilla war (Kenya, Chad, Ethiopia, Zaire) or civil war (Zaire, Nigeria), or when power struggles threaten to degenerate into ethnic conflict (Uganda, 1966). By and large, however, African armies spend most of their time doing what armies everywhere do — drilling, maneuvering, and other practicing of martial skills.

The variables that correlated best with military intervention are shown in Table 3. An unanticipated result is the rather minimal extent (22% of the variance) to which no intervention, unsuccessful intervention, and successful intervention are explained. The first and last measures may be taken as temporary ones. If the officer corps had not been Africanized, the possibility of a coup would have been diminished. This is scarcely surprising; expatriate officers are simply not likely to lead a coup attempt and their presence probably acts as a deterrent to local officers (the *Force Publique* mutiny in 1960 is not an exception). Similarly, ex-colonial power retention of military bases is a restraining factor. The other two variables are more promising. A lower rate of

TABLE 3:   MILITARY VARIABLES AND

MILITARY INTERVENTION

	Multiple r
*Existence of former metropole military bases, 1964	.26773
*Percentage change in total armed forces, 1963 to 1967	.34286
*Total defense budget, 1967	.39811
Africanization of the army officer corps at Independence	.46922
	r^2= .22017

Data Source: Northwestern University "Black Africa" project.
* Simple correlation with dependent variable is negative.

change in size of armed forces and a smaller total defense spending level are associated with higher levels of intervention. This could be interpreted as a defensive reaction by the military to a perception that they are undervalued by politicians. The explanatory power of the variables, however, is not high enough for this to be more than suggestive.

Some relationship between internal security forces vis-a-vis the regular armed forces and military intervention was expected. The creation of a countervailing institution of force seems a reasonable and rational tactic for political leaders with a nervous eye on their generals and colonels. This sort of independent variable produced minimal correlations with military intervention. Yet, this relationship has been held responsible for the timing of many coups and perhaps the incidence of some (Decalo, 1973; First, 1970; Welch, 1970). Finally, two types of external influence may be considered. Of the variables related to military aid, only "the existence of former metropole military bases, 1964" was moderately discriminatory. Data relating to several aspects of general foreign aid did, however, produce interesting results and are presented in Table 4. The last three variables are negatively correlated, again providing some evidence that those countries with fewer economic resources are more likely to have military intervention.

CONCLUSIONS

The best advice that one could offer to African politicians who would like to serve out their alloted term of office peacefully is, (a) do not have an army, a solution chosen so far only by Gambia, Swaziland, Botswana and Lesotho, (b) retain a visible military presence from the former colonial power, and (c) allow the military to feel appreciated and rewarded by increasing its size and budget. The third tactic, of course, has its own risks and the second course would leave

TABLE 4:   FOREIGN AID, FOREIGN TRADE,

AND MILITARY INTERVENTION

	Multiple r
United States aid as a percent of U.S. aid to Africa, 1964	.40694
*Per capita aid from ex-metropole, 1963	.48343
*Per capita aid from ex-metropole, 1961	.59265
*Percentage change in U.S. aid per capita, 1962-1966	.61283
	$r^2=$ .37556

Data Source: Northwestern University "Black Africa" project.
*Negative simple correlation with the dependent variable.

the politician open to charges of being a neo-colonial stooge, a tool of the imperialists, etc. It is not an easy choice; for many nations the second option has been foreclosed by events, and rumors of the first (as a serious policy choice) would probably result in an immediate coup d'état.

Societal conditions (as economic or social indices) do not seem to be an important determinant of this form of political instability. Given the nature of the phenomenon examined, such a conclusion is perhaps inevitable. None-theless, our exercise is essential if only because so many social scientists have suggested that some other conclusion is equally inevitable. My own working hypothesis is that the coup d'état is an elite event pure and simple, that its sources must be found within the behavior and motivations of the elites and aspiring elites. Politics is an oligarchical activity in these states; it is within the small group who play the game that we must look for explanations.

To sum up the statistical analysis, and to give greater focus to the theoretical implications of the paper, the best discriminating variable from each of the previous tables (and the analyses reported without accompanying tables) were combined in a final step-wise regression. These eight variables (the "U.S. aid to Africa" fell below the critical partial value) account for slightly over sixty per cent of the variation in the incidence of military intervention. Although the results appear somewhat disjointed, closer inspection suggests a pattern of increasing political rigidity leading to the attempt, by dissident elites, to break through by way of a coup d'état. The life span of a party may not only spell institutionalization, it may also spell ossification. If the latter, new recruits to the party or to government service are confronted with a relatively entrenched and unyielding political elite. If competition within the party is stifled, if the possibility of effecting political change through legal channels seems remote, then the prospect of effecting change via the quick, relatively bloodless, coup d'état becomes appealing. It should be noticed that this apparent rigidity in the political sphere is

TABLE 5:   CORRELATES OF MILITARY

INTERVENTION

	Multiple r
Number of years from date of founding of the first political party to 1967	.43877
Percent of the population in cities of more than 20,000 inhabitants, 1965	.59430
Percent of labor force engaged in subsistence agriculture	.66477
Direct taxes as a percent of total government revenue, 1966	.72099
*Total number of political party splits and mergers, 1957 to 1967	.74551
*Existence of former metropole bases, 1964	.76610
Armed forces per 100,000 population, 1967	.78392
*Percent change in total armed forces, 1963 to 1967	.78440

$$r^2 = .61529$$

Data Source: Northwestern University "Black Africa" project.
*Indicates a negative simple correlation with the dependent variable.

accompanied by changes in the society — particularly a strong shift from rural to urban residence and probably an increase in the wage-earning sector of the economy (as measured by the change in direct taxes).

The intervening variable we need for more comprehensive analysis would measure the coercive ability of the government. Armed forces are only a partial measure of that ability. Yet some measure must be found of the level of force, and the willingness to use it, that so often seems to stand between an expanding society and economy, and a static political system. The method employed to derive the results in Figures 1 and 2 suggest the analytic potential of this approach. The measurement of coercive and instability events at the elite and public ("mass") levels added an important dimension to the explanation of coups d'état and we suggest that it is equally promising as a predictive variable. Future research should focus on this factor, coercive ability and potential, as the next stage in analysis of the African political process.

REFERENCES

Ake, Claude
        1967   A Theory of Political Integration. Homewood, Illinois: Dorsey Press.
Bates, Robert H.
        1974   "Ethnic Competition and Modernization in Contemporary Africa". Comparative Political Studies. 6 (January):457-484.

Bienen, Henry
    1968   "Public Order and the Military in Africa: Mutinies in Kenya, Uganda, and Tanganyika". Pp. 35-70 in Henry Bienen (ed.) The Military Intervenes: Case Studies in Political Development. New York: Russell Sage Foundation.

Bretton, Henry L.
    1973   Power and Politics in Africa. Chicago: Aldine Publishing Co.

Decalo, Samuel
    1973   "Military Coups and Military Regimes in Africa". Journal of Modern African Studies, 11: 1:105-127.

Feierabend, Ivo K. and Rosalind L. Feierabend
    1966   "The Relationship of Systemic Frustration, Political Coercion, International Tension and Political Instability: A Cross-National Study". Paper presented to American Psychological Association. New York (September).

Feit, Edward
    1968   "Military Coups and Political Development: Some Lessons from Ghana and Nigeria". World Politics, 20 (January): 179-193.

First, Ruth
    1970   The Barrel of the Gun. Harmondsworth: Penguin.

Green, Reginald H. and Ann Seidman
    1968   Unity or Poverty? The Economics of Pan Africanism. Harmondworth: Penguin.

Hakes, Jay E.
    1973   "Weak Parliaments and Military Coups in Africa: A Study in Regime Instability". Sage Research Papers in the Social Sciences (Comparative Legislative Studies Series, No. 90-004). Beverly Hills and London: Sage Publications.

Huntington, Samuel P.
    1965   "Political Development and Political Decay". World Politics 18 (April):386-430.
    1968   Political Order in Changing Societies. New Haven: Yale University Press.

Janowitz, Morris
    1964   The Military in the Political Development of New Nations. Chicago: The University of Chicago Press.

Kautsky, John H.
    1964   "The Military in Underdeveloped Countries". Economic Development and Cultural Change 12 (July): 436-443.

Lloyd, P.C. (ed.)
    1966   The New Elites of Tropical Africa. London: Oxford University Press for the International African Institute.

McGowan, Patrick J. and Robert I. Lewis
    1973   "Culture and Foreign Policy Behaviour in Black Africa: An Exploratory, Comparative Study". Paper presented to the American Political Science Association New Orleans (September).

McGowan, P.J., J.G. Kean and R. Morje
    1972   "A Manual and Codebook for the Identification, Abstraction, and Coding of Foreign Policy Acts". Syracuse:AFRICA Project Research Report Number 1.

McKown, Roberta E. and Robert E. Kauffman
    1973   "Party System as a Comparative Analytic Concept in African Politics". Comparative Politics 6: (October):47-72.

Mazrui, Ali A.
    1972   Cultural Engineering and Nation-Building in East Africa. Evanston: Northwestern University Press.

Melson, Robert and Howard Wolpe
    1970   "Modernization and the Politics of Communalism: A Theoretical Perspective". The American Political Science Review 64 (December):1112-1130.

Morrison, D.G. and H.M. Stevenson
    1972a   "Integration and Instability: Patterns of African Political Development". The American Political Science Review 66 (September):902-927.
    1972b   "Political Instability in Independent Black Africa: More Dimensions of Conflict Behaviour Within Nations". The Journal of Conflict Resolution 15 (September):347-368.

Morrison, D.G., R.C. Mitchell, J.H. Paden and H.M. Stevenson
    1972   Black Africa: A Handbook for Comparative Analysis. New York: The Free Press.

Nellis, John R.
    1970   "A Model of Developmental Ideology in Africa: Structure and Implications". Sage
              Professional Papers (Comparative Politics Series, No. 01-007). Beverly Hills and
              London: Sage Publications.
O'Connell, James
    1967   "The Inevitability of Instability". The Journal of Modern African Studies 5
              (September):181-192.
Pye, Lucian
    1966   "Armies in the Process of Political Development", Aspects of Political Development.
              Boston: Little, Brown and Co.
Raser, John R.
    1966   "Personal Characteristics of Political Decision-Makers: A Literature Review".
              Philadelphia: Peace Research Society Papers, 5.
Rosenau, James
    1964   International Aspects of Civil Strife. Princeton: Princeton University Press.
    1969   Linkage Politics. New York: The Free Press.
Schwartz, David
    1973   Political Alienation and Political Behavior. Chicago: Aldine Publishing Co.
Scolnick, Joseph M. Jr.
    1974   "An Appraisal of Studies of the Linkage between Domestic and International
              Conflict". Comparative Political Studies 6 (January):485-509.
Shils, Edward
    1960   "The Intellectuals in the Political Development of New States". World Politics 12
              (April):329-368.
Stallings, Barbara
    1972   "Economic Dependency in Africa and Latin America". Sage Professional Papers
              (Comparative Politics Series, No. 01-031). Beverly Hills and London: Sage
              Publications.
Taylor, Charles Lewis and Michael C. Hudson
    1972   World Handbook of Political and Social Indicators, 2nd edition. New Haven: Yale
              University Press.
Welch, Claude E.
    1970   "The Roots and Implications of Military Intervention". Pp. 1-59 in Claude E. Welch
              (ed.) Soldier and State in Africa. Evanston: Northwestern University Press.
Zolberg, Aristide R.
    1966   Creating Political Order: The Party States of West Africa. Chicago: Rand McNally.
    1968a   "The Structure of Political Conflict in the New States of Tropical Africa". American
              Political Science Review 62 (March):70-87.
    1968b   "Military Interventions in the New States of Tropical Africa: Elements of Comparative
              Analysis". Pp. 71-98 in Henry Bienen (ed.) The Military Intervenes. New York: Russell
              Sage Foundation.

National Studies

11

CONVERGENCE, ISOMORPHISM, AND INTERDEPENDENCE AT THE CIVIL-MILITARY INTERFACE*

DAVID R. SEGAL, JOHN BLAIR

University of Maryland

FRANK NEWPORT

University of Missouri

SUSAN STEPHENS

University of Indiana

The literature of military sociology dealing with the convergence of civilian and military institutions in modern society asserts that although structural isomorphism may never be attained, the trend is in that direction. It further asserts that this hypothesized convergence is characterized by a breaking-down of the boundary between the civil and the military. We suggest that particularly in an era of all volunteer armed forces, which is the emerging pattern in the industrial nations of the west, the trend is no longer toward convergence and may be one of divergence. Convergence can be seen as making the military functionally independent of its host society and insulated from it, whereas the enforcement of more specifically military definitions of the armed services force them to maintain open boundaries and enter into exchange relationships with their host society. Data relating to the military family, occupational structure, and research management are presented as examples of empirical approaches to the convergence phenomenon.

The relationship between civilian and military institutions in industrial societies has long been of interest to sociologists. The military sociology of the 1960's stressed the increasing similarity of military and civilian sectors of American society. Thus, Janowitz (1965:17) argued that "to analyze the contemporary military establishment as a social system, it is . . . necessary to assume that for some time it has tended to display more and more of the characteristics typical of any large-scale nonmilitary bureaucracy." At the same time, however, there was a recognition that common technologies, leading to common organizational forms, could not lead to total elimination of the fundamental difference between that which is military and that which is civilian.

Although stressing the increasingly similar occupational structures of civilian and military sectors (see Lang, 1964:45) and postulating that on

---

* An earlier version of this paper was presented at the annual meeting of the International Studies Association, New York, March 16, 1973. We are indebted to Jerzy Wiatr and Charles C. Moskos, Jr., for their comments at that time. The views presented in this paper do not necessarily reflect those of the Army Research Institute or of the University of Michigan.

the basis of these similarities civilian and military organizational forms must converge as well (see Grusky, 1964:84), military sociology has not asserted that total convergence would be achieved at some point, or that structural isomorphism would be achieved. Rather, the convergence function has been conceived, at most, as an asymptotic one, with military and civilian structures becoming increasingly similar, but failing to reach a point of intersection. (Segal and Segal, 1971; Segal, 1972). Other scholars in fact see the function describing civil-military convergence as tangential rather than asymptotic. Moskos (1970:170), for example, suggested that "the over-two-decade-long institutional convergence of the armed forces and American society is beginning to reverse itself . . . (and) that the military in the post-Vietnam period will increasingly diverge along a variety of dimensions from the mainstream of developments in the general society". A third position posits limits on the asymptotic function, implying that rather than constantly converging under the force of technological development, military and civilian organizational forms will reach a point prior to intersection at which further convergence will be precluded by the basic distinction between the military and the civilian. Thus, pointing out that even in highly technological warfare, conventional military units and the traditional military role must be maintained, and that in an age of deterrence the management of violence is still the prime military mission, Janowitz (1971:21) argues that "the narrowing distinction between military and nonmilitary bureaucracies can never result in the elimination of fundamental organizational differences." Most recently, Moskos (1973) has suggested that the military may at the same time be convergent with and divergent from civilian society depending on the empirical indicators used — a model that he labels "segmented" or "plural". Divergence will be most apparent in combat arms, he suggests, and convergence in technical support agencies. We shall propose below an alternative framework for viewing the convergence problem.

THE TWO FACES OF CONVERGENCE

It must be noted at the outset that scholars concerned with the convergence phenomenon differ not only in the degree to which they see convergence occurring but also in their projections of what the social system would look like if convergence were in fact to take place. The major area of disagreement is on whether the civil or the military will dominate the merged structure. Two opposing positions are apparent here. On the one hand, Lasswell's garrison-state hypothesis, which was the first major projection of civil-military convergence in modern American social science, sees the development of new military technologies that make the risk of being a civilian in wartime almost as great as that of being a military man; these technologies lead to a merged civil-military social structure dominated by military men in pursuit of military objectives (see Lasswell, 1962). On the other hand, the argument is made that contrary to Lasswell's position, the convergence that has taken place thus far has led not to a militarization of civilian institutions but rather to a civilianization of the military institutions (Biderman and Sharp, 1968:397). It seems premature at this point to assert that one or the other of these positions is correct. Such a decision presumes that convergence has already been demonstrated. However, the convergence phenomenon today has the status of an interesting hypothesis in military sociology, not that of an assumption. We shall therefore be concerned here simply with the horse, and leave the cart for another occasion, remaining mindful that if convergence is demonstrated, it cannot be interpreted either as a demonstration of civil ascendency over the military or vice versa without additional analysis.

MODELS OF CONVERGENCE

The study of civil-military convergence is burdened by both conceptual and operational ambiguity. Two scholars using the term convergence may well mean very different things, and a third, interested in the reciprocal interpenetration of the civil and the military, might be referring to either of the first two phenomena, or to some third process altogether. And two scholars who use the same term and mean the same thing by it may nonetheless come to different conclusions if one studies formal organizational properties and the other occupational distributions in the two sectors.

At the conceptual level, two different types of relationships between the civil and the military need to be specified. It is necessary to distinguish the *structural convergence* of civilian and military institutions from the *interdependence* of these institutions. It is proposed that these two aspects of the convergence phenomenon are negatively correlated with each other. Assuming that there is some set of functional requirements that must be fulfilled for any social system, civilian or military, then the more structurally similar the military is to civilian society in terms of organizational characteristics, occupational structure, etc., the more capable it is of sustaining itself as an independent entity without depending on the civilian sector. Hence, the greater the degree of structural convergence, the more isolated the armed forces may become from civilian society. The greater the constraints placed on such convergence by emphasis on purely military activities, by contrast, the more dependent the armed forces will be on the civilian sector for non-combat activities, and the more permeable will be the boundaries between military and civilian institutions.

CONVERGENCE WITH WHAT?

One of the issues that must be faced in discussions of civil-military convergence is what structures in civilian society the military is hypothesized to be converging with. Is the referent an ideal-typical large scale non-military bureaucracy, or is it the total civilian sector of society? While much of the rhetoric of convergence has been presented with a view toward the former kind of comparison, what seems crucial to us is the latter. As noted above, underlying the issue of convergence is the problem of boundary permeability, which is central to the understanding of civil-military relations. Huntington (1957) points out, for example, that objective civilian control of the military is facilitated by structurally maintaining a sharp distinction between that which is military and that which is civilian. By civilian, he means not a single corporate entity, but rather the collection of nonmilitary social institutions. To the degree that a military institution becomes structurally similar to its host society, it may also become self-sufficient. Under these conditions, civil-military relations move from Huntington's "objective" to his "subjective" model of control. The linkages through which subjective control is maintained are weak, however (Segal, 1974), and the military may become increasingly independent of its host society.

"FAMILY ECOLOGY" AS AN INTERFACE PROCESS

There are institutions in American society that may be seen as helping to bridge the boundary between military and civilian sectors. Bramson (1971), for example, has discussed the way the Examination and Induction Center, under a system of conscription and enlistment, served both to bring into the military people who did not want to be there, and to keep out people who did but who were defined by the military as unacceptable for any of a number of reasons. In a more long-term sense, the family can also be viewed as an interface institution, giving the man who spends his working hours on a military base an anchor point in civilian society. The company town of the early twentieth century prevented the family from serving such a boundary function by incorporating it into the company system. The trend in the American economy, however, has been away from company towns, with the family operating as a more autonomous system entering into exchange relationships with economic organizations. With the movement away from company towns, the company and its host community have become more interdependent (see Parsons, 1960).

The relationship between the military as a corporate entity and the families of its employees has gone in the opposite direction from that of civilian economic organization. The military family did not really exist historically. Most soldiers were not married except for more senior officers, and their wives and families could only rarely live with them on a military post if they were married. Women living in communities outside the base, and in some cases female employees, provided certain marital functions (Little, 1971). Until the beginning of World War II, this was true except during times of national mobilization. Even then, families were far away and little was provided for their support.

During the mass mobilization of World War II and in the cold war period after that, as the function of armies changed, large numbers of married men were brought into the military and for the first time assistance to families in terms of allowance and limited medical care was made available. Because of housing shortages on post, most families lived in cities, and the majority of economic transactions still occurred off post. For many military men their daily trip to the post for their duties resembled the daily trip to the factory or office for others. Increasingly the soldier was a family man and community member. True, he moved more than others and his collar was green or brown rather than blue or white, but there was considerable parallelism in structure and interdependence in activities between the military and civilian sectors.

But what about the present-day military family? How is it similar to or distinct from its civilian counterpart? First, the trends in assistance

nd support to the family which have come to characterize the post
World War II period have continued and expanded in scope. To attempt to
measure this trend, one could consider a wide range of empirical indi-
ators. For example, one might want to look at the change in family
allotments (eligibility and amount), medical care for dependents (on and off
post), welfare services (such as the Army Community Service), provision

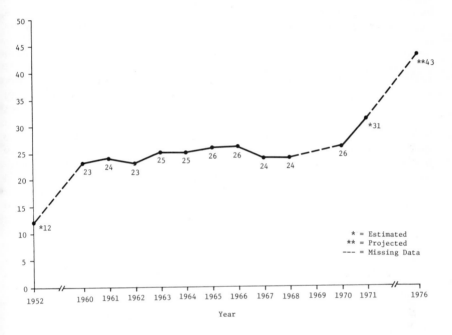

FIGURE 1.   Percentage of military families in adequate
military (owned and controlled) housing[1]

[1]The data for 1961-1968 come from U.S. Department of Defense Annual Reports for the respective fiscal years. The percentage represents the proportion of
military families in adequate family housing units owned and controlled by the
military. The number of military families was operationally defined as the number
of wives listed as military dependents of the total DOD military personnel. For
1952, the percentage was estimated based on 200,000 reported housing units (U.S.
DOD Annual Report, 1952) and on an estimate made of the number of families which
was based on the 1952 total personnel strength using the wives to total personnel
ratio of 1967, a year with similar troop strength and war mobilization. For 1960,
the number of wives was estimated using the wives to total personnel ratio of
1961; the number of housing units was given in the annual report. For 1970, the
data on the number of families and the number of adequate housing units came from
U.S. House hearings (1972:106). For 1971, the number of housing units is from
U.S. House hearing (Ibid.) and the number of families was estimated based on the
ratio of families to personnel in 1970. This probably underestimates the number of
families — and increases the proportion given — because the reduction in force
between 1970 and 1971 probably involved young, single men disproportionately.
The 1976 figure is based on projected family and housing unit figures for 1976
(U.S. House, 1972:106).

of on-post consumer goods facilities (PX and commissary), or entertain-
ment facilities (clubs, athletic facilities, movie theaters, etc.).

As the data presented in Figure 1 show, the percentage of families in
military-owned and controlled housing across time has shown a constant
upward trend. Through the decade of the 1960's, there was a relatively
stable plateau varying between 23 and 26 percent of military families.
This was an increase from the decade of the 1950's, and another major
increase is projected in the 1970's. Were data available for earlier periods,
the change would probably be even more striking. The trend is clear,
however, and would be upward in the future even if no new housing were to
be built — at least until the number of personnel and their families
decreases to its low point in the all-volunteer Army. Thus, the Army
family has been increasingly relocated from the civilian to the military
community. More importantly, given the decrease in civilian company
towns, were we to graph difference scores rather than raw percentages,
the curve would be changed by a considerable power. Equally important
is that 75 percent of the FY 1972 building program was devoted to
enlisted rather than officer housing. This too is in direct contrast to
civilian corporations which, to the extent that they see to the housing
needs of their personnel, seem to confine their concerns to management
rather than assembly-line strata (Jennings, 1970). The personnel problems
of the all-volunteer Army do not focus on an inability to get general
officers to remain in service. Rather, it is the retention of qualified
enlisted men that is problematic, and with an increasingly large proportion of the enlisted force married, the Army cannot afford to compete
with the family for the loyalty of the soldier. The enlisted family is
therefore being increasingly brought within the Army system (Norbo
et. al., forthcoming).

OCCUPATIONAL DISTRIBUTIONS

Much of the argument on civil-military convergence has been concerned with occupational structures. Early reports indicated increasing
similarity between the military and the civilian in this regard (see Lang,
1964), but made little comment on the implications of that similarity.
However, data presented both by Biderman and Sharp (1968) and by
Wool (1968) suggest that this convergence is not taking place. Biderman and
Sharp see important limitations on the "transfer value" of military skills
to civilian life, and Wool points out that the military remains a specialized
structure, with large numbers of men engaged in activities that are only
slightly represented in the civilian occupational structure.

Wool reminds us that while occupational convergence has taken place
in the past, the military remains a very specialized structure with
markedly different distributions of individuals in categories of occupations.
These differences include the absence of sales and farm workers in the
military, the concomitant absence of ground combat troops in the civilian
structure, and much greater number of mechanics in the military in
comparison to the civilian sector. In short, there is by no means a
structural convergence between the two sectors.

In very broad terms, there have been some similar trends in the
civilian and military sectors: increases in skilled and technical jobs,

decreases in combat and farm occupations, increases in white-collar jobs,
growth of the tertiary sectors. The frequencies of certain occupations in
the two sectors remain different, and most of the change that did occur
took place between World War II and the mid-1950's. Thus, while we can
assert that a general convergence in occupational structure took place
historically, it cannot be projected into the future.

Figure 2 presents absolute difference scores between the proportion
of the civilian labor force and the proportion of the military labor force
in three broad categories of occupations: white collar (excluding farm and

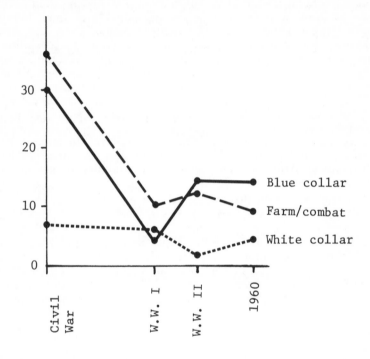

SOURCE: Wool, 1968, p. 52.

FIGURE 2.   Differences between civilian and military sectors
            in percent of labor force engaged in white collar,
            blue collar, and combat/farm occupations.

combat occupations); blue collar; farm and combat occupations. This last category might be seen as the declining primary sector of the civilian and military organizations, respectively. At the time of the Civil War, 90.4 percent of our active duty force was categorized in combat occupations. By 1960, this figure had fallen to 16.3 percent. Less dramatically, at the time of the Civil War, 53 percent of the male civilian labor force was engaged in farm occupations as against 6.3 percent in 1960. Despite a continuing decline in the primary sector, and despite the fact that between the Civil War and 1960 the military overtook and surpassed the civilian sector in the proportion of its labor force involved in administrative and clerical occupations, the difference between the percentage in blue collar occupations in the two sectors has remained relatively constant in the post-World War II years, after a convergence in the percentages for pre-World War I. The difference between the percentage in white collar occupations, after declining prior to World War II, is now increasing moderately.

The consideration of occupational convergence between the military and civilian sectors raises again the problem of system boundaries. Lang (1972) sees the primacy of combat orientations as the basis for a military career diminishing as the need for personnel in the tertiary sector increases. This would, in theory, reduce the discrepancy between that which is military and that which is civilian (cf. Segal, 1972). Because of the inertia of traditional concepts of the military career, however, the military institution has difficulty fitting its skill distribution to its needs. Lang (1972) suggests three alternative means of dealing with the problem: lateral recruitment, use of paraprofessionals, and contract. The first two involve bringing people who are not military professionals into the structure of military management, and would probably contribute to structural convergence. The latter defines as outside the military sphere tasks that are not performed by military personnel, thereby asserting system boundaries and contributing to interdependence. Lateral entry has fallen into disuse in the post-World War II years. The paraprofessional model is approximated today only in the Air Force, and there only at junior grades. The contract model, by contrast, has traditionally been, and continues to be, the major means by which the military secures services. With the transition to an all-volunteer force, and with a diminution in the size of the active duty force, we might anticipate that an increasing number of tasks will be defined as non-military and outside of the boundaries of the military system, and will be performed by civilians on a contract basis.

Our own interpretation of the data is that the boundary is indeed distinct, and that in an era of shrinking uniformed personnel resources, the military will increasingly diverge from civilian occupational structure and move toward its primary mission — combat readiness — the increasingly complex technology of combat notwithstanding. The implications of this structural divergence appear to be the increased contact and interpenetrability between the military and civilian society which is necessary if the military is to continue to exist. The civilian sector is still responsible for the manufacture of clothing, equipment, bombs, weapons, tools and so on for the military. Food must be grown by the civilian sector and sold to the military. Services for military personnel, such as barber shops, auto mechanics, and Bible salesmen, must be provided from the civilian sector (although the military continues to provide ministers, doctors, and dentists for its personnel). All of this dictates that there must be a large amount of interaction between the military and civilian spheres. A useful example of a completely independent military is provided by US military installations in foreign countries, where most equipment and supplies are sent from the United States and there is minimal contact between the military personnel and the indigenous economy. Here the American military for all intents and purposes is functionally independent by virtue of being able to fulfill its own needs (see Wolf, 1969). It appears, then, as if the relative lack of convergence between the occupational structures of the civilian and military means that there is still a great deal of contact between the two, and that the military in this country has not become independent of the civilian work force and economy.

RESEARCH AND DEVELOPMENT

Technology has been postulated to be the motor that runs the convergence machine, and research and development (R&D) is the handmaiden of technology. Indeed, given the dependence of a wide range of organizations, the military among them, on modern technology, we might expect civil-military convergence in the R&D area even if it occurred nowhere else.

Recently sociologists interested in organizational analysis have used an open-system approach in studying the internal structure and functioning of organizations. Characteristics of the open-system perspective are a reconceptualization of organizational boundaries as problematic and an emphasis on external variables as the primary agents of social change (Hirsch, 1973; Katz and Kahn, 1966). In particular, Thompson (1967) argues that the structure of all organizations is designed to protect the production or technological core from environmental influences. Therefore, it will be non-production units such as marketing, distribution, and research and development which will be involved in exchanges with the environment. The key aspects of these boundary-spanning roles are obtaining intelligence on probable future demand, on continued availability of raw materials, and on the relative merits of product innovations, and carrying out policy decisions in sales, distribution, and product development and production (Hirsch, 1973). The primary characteristics attributed to the environment in this approach are its complexity and relative unpredictability. This environment includes, for military as well as for civilian industrial organizations, rapidly changing technology and demands for organizational output. Research and development is most commonly seen as an organizational attempt to manage the uncertainty posed by a complex and changing environment through prediction and control of innovation and demand. The military as well as civilian and other governmental organizations engages in R&D in response to environmental threats to organizational control over the production process in a broad sense). The simple convergence hypothesis would therefore predict that the military organization would increasingly resemble other organizations in R&D expenditures as a proportion of total resources, in undertaking more non-military-specific research especially in management and other general skills and techniques, and in the amount of research done internally (not contracted out to other organizations).

What are aspects of the R&D process which might be relevant to the convergence hypotheses? Four key parameters might be the number and distribution of manpower resources devoted to R&D, similar measures for financial resources, fields of study within which research is undertaken, and the organization of research, especially the distribution between in-house and contracted research. The civilian benchmark against which to test convergence might be civilian government agencies or civilian private enterprises. It is necessary to establish both theoretically and empirically the position of these benchmarks in order to demonstrate convergence by the military.

What would be the consequences for interaction of the military with its environment if convergence with one or another of the civilian models were demonstrated? To the extent that the civilian organization is autonomous in its research activities and to the extent that the military converged with that model, military R&D could operate autonomously of its environment. To the extent that in-house military R&D employs only military research personnel, allots a reasonable (in comparison with other organizations) amount of resources to research, and covers all relevent or necessary fields of inquiry, military R&D is self-contained and needs little or no interaction with most civilian research-related organizations to carry out its functions.

Figure 3 presents mean indices of dissimilarity for R&D expenditures as a proportion of the total budget among the American armed services (computed for each pair of services and averaged), for the Department of Agriculture and for the Department of Health, Education and Welfare as civilian governmental agencies for comparative purposes, and between the armed services and the civilian agencies (computed for each service-civilian agency pair and averaged). It is clear that the two governmental agencies are more dissimilar from each other than the three armed services are among themselves. Moreover, the secular trend among the armed services seems to be toward greater similarity, whereas the trend between HEW and Agriculture seems to be toward greater dissimilarity, with the exception of 1969. Most importantly, dissimilarity is greatest in the military-civilian comparisons, and this dissimilarity does not seem to have decreased through the decade of the 1960's.

In the R&D field, the boundary maintenance problem can be approached by considering the degree to which the military conducts such activities in-house, rather than having it done by outside contractors. The former model more closely approximates the activities of civilian enterprises that are highly dependent on technological development, and hence might be seen as contributing to structural convergence. Carrying out R&D activities on a contract basis contributes to a stricter definition of the division of labor between military and civilian sectors, and hence militates against convergence and reflects interdependence.

While according to table 1 there are differences among the branches of the American military and fluctuations over time in the degree to which R&D activities are carried out in-house, no clear case can be made for convergence, and a mild case can be made for interdependence. The Air

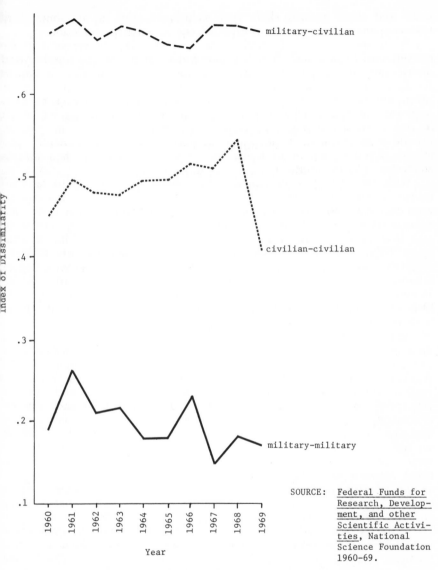

FIGURE 3.   Indices of dissimilarity among and between
            U.S. armed services and governmental agencies
            in R and D expenditures, 1960-1969.

Force, which through the decade of the 1960's grew from having the smallest R&D obligations relative to its budget among the services to having
the greatest, performed about 13 percent of its R&D activity in-house at
both the beginning and the end of the decade, with fluctuations in between.
The Navy experienced similar overall stability, although the proportion of
its total R&D budget which was spent within the organization was more
than 30 percent throughout the ten year period. The Army, on the other

hand, was the only service to show a secular trend in these data. It decreased its internal R&D activity from 40.7 percent in 1960 to 34.5 percent in 1969. The comparison organizations in table 1, HEW and the Department of Agriculture, show an intermediate picture. The latter conducted most research within the organization, drawing to a much smaller extent on non-governmental resources, while the former showed a moderate decline in in-house research as a proportion of the total R&D budget, from about 26 percent to about 19 percent. While it is impossible from these data, to demonstrate conclusively either convergence or divergence, the relatively small total amount of in-house research conducted by the Navy and the Air Force and the decrease in the amount conducted by the Army are suggestive of military-society interchange and interdependence, and therefore, structural divergence.

TABLE 1.   INTRAMURAL R&D AS PERCENT OF TOTAL R&D OBLIGATIONS

Fiscal Year	Army	Navy	Air Force	Agriculture	HEW
1960	40.7	31.1	13.7	71.3	25.5
1961	43.7	30.8	9.0	72.5	22.7
1962	40.8	38.4	11.6	69.1	21.0
1963	34.2	40.6	10.4	70.1	20.1
1964	33.1	35.8	13.0	68.9	19.3
1965	34.3	36.6	14.0	67.9	18.6
1966	35.5	45.5	14.1	69.9	17.9
1967	32.7	32.8	13.9	69.1	17.8
1968	38.9	32.9	14.6	71.9	17.7
1969	34.5	33.4	13.1	73.2	18.8

Source: Federal Funds for Research, Development, and Other Scientific Activities, National Science Foundation, 1960–1969.

DISCUSSION

Where previous discussions of the civil-military convergence phenomenon have tended to view such convergence as contributing to the permeability of the boundary of the military system, we suggest that the greater the degree of structural convergence, the less dependent the military is on its host society, and the more insulated it may become from civilian sensibilities (see Moellering, 1973). Empirical indicators of structural convergence of civilian and military sectors examined here do not in the aggregate support the hypothesized convergence. By attempting to bring the pattern maintaining functions of the family within the military system, for example, the military is becoming more structurally similar to the civilian community and is therefore becoming a more closed system. The continuing dissimilarity of the civilian and military occupational structures and the continuing reliance of the military on civilian R&D activities, however, do indicate a lack of structural convergence and the concomitant necessity of the military to maintain itself as a more open system.

The continued lack of similarity between civilian and military occupational structures despite convergence during some historical periods, maintaining the military's need for civilian employees and services, and the handling of a good deal of the research and development on a contract rather than an intra-mural basis, seem to suggest a strengthening of the distinction between what is military and what is civilian through the mechanism of differentiation in function. By more clearly defining the boundary between the military and the civilian, the military is able to maintain itself as a more open system. Where Lang (1973) sees a blurring of the civil-military boundary associated with increased military dependence on civilian expertise, we see a reaffirmation, in the current decade, of a traditional division of labor that perhaps did get blurred in the early 1960's.

It might be hypothesized that a healthy relationship between the military institution and the democratic society it protects seems to require that the military function be narrowly defined so that the military is functionally dependent upon civilian institutions which can, in turn, exercise some control over it. It may be that under an all-volunteer system it is especially important for the military to self-consciously integrate itself into civilian society, and that a clearer definition of the boundaries of the military system must be developed precisely so that the military institution can be maintained as an open system (Janowitz, 1973). On the other hand, others, most notably the critics of the "military-industrial complex" have argued that this type of symbiotic relationship instead of being healthy, creates a degree of interdependence with civilian and military interests so interwined that military (and political) policy is at least partly dictated by corporate needs and vice versa. Either relationship could be conceived as injurious to democratic values and processes. An insulated military, able to function by itself, could possibly be in a position to operate independently either within this country or on the international scene. The interdependent military, conversely, raises the possibility of military activities controlled not by the nation as a whole, but by some form of power elite. In either event, the exact nature of the civil-military interface must be made explicit if questions such as these are to be answered.

From this perspective, Moskos' (1973) "segmental" model of convergence, while conceptualizing military personnel systems as evidence for divergence from the civilian occupational structure, has different consequences for the problem of interdependence. The combat army, as the traditional nucleus of military operations, has become increasingly mission oriented and wholly staffed by personnel in uniform trained in combat specialties. It is here that divergence from civilian society takes place. The support agencies, by contrast, in an era of fewer enlistees and no conscripts, may become increasingly dependent on civilian employees or on services performed contractually by civilian organizations. Alternatively, one may view the segmental model in terms of two armies: a combat army, oriented to the combat mission and structurally divergent from civilian society, and a support army, similar in structure to civilian institutions (Hauser, 1973). The combat army in this case would be functionally dependent on the support army rather than on the civilian sector, and thus its relationship to civilian society would be at one remove.

A similar phenomenon arises with regard to the military family. At the level of complex organizations, there is structural divergence in comparison to corporations and company housing and other services for employees and their families. However, the military installation represents a structural convergence with regard to the facilities and processes found in civilian communities (see Clark, 1968). Increasing incorporation of the entire family into a military base environment, where military supervised and controlled institutions mediate in the soldier's contact with the civilian sector, removes the individual aspects of the military-civilian interface and leaves a situation in which the actors are not individuals but organizations — for instance, military procurement offices and civilian supply corporations instead of individual consumer and retailer. Thus civil-military interdependence is increased at the institutional level but decreased at the level of the individual soldier and his family. Whether these relationships at one remove between the military and the surrounding society present threats to civilian ascendancy and control or increase high-level military recognition of and adjustment to dependence on the civilian sphere is another question which, at present, remains unresolved.

REFERENCES

Biderman, Albert D. and Laure M. Sharp
    1968 "The Convergence of Military and Civilian Occupational Structures." American Journal of Sociology 73 (January):381-399.
Bramson, Leon
    1971 "The Armed Forces Examining Station." Pp. 185-220 in Charles C. Moskos, Jr. (ed), Public Opinion and the Military Establishment. Beverly Hills: Sage Publications.
Clark, Terry N.
    1968 Community Structure and Decision-Making: Comparative Analysis. San Francisco:Chandler Publishing Company.
Grusky, Oscar
    1964 "The Effects of Succession." Pp. 83-111 in Morris Janowitz (ed.), The New Military, New York: Russell Sage Foundation.
Hauser, William L.
    1973 America's Army in Crisis. Baltimore: Johns Hopkins University Press.
Hirsch, Paul M.
    1973 The Organization of Consumption. Unpublished Ph.D. dissertation, The University of Michigan.

Huntington, Samuel
  1957 The Soldier and the State. Cambridge: Harvard University Press.
Janowitz, Morris
  1965 Sociology and the Military Establishment, revised edition. New York:
        Russell Sage Foundation.
  1971 "The Emergent Military." Pp. 255-270 in Charles C. Moskos, Jr. (ed.),
        Public Opinion and the Military Establishment. Beverly Hills: Sage
        Publications.
  1973 The U.S. Forces and the Zero Draft. Adelphi Papers 94. London:
        International Institute for Strategic Studies.
Jennings, Eugene E.
  1970 "Mobicentric Man." Psychology Today 4(July):34ff.
Katz, Daniel and Robert Kahn
  1966 The Social Psychology of Organization. New York: John Wiley & Sons, Inc.
Lang, Kurt
  1964 "Technology and Career Management in the Military." Pp. 39-81 in
        Morris Janowitz (ed.), The New Military. New York: Russell Sage Foundation.
  1972 "Military Career Structure: Emerging Trends and Alternatives."
        Administrative Science Quarterly 17 (December):487-498.
  1973 "Trends in Military Occupational Structure and their Political Implica-
        tions." Journal of Political and Military Sociology 1 (Spring):1-18.
Lasswell, Harold D.
  1962 "The Garrison-State Hypothesis Today." Pp. 51-70 in Samuel P. Hunting-
        ton (ed.), Changing Patterns of Military Politics. New York: Free Press of
        Glencoe.
Little, Roger W.
  1971 "The Military Family." Pp. 247-271 in R.W. Little (ed.), Handbook of
        Military Institutions. Beverly Hills: Sage Publications.
Moellering, John H.
  1973 "The Army Turns Inward." Military Review 53 (July):68-83.
Moskos, Charles C., Jr.
  1970 The American Enlisted Man. New York: Russell Sage Foundation.
  1973 "The Emergent Military: Civil, Traditional, or Plural?" Pacific
        Sociological Review 16 (April):255-280.
Norbo, Gary J., Richard S. Seeberg, William L. Wubbena, Jr., David R. Segal,
        Mady W. Segal, and Robert F. Holz
  (Forthcoming) Changes in the Structure of Army Families. Carlisle Barracks:
        U.S. Army War College.
Parsons, Talcott
  1960 Structure and Process in Modern Societies. New York: Free Press.
Segal, David R. and Daniel H. Willick
  1968 "The Reinforcement of Traditional Career Patterns in Agencies Under
        Stress." Public Administration Review 28(January-February):30-38.
Segal, David R. and Mady W. Segal
  1971 "Models of Civil-Military Relationships at the Elite Level." Pp. 279-292
        in M. Van Gils (ed.), The Perceived Role of the Military. Rotterdam:
        Rotterdam University Press.
Segal, David R.
  1972 "Civil-Military Differentiation in the New Industrial State." Sociological
        Focus 6 (Winter):45-58.
  1974 "Structural Linkages Between Civilian and Military Sectors of American
        Society." Paper presented at the 8th World Congress of Sociology. (August):
        Toronto.
Thompson, James D.
  1967 Organizations in Action. McGraw-Hill: New York.

U.S. Department of Defense
  1952-   Annual Reports, Fiscal Years 1952-1968. Department of Defense Wash-
  1968   ington, D.C.: Government Printing Office.
U.S. House of Representatives
  1972   "Military Construction Appropriations for 1973." Hearing before a Sub-
          committee of the Committee on Appropriations, 92nd Congress, 2nd Session,
          Part 1. Washington, DC.: Government Printing Office.
Wolf, Charlotte
  1969   Garrison Community: A Study of an Overseas American Military Colony.
          Westport, Connecticut: Greenwood Publishing Company.
Wool, Harold
  1968   The Military Specialist. Baltimore: Johns Hopkins University Press.

12

CIVIL-MILITARY RELATIONS IN GREECE: 1909-1974*

GEORGE A. KOURVETARIS

Northern Illinois University

Using Moskos' conceptual framework of convergent, divergent and segmented patterns, an effort is made to delineate civil-military relations in the socio-political history of modern Greece. Commencing with the revolt of 1909, seven landmarks of civil-military relations that contributed to the shaping of modern Greek socio-political history are identified and briefly discussed. The analysis shows that Greece has undergone a process of convergent, divergent, and segmented patterns in civil-military relations. Convergence between armed forces and society stands out as the most important deterrent against military intervention in the political and social processes of modern Greece.

The assumption of political roles by the armed forces in a substantial number of countries particularly since the end of World War II has sparked a sustained and growing interest in comparative analyses and case studies of military institutions. Although military intervention in the developing nations of the Third World (with a few exceptions) has been somewhat taken for granted by western writers (Pye, 1961; Johnson, 1964; Huntington, 1957 and 1968; Janowitz, 1964; Rustow, 1963; Perlmutter, 1969; Finer, 1962; Lieuwen, 1962; Ben-Dor, 1973), the assumption of political leadership by the Greek military in 1967 and the recent collapse of the military rule have drawn great attention. Much of the anxiety has been expressed by those who are honestly committed to seeing democracy restored in Greece and in whatever country it has been denied.

The present analysis will first briefly trace the linkages between armed forces and society in the modern socio-political history of Greece. It will then apply Moskos' (1973) conceptual framework and analyze the convergent, divergent, and segmented features of military and civilian/political structures with the emphasis on the role of the military in Greek politics in the 20th century.

Briefly stated, Moskos' framework contains three components: the "convergent" which seeks to bring the military institutional structures closer to the civilian; the "divergent or traditional military," which emphasizes the increasing differentiation between military and civilian social structures and seeks a greater autonomy on the part of the former; and "the segmented"

*A version of this paper was originally presented at the biannual Symposium of Modern Greek Studies Association held at Columbia University on November 9-11, 1973. The author wishes to express his gratitude to Peter Karavites, Catherine Papastathopoulos, Nicholas Michas, Panos Bardis, and Betty Dobratz for their invaluable suggestions and comments. It must be stressed, however, that the usual caveat that the author alone accepts the responsibility for the interpretations and analyses is especially relevant here.

military, which is both an effort at synthesis and a compartmentalization of civilianized and traditional trends, with some areas stressing convergent and others favoring divergent features. While others exist, Moskos identifies four major levels of variation on civil-military issues in this framework: "social recruitment/social composition" (whether or not armed forces are representative of the broader society); "institutional" parallels (or discontinuities) between military and civilian structures; occupational/professional differentiation; and ideological contrasts between civilian and military men. Despite its typological character and greater applicability to the American armed forces and society, Moskos' conceptual framework also seems appropriate for an analysis of the Greek armed forces and society.

GREEK ARMED FORCES AND SOCIETY

For the purposes of clarity, seven chronological periods of civil-military relations (commencing with 1909 to the present) will be identified. In the judgment of this writer these periods contain certain major landmarks in the socio-political history of modern Greece. Further, one can recognize an intense linkage and interpenetration of armed forces and society at different points in time. From her inception as a new independent nation (1827) up until the first quarter of the 20th century, Greece was struggling to find her new role, build her institutions, expand her frontiers, and develop a sense of nationhood and national integration. Six salient factors characterized armed forces and society prior to the 19th century: a lack of central and unified military leadership, insufficient funds, frequent military intervention in politics and vice versa, corrupt and inefficient political governments, the deadlock between the government and the King over domestic and foreign issues, and the general "romantic" orientation and non-professionalism of military and civilian institutions of the times. Unlike Western European armies, the Greek officer corps did not evolve from a feudal/aristocratic tradition. Both exogenous and indigenous socio-political and military influences and events contributed to the development, organization, and subsequent professionalization of the Greek armed forces.

Civil-Military Relations (1909-1913): Convergence. It must be emphasized that the major socio-political crises and changes in modern Greek society are intertwined with Greece's armed forces. It is within this context that the role of the military in Greece must be assessed. The emergence of Greece as a sovereign nation must be seen as a result of her ability to establish viable political and military organizations. Tsakonas (1967) argues that the military revolution of 1909, which was spearheaded by young, idealistic officers, heralded the beginning of modern Greece. During the 1909 revolution and the subsequent Balkan Wars of 1912 and 1913, civil-military relations showed trends of consensus along political, ideological, and institutional/organizational levels.

At the national political and military levels, the cooperation between Eleftherios Venizelos, the charismatic political leader of the Liberal Party, and that of King Constantine I (as commander-in-chief of the armed forces) resulted in an unprecedented desire to achieve national unity and redeem the remainder of the Greek population still under Turkish rule. At the ideological level both the ideas of "nationalism" and that of *Megale Idea* (to recover

Constantinople and restore Byzantium from the Ottoman conquest of 1453) were the unifying elements of political and military leadership which had their antecedents in the spirit of Greek National Revolution of 1821 and its aftermath. During this period, the emerging Greek nation followed an irredentist policy to regain its Northern territories — a long, national, and legitimate claim of Greece's foreign policy. The political leadership was consistent with the military heroic self-images and national aspirations and objectives (Kourvetaris, 1971a).

The revolution of 1909 was spearheaded in the name of social and political change: to increase the role of the military in "the making of the new nation," to modernize and re-organize the political and military structures, to eliminate corruption and nepotism in public and military life, and to uplift the officers' shattered morale due to the ill-fated war of 1897 with Turkey. Besides this evidence suggesting a "convergence" of military and civilian structures and values at the turn of the century, some additional indicators of this "convergence" can be cited: the emergence of sociology as a social reform movement and the establishment of the first sociological society in 1908-1915; the high legitimacy of military and political institutions; and the hundreds of Greeks of the diaspora (especially from the United States) who voluntarily returned and enlisted to fight in the Balkan Wars.

2. *Civil-Military Relations (1914-1936): Divergence.* The conceptual antithesis of the "convergent military" is the divergent one that stresses differences between armed forces and society. With the onset of World War I, a constitutional crisis developed that led to a national political schism over the issue of whether Greece should participate in the war on the side of the Entente or whether it should remain neutral. The military was split as was the rest of society into two rival camps, the "Royalists" and "Venizelists." The Royalists supported King Constantine and favored neutrality while the Venizelists favored entrance into the war. The Entente powers resolved the deadlock by overthrowing the pro-royalist Athens government, forcing King Constantine I into exile, and helping Venizelos and his followers to regain power. Needless to say, all the pro-royalist elements were purged from the military. This national schism resulting from the inability of the civilian-military leadership to reach a consensus left its imprint on the social and political life of Greece even to the present.

While World War I was over by 1918, Greek troops, encouraged and supported by the allies, landed in Asia Minor in 1919. Three years later, the military expedition to realize the old-time dream of *Megale Idea* resulted in a fiasco. In Greece proper, the Venizelists lost the national elections to the Royalists and the King was recalled to the throne. A host of factors contributed to Greece's new plight: bifurcation of civil-military leadership; the political ambivalence of the Entente powers; the almost total reliance of Greece on allies who withdrew their support when Venizelos and his followers failed to win the election; Greece's unrealistic commitment to *Megale Idea* which was incompatible with the interests of the Entente powers; the rivalries and discord of the Entente powers themselves; Russia's policy against Greece; and above all, the rise of the Turkish nationalism under the leadership of Kemal Ataturk.

Following the debacle in Asia Minor, a series of coups and counter-coups engineered by Venizelist and Royalist officers respectively resulted in the dissolution of the monarchy and the republicanization of the armed forces During the 1920's, civil-military relations were divergent partly because the Asia Minor debacle resulted in a series of national political crises, the most important being the execution of the six officers and political leaders allegedly held responsible for the failure in Asia Minor. At the societal level a massive displacement and exchange of populations between Turkey and Greece had both positive and negative ramifications in the social, economic, demographic, and political sectors of Greece.

At the military institutional level efforts to re-organize the military and reinstate the officers who had been dismissed during the schism between "Royalists" and "Venizelists" had limited success. The divergence between armed forces and society was further aggravated by the repeated deadlock between the two political groupings over domestic issues. The most prominent of these problems were the uprooting of one and a half million Greeks from Asia Minor and the emergence of the Communist Party, which largely was a consequence of the socioeconomic plight of the uprooted Greeks. The political deadlock between the two major national parties led to a military coup in 1935 by Royalist officers. The ascendancy of royalism in the armed forces and in politics was followed by purging all Republican officers in the military and in the civil service. In 1936 General Paggalos restored the Monarchy while General Metaxas abolished the parliament and political parties and assumed dictatorial powers.

3. *Civil-Military Relations (1936-1940): Convergence.* Despite Metaxas' authoritarian rule, the dissolution of political parties, and the repression of Communists by the Metaxas' regime, the Greek nation by 1940 was unified behind its armed forces, the King, and the Metaxas' government. The axis military machine and the design for world domination, coupled with the Italian ultimatum that Greece allow the Italian forces to cross Greece's Northern borders, resulted in convergence of armed forces and society. The refusal of Greece in the historic "OHI" (NO) and the subsequent Italian declaration of war against Greece in October, 1940 found the Greek armed forces and society united against the axis.

During World War II, the armed forces and society showed determination and "national purpose" reminiscent of the Balkan Wars. Since the Axis' military machine had been sweeping over Europe, the Greek armed forces' resistance and subsequent victory against the Italian forces on the Albanian front in 1940 were heralded both in Greece and in the West as the first victory for the allies in Europe.

4. *Civil-Military Relations (1941-1949). Segmented.* The German invasion and subsequent occupation of Greece (1941-1943) left the country without genuine political and military leadership. Civil-military relations during the decade of the 1940's and until the early 1950's reflected the fragmentation between armed forces and society. The dismantling of the Greek national army by the occupation forces is an indicator of the segmented model of civil-military relations. A substantial number of officers and servicemen escaped and joined the allies who were fighting against the axis forces in the Northern African, near Eastern, and Italian fronts, but the majority of the officers remained in Greece fighting the occupation forces and later the Communists.

The most salient development during the German occupation was the revival of the Greek Communist Party (K.K.E.). In 1941, the K.K.E. established the National Liberation Front (E.A.M.) and its military arm, the Greek Popular Resistance Army (E.L.A.S.) whose initials almost reproduced the Greek word for Hellas. The E.A.M./E.L.A.S. organization, in part due to its ideology, objectives and early recruiting policies including the presence of some Republican and ex-army officers, enhanced its image as a patriotic and national liberation movement against the occupation forces.

While initially the E.A.M./E.L.A.S. and the Republican forces cooperated against the occupied forces, later they split. One of E.A.M./E.L.A.S.' political and military objectives was to undermine the Republican resistance movement, both in Greece and among the expeditionary Greek forces in the Near-Eastern front. In Greece proper, the Republican resistance movement was represented by E.D.E.S. (National Republican Greek League) under the leadership of General Napoleon Zervas and the 5/42 regiment led by Colonel Psaros. (The latter was dissolved in April, 1944 after its leader was assassinated.) A large number of men in both of these organizations were ex-army officers.

While these developments were taking place in Greece, in 1943 a number of unsuccessful mutinies incited by left-leaning officers were reported in Alexandria. Counterinsurgency and army conspiratorial groups were formed both in Greece and in the near East to combat communism.

A special British force known as the Allied Military Mission arrived in Greece in 1942. Mixed groups of both E.D.E.S. and E.L.A.S. bands co-operated with the British. The British mission remained in Greece and solicited the assistance of all guerrilla bands regardless of their political affiliations as long as they agreed to fight the axis. In July, 1943, the E.A.M./E.L.A.S. group signed a "National Bands Agreement" which provided for the establishment of a joint Greek headquarters for all resistance forces under the allied commander in the near-East.

In March, 1944, the E.A.M./E.L.A.S. group created the Political Committee of National Liberation (P.E.E.A.) which invited radical but non-communist personalities to participate. The principal aim of this maneuver was to undermine the position of the Greek government in Cairo and to give the impression of a popular revolution through peaceful and political channels.

One can briefly mention the causes which split the Communist and Republican guerrilla forces: (a) the creation of the political committee known as the Communist government in the mountains whose aim was to undermine the position of the Greek government abroad, (b) the constitutional question of whether the King should or should not return before the constitutional issue had been submitted to plebiscite, and (c) the military mutinies in Alexandria.

George Papandreou, a Republican/Liberal politician, headed the Greek government in Cairo in 1943 and urged the British not to leave Greece after the departure of the occupation forces. About the same year, Papandreou managed to call the Lebanon Conference which was attended by representatives of the major resistance movements. According to the provisions of the conference, a new government of national unity was to be established along with the re-organization of a national Army and the unification of all guerrilla units under its control. Despite the Lebanon agreement, the Communists refused to disarm because a) they were encouraged to continue the guerrilla warfare by Tito, who hoped to control all of Macedonia, b) they realized that the British Military

Mission and the returning Greek expeditionary brigades were too small to fight them, and c) they were supported by the USSR. Convinced that they had the power to gain control of Greece, they launched an armed attack on Athens in December, 1944 but they failed to seize power.

In December, 1945, the Varkiza Agreement ended hostilities. The Communists agreed to disarm because they had been informed through a Soviet Military Mission that Churchill and Stalin had agreed that Greece was to remain under a British sphere of influence in exchange for assigning Poland to the Russian sphere of influence.

In 1946, a full fledged guerrilla movement began in Greece. Despite the Communists early successes, the political tide was running against them. The Conservative/Populists (Laikon Komma) won the elections of 1946 which were supervised by an international committee. A plebiscite was held that brought back King George II. Liberals and Populists co-operated and supported the King in their anti-communist stand. On the international scene, an investigating committee on Balkan affairs reported to the General Assembly of the United Nations that Albania, Yugoslavia and Bulgaria actively supported the guerrilla movement in Greece. In 1947, the U.S. Congress approved the Truman Doctrine which provided American military assistance to Greece and Turkey. This marked the beginning of American penetration in Greece. Two years later in 1949, the battle against the guerrilla forces ended under the military leadership of Marshal Alexandros Papagos, an ex-army general and veteran of the Italian War. The Communists were defeated at the E.L.A.S. stronghold in the mountains of Grammos and Vitsi.

5. *Civil-Military Relations (1950-1963): Convergence.* The advent of the 1950's marked the end of a decade and a half of catastropic events including a dictatorship, the Greco-Italian War, the German occupation, and the civil war that left the country in economic, political, and social ruins. The defeat of the Communists by the national army in 1949 enhanced the image and status of the military and contributed to an increase of its role in Greek society and politics.

Through the Marshall plan, the Truman Doctrine, and private programs, Greece began a vigorous program of re-construction and recovery. However, most American aid to Greece from 1947 to 1954 was spent for the re-organization and modernization of the Greek armed forces. During the 1950's a convergence between the armed forces, the King, and the major national political parties occurred along an anti-Communist ideological position.

The major political formations of right, center, and left resumed with different labels. The Conservative Populists *Laikon Komma* (right) gave way to the Greek Rally (1951) *Ellinikos Synagermos* headed by Papagos. In turn it was replaced by the National Radical Union (ERE) *Ethniki Rizospastiki Enosis* founded by Constantinos Caramanlis (1956) and later headed by Panagiotis Canellopoulos (1963). Included in the political right was the Progressives, a minor right wing party and a personal vehicle of Spyros Markezinis who originally was with the Greek Rally and served as the Minister of Coordination. Markezinis was considered the major architect of the economic miracle of Greece in the 1950's. Despite its close alliance with ERE, the Progressives maintained their separate parliamentary identity.

Between 1952-1963, the right maintained a decisive parliamentary majority and a popular vote ranging between 44 and 50%. During the conservative supremacy, the major opposition group was found in the Center (although an electoral quirk gave the Left the second largest parliamentary representation in 1958). The Center was the political progeny of the Liberal Party *Phileleronthero Komma,* that was originally founded by Eleftherios Venizelos, the charismatic political leader and nationalist from the island of Crete. For a period in the early 1950's the Center spectrum of Greek politics was shared by three parties: the Liberals continuing under the old label and headed by Sophocles Venizelos, the son of Eleftherios Venizelos; a personal party of George Papandreou; and the National Progressive Center Union (EPEK), a liberal coalition headed by a retired General Nicholas Plastiras and a former premier Emmanuel Tsouderos in 1950 and 1951.

When Prime Minister Pagagos died in 1955, he was succeeded by Constantinos Caramanlis, the hand-picked choice of the King and the minister of public works in the National Rally Party. The Caramanlis government faced many problems created by the war, the occupation forces, and the Communist movement. In spite of these problems and cleavages, the Caramanlis government was strong enough to continue a vigorous program of social and economic reconstruction. Even his critics and detractors agree that Caramanlis and his party gave the most durable post World War II government in Greece. During that time, Greece was admitted to the Council of Europe, became a bona fide member of NATO, an associate member of the European Common Market, and Cyprus won her Independence from Britain. It is rather ironic that the same issues that pre-occupied the Caramanlis government in the mid-1950's and early 1960's have re-emerged in the mid-1970's. Some of these issues were inherited from the military regime in 1974. Needless to say, this included the "Cyprus Tragedy." Yet one can trace the seeds of the present discord and stalemate in "Cyprus" in the London and Zurich accords of 1960 in which the Caramanlis Government was a signatory to those agreements along with Turkey and England.

During the Caramanlis era a convergence between armed forces and society was achieved. Both the military and the King supported the policies of the Caramanlis government which in turn did not question the influence of the military or the King in national politics. More concretely all major social institutions (i.e., military, economic, educational, religious, familial, and political) and civil bureaucracy engaged in a concerted effort to reconstruct the Greek nation and solve the social problems generated by the decade of the 1940's. The armed forces played a pivotal role in providing technical and manpower resources in this effort. The behavior of Greek Communists was repudiated by the people and national political leaders alike. Civil-military groups adopted a policy of strong anti-Communism that was also consistent with the ideology of cold war in the west and in the Atlantic community. All national parties except the far left (EDA) endorsed a pro-Western, pro-American, and pro-NATO national policy and supported the principle of self-determination for Cyprus.

In 1963, Caramanlis and his government was forced to resign. His resignation was precipitated first by a dispute with King Paul over the timing of the latter's state visit to England. The Caramanlis government argued that such a visit was not in the best interests of Greece at that time. Second, the Caramanlis government was accused of being morally responsible for the death of the EDA deputy Lambrakis who was attacked by extreme rightists at a left wing rally in Salonica. Third, the Caramanlis government was shaken by a sex scandal which implicated the ecclesiastical leadership of the national church of Greece and forced the resignation of the archbishop. Added to these was the contention of the liberal politicians and the press that both the military and the King were exercising extra-parliamentary powers and influence in national politics. Given these issues a climate of new political and social change was created in Greece. At the same time the Kennedy administration indicated it would support a more liberal government thus fostering the rise of the Center Union.

   6. *Civil-Military Relations (1963-1967): Divergence.* The model of convergence in civil-military relations was running its course by the early 1960's. The resignation of the Caramanlis government in 1963 was followed by George Papandreou's ascent to power. Papandreou was a protege of Eleftherios Venizelos and headed the Center Union Party that was the progeny of the old Liberal Party. In 1961 Papandreou succeeded in uniting the two factions of the Centerist groups into a single Center Union Party although he was unable to win the elections in that year. In 1963 the Center Union won a plurality and Papandreou became Prime Minister. In 1964 Papandreou called for new elections in which his party won 173 of 300 seats in parliament. ERE, in coalition with the Progressives of Markezinis, received 105 seats and EDA 22. The Center Union had made gains in both its left and right wings. It must be noted that the coming to power of the Center Union and George Papandreou in particular after almost twenty years of political oblivion created mixed feelings among the military, the King, and the more conservative forces in Greek society, especially the business community, the church, and civil bureaucracy.

   In spite of Papandreou's popular support and political strength in the parliament, he was faced with a number of conflicts and crises — some generated from within his own party, some from the personality of the man himself, and some from other political and social forces in Greek society (e.g., the military and the King). By March, 1965 George Papandreou was convinced that he was in control of neither the army nor his own party and government, although he seemed to have the popular support.

   The evidence suggests that during 1963-1967 or prior to the military coup, armed forces and society can be genuinely characterized as divergent. The most salient issues during the short tenure of Papandreou's premiership can only be briefly summarized here, but it seems the political stalemate and procrastination between and among different forces created the mood and rationale for military intervention one month prior to the scheduled national elections.

   The nature of legitimacy for both major national parties was more of a charismatic rather than legal/rational type. Legg (1969 and 1973) argues that Greek political parties with the exception of the Left have generally been of polyarchic and personalist types. The major political conflict was usually at the level of the party leader himself. While the Center Union revealed a concern for modernizing the political, civil, and military bureaucracies, it was embroiled in a number of issues that attenuated its ability to achieve these ends.

On the domestic and national scene, first a constitutional question and crisis was raised by George Papandreou himself over the issue of the Minister of Defense. In order for Papandreou to exercise greater "civilian control" over the military, he demanded the resignation of his Minister of National Defense. However, the minister refused to resign. In the past the military and the King had exerted greater influence over this ministry. Confident of his popularity and of his majority in parliament, George Papandreou challenged the legitimacy of the King and insisted that the "King must reign whereas the people must rule" through their representatives.

Although George Papandreou believed in the principle of "civilian rule" over the military, his recommendations for the appointment of ministers had to be approved by the King according to the 1952 Constitution. Because of this dispute, George Papandreou resigned and called for new national elections immediately. A series of futile attempts initiated by the King and his advisors to form a new government failed, and finally the King was forced to set new elections for May 21, 1967 (almost a year and a half following Papandreou's resignation).

Following World War II and the defeat of the Communists, Greece was singularly dominated by the political right. Although the stated policy of the Center Union was pro-NATO, pro-Western, pro-king, and pro-military, George Papandreou and especially his son Andreas, a former professor of Economics in American universities and a deputy and contestant for the leadership of the Center Union, were rather critical of these institutions and the policies of the United States toward Greece and Cyprus. (One can argue that in view of the recent pro-Turkish attitude of the U.S. foreign policy over the Cyprus crisis, the Center Union and Andreas Papandreou in particular were accurate in their criticisms of both NATO and the United States.)

Furthermore, the perceived threat by the military that a victory by the Center Union would upset the officers' careers and reduce the military/defense budget contributed to even greater alienation of the military from the policies of the Center Union. At the same time the discovery of an alleged left-wing conspiratorial group known as ASPIDA (shield) became the *cause celébre* which further aggravated the already tenuous situation and embarrassed both the military leadership and the Papandreou government.

In 1964, the younger Papandreou was elected to parliament. It is true that some of Papandreou's fervent supporters saw him as a new force in Greek politics. In fact, Andreas Papandreou attempted to modernize and professionalize the Center Union Party by introducing American ideas from the "New Deal" and "New Frontier" political platforms. However, the detractors of the younger Papandreou regarded him as an interloper who used his father's political sagacity for dynastic succession to the leadership of the Center Union. Resentment arose not only among Papandreou's political adversaries but among the political co-leaders within his own party. This resentment culminated finally in the split of the Center Union and withdrawal of many deputies who became known as apostates from Papandreou's party during the caretaker governments (appointed by the King).

On the international scene, the Cyprus issue, which almost developed into a full-blown war between Greece and Turkey in 1964, aggravated even further the civil-military relations between the two nations and increased Greece's isolation from NATO and the United States, both of which rather favored Turkey or did not favor self-determination or union (enosis) of Cyprus with Greece.

7. *Civil-Military Relations 1967-1974: Civil-Military Administrative Alliance — Cohesion Without Consensus.* Feit (1973) proposes a cyclical model through which military regimes pass: the military take-over, the military-civilian administrative alliance — cohesion without consensus or the praetorian regime, and finally the downfall and replacement. This model can be applied to the 1967-1974 period in Greece. In this last section an effort will be made to sketch the major developments and changes from the 1967 military coup up to the Cyprus crisis and the re-establishment of civilian government in Greece. The 1967 coup in particular has been discussed by many writers (Doumas, 1968; Gregoriou, 1969; Kousoulas, 1969; Brown, 1971; Moskos, 1971; Kourvetaris, 1971a, b, c; Clogg and Yannopoulos, 1972; Feit, 1973; Legg, 1969 and 1973).

In countries where armies have not fully accepted the "principle of civil supremacy" in politics, and whenever civilian political elites are incapable of creating a viable political system for social and economic change, the military may usurp political power. Increased professionalism does not necessarily reduce the propensity of the Greek military for political intervention. On the contrary, the political awareness and influence of the Greek military grew with an increase of professionalism and a broadening of the social base of recruitment of the officer corps. Because the officer corps views itself both as a professional organization and national cultural/societal institution, it believes it represents both the social aspirations of the people and national interests (see Kourvetaris, 1971a:1056). Historically, in Greece as in other nations, the primary mission of the armed forces is to provide military leadership in defending the sovereignty of the state and the national interests. In exercising its role in Greek society the military has also assumed political roles during periods of political and national crises. The assumption of political roles by certain officers in 1967 was carried out by officers who eventually relinquished their military commissions and did not return to the military.

For reasons of parsimony one may underscore the following changes and dramatic events in the period (between 1967-1974) with little further elaboration. At the domestic and national levels, the abolition of the institution of monarchy and declaration of Greece as a republic was one of the most significant changes in the modern constitutional political history of Greece. While the Papadopoulos regime initiated this change in 1973, it was later (1974) legitimated by the civilian government of Caramanlis through a national referendum in which the overwhelming majority of the Greek people (about 2 to 1) voted in favor of the republic.

At the domestic scene the student revolt at the prestigious Polytechnic School in Athens and the subsequent killings of a number of students sparked a series of events which contributed to the counter-coup of November 24, 1973 and the restoration of civilian democratic rule in the second half of 1974. While dramatic civil-military changes were taking place in Greece proper, there occurred the abortive coup and assassination attempt against President Makarios by Greek army officers and Greek Cypriot national guardsmen and the subsequent brutal invasion of Cyprus by Turkish forces. When NATO equipped Turkish forces occupied over 40% of the island, Greece in protest withdrew from the military wing of NATO because the alliance made no effort to prevent the aggression of one of its members against another.

Ironically, the tragic events in Cyprus became the catalyst which brought about the end of military rule and the restoration of civilian rule and democratic processes in Greece. The self-exiled former prime minister of Greece, Caramanlis, was recalled from Paris by the military to lead the nation in a time of profound national tragedy second only to the Asia Minor debacle of the 1920's. Armed forces and society moved from a cohesion without consensus model of civil-military relations to one of partial convergence against an expansionist and aggressive Turkey. The agonizing events in Cyprus and the mobilization of the Greek armed forces brought Greece and Turkey for the third time to the brink of a full-blown war (the other two in 1964 and 1967).

On November 17, 1974, Caramanlis and his "New Democracy" Party won the national elections by both a majority of popular vote and 220 out of 300 seats in the parliament. The Cyprus tragedy, economy, and the trial of the protagonists of the 1967 and 1973 coups became the major preoccupations of Caramanlis's government. Whether or not the Caramanlis forces and those from the opposition parties will be able to extricate the Greek nation from these crises remains to be seen.

Greece is pursuing an economic and industrial development through political stability at home and cooperation and reapproachment with her natural neighbors in the Balkans, Mediterranean and Middle Eastern nations. Concurrently, she is following a policy of integration into the Common Market and is seeking economic support from the Western and American nations. It is my judgment Greece in the late 1970's will focus on the industrialization (particularly tertiary sector of her economy), strengthening her political and democratic institutions, modernizing her armed forces, and promoting mutual understanding, cooperation, and peaceful co-existence with all nations including those with dissimilar socio-political and economic systems. The aggressive and expansionist policy followed by Turkey in Cyprus and her bellicose language and threats against Greece over the Aegean have resulted in a partial convergence of armed forces and society. It is my contention that discipline and confidence in the military and civilian leadership are being restored.

SUMMARY AND CONCLUSION

In this analysis an effort has been made to delineate the patterns of civil-military relations in Greek society by applying Moskos' conceptual framework of convergent, divergent, and segmented patterns. This analysis indicates that the greater the level of convergence of armed forces and society and the greater the external threat, the less the propensity for military intervention in politics. Civil-military relations in the periods preceding World War I (1908, 1912, and 1913), prior to World War II up to 1940 and the decade of 1950's were characterized as converging with both military and political leadership united in their national objectives and ideology. This convergence was generated and sustained by external threat and internal conditions and cleavages of the

Greek social structure. During these periods the role of the military increased in Greek society and its legitimacy was not questioned.

On the other hand, divergence between civilian and military elites at the political/ideological levels seems to increase the propensity for military intervention in Greek politics. For example, the military interventions of 1908, those in the decade of the 1920's and mid 1930's, and the more recent one in the late 1960's were precipitated because of ideological divergence between civilian and military elites and national issues. Thus, the pattern of civil-military relations during 1963 and 1967 was divergent. In the middle 1960's the political power of the Radical Union that dominated the national scene for almost a decade was challenged by the Center Union. The ascent to power of the Center Union was problematic, and it found itself embroiled in a series of crises. These crises were generated from within and from without the Center Union itself and reached a climax in the military intervention of 1967.

The coercive intervention of the military in Greek politics did not bring about either a convergence or a divergence pattern of civil-military relations but rather a segmented model, a forced cohesion without consensus. Despite the civilianizing and politicizing trends of the military regime by the early 1970's (e.g., the replacement of ex-army officers by civilians in key positions in the government, the setting of dates for political parties and elections), the trend was abruptly discontinued by the November 24, 1973 counter-coup in which Papadopoulos was ousted by his own fellow officers such as Ioannides who were subsequently responsible for the attempted Cyprus coup. When the military could not handle the Cyprus issue, Caramanlis was invited back.

In the 1974 parliamentary elections, after almost a decade of authoritarian military rule, interrupted political life and crises and despite new emerging political forces and issues, once again one can discern three distinctive political formulations very much reminiscent of Greek politics a decade earlier although with different labels. Thus the ERE of the 1960's becomes the New Democracy of the mid-1970's headed by Caramanlis, the present Prime Minister of Greece. Like before the Center Union emerged into two splinter parties — the Center Union-New Forces headed by George Mavros, a liberal former Minister and Deputy Premier, and the Pan-Hellenic Socialist Movement led by Andreas Papandreou. The United Left (former EDA) party is at the far left of the continuum.

In view of the new political and social developments during the mid 1970's both in Greece proper and Cyprus, one can only speculate that the emerging model of civil-military relations in the late 1970's will be segmented with some aspects of the military organization becoming more similar to the civilian and some parts diverging from society. Whether or not this trend in civil-military relations is predicated on "the principle of civilian supremacy" and "non-military intervention" may be seen in the immediate future.

REFERENCES

Ben-Dor, Gabriel
1973   "The Politics of Threat: Military Intervention in the Middle East."
        Journal of Political and Military Sociology 1 (Spring):57-69.
Brown, James
1971   "The Military in Politics: A Case Study of Greece." An unpublished Ph.D.
        dissertation, State University of New York at Buffalo.
Clogg, Richard and George Yannopoulos (eds.)
1972   Greece Under Military Rule. London: Secker and Warburg.
Doumas, Christos
1968   "Crisis, Revolution, and Military Rule in Greece: A Tentative Analysis."
        Southern Quarterly 6 (April):255-288.
Feit, Edward (ed.)
1973   The Armed Bureaucrats. Boston: Houghton Mifflin Co.
Finer, S.E.
1960   The Man on Horseback: The Role of the Military in Politics. New York: Fred
        A. Praeger.
Gils, Van M.R.
1971   The Perceived Role of the Military. Netherlands: Rotterdam University
        Press.
Government Gazette
1968   "Ministry of National Defense and Administration of the Armed Forces."
        Order No. 58, issue of paper 295, December, Government Gazette.
Gregoriou, Georgios J.
1969   "Greece: Problem in Political Change and Democratic Development, 1821-
        1967." An unpublished Ph.D. dissertation, New York University.
Huntington, Samuel P.
1957   The Soldier and the State: The Theory and Politics of Civil Military
        Relations. Cambridge: Harvard University Press.
1968   Political Order in Changing Societies. New Haven: Yale University Press.
Janowitz, Morris
1964   The Military in the Political Development of New Nations: A Comparative
        Approach. Chicago: University of Chicago Press.
Janowitz, Morris and Jacques Van Doorn (eds.)
1971a   On Military Ideology. Netherlands: Rotterdam University Press.
1971b   On Military Intervention. Netherlands: Rotterdam University Press.
Johnson, John
1964   The Military and Society in Latin America. Stanford: Stanford University
        Press.
Kornhauser, William
1969   "Revolutions." Pp. 404-442 in Roger W. Little (ed.), A Survey of Military
        Institutions. Volume II, The Inter-University Seminar on Armed Forces and
        Society.
Kourvetaris, George A.
1971a   "Professional Self-Images and Political Perspectives in the Greek Military."
        American Sociological Review 36 (December):1043-1057.
1971b   "The Greek Army Officer Corps: Its Professionalism and Political
        Interventionism." Pp. 153-201 in Janowitz and Van Doorn (eds.), On
        Military Intervention. Netherlands: Rotterdam University Press.
1971c   "The Role of the Military in Greek Politics." International Review of History
        and Political Science 8 (August):91-114.
Kousoulas, George
1969   "The Origins of the Greek Military Coup, April 1967." Orbis 13 (Spring):332-
        358.
Legg, Keith R.
1969   Politics in Modern Greece. Stanford: Stanford University Press.
1973   "Political Change in a Clientelistic Polity: The Failure of Democracy in
        Greece." Journal of Political and Military Sociology 1 (Fall):231-246.

Lieuwen, Edwin
    1962   "Militarism and Politics in Latin America." In John Johnson (ed.), The Role
            of the Military in Underdeveloped Countries. Princeton: Princeton Univer-
            sity Press.
Markezinis, Spyros
    1966   Politiki Istoria Tis Neoteras Ellados (Political History of Modern Greece).
            Volume 4, Athens, Greece: Papyros Publishing Company.
Moskos, Charles C., Jr.
    1971   "The Breakdown of Parliamentary Democracy in Greece, 1965-67." The
            Greek Review of Social Research 7-8:3-15.
    1973   "The Emergent Military: Civil, Traditional, or Plural?" Pp. 536-550 in Frank
            Trager and Philip Kronenberg (eds.), National Security and American
            Society. The National Security Education Program: The University Press of
            Kansas.
Papacosma, Solon Y.
    1971   "The Greek Military Revolt of 1909." An unpublished Ph.D. dissertation,
            Indiana University.
Perlmutter, Amos
    1969   "The Praetorian State and the Praetorian Army: Toward a Taxonomy of
            Civil-Military Relations in Developing Polities." Comparative Politics 1
            (April):382-404.
Pye, Lucien W.
    1961   "Armies in the Process of Political Modernization." European Journal of
            Sociology 2:82-92.
Rustow, D.A.
    1963   "The Military in Middle Eastern Society and Politics." In S.N. Fisher (ed.),
            The Military in the Middle East: Problems in Society and Government.
            Columbus, Ohio: State University Press.
Smokovitis, Demetrios
    1973   "Sociological Problems of the Armed Forces in Greece." An unpublished
            dissertation submitted in the Panteios Supreme School of Political Science,
            Athens, Greece.
Tsakonas, Demetrios G.
    1967   Koinoniologia Tou Neou-Hellenikou Pnevmatos (Sociology of the New
            Hellenic Spirit). Athens: Ellinika Grammata.

13

CIVIL-MILITARY RELATIONS AND MILITARY RULE: BRAZIL SINCE 1964

BRUCE R. DRURY

Lamar University

Social scientists contend that prolonged, effective government by the armed forces in a developing nation is improbable because of the inability of the officers to act as proficient political brokers vis-a-vis the major civilian groups within the society. The experience of Brazil, 1964-1970, indicates that the success of military rule may be enhanced by the following factors. First, if interest associations are weak and subservient to the State, there may be no effective opposition to military rule. Second, if the boundaries of the military institutions are fragmented, the officers may acquire extensive political and administrative experience while remaining somewhat insulated against societal cleavages. Third, if the armed forces can acquire institutional pride and a generally accepted political doctrine, the officers may gain the confidence needed to assume an expanded political role and the armed forces may be able to sublimate or avoid profound internal conflicts.

INTRODUCTION

On March 31, 1964, the Brazilian armed forces executed a bloodless coup d'etat against the constitutional government of President João Goulart. Such intervention by the military was not uncommon in Brazilian politics, but the retention of power for an indefinite period was not in accord with the tradition of the armed forces as the "moderating power." As the moderating power the military officers viewed their institution as the final authority in political conflicts, charged specifically with preventing the imposition of radical solutions to political problems. Once a compromise had been engineered by the officers, political authority was returned to civilians (Johnson, 1964: 177-223; Pedreira, 1964: 38-40). In 1964, however, the Brazilian generals decided that limited intervention was no longer sufficient to prevent the dissolution of the political and administrative structures (Wald, 1966: 41-42). They perceived that the crisis which confronted the political system could be resolved only by an extended period of military rule during which the system would be rebuilt.

Decisions of the type made by the Brazilian generals are not unusual in the so-called developing nations. Political crises are common occurrences in such nations and military intervention is often a common reaction. But while the causes of intervention have been extensively analyzed, the research directed toward military rule has been limited. Generally social scientists have contended that prolonged effective government by the armed forces is improbable because of the assumed inability of the officers to act as proficient political brokers vis-a-vis the major civilian

233

groups within the society. This belief often causes scholars to predict that attempts at direct rule by the military, such as the effort begun in Brazil in April of 1964, would inevitably result in a process of increasing governmental instability and ineffectiveness.

The premise that military officers cannot act as effective political brokers seems to be based upon three often unverified assumptions. First, it is argued that in many developing societies, interest associations will not tolerate the type of authoritarian control typical of a military regime. Second, either military institutions are too insulated from the civilian society for the officers to master the problem of working with civilian groups or the armed forces are too open and thus suffer from the same cleavages that caused the conflict in the society at large. Third, it is assumed that military officers understand little of the social, economic and political problems which they would have to confront as rulers and thus do not have generally accepted prescriptions for the problems. Without an accepted doctrine it is assumed that cleavages would develop within the armed forces over policy questions and that these cleavages would destroy the unity and coherence of the military regime.

It is the purpose of this paper to use an analysis of civil-military relations in Brazil to examine the validity of these assumptions and to test a set of variables which seem to be better indicators of persistent military rule.

THE VARIABLES

The first variable relates to the strength and autonomy of interest associations. If interest groups are autonomous, then the first assumption is likely to be true. If they are weak and subservient to the State, however, there may be no effective opposition to military rule. The second variable is concerned with the nature of institutional boundaries. If the boundaries of the armed forces institutions are integral or permeated, then one of the alternatives in the second assumption may be correct. If, on the other hand, the boundaries are fragmented, then the officers may acquire extensive political and administrative experience while remaining insulated against societal cleavages. The third variable examines the presence of a political doctrine for the officer corps. If the armed forces can acquire a set of generally accepted prescriptions for political, economic and social problems, then the officers may gain the confidence needed to assume an expanded political role. Absence of such a doctrine might result in destructive conflicts within the officer corps.

Prolonged military rule requires the soldiers to create a support base that would extend beyond the barracks. In most societies which are susceptible to military intervention, widespread support is not necessary for the mere overthrow of the existing government. First of all, the armed forces with their discipline, organization, and firepower are well-equipped for the task of seizing power (Janowitz, 1964: 31-40; Finer, 1962: 6). Secondly, developing nations generally exhibit a heterogeneity of elite groups and several coexisting forms of legitimacy, and this often assures the armed forces of some civilian support, especially in a crisis situation. Such societies have many "power contenders," each of which has its own means of demonstrating its power capability (Anderson, 1967: 93-101).

With no single universally accepted means for resolving conflicts, one or more power contenders may support a military solution (Huntington, 1968: 194-198; Janowitz, 1964: 29).

In *The Soldier and the State* Huntington (1957: 84) argued that professionalism will decrease the political involvement of military men. Although Huntington (1968: 193) has rejected his earlier contention, it is still accepted as valid by many advocates of military assistance training. Current evidence, however, indicates that the propensity for political activity seems to increase as the soldiers become more professional in their roles as guardians of the national security. The career military officer is both a professional soldier and a public servant. The professional role dictates an obedience to the political regime (and thus no political activity), but, at the same time, the role gives the officer access to the means of violence. The servant role requires the officer to protect the "national interest" and thus may allow the officer to judge the political output of the regime (Fidel, 1970-1971: 24-25; Janowitz, 1965: 233-237). The addition of the servant role may decrease the aloofness of the heroic soldier and make him more aware of the effects of public policy to the point that he may wish to intervene in order to repair a disrupted political system (Kourvetaris, 1971: 1053-1054).

Professionalism in the military has expanded to include the necessity for an awareness of the effect of domestic policy upon national security. The Cuban Revolution and fear of communist opportunism during political crisis have caused the armed forces of developing nations to extend the concept of security to encompass all aspects of social and political life (Gutteridge, 1965: 133; Stepan, 1971: 173; Feit, 1973: 6-8). A perceived fear of a communist take-over encouraged the Brazilian generals to act in 1964. A similar fear of communist success prompted the Greek colonels to take power in 1967 (Kourvetaris, 1971: 1054). Fear of an anticipated consolidation of popular groups into an unmanageable political force pressed the Peruvian army into action in 1968 (Cotler, 1970-1971: 101-102). Economic chaos brought military intervention into Ghanaian politics in 1966 and 1971 (Welch, 1972: 212-214). Political chaos and corruption were used to justify the military coup of January, 1966 in Nigeria (Welch, 1972: 216-217; Luckham, 1971b: 402-403).

Professionalism may also prompt soldiers to intervene in defense of institutional interests which the soldiers relate to their national security function. Some of the armies of the new African states have intervened because of job competition or defense budget considerations (Welch, 1972: 220-221; Lee, 1969: 89-97; Lofchie, 1972: 30-31). In some praetorian societies in Latin America, civilian regimes have been able to buy military support with salary increases, budget increases, and fringe benefits. Economic problems and progressive social legislation, however, quite often threaten to dilute the privileges of the military officers and weaken the military capability of the armed forces, and thus encourage military intervention (Needler, 1966: 618; Baker, 1967: 7-8). It is significant that the proportion of the national budget allocated to the Brazilian armed forces dropped six percentage points in the two years prior to the

1954 attempted coup d'etat and dropped to an all-time low in 1964.[1] Intervention based on the protection of institutional or personal interests does not, of course, elicit much support from civilian groups, but institutional interests may provide the level of military cohesion that will allow the armed forces to intervene in a crisis situation.

Armies can overthrow governments because of their near monopoly over the means of violence. Support is necessary for a coup d'etat, but the threat of violence is the critical factor. Armies are generally successful in attempts to overthrow governments because they are crisis organizations and a coup is similar to the type of crisis activity for which they train. For example, the 1967 coup in Greece followed a NATO contingency plan (Feit, 1973: 121-122). This crisis orientation that facilitates intervention by the military, however, is the very factor that works against rule by the military. As Janowitz (1964: 28) contends, military officers lack the leadership skills required for bargaining and political communications, and they are thus doomed to failure as rulers because they will never compromise. Huntington (1968: 221) argues that this is especially true in nations experiencing the first phases of mass politics. When popular organizations threaten the system, the armed forces will act as a conservative force in order to create or preserve a political context which is more open and rational than that of an oligarchical system and which does not threaten military status as a result of the social reforms of a mass democracy (Huntington, 1968: 224; Finer, 1962: 47).

In all developing nations except those with oligarchical systems, Huntington puts the military in an essentially negative role and seems to conclude that political change can be accomplished only by external intervention or a social revolution. In particular, Huntington and others contend that most Latin American societies are too advanced to allow effective military rule because of the officers' inability to become accomplished political brokers (Huntington, 1968: 228-229; Lieuwen, 1962: 155; Horowitz, 1968: 64).

In spite of the argument against a solution by military reform, the armed forces are in power in many transitional states of Latin America, Asia, and Africa, and there is little evidence to suggest that they will voluntarily fade from the political picture or that other social groups will be able to dislodge them forcibly. If the armed forces cannot be pushed out of the political arena in states that are in the middle stages of political modernization (for example, South Korea and Greece), then perhaps Huntington has oversimplified the situation by stating that the soldiers could not be effective rulers in such situations.[2] Huntington's generalization appears to assume that societies in the middle stages of

---

1. The defense share decreased from 32.5 percent of the total budget in 1952 to 26.5 percent in 1954 and then rose to 29 percent in 1957. From there it decreased steadily to a low of 14 percent in 1964 and then jumped to 20.9 percent in 1965 and 25 percent in 1967.

2. Huntington's contention that soldiers are radicals in societies experiencing the first stages of modernization also appears to be an oversimplification according to the evidence provided by Price (1971: 378-379).

development have well-developed and autonomous interest organizations that will thwart the efforts of middle-class military leadership to effect political change.

The assumption of autonomy is questionable. In the development of the Western European states, religious, cultural, or class phenomena were the prime movers in the creation of political parties and their parallel interest organizations. In societies where such profound cleavages do not exist, interest organizations, especially those with a mass membership, have been slow to develop unless some factor not directly related to politics, such as an economic or social benefit, was present (Olson, 1965: 132-159). In developing nations, reformist regimes that seek to establish bases of support or to emulate the more politically developed nations often sponsor and subsidize the formation of mass-based interest organizations. In this manner both the peasant and labor "sectors" were created in Mexico and have largely remained captives of the regime since their creation (Gonzalez Casanova, 1970: 14-17). Similarly in the urban slums of Venezuela, political mobilization has generally been initiated by outsiders — political party workers, labor union leaders, and especially people connected with government agencies (Ray, 1969: 81-83).

Where popular urban and agrarian groups are mobilized for political action (i.e., politicized) by personalistic leaders or representatives of other political organizations, the popular organizations generally lack autonomy. Thus, it seems possible that a military regime could de-politicize these groups by removing or co-opting the leadership while middle-class groups or the soldiers themselves are developing stable institutions for protracted political control.

Another assumption which apparently causes scholars to doubt the ability of the military to effect reform is that military officers are thought to have little experience in entrepreneurial or brokerage roles. Where boundaries of the military organization are integral (i.e., relations with the outside environment are under strict control of the command hierarchy), the assumption often is correct, but the boundaries appear to be fragmented in many developing nations and thus military men find that extensive interaction with civilian groups is possible (Luckham, 1971a: 27-33). Boundary fragmentation tends to increase as the soldiers become more cognizant of the effect of political and economic policies upon national security.

Moreover, where the fragmented boundaries have allowed military officers on active duty to perform roles ordinarily reserved for civilians — nonmilitary bureaucratic tasks, management of economic enterprises, teaching, nonmilitary construction management, etc. — the entrepreneurial experience apparently enhances the ability of the military leaders to provide solutions to the mobilization-institutionalization gap. Especially when the military does not have a strong partisan position, an entrepreneurial military regime may have "success in establishing order and security, the repression of insurgent minorities, the drive for the foundation of new economic enterprises, the elimination of traditional political parties and the establishment of the new political frameworks" (Lissak, 1967: 254-255). Military governments, by redirecting investments, limiting consumption, and/or frustrating redistribution of wealth, have been remarkably successful in achieving high rates of economic growth (Horowitz, 1971: 44-47).

The contention that a military regime in an advanced developing nation must mobilize mass participation in order to maintain power (Huntington, 1968: 241; Janowitz, 1964: 29) can also be countered by stating that the military needs only to control or co-opt the relevant political forces of the society. If military leaders have extensive political contacts and experiences, the calculations which convince the leaders that a military take-over is feasible "may include the assumptions or experiences that masses in a particular country are neutral, negligible, or easily manipulable" (Wilner, 1970: 268). Certainly the acquisition of managerial skills by the "military manager" and the political awareness of the professional national security manager gives the military officer the confidence that he can use the political resources at his disposal to secure sufficient support (Kourvetaris, 1971: 1055-1056).

Furthermore, it may be reasonably easy for the military rulers to elicit at least passive support from strategic groups. The reformist doctrine of the new type of military ruler may be sufficiently attractive to some groups to counter their dislike for coercion and control (Miguens, 1970-1971: 8-11; Einaudi, 1969: 8-10). If the military government produces policy, it will also earn the support of the civilian bureaucracy, for as Feit states: "Bureaucrats of all kinds will accept rulers who rule, whether good or evil, for not to do so would threaten the very principle [discipline] on which organizations rest" (1973: 11).

CIVIL-MILITARY RELATIONS IN BRAZIL

The coup d'etat of March 31, 1964, in Brazil marked the end of the arbiter role for the Brazilian armed forces and the beginning of a new role as ruler. Contrary to the pessimistic prognosis of Huntington, the factors which have allowed military men to govern Brazil for some ten years should allow the existence of a relatively stable and effective military regime for several years to come. First of all, interest associations have not been able to match the influence of clientelistic politicians. Interest associations do exist in Brazil, but the primary means of securing the desired governmental action is through the clientage system (Leff, 1968: 118-131). This situation insulates the government from group pressures and thus gives the government greater freedom for policy innovations since political goods are allocated on an individual rather than on a sectoral basis. The government has more discretionary options in dispensing rewards because value allocations are treated as rewards or favors and not as services which are owed to the client (Scott, 1972: 14-15).

The patron-client relationship also gives the government a means of controlling incipient opposition elements. Since the patron's position depends upon his ability to deliver collective goods to his clients, the government may block the patron's access to the administrative structure, thereby weakening his control over his supporters. Where an institutionalized interest association would search for a new point of access (perhaps within an organized opposition group), in a clientelist system the clients search for a new patron.

The interest associations that do exist in Brazil have presented little difficulty for the military government. The associations which might logically oppose a military regime enjoy little autonomy. Urban labor in Brazil was brought into the political arena by the corporatist Estado Novo of Getulio Vargas (1937-1945) and has not been able to break out of that control (Weffort, 1970: 390-391). Urban labor syndicates are controlled by *pelegos* — clientelists who play the role of labor advocates but generally serve the government (Schmitter, 1971: 188-194). Rural workers' syndicates also have a potential for strong opposition. At the time of the 1964 coup, however, these groups were neither intensively nor extensively organized, and, in general, they were "follower" groups — successors to the patriarchical leader-follower arrangements of the traditional culture (Galjart, 1964: 3-4). Just as the government was able to substitute loyal *pelegos* in urban labor syndicates for those whose loyalty was questionable, the unequal nature of the leader-follower arrangement in peasant groups also allowed the substitution of loyal leaders, who then consolidated their positions through access to the administrative structure.

The only truly autonomous opposition association in 1964 was the students' organization, which proved troublesome, but because of its limited membership was isolated and repressed. Other interest associations such as employers' and commercial associations enjoyed autonomy, but they were generally in agreement with the goals of the military regime, especially in reference to developmental policy and the need to control the mobilization of urban and rural workers (Einaudi and Stepan, 1971: 88-89). Thus, the industrial, commercial, and agricultural elite have been co-opted by the policies of an authoritarian military regime; urban and rural workers' groups were co-opted by a carrot-and-stick approach of payoffs for cooperation and coercion for noncooperation; and other groups, such as students, were repressed or ignored.

Another factor which should enhance the ability of the Brazilian armed forces to control and direct the political system is the fragmentation of institutional boundaries. The moderator role which traditionally accrued to the military after the fall of the monarchy is evidence of some boundary fragmentation. In the political crises of 1930, 1945, 1954, and 1964, many civilians openly requested military intervention to restrain or to overthrow the existing government (Stepan, 1971: 93-115). As the crisis heated up in late 1963 and early 1964, civilian demands for military intervention were common and were matched by complaints coming from within the armed forces. Middle- and senior-grade officers objected to the effect of inflation upon their salaries, the chaotic state of the national economy, the growing use of violence by rural and urban popular groups, the politization of promotions, the acceptance of open communist activity, and the granting of amnesty to rebellious enlisted men (Einaudi and Stepan, 1971: 78-80).

The expanded conception of national security further fragmented military boundaries. Military officers became aware of the political, social, and economic context of national security, and some favored military action to set up a strong government which would end the recurring crises (Pedreira, 1964: 41). The vehicle for imparting this new awareness was the Escola Superior de Guerra (ESG), organized in 1949.[3] Generally attended by the more ambitious and intelligent officers, the ESG imbued its students with the necessity for a moral and economic redemption of Brazil, which would enable the nation to take its rightful role in the struggle of the "Christian West" against the "Communist East." Students of the ESG heard lectures from distinguished scholars and, in study groups, formulated policy programs for dealing with security and developmental problems (Schneider, 1971: 245-251).

In addition to expanding the intellectual horizons of military officers, the ESG experience also fostered contact with the political and economic power structure. Stepan (1971: 177) reports that by 1966 the list of ESG graduates included 599 military officers, 224 businessmen, 297 members of the federal bureaucracy, 39 federal congressmen, 23 state and federal judges, and 107 professionals such as professors, writers, economists, doctors, and clergymen. The contacts made during the year-long course are maintained through an alumni association which publishes a journal and holds periodic meetings and seminars to study new problems (Schneider, 1971: 250-251).

At the administrative level, military boundaries have been fragmented since the Estado Novo period. Active duty and retired general officers often hold cabinet positions (Baker, 1967: 78). Brazilian army officers have extensive experience in administrative roles through service in frontier settlements, civic-action construction projects, civic-action health and sanitary advisory programs, management of critical industrial facilities, and participation in research and planning councils (Manwaring, 1968: 90-95). The army provides top executives for the National Steel Company, Brazil's largest steel-producing enterprise; the Rio Doce Company, the major ore producer and shipper; and Petrobras, the government oil monopoly. Air Force officers are prominent as top management officials in civilian factories, airlines, the weather service, and airport administration. Naval officers are involved in shipping concerns, port facilities, and the development of tele-communications and nuclear energy (Baker, 1967: 95-96). Johnson (1964: 211-212) reports that in 1961 approximately 1,100 Brazilian military officers were on detached duty, serving in civilian positions in national, state, and local government. The size of the military budget is also an indication of the scope of activity of military officers. Although the armed forces comprised 0.3 percent of the population in 1965, the military budget was equal to 3 percent of the gross national product of Brazil (Moreira da Silva, 1966: 59).

The fragmented boundaries of the Brazilian military have given the officers not only experience in administration and policy formulation but also a feel for the necessity of maintaining political support. Furthermore, this experience apparently gave the officers confidence that they could be both effective administrators and political brokers. Such con-

---

3. The Escola Superior de Guerra (Higher War College) was organized by a group of officers who had studied at the French War College. This "Sorbonne" group included Humberto de Castelo Branco who was to become the first president of the military regime.

fidence indeed seems to be an important factor in whether or not the armed forces will remain in power after a coup. Einaudi and Stepan (1971: 75-76) contend that the Brazilian generals were content with the moderator role prior to the 1960's because they had relative confidence in the ability of civilians to rule and also little confidence in their own political capability. The recurring crises from 1961 to 1964 destroyed the generals' confidence in civilian rule; and the administrative experience enhanced the generals' confidence in themselves.

Also adding to the generals' confidence were foreign contacts and the acquisition of a developmental doctrine. Brazil was the only Latin American nation to send ground combat troops to participate in World War II. After a fitful start, the Brazilian Expeditionary Force (FEB) enjoyed great success against the German forces in Italy. From this experience, the Brazilian armed forces earned a new status as the defenders of democracy and national honor and acquired a panoply of heroes and heroic experiences. In addition, the officers who served in the FEB developed a strong appreciation for the necessity of planning, unity, and cooperation and became open admirers of the political and economic organization of the United States (Stepan, 1971: 242-248).

The FEB experience also impressed its participants — many of whom went on to be the organizers of the ESG — with the importance of the social, economic, and political requisites for a modern army. As the Cold War became the dominant factor in international politics, the relationship between national development and national security gained more emphasis. The Cuban Revolution and the threat of internal war further expanded the social and political basis for national security. The doctrine of the ESG identified the defense of the "Christian West," in general, and Brazil, in particular, with a strong national economy and a stable political and social structure. Thus, General Golbery (1967: 198) warns that "indirect Communist aggression . . . capitalizes on local discontents, the frustrations of misery and hunger, and just nationalist anxieties." As the ESG studied the developmental and security aspects of inflation, agrarian reform, electoral and party systems, transportation, and education, as well as internal and conventional warfare, there began to develop a military-political prescription. This doctrine, although not universally accepted by all military officers, gained more acceptance as the political crisis deepened (Einaudi and Stepan, 1971: 83-84), and it was apparently the existence of the doctrine that gave the generals the requisite confidence to retain control of the government.

The fragmentation of the armed forces' institutional boundaries will often increase the soldiers' confidence in their ability to govern, but it may also be detrimental to military rule since fragmentation may "reduce the army's cohesion, the unity of its authority, and its ability to bargain and seek its interests as a single monopolistic group" (Luckham, 1971a: 14). Permeated boundaries subject the military to the same conflicts which exist in the civilian sector. Armed forces which have fragmented boundaries are less involved in such conflicts (that is, they are somewhat insulated from these conflicts), but increased awareness of politics may result in a replication of societal cleavages within the armed forces.

Factionalism has not been an unusual phenomenon in the Brazilian armed forces. The *Tenente* revolt of 1922 was the product of dissension between reform-minded junior officers and entrenched generals who served the interests of the landed oligarchy. Following World War II a cleavage existed concerning policy alternatives for national development, with the nationalist faction of officers favoring development by Brazilians only and the right-wing Democratic Crusade wanting development by the quickest means possible. Between these two factions was the legalistic group that generally opposed overt military involvement in political affairs, and it was this group which put the conflict in limbo after 1955 by disciplining many of the leaders of the other two factions.

Following the precipitous resignation of President Quadros in 1961, the conflict resurfaced around the issue of the perceived threat of communism, with the legalists again serving as the pivotal group between the nationalist left and the anti-communist right. By the end of 1963, however, the ineffective leadership of Joao Goulart, whom the leftist officers had supported, had alienated most of the officer corps and the few leftists who continued to support Goulart were isolated. A vast majority of the military officers saw communism and govern-mental corruption as increasing severe threats to the security of the nation (Einaudi and Stepan, 1971: 84). The legalists had been driven into the right-wing activist camp and the left nationalists were so isolated that they were easily purged following the coup d'etat. The unity and cohesion which existed in early 1964 was short-lived, however, and a new cleavage soon developed within the majority anti-communist right-wing faction.

The major points of difference in the new cleavage between the ESG officers and the authoritarian nationalists[4] involved the following issues: the role of private foreign capital, the means for dealing with the threat of communism, the relationship with the United States, the length of military rule, and the extent of political purges (Einaudi and Stepan, 1971: 90). This conflict within the military was to be the major problem for military rule in Brazil. Yet the mere fact that this was to be the major problem is highly significant. The officers seldom questioned their ability to rule; they only questioned how to rule. Civil-military rela-tions in Brazil had reached a point where the officers were confident that they could manipulate their political resources in such a way as to maintain the requisite support for staying in power. Policy questions would result in occasional open conflicts that would give the civilians faint glimmers of hope, but the resolve of the officers was to stay in power until their job was completed.

CONCLUSION

The examination of the Brazilian case demonstrates the validity of the

---

4. The core of the *Cruzada Democratica* had split into essentially two groups. One group, closely associated with the ESG, espoused a tutelatory democracy that would foster economic development with the help of private domestic and foreign capital. The other group was less interested in democracy and development and more interested in a moral redemption and the control of communism.

variables. First, the weak and subservient nature of interest associations in Brazil has limited the effectiveness of opposition to military rule. This has allowed the military regime to co-opt or repress potential or actual opposition groups. Second, the fragmented boundaries of the military establishment provided the Brazilian officers with extensive experience in political and administrative roles while at the same time somewhat insulating the armed forces against the destructive effects of societal cleavages. This insulation was not at all complete but it was sufficient to keep internal conflicts at a manageable level. Third, the acquisition of institutional pride and expertise through the formulation and acceptance of a developmental doctrine has given the Brazilian officer the requisite confidence for the assumption of an expanded political role. Because the doctrine provided a generally accepted set of goals for the military regime, internal cleavages, although not insignificant, have been contained.

In terms of short-run political stability and economic development the military has been significantly successful in ruling Brazil since 1964. Political unrest has been reduced to a manageable level through the use of repressive and co-optive techniques, and crises of succession have been confined within the boundaries of the armed forces. Inflation is still a problem but it has been reduced to an almost tolerable level. Even though little has been done to equalize or redistribute income, the growth of the economy by an average annual rate of 10 percent over the last five years is an impressive accomplishment. The political stability and economic gains under military rule have been made at the expense of progressive political and social change, however. Brazilians are not allowed to participate in political decisions and the atmosphere of repression includes press censorship and the imprisonment, exile, and occasional torture of political dissidents.

The experience of Brazil indicates that the armed forces can provide relatively stable and, depending on one's values and priorities, effective government in a developing nation under certain conditions. It also makes clear that the phenomenon of military rule deserves more extensive research.

REFERENCES

Anderson, Charles W.
    1967   Politics and Economic Change in Latin America: The Governing of Restless Nations. Princeton: Van Nostrand.
Baker, Ross K.
    1967   A Study of Military Status and Status Deprivation in Three Latin American Armies. Washington, D.C.: Center for Research in Social Systems.
Cotler, Julio
    1970-   "Political Crisis and Military Populism in Peru." Studies in Comparative International Development 6:95-113.
    71
Einaudi, Luigi R.
    1969   The Peruvian Military: A Summary Political Analysis. Santa Monica, California: The RAND Corporation RM-6042-PR (May).
Einaudi, Luigi R. and Stepan, Alfred C., III
    1971   Latin American Institutional Development: Changing Military Perspectives in Peru and Brazil. Santa Monica, California: The RAND Corporation R-586-DOS (April).

Feit, Edward
1973 The Armed Bureaucrats: Military-Administrative Regimes and Political Development. Boston: Houghton Mifflin.
Fidel, Kenneth
1970- "Military Organization and Conspiracy in Turkey." Studies in Compara-
71 tive International Development 6:19-43.
Finer, S. E.
1962 The Man on Horseback: The Role of the Military in Politics. New York: Praeger.
Galjart, Benno
1964 "Class and 'Following' in Rural Brazil." America Latina 7 (July/September): 3-24.
Golbery (General) do Conto e Silva
1967 Geopolitica do Brasil. Rio de Janeiro: Livraria Jose Olympio.
Gonzalez Casanova, Pablo
1970 Democracy in Mexico, Danielle Salti, trans. New York: Oxford University Press.
Gutteridge, William
1965 Institutions and Power in New States. New York: Praeger.
Halpern, Manfred
1962 "Middle Eastern Armies and the New Middle Class." Pp. 277-315 in John J. Johnson (ed), The Role of the Military in Underdeveloped Countries. Princeton: Princeton University Press.
Horowitz, Irving Louis
1968 "Political Legitimization and the Institutionalization of Crisis in Latin America." Comparative Political Studies 1 (April): 45-69.
1971 "The Military as a Subculture." Pp. 41-51 in Abdul A. Said (ed), Protagonists of Change: Subcultures in Development and Revolution. Englewood Cliffs: Prentice-Hall.
Huntington, Samuel P.
1957 The Soldier and the State: The Theory and Politics of Civil-Military Relations. Cambridge: Harvard University Press.
1968 Political Order in Changing Societies. New Haven: Yale University Press.
Janowitz, Morris
1964 The Military in the Political Development of New Nations: An Essay in Comparative Analysis. Chicago: University of Chicago Press.
1965 "The Armed Forces and Society in Western Europe." European Journal of Sociology 6 (August): 225-237.
Johnson, John J.
1964 The Military and Society in Latin America. Stanford: Stanford University Press.
Kourvetaris, George Andrew
1971 "Professional Self-Images and Political Perspectives in the Greek Military." American Sociological Review 36 (December): 1043-1057.
Lee, J. M.
1969 African Armies and Civil Order. New York: Praeger.
Leff, Nathaniel H.
1968 Economic Policy-Making and Development in Brazil, 1947-1964. New York: Wiley.
Lieuwen, Edwin
1962 "Militarism and Politics in Latin America." Pp. 131-163 in John J. Johnson (ed), The Role of the Military in Underdeveloped Countries. Princeton: Princeton University Press.
Lissak, Moshe
1967 "Modernization and Role Expansion of the Military in Developing Countries." Comparative Studies in Society and History 9 (April): 233-255.

Lofchie, Michael F.
    1972   "The Uganda Coup." The Journal of Modern African Studies 10 (May):
            19-35.
Luckham, A.R.
    1971a "A Comparative Typology of Civil-Military Relations." Government and
            Opposition 6 (Winter): 5-35.
    1971b "Institutional Transfer and Breakdown in a New Nation: The Nigerian
            Military." Administrative Science Quarterly 16 (December): 387-405.
Manwaring, Max Garrett
    1968   The Military in Brazilian Politics. Ph.D. Dissertation, University of
            Illinois.
Miguens, Jose Enrique
    1970- "The New Latin American Military Coup." Studies in Comparative In-
    71   ternational Development 6:3-15.
Moreira da Silva, Paulo de Castro
    1966   "As Ativadades Paralelas das Forces Armadas." Cadernos Brasileiros
            8 (November-December): 59-64.
Needler, Martin C.
    1966   "Political Development and Military Intervention in Latin America."
            American Political Science Review 60 (September): 616-626.
Nun, Jose
    1968   "A Latin American Phenomenon: The Middle-Class Military Coup."
            Pp. 145-185 in James Petras and Maurice Zeitlin (eds), Latin America:
            Reform or Revolution? Greenwich, Connecticut: Fawcett.
Olson, Mancur, Jr.
    1965   The Logic of Collective Action: Public Goods and the Theory of Groups.
            Cambridge: Harvard University Press.
Pedreira, Fernando
    1964   Marco 31: Civis e Militares no Processo da Crise Brasileira. Rio de
            Janeiro: Jose Alvaro.
Price, Robert M.
    1971   "Military Officers and Political Leadership: The Ghanaian Case."
            Comparative Politics 3 (April): 361-379.
Ray, Talton F.
    1969   The Politics of the Barrios of Venezuela. Berkeley: University of Cali-
            fornia Press.
Schmitter, Phillippe C.
    1971   Interest Conflict and Political Change in Brazil. Stanford: Stanford Uni-
            versity Press.
Schneider, Ronald M.
    1971   The Political System of Brazil: Emergence of a "Modernizing" Authori-
            tarian Regime, 1964-1970. New York: Columbia University Press.
Scott, James C.
    1972   Comparative Political Corruption. Englewood Cliffs: Prentice-Hall.
Stepan, Alfred
    1971   The Military in Politics: Changing Patterns in Brazil. Princeton: Prince-
            ton University Press.
Wald, Arnold
    1966   Desenvolveimento, Revolucao e Democracia. Rio de Janeiro: Editora
            Fundo de Cultura.
Weffort, Francisco C.
    1970   "State and Mass in Brazil." Pp. 385-406 in Irving Louis Horowitz (ed),
            Masses in Latin America. New York: Oxford University Press.
Welch, Claude E.
    1972   "Praetorianism in Commonwealth West Africa." The Journal of Modern
            African Studies 10 (July): 203-222.
Wilner, Ann Ruth
    1970   "Perspectives on Military Elites as Rulers and Wielders of Power."
            Journal of Comparative Administration 2 (November): 261-276.

14

TECHNOLOGY AND POLITICAL
RELIABILITY IN THE
EAST GERMAN MILITARY*

DALE R. HERSPRING

Department of State

Focusing on the East German armed forces, this paper analyzes the effect increasing reliance on modern technology has had on civil-military relations in the GDR. The Party's response to modern technology in the armed forces was threefold; first, the Party provided its political representatives with technical training; second, it increased the politicization of regular officers; and third, it developed political control structures to assure that a commonality of interests between its political and regular officers will not develop to the point where the military might act as a unit against the Party. The article concludes that even though these political control structures may not be completely effective in the future, the armed forces are so heterogeneous in their interests and so politicized in their orientation that there is little danger they will ever act as a unit in opposing Party policies.

The problem of how to effect a viable relationship between the Party and the armed forces in an increasingly technical military is an important area of concern to party leaders in Communist systems. Kolkowicz (1971), for example, has argued that increasing reliance on modern technology has forced the CPSU to grant the Soviet armed forces greater institutional autonomy. Odom (1973), on the other hand, maintains that increased technology is having little or no affect on the Soviet Party's ability to control the military.

The NVA (*Nationale Volksarmee* or National People's Army) is one of the most modern in all of Europe (International Institute of Strategic Studies, 1974). In addition to a modern air force, it possesses a small, but modern navy and an army of 100,000 divided into six divisions, four of motorized infantry and two of armor. As a result of its strategic geographical location and its high marks earned in past maneuvers, the Soviets have supplied the NVA with some of the most modern equipment and consider it an important addition to Soviet forces stationed in the GDR.

In view of the highly technical nature of the NVA, it would appear, based on Kolkowicz's research, that the ruling SED (*Sozialistische Einheitspartei Deutschlands* or Socialist Unity Party) would have been forced to make concessions to the demands of modern technology and its practitioners. A recent study by this writer (Herspring, 1973) indicates, however, that although some concessions were in fact made, the Party has not been forced to grant the

---

*The views expressed in this article are those of the writer and do not represent official U.S. Government policy.

NVA greater institutional autonomy. This suggests that Odom's findings for the USSR more closely describe the East German situation than do Kolkowicz's. In order to better understand the reasons for this situation, it might be useful to look at the Party's reaction to increased technology by focusing on the way it has handled the political reliability and technical qualifications of its officer corps.

During the seven years of its existence (1949-1956) as the KVP (*Kasernierte Volkspolizei* or People's Police Quartered in Barracks), the predecessor of the NVA, the Party assumed a low profile. Cognizant of the hostility with which large segments of the population, including some members of the military, viewed it and limited by the easy escape route open to discontents through Berlin, the Party adopted a policy aimed at neutralizing hostility toward the regime. Political control mechanisms such as the military party organization were present. Nevertheless, no attempt was made to force officers to participate in political activities. Those who were not against the Party were considered its allies.

This situation changed in 1956 with the Hungarian uprising, shortly after the founding of the NVA. Cognizant of the low degree of normative commitment on the part of its own officer corps and aware of the large number of Hungarian officers who went over to the insurgents, the SED party leadership decided it would no longer sanction political neutrality.

Yet, while placing greater emphasis on politicizing the armed forces, the SED leadership nevertheless took care to avoid escalating political requirements to the point where they would make technological growth impossible.[1] Although the importance of a politically reliable military was upper most in their minds, party leaders made it abundantly clear that they were interested not only in "red" military officers, but in "expert" political officers as well. Only by combining both technical competence and political reliability would it be possible to become one of the most modern and politically reliable members of the Warsaw Pact, a position which would strengthen the East German hand in relations with the Soviets.

THE POLITICAL OFFICER AND TECHNOLOGY

The attempt by Communist parties to maximize military efficiency and political control through the use of political officers (or political commissars as they were formerly called), has resulted in tensions between professional soldiers and these officers ever since they were first introduced in the Red Army in 1918. Modern technology has made resolution of this conflict even more difficult. The more complex the weapons systems involved, the more difficult it becomes for the non-specialist to understand either their operation or the problems associated with their deployment. As a consequence, the political officer who is not a technician may unintentionally sabotage the efficient operation of a unit through his ignorance. This in turn may also create dissension between him and the regular officer with whom he is supposed to

---

1. Technical growth at this time was also of great importance. The military had just released most of the former members of the *Wehrmacht* who had served as the bulk of its technical specialists. In addition, the overall educational level of the officer corps was abysmally low. For example, only 10.7% had attended a three year officer's training school, over 79% had not gone beyond the basic school and only 2.0% possessed an academic degree (Herspring, 1973).

work closely. The technically incompetent political officer may also find himself unable to relate to his charges in a manner with which they can identify and in terms they can understand.

In the Soviet Union, shifts in emphasis on politicization or military efficiency have brought forth structural changes to modify the authority relationships between military and political officers (Fainsod, 1967:463-500). For example, fear of German military prowess in 1940 resulted in the abolition of the position of political commissar and his replacement with that of assistant commander for political work. In 1941, concern over the large scale surrenders and the collapse of resistance in the face of the German onslaught led to reinstatement of the political commissar. Finally, in 1942, confident that political control had been reestablished, political commissars were again dropped and assistant commanders for political work reintroduced. The Soviets have also varied the level within the military organization to which political officers are assigned. For example, in 1955 the position was abolished at the company level (Fainsod, 1967:483; Garthoff, 1966:51).

Interestingly, the East Germans have never undertaken this type of structural change. At the time of the founding of the KVP in 1949, political officers were assigned down to the company level. This practice was carried over to the NVA after its inception in 1956 and has continued to the present day.

In order to deal with the problem of raising the technical qualifications of political officers, the Soviets have placed increased emphasis on the technical qualifications of young political officers (Fainsod, 1967:486, Jones, 1974:97). In addition, they have employed a policy aimed at interchanging military and political officers in order to provide each with a better understanding of the problems faced by the other (Fainsod, 1967:486, Wolfe, 1968:129).

It is these latter, non-structural approaches to the problem which most closely parallel the methods utilized by the East Germans. The majority of the political officers who entered the newly created NVA in 1956 had been members of the KVP. Most of them had attended a political officer training school for between one and two years where a minimum of time was devoted to technical subjects. To meet the need for a better educated political officer corps, one of the first steps taken upon creation of the NVA was the establishment of a political officer training school in Berlin-Treptow. At the same time, the length of study required for future political officers was lengthened from two to three years. It was hoped that the additional time would better enable the future political officers to learn the techniques necessary to make their dogma credible in an increasingly technical military.

In an attempt to procure individuals with a better understanding of military hardware, an instruction was issued in 1957 which stated that henceforth, "cadre from the best and most active soldiers and NCO's from units are to be selected and sent to the Political Officer Training School" (Autorenkollektiv, 1969:90). Thus political officers began to be drawn from men with at least a basic familiarity with many of the military's increasingly complex weapons systems.

Nevertheless, these changes proved insufficient. The technical background of the former enlisted men and NCO's was inadequate to enable them to deal satisfactorily with their technical colleagues. Even attempts by the political officer training school to supplement their lack of technical training with special courses covering some aspects of military procedures and technology failed. Faced with numerous complaints by military officers frustrated by their inability to work with technically incompetent political colleagues, the SED closed down the school in 1961 (Forester, 1972:181). From then on, individuals wishing to become political officers had two options. They could attend one of the military officer training schools and emphasize political subjects, or once they were commissioned as military or naval officers they could be selected for special political studies or take correspondence courses. Successful completion of these courses would be followed by service as political officers (Greese and Voerster, 1966:42).

Regardless of which path was selected, the aspiring political officer would be required to attend a regular officer training school, where he would be expected to be technically qualified like any other graduate. Thus a political officer, like his military counterpart, who attended the Army's Ernst Thälmann Officer Training School would be expected to qualify as a squad leader in one of the army's major areas of specialization, i.e. motorized infantry, armor or communications.

Reliance on military officers whose political training was gained primarily from short-term courses to fill positions as political officers continued until 1970. Although the Party had succeeded in producing political officers who were technically qualified, it was felt that their political qualifications left much to be desired. Consequently, a political officer school, later named the Wilhelm Pieck Military-Political College, with the status of a university (*Hochschule*) was established in Berlin in 1970.[2] This school, it was hoped, would provide its graduates with a thorough knowledge of political subjects to complement their technical expertise. As General Hoffmann (1970:12), the Minister of Defense and head of the NVA, put it at the time the school was established:

> Old experiences and good will no longer suffice to lead ideological work with sufficient quality. Only when our commanders and political officers possess advanced scientific knowledge as well as the necessary educational ability and skills will it be possible to do justice to the increasing demands of work with the masses.

Although specific details concerning this school are not available, it is apparently aimed at training graduates of the officer training schools, who have served in the field for a couple of years as political officers at the company and battalion level. Presumably, individuals selected to serve as political officers would attend this school for at least a year and from all appearances probably longer. The opportunity also exists for selected individuals to continue beyond this one year course and obtain the academic degree of a diploma in social science (*Diplomgesellschaftswissenschaft*). In addition to training young officers for work as political officers, this college also offers short courses for higher ranking officers.

To fulfill his role, the political officer now receives both high quality technical training and courses designed to provide not only a sophisticated knowledge of Marxism-Leninism, but an understanding of pedagogical techniques for its dissemination as well. Only thus, the SED decided, could it expect political officers to carry out party policy intelligently and present party dogma in a way which would appeal to the highly educated technicians with which they were increasingly confronted.

---

2. The other four officer training schools, the Ernst Thälmann Army Officer School, Franz Mehring Air Force Officer School, the Karl Liebknecht Naval Officer School and the Rosa Luxemburg Border Troops Officer School were also accorded the status of a university in 1970.

THE MILITARY OFFICER AND IDEOLOGY

While the SED worked to improve the performance of political officers, it was also concerned with cultivating a high degree of political reliability among NVA military officers. Party leaders resisted the temptation to throw caution to the wind and place their entire emphasis on raising the technical qualifications of their relatively incompetent officer corps. The SED leadership decided that military officers must also be politically reliable.

For members of the KVP, all performance measures such as political qualifications, leadership ability and technical competence appear to have been weighted equally in determining the selection and promotion of officers to all but the very highest levels where political considerations were paramount. In fact it was even possible for a military officer to remain uninvolved in political activities and be promoted, provided he was a good technician and not openly hostile to the Party.

With the creation of the NVA, and the events in Hungary, the Party quickly shifted its attention to an officer's political qualifications. Officers who had tended to view themselves primarily as technical experts with little or no time for party activities were severely reprimanded. In addition, a resolution by the SED Politbüro establishing "regulations for the Role of the Party in the NVA" made it very clear that only politically active officers had a future in the NVA. As one East German political officer (Borning, 1958:1) put it:

> The practice shows, however, that political and military training have been separated from one another, that some comrade officers believe that they are military "specialists" (*Fachleute*) and that political work, the education of their subordinates, is the task of the political officer. This tendency was strengthened because the party organization exerted so little influence on military training and education. In the resolution of the Politbüro, the demand was stated decisively that each officer must, in the first place, be a political functionary who carries out his work on behalf of the Party.

To insure the political activism of military officers, emphasis was placed on work by the military in various sectors of the civilian economy such as industry, harvesting crops and public works. In theory, this program is not unlike those of China and some other Eastern European countries, most notably Rumania. In practice, however, in spite of the large amount of attention given to such projects in the East German press, their own figures for the years for which data are available indicate that the total amount of time devoted to such projects never exceeded more than one percent of the total working hours available to the military (Herspring, 1973). Although it is not possible to say with certainty why the Party has been willing to accept such a low level of involvement by the military in the civilian sector, two factors seem to be of primary importance. First, the highly developed state of the East German economy necessitates the use of such labor for only limited projects, and second, the Party has enough other techniques available to make such work unnecessary in its effort to politicize the NVA.

Another measure used by the Party was the requirement that all officers and in particular military officers must have spent some time working in the civilian economy or as the East Germans call it, the productive process. Those officers who had not had the "opportunity" to do such work would be required to spend up to six months in either agriculture or industry (Ulbricht, 1958:41). The program sought to prevent a resurgence of a feeling of superiority or alienation within a German military clique toward civilian society. This policy is no longer operative because all entering students at officer training schools are graduates of the East German polytechnic educational system. It does, however, appear to have served its purpose. Those who do not show the proper amount of "enthusiasm" for such work either while in the polytechnic educational system or while performing their civilian work as members of the military will not be permitted to make the military a career.

One of the most important prerequisites for assuring participation by the military officer in party activities is party membership. Fully aware that increasing the percentage of party members in the NVA officer corps would bring in many opportunists and careerists, the Party nevertheless felt that the increased control it would have over military officers by making them subject to party as well as military discipline justified such a move. As a consequence, the Party applied increased pressure on officers to become party members. The proportion of officers who were party members rose accordingly from 79.5% at the time the NVA was founded to over 98.0% by the end of 1973 (Herspring, 1973). Pressure to join the Party has not been limited to technical and combat officers. Even military physicians and veterinarians have been forced to form party groups where they spend their time discussing subjects such as the advantages of socialized medicine over the more capitalistic style of medicine prevalent in the West.

Of the policies the Party introduced to politicize military officers, its emphasis on political factors for promotion and the introduction of part-time ideological courses are probably the most important. The instructions introduced in 1958 made the military officer responsible for both the military and political performance of his unit. Now, instead of being able to blame the political officer, if, for example, political indoctrination lectures were not stimulating, the military officer bears primary responsibility. While blame for failures in this area is shared by the political officer, it is particularly damaging to the military commander's chances for promotion since as a socialist military officer he is expected to combine a good knowledge of military technology with a high level of socialist consciousness.

Along with the stress it placed on officers' political consciousness, the Party soon realized that it would have to supply these officers with the necessary theoretical knowledge if they were going to bear responsibility in the political as well as military spheres. Consequently, the Party made part-time political education courses mandatory in 1963. Up to this time, political indoctrination courses had been voluntary, similar to the situation in the Soviet Union in the mid-fifties (Garthoff, 1966:51). The first segment of the mandatory officer indoctrination program, called "Further Education in the Social Sciences (*gesellschaftswissenschaftliche Weiterbildung*)," was to last three years. Participants attended one study session a week. In addition to attending classes, officers were also required to read extensively and write seminar papers.

After the first segment of the program studying the basis of Marxism-Leninism came to an end in 1966 with a rather elaborate set of oral and written examinations, a second course was introduced which dealt with the history of the German Worker's Movement. A third segment was introduced in 1969 and dealt with problems of a more general nature such as the Socialist Commonwealth and the struggle between socialism and imperialism. A fourth segment began in 1972, although details on its content are not available. As a result of this program, military officers hoping to get ahead have to show not only their enthusiasm for party activities, but their knowledge of its ideology, history and positions on various subjects as well.

Tighter control over military promotions further increased party influence over military officers. In order to provide the Party with a firm basis upon which to evaluate an officer's technical and political qualifications for promotion, a set of efficiency reports were introduced in 1964. While previously an individual's commanding officer had been expected to enter a sentence or two concerning his political qualifications and enthusiasm in his record, the new forms, filled out every four years, called for extensive comments regarding both his technical and political performance. Those not considered either technically or politically qualified would not be promoted.

These efficiency reports have become increasingly important to a military officer's career. This became particularly apparent in the forms for the 1972 efficiency reports which linked promotion closely to the information provided, particularly in regard to attendance at various educational and training institutions in the GDR and Soviet Union. For example, in order to be promoted to senior ranks in the NVA, it is necessary for an officer to attend the Friedrich Engels Military Academy in Dresden. The individual's commanding officer, in close consultation with the military party organization, must make a recommendation concerning an individual's technical and political qualifications for attendance at the academy. Should he fail to be recommended, he could be demoted or released from the service, or if he is a borderline case, remain in the service without any hope of aspiring to high level ranks. The situation is even more critical for a technical specialist. Many positions require that their occupant have completed a special school. In determining whether or not to send an individual to that school, his superiors are now required to take into consideration his political performance. Consequently, even though he may have already attended the academy or a similar one in the Soviet Union, he may find himself denied a command position because he failed to complete the appropriate school.

Insofar as the future is concerned, studies carried out among officer cadets in the GDR during the mid-sixties confirm that, contrary to Party hopes, the tendency of military technicians to lack enthusiasm for political studies and activities still exists. When asked why they had decided on a military career, for example, air force cadets replied, "because we like modern technology" (Wahnelt and Flau, 1967:4-5). Likewise, cadets at the army's Ernst Thälmann Officer Training School listed political studies as their least interesting course (Lüttke and Mahn, 1966:1424). This suggests that the Party will have to continue to emphasize the importance of political training to military officers just as it will have to place continued stress on the importance of technical training for political officers if it hopes to produce officers highly competent in both areas.

THE PARTY AND POLITICAL AND MILITARY OFFICERS

Assuming that the Party has been successful in narrowing the conceptual gap between military and political officers, there is still a question of the effect this move toward convergence may have on the relationship between the Party and the armed forces. Will a commonality of interests and outlook produce political and military officers who empathize with each other's problems and create a strong sense of what Huntington (1959:10) has called corporateness of sufficient intensity that party directives which they perceive detrimental to the fulfillment of the NVA's mission are ignored or diluted? To assure that such a situation never arises, the Party has developed two closely related structures.

One of these structures is the military party organization.[3] Although the military party organization has been present in the East German armed forces since their founding in 1949, its activities were often ignored, in particular by military officers. The 1958 resolution of the Politbüro, in addition to increasing pressure on the military officer to become involved in party activities also expanded the role of the military party organization.

Up to this time, the smallest party unit, the basic organization (*Grundorganisation*) was formed only as far down into the NVA organizational structure as the regimental level. Most of the Party's activities, however, took place further down in the organizational structure - primarily at the company level. Consequently, the Party was often forced to rely almost entirely on the political officer for direction and comments regarding the effectiveness of political activities such as political indoctrination. To counteract this situation, the Party established party groups (*Parteigruppen*) down to the company level creating a situation similar to that prevalent in the USSR (Fainsod, 1967:486). This meant that the Party was now organizationally present at the most important level of military and party activity.

In 1963, the Party moved to further strengthen the effectiveness of the military party organization by lowering the level to which the basic organization is present down to the battalion and independent company. In addition, party groups were extended to include platoons as well as non-independent companies. As a result, the military party organization was now present down to the very smallest unit of the NVA, a situation which has continued to the present day.

The authority of the respective military party organizations is considerable. They may require the recall of any political or military officer at their level who fails to give evidence, either individually or collectively, of a willingness to properly implement party directives. This means that even a company commander and his political deputy must be careful to follow party instructions.

The second structure utilized by the Party to insure that its directives are carefully followed are the political organs (*Politorgane*). The task of these organs, which are very similar in structure to those of the Soviet military (Wolfe, 1968:129), is to direct all political work within the NVA. This includes among other things, setting up courses for and directing the carrying out of political indoctrination courses, making certain that party directives are followed, and supervising political cadres. Although they too existed prior to 1958, the political organs were loosely organized, and as a result, the coordination of activities at various levels left much to be desired. Although the 1958 resolutions of the Politbüro affirmed the importance of the political organs in regulating and supervising party activities, little was done to effectively improve their performance.

In 1963 another attempt was made to strengthen the authority of the political organs by making them responsible for activities down to the basic organization. This meant they had to increase the frequency and expand the

---

3. The SED is the only one of East Germany's five political parties which is permitted to organize in the military.

scope of their inspections and supervisory activities considerably. In spite of this added authority, however, the Party remained unsatisfied with efforts in this area. Finally, in 1967, a Central Party Directorate (*Zentrale Parteileitung* or ZPL) was established. This structure, manned jointly by representatives of the political organs and military party organization, has the task of coordinating sections not only of the basic organization, but those of party groups as well. As a result, it has been possible for the political organs to supervise and report on party activities at even the lowest levels. Through the increased authority enjoyed by both of these structures, it is highly unlikely that political or military officers will be able to circumvent party directives without seriously damaging their careers in the NVA.

CONCLUSION

Although it would appear that the Party has been successful in developing not only political officers with technical skills and technical officers who are politically active, but supervisory organs to monitor their behavior as well, the Party still faces a potentially serious problem. Just as it was important for the Party to develop techniques to counteract any tendencies on the part of regular and political officers to cooperate too closely as a result of their increased empathy for each other's problems, thereby circumventing party policy, it will also be necessary for the Party to develop a means of avoiding the rise of a coalition of generals and admirals who may have ideas different from those of the Party on military matters. Up to now, this has not been a serious problem. All four of the currently highest ranking officers in the NVA, for example, are in their positions primarily because of political qualifications. One is a member of the Politbüro, two are members of the Central Committee, and one is a candidate member of the Central Committee.

Karl-Heinz Hoffmann, a member of the Politbüro, is the Minister of Defense and an army general. Although a veteran of the Spanish Civil War and a graduate of a Soviet military academy, he is far from being a trained technician. He is, however, a dedicated Marxist-Leninist and from all reports, an outstanding manager. His heir-apparent, Heinz Keßler, a colonel general, and chief of the Main Staff, is also a graduate of a Soviet military academy. Although he was formerly commander of the air force, he also lacks a technical background. In fact, his elevation to this important position is probably more due to his close personal relationship with Honecker, stretching back to the days when they were both in the Free German Youth movement, than his military expertise.

Waldemar Verner, head of the Main Political Administration and an admiral, is one of the most technically deficient members of the NVA.[4] He appears to owe his position primarily to his brother who is a member of the SED's Politbüro. Herbert Scheibe, a lieutenant general and director of the Central Committee's Section on Security Questions, appears to be in line for Verner's job when he retires. Formerly a political officer, he has also served as a regular officer in the air force in addition to attending a Soviet military academy. Yet, although he has held jobs in both the technical and political areas, he too appears to lack significant technical training. Consequently,

---

4. As an East German said to this writer, "Professional sailor? Nonsense, he can't even swim." (Berufssoldat? Quatsch, er kann nicht mal schwimmen).

although he most closely approximates the model of a "socialist" officer of the four discussed here, it would be difficult to list him as a technically qualified political officer.

Although it is of course possible that the Party could continue to recruit its top generals from the ranks of the politically active, this does not appear likely. The NVA has given no indication in its admittedly short history of an inclination to bring civilians into the upper ranks of the military.[5] Assuming that it continues to follow this policy and further that it continues to demand that *all* officers, whatever their main area of specialization, be both technically qualified and politically active, then it is only a matter of time before the leadership of the NVA passes into the hands of "socialist" admirals and generals. How will this affect the relationship between the Party and the military? The political organs and military party organization will be of limited utility to the Party, particularly since they will probably be headed by officers who would be part of this hypothetical "coalition."

Odom's (1973) suggestion that the dichotomy between technology and ideology is not as serious as often thought may supply a partial answer to this question. It is true that the military often resents the primacy which the Party appears to place on politicization in the NVA. On the other hand, however, it is also accurate that some party leaders feel too much attention is paid to technical factors and not enough to politics. Yet, both appear to accept the need for the other.

The NVA is primarily a political organization. There is no room in the NVA for an apolitical technocrat. This is constantly stressed not only in the military press, but in daily lectures and part-time ideological courses as well. The same is true insofar as technical knowledge is concerned. There is no longer any room for the technically incompetent political officer. All military officers, however, appear to accept the need for Party primacy - even though they may disagree with some aspects of some policies. Hence the likelihood of an East German officer contemplating actions different from those advocated by the Party appears small.

Even if several officers did decide to oppose a particular party policy, there is very little likelihood that they could mobilize the armed forces to act as a corporate body. The NVA, like other military units, is not a monolithic organization. In the day to day bureaucratic battles over resource allocation and policy implementation, the various competing services can be expected to look outside their own service and even outside the military community for support. As a result, rather than a military vs. Party confrontation, one would probably see one part of the military on one side aligned with a component of civilian society, while the remainder either remained neutral or aligned themselves with other components of society.

This suggests that, at present at least, the coming of the "socialist" admirals and generals will not seriously affect the present relationship between the Party and the armed forces. These individuals, although they will be professional soldiers, will also be party members, who accept party primacy and evidence obedience in carrying out its instructions regardless of whatever institutional loyalties they may feel.

---

5. The one possible exception is Stoph who headed the NVA from 1956 to 1960 when Hoffmann took over.

REFERENCES

Autorenkollektiv des Deutschen Instituts für Militärgeschichte (Author Collective of the German Institute of Military History)
  1969   Zeittafel zur Militärgeschichte der Deutschen Demokratischen Republik, 1949 bis 1968 (Chronological Table of Military History of the German Democratic Republic, 1949 to 1968). Berlin: Deutscher Militärverlag.

Borning, Walter, Colonel
  1958   "Unter Führung der Partei erringen wir Erfolge" (We achieve Successes under the Leadership of the Party). Volksarmee, June 24, 1958:1.

Fainsod, Merle
  1967   How Russia is Ruled. Cambridge: Harvard University Press, rev. ed.

Forster, Thomas M.
  1972   Die NVA - Kernstück der Landesverteidigung der DDR (The NPA - Basis of the Defense of the GDR). Köln: Markus Verlag.

Garthoff, Raymond A.
  1966   Soviet Military Strategy. New York: Praeger.

Greese, Karl and Voerster, Alfred
  1966   "Probleme der Auswahl und Föderung der Offizierskader in der NVA, 1958-1963" (Problems of Selection and Promotion of Officer Cadre in the NPA, 1958-1963). Zeitschrift fur Militärgeschichte 1:32-47.

Herspring, Dale R.
  1973   East German Civil-Military Relations: The Impact of Technology, 1949-1972. New York: Praeger.

Hoffmann, Heinz, General
  1970   "Siebziger Jahre Setzen hohe Maßstäbe für die Marxistisch-leninistische Bildung, für die Erziehung, Lehre und Forschung" (The Nineteen Seventies require high Standards for Marxist-Leninist Training, for Education, Teaching and Research). Parteiarbeiter Special Issue:2-14.

Huntington, Samuel
  1964   The Soldier and the State. New York: Vintage.

International Institute of Strategic Studies
  1974   The Military Balance, 1974-1975. London: International Institute of Strategic Studies.

Jones, Christopher D.
  1974   "The 'Revolution in Military Affairs' and Party-Military Relations, 1965-70." Survey 20 (Winter):84-100.

Kolkowicz, Roman
  1971   "The Military." Pp. 131-169 in Gordon Skilling and Franklyn Griffiths (eds.), Interest Groups in Soviet Politics. Princeton: Princeton University Press.

Lüttke, H., Lieutenant Colonel and Mahn, S., Lieutenant Colonel
  1966   "Erfahrungen bei der Verbesserung der Bildungs- und Erziehungsarbeit durch Klassenanalysen" (Experience Associated with Improvement of the Educational and Training Work as a Result of Class Analysis). Militärwesen 10:1420-1432.

Odom, William E.
  1973   "The Party Connection." Problems of Communism 22 (September-October):12-26.

Ulbricht, Walter
  1958   "Zur Eröffnung der ersten sozialistischen Militärakademie in der Geschichte Deutschlands" (On the Occasion of the Opening of the First Socialist Military Academy in the History of Germany). Militärwesen Special Issue:5-47.

Wahnelt, R., Major and Flau, E. Major
  1967   "Die Notwendigkeit richtiger Vorstellungen über die gesellschaftliche Rolle des Offiziersberufs" (The Necessity for a Correct Understanding of the Social Role of the Officer's Profession). Luftverteidigung 2:3-12.

Wolfe, Thomas W.
  1968   "The Military." Pp. 112-142 in Allen Kassof (ed.), Prospects for Soviet-Society. New York: Praeger.

Methodological Issues in Military Intervention

15

MILITARY INTERVENTION:
A METHODOLOGICAL NOTE

LEE SIGELMAN

Texas Tech University

This note examines five indicators of the extent of military interven-tion in the domestic political order. Although some of the indicators have been extensively employed in cross-national research, all are found to be lacking in sensitivity (the ability to make distinctions among roughly similar cases) and validity (as measured by the convergence test). A composite intervention measure, the Military Intervention Index (MII), is derived by the simple expedient of combining the five indicators — computing percentile scores for each of 88 nations on each indicator and then computing an overall mean percentile scale. The MII is found to be far more sensitive and a good deal more valid than any of the individual indicators. Although it is still far from a perfect measure of intervention, the MII is a substantial improvement over existing indicators; use of the MII in cross-national research could well contribute to the accumulation of well-documented findings concerning the political role of military systems.

Recent years have witnessed an explosion of literature on the causes, correlates, and consequences of military intervention in the domestic political order. Beyond the important theoretical contributions of Finer (1962), Huntington (1964), Janowitz (1964), and others, the intervention literature has featured a commitment to the sort of hypothesis-testing on a broad cross-national scale that is all too rare in comparative study (see, e.g., Feldberg, 1970; Fossum, 1967; Hoadley, 1973; Needler, 1966; Nordlinger, 1970; Putnam, 1967; Schmitter, 1973). Despite this commit-ment to rigor, however, students of intervention have yet to satisfactorily resolve a key problem — how to measure military intervention. Many indicators of intervention have been offered, but each, as we shall see, suffers certain disabilities. The intent of this brief note is to assess these indicators and to offer a new, hybrid approach to the measurement of intervention.

INTERVENTION INDICATORS: AN ASSESSMENT

There is no lack of consensus on the meaning of "intervention." Most scholars would concur with Samuel Finer's (1962:23) definition of inter-vention as "the armed forces' constrained substitution of their own poli-cies and/or their persons, for those of the recognized civilian authori-ties." But how to *measure* intervention? The problem for comparativists is to develop valid and discriminating measures, and here, unfortunately there is little consensus.

Although most cross-national studies of intervention have relied on the indicators put forward by Adelman and Morris (1968) or Banks and Textor (1963), these are not the only potentially useful scales. A broad cross-section of nations have been classified according to the political role of the military in at least five different works:

(1) Adelman and Morris' (1967) "political strength of the military" scale, an eight-point judgmental index of the level of military intervention in 74 less developed systems in the early and middle 1960s.

(2) Banks and Textor's (1963) three-point "political participation by the military" scale, for 115 nations in the early 1960s.

(3) Coleman's (1960) two dichotomous ratings of military "over-participation" in the performance of political and governmental functions, which, when combined into a single scale, present a three-point index of military intervention in 76 less developed systems, circa 1960.

(4) Finer's (1970) twelve-category classification of regime types, which, by collapsing the fifth through twelfth categories, can be converted into a five-point intervention index for 125 nations as of the 1960s.

(5) Banks' (1971) three-category classification of regime types according to the political role of the military in 135 nations, yearly from early in the nineteenth century to 1966, which, when scores are aggregated from 1956 to 1966, indexes intervention for a period which roughly corresponds to that covered by the other indicators.

In assessing the utility of these scales, two shortcomings must be recognized. First of all, the scales lack *sensitivity*. Any instrument's discriminatory power is limited, but in the case of intervention measures, insensitivity seems to have been carried to an extreme — especially by the dichotomies and trichotomies among the five indicators. Insufficient sensitivity would not necessarily pose an important problem, except that it constitutes a source of measurement error: crude distinctions group unlike cases (see Kaplan, 1964: 199-200). Secondly, the scales seem very *idiosyncratic*. As indicators of the same underlying concept, military intervention, the five scales ought to be very highly intercorrelated; this is what is meant by the "convergent validity" of a measure — the extent to which it is related to other indicators of the same concept. But in this regard, the performance of the five indicators is not very impressive. As Table 1 demonstrates, the correlations between pairs of indicators are often distressingly low: almost half are beneath the .4 level, and only one tops .6. Moreover, only one of the indices — Adelman and Morris' — displays an average correlation which is at all impressive, and this is largely a function of the magnitude of its correlation with the Banks-Textor measure (which, not so coincidentally, Adelman and Morris (1967:75) say they consulted in creating their own variable).

In sum, presently-available intervention indicators are neither as sensitive nor as valid as one might wish. This situation is doubly problematic, in that indicators may be relatively sensitive, or they may be relatively valid, but they are very unlikely to be *both* sensitive *and* valid. The Banks index, for example, has the greatest power of discrimination, but the lowest average correlation. The Banks-Textor

TABLE 1.   INTERCORRELATIONS BETWEEN FIVE INDICATORS
            OF MILITARY INTERVENTION[a]

	(1)	(2)	(3)	(4)	(5)
1) Adelman-Morris	---	.591	.493	.478	.778
2) Coleman		---	.375	.381	.592
3) Finer			---	.597	.353
4) Banks				---	.312
5) Banks-Textor					---
Average Correlation	.585	.485	.455	.442	.509

[a]The correlation coefficient is Kendall's tau, an ordinal measure
of association.

measure, which scores relatively high on the convergence test, is extremely insensitive. Surely the best available measure of intervention, by
these criteria, is Adelman and Morris'. But although the performance
of this indicator is impressive compared to the other available indicators,
it is hard to believe that military intervention cannot be measured with
substantially greater sensitivity and validity.

MEASURING INTERVENTION:
A SIMPLE COMPOSITE APPROACH

Quantitative cross-national studies of intervention are thus beset with
pressing measurement problem. Given the low to moderate correlations
between alternative intervention indices, findings may be "indicator-
specific"; that is, empirical findings about intervention derived when one
indicator is used may not be valid for other measures. A simple solution
would be to construct a composite intervention indicator, one which is
more closely related to each individual index than the indices are to
one another. That is, where individual measures are bedeviled by idio-
syncracy, combining several of the measures can cancel individual
idiosyncracies and thus enhance validity; such a procedure in effect
presents a "lowest common denominator" from a measurement perspective — analogous to (though less sophisticated than) index construction
through factor analysis. Moreover, aggregating several indicators rather
than relying on a single indicator permits much finer discriminations to
be made.

Creating a composite intervention measure is quite simple. Because
the scope of two of the indicators is restricted to "third world" nations,
it was necessary to drop European and North American nations from the
analysis; this left the 88 Latin American, African, Middle Eastern, and
Asian nations which are listed in Table 2. The primary methodological
problem here, as in all composite indices, was settling on a procedure

TABLE 2. MILITARY INTERVENTION INDEX SCORES AND RANKS FOR 88
NATIONS

Rank	Nation	MII Score	Rank	Nation	MII Scor
1	Burma	89.1	46.5	Afghanistan	43.
2	Syria	89.0	46.5	Ethiopia	43.
3	Sudan	88.0	46.5	Lebanon	43.
4	Pakistan	87.0	46.5	Senegal	43.
5	Argentina	86.6	49	Mali	43.
6	Thailand	85.4	50	Somali Rep.	43.
7	Iraq	84.9	51	Rhodesia	42.
8.5	Congo, Kinshasa	83.8	52	Cambodia	40.
8.5	El Salvador	83.8	54	Mongolia	39.
10	Algeria	83.2	54	North Korea	39.
11	Peru	81.6	54	North Vietnam	39.
12	Honduras	80.8	56	Libya	39.
13	Guatemala	78.5	57	Saudi Arabia	37.
14	Egypt	76.2	58	Liberia	36.
15	Brazil	73.7	59	Kenya	34.
16	South Korea	73.2	60.5	Guinea	34.
17	Paraguay	72.0	60.5	Mexico	34.
18	Nicaragua	71.9	62	Malaysia	32.
19	Indonesia	69.2	63	Chad	31.
20	Haiti	68.0	64	Kuwait	30.
21.5	Dominican Rep.	66.4	65.5	Mauritania	28.
21.5	South Vietnam	66.4	65.5	Rwanda	28.
23	Yemen	65.6	67.5	Malawi	27.
24	Venezuela	62.1	67.5	Zambia	27.
25	Bolivia	60.5	76.5	Cameroun	27.
26	Ecuador	59.6	76.5	Ceylon	27.
27	Turkey	58.9	76.5	Chile	27.
28	Togo	58.7	76.5	Costa Rica	27.
29	Panama	58.2	76.5	Gabon	27.
30	Laos	57.7	76.5	India	27.
31	Taiwan	55.9	76.5	Israel	27.
32.5	C.A.R.	55.3	76.5	Ivory Coast	27.
32.5	Upper Volta	55.3	76.5	Morocco	27.
34	Burundi	53.6	76.5	Niger	27.
35	Jordan	50.6	76.5	Philippines	27.
36	Nepal	50.2	76.5	Sierra Leone	27.
37	Nigeria	48.8	76.5	Tanganyika	27.
38	Cuba	48.6	76.5	Tunisia	27.
39	Iran	48.0	76.5	Uganda	27.
40	Ghana	47.8	76.5	Uruguay	27.
41	Dahomey	47.4	86	Jamaica	26.
42	Colombia	47.3	86	Japan	26.
43	Congo, Brazza.	47.2	86	Trinidad	26.
44	South Africa	44.2	88	Malagasay	26.

for combining the various indicators. Of course, such techniques, e.g.
t-scoring, z-scoring, factor analysis, abound. In the present case, how
ever, it was decided that, because of the ordinal nature of the five indi
cators, the most appropriate technique would involve computing percen
tile scores for each nation on each indicator, and then computing an
overall mean percentile scale. (Percentile scores rather than simple rank

were used in computation because of the differing lengths of the five series, caused by missing data. Finsterbusch (1973) employed precisely the same method in creating overall indices of the level and rate of modernization in 69 nations.) Each nation's rank and score on this scale, called the Military Intervention Index (MII), are displayed in Table 2.

Obviously there is a great deal of variability among nations on the MII. Of course, the theoretical maximum and minimum values of the MII (100.0 and 0.0) are not attained by any of the 88 nations examined here. But there is an obvious stratification on the MII, ranging from a relatively small set of nations which score very high, to a larger class of nations in the middle range, and finally to a large group of nations in which the military plays a minimal political role. Moreover, as Table 3 reveals, there is also a clear stratification among geographic regions, with Latin America, the Middle East, and Asia, in that order, all displaying appreciably higher intervention scores than did Africa in the 1960s. However, Table 3 also indicates a good deal of heterogeneity within regions, which suggests that it is dangerous to characterize a nation by the central tendency of the region of which it is a member.

TABLE 3.   MILITARY INTERVENTION SCORE MEAN, RANGE, AND
STANDARD DEVIATION, BY REGION

Region	N	Mean MII Score	Range	Standard Deviation
Latin America	22	57.68	26.5 - 86.6	21.14
Africa	36	41.37	26.1 - 88.0	16.64
Middle East	12	54.58	27.3 - 89.0	20.58
Asia	18	51.93	26.5 - 89.1	21.91

Does the performance of the MII measure up against that of the five individual indicators? Inspection of Table 2 should reveal the substantial increase in sensitivity which is gained by a composite approach. The 88 nations represented in Table 2 are ranked on a scale which contains 60 discrete steps — a huge improvement over any of the five indicators. In this sense, the MII is far less crude than the indicators. Whereas the five indicators permit only the broadest of comparisons to be made, the MII differentiates between cases which are roughly similar, but not identical. Of course, there is always the danger of spurious precision. The temptation to label the Burmese military as clearly more highly interventionist than the Syrian must be stoutly resisted. But Table 2 does provide clear warrant for labelling the Burmese military more highly interventionist than the South Korean, the Syrian than the Egyptian, and the Argentine than the Nicaraguan. Significantly, these are precisely the sorts of distinctions which cannot be made by the five individual indicators, because each lumps roughly similar cases together in very broad categories.

TABLE 4.   CORRELATIONS BETWEEN THE MII AND THE FIVE INTERVENTION
            INDICATORS*

Indicator	Correlation with MII
Adelman-Morris	.744
Coleman	.629
Finer	.610
Banks	.598
Banks-Textor	.666
Average Correlation	.649

*The correlation coefficient is Kendall's tau, an ordinal measure of association.

But what about the validity of the MII compared to the five indicators? Table 4 presents the correlations of the MII with each of the component indicators. Each of the correlations is at least in the vicinity of .6. The MII's correlation with each indicator is always far above the indicator's average correlation and, more significantly, the MII's average correlation is easily higher than that of any of the indicators. Each of the five component scales contributes substantially to the overall intervention score. In sum, not only is the MII much more discriminating than any of the indicators, it is also, by the test of convergence, substantially more valid.

Naturally, the MII is still neither as sensitive nor as valid as we would wish. Moreover, it is restricted in application to the early and middle 1960s. Nonetheless, we hope that by pointing up some of the inadequacies of available intervention indicators and by offering a simple composite intervention index, this brief note may contribute to the accumulation of well-documented findings on the political role of military systems.

REFERENCES

Adelman, Irma and Morris, Cynthia Taft
    1967   Society, Politics, and Economic Development. Baltimore: Johns Hopkins.
           Press.
Banks, Arthur S.
    1971   Cross-Polity Time Series Data. Cambridge: MIT Press.
Banks, Arthur S. and Textor, Robert B.
    1963   A Cross-Polity Survey. Cambridge: MIT Press.
Coleman, James S.
    1960   "The Political Systems of the Developing Areas." Pp. 532-576 in Gabriel
           Almond and James Coleman (eds.), The Politics of the Developing Areas.
           Princeton: Princeton University Press.

Feldberg, Roslyn L.
   1970   "Political Systems and the Role of the Military." Sociological Quarterly
          11 (Spring): 206-218.
Finer, Samuel E.
   1962   The Man on Horseback. New York: Praeger.
Finer, Samuel E.
   1970   Comparative Government. New York: Basic Books.
Finsterbusch, Kurt
   1973   "Recent Rank Ordering of Nations in Terms of Level and Rate of Develop-
          ment." Studies in Comparative International Development 8 (Spring): 52-70.
Fossum, Egil
   1967   "Factors Influencing the Occurrence of Military Coups d'Etat in Latin
          America." Journal of Peace Research 3: 228-251.
Hoadley, J. Stephen
   1973   "Social Complexity, Economic Development, and Military Coups d'Etat
          in Latin America and Asia." Journal of Peace Research 9:119-120.
Huntington, Samuel P.
   1964   The Soldier and the State. New York: Random House.
Janowitz, Morris
   1964   The Military in the Political Development of New Nations. Chicago: Uni-
          versity of Chicago Press.
Kaplan, Abraham
   1964   The Conduct of Inquiry. San Francisco: Chandler.
Needler, Martin C.
   1966   "Political Development and Military Intervention in Latin America."
          American Political Science Review 60 (September): 616-626.
Nordlinger, Eric A.
   1970   "Soldiers in Mufti: The Impact of Military Rule Upon Economic and
          Social Change in the Non-Western States." American Political Science
          Review 64 (December): 1131-1148.
Putnam, Robert D.
   1967   "Toward Explaining Military Intervention in Latin American Politics."
          World Politics 20 (October): 83-110.
Schmitter, Philippe G.
   1973   "Foreign Military Assistance, National Military Spending and Military
          Rule in Latin America." Pp. 117-188 in Philippe Schmitter (ed.), Military
          Rule in Latin America. Beverly Hills: Sage Publications.

16

MILITARY SIZE AND POLITICAL INTERVENTION

LEE SIGELMAN

Texas Tech University

This note analyzes the proposition, advanced by Edward Feit in The Armed Bureaucrats, that smaller armies are more likely than larger ones to intervene in the domestic political order in nations of the "third world." Several different tests of the hypothesis are attempted, but each turns up results that directly contradict Feit's proposition.

In his recent survey of the modernizing role of the military, Edward Feit (1973) offers a proposition which, if validated, would add a new dimension to our understanding of the factors underlying military intervention in nations of the "third world." Feit asserts that there is an *inverse* relationship between the size of a nation's military force and the extent to which the military intervenes in the domestic political order. That is, according to Feit, smaller armies are more likely than larger ones to intervene. Although this idea is by no means the central insight of Feit's far-ranging and authoritative work, it is interesting and novel enough to warrant the attention of scholars interested in intervention.

Three factors are said by Feit to promote this greater proclivity for intervention on the part of smaller militaries:

(1) Small size facilitates *communication* among different army units. It makes it easier for the vital linking ranks — those of field grade — to function as a body, to form interest groups and clubs, and to coordinate the movements of troops under their command.

(2) Partially as a result, smaller armies achieve a particular *mental set,* characterized by a sense of corporate identity, distrust, and concern with order both in the army and in the society as a whole.

(3) A small army can play only a limited role as an instrument of foreign policy. Thus, smaller armies are characterized by *goal displacement,* with the traditionally secondary role of the military — maintaining internal order — becoming the main concern of the small army (Feit, 1973:6-7).

To this point, no systematic investigation of the relationship between military size and intervention has been undertaken. Feit's own study focused on the role of the military in six nations (Argentina, Burma, Egypt, Greece, Pakistan, and Spain). On the basis of his intensive examination of these cases, Feit concluded that there was support for the small size-military intervention thesis, but warned that "complete acceptance" of the thesis would have to await further investigation (Feit, 1973:172). The purpose of this note is to provide just such an investigation.

A necessary preliminary to examining Feit's hypothesis is generating measures of military size and intervention:

Military Size. As suggested by Feit, we indexed military size by the Military Participation Ratio (MPR) — the proportion of the working-age population which is in the military. MPR data for 1965 are available for a broad cross-section of nations (Taylor and Hudson, 1972), whose scores range from highs of 17.7% in Switzerland and 16.4% in Israel to a low of 0.0% in several nations, including Costa Rica and Kuwait.[1]

Military Intervention. Elsewhere, we have criticized existing measures of intervention for their lack of sensitivity and validity, and have created a composite index of intervention in the 1960s which improves substantially on these measures (Sigelman, 1974). Percentile scores for 88 Latin American, African, Middle Eastern, and Asian nations were computed on each of five available intervention indicators (see Adelman and Morris (1967); Banks (1971); Banks and Textor (1963); Coleman (1960); and Finer (1970)); these scores were then combined into one overall mean percentile scale, called the Military Intervention Index (MII).[2]

FINDINGS

Are military size and intervention, thus measured, correlated significantly, and, as Feit suggests, in an inverse direction? Correlation of the MPR and the MII for the 88 nations produced a Kendall's tau value of $+.247$ ($p < .001$). So the two indices are significantly related — but, contrary to Feit's prediction, positively, not negatively. Nor, although the magnitude of the correlation fell, did the relationship become inverse when a control for geographic region was instituted (see Table 1).

However, testing the size-intervention relationship in this fashion overlooks an aspect of Feit's argument — the manner in which he deals with military size. Rather than conceiving of size, as tapped by the MPR, as an interval, or even an ordinal-level variable, Feit treats it as a simple dichotomy. An "arbitrary but reasonable standard for the size of a small army," according to Feit (1973:6), can be set at an MPR of less than 1%. On this basis, we reexamined the MPR-MII relationship over all 88 nations and for three of the four regions. (Not a single African nation had an MPR of 1% or above, so the hypothesis could not be tested there.) The results here (see Table 2) were quite similar to those obtained above. For the 88 nations, a difference, which barely failed to reach the .05

---

1. These data refer to military personnel actually on duty, including paramilitary forces where significant. Taylor and Hudson exclude reserve forces except in Switzerland. where the national militia includes all able-bodied males, and Israel, where reserves account for a high proportion of the readily-mobilized fighting force (Taylor and Hudson, 1972:20).

2. More detailed information on the operationalization of this variable can be found in Sigelman (1974). The five indicators which were combined to form the MPR are all "soft" or judgmentally-based measures. Any number of approaches to measuring intervention have been tried, including most frequently, counting the number of military coups over a certain time span. Here, however, the interest was in the military as a continuing political force rather than as an intermittent disrupter. Though each of the judgmental indices, taken individually, suffers from certain problems, the five measures in combination present a reasonably strong index of the continuing role of the military in politics.

TABLE 1.   THE RELATIONSHIP BETWEEN MILITARY
            SIZE AND INTERVENTION, BY REGION[a]

Nations	N	Correlation	P
Entire Sample	88	+.247	.001
Latin America	22	+.149	.166
Africa	36	+.075	.261
Middle East	12	+.199	.185
Asia	18	+.254	.070

[a]The coefficient is Kendall's tau, an ordinal measure of association.

significance level, in MII scores emerged between nations with smaller and larger militaries; but again, this difference was in the opposite direction from that predicted by Feit. Disaggregating the 88 nations by region produced differences which were less pronounced but which still ran directly counter to Feit's hypothesis.

Finally, having failed to verify Feit's hypothesis by these means, we tried still a third approach. As noted above, Feit himself suggested the MPR as a measure of military size, but it seems possible that an absolute measure of size may be more appropriate. On the basis of the MPR, India, for example, would be considered to have a small military (MPR = 0.37%); but given that India's military force totals one million men (by far the largest in the present analysis), are Feit's arguments about smallness — that it facilitates communication, encourages a particular mental set, and leads to goal displacement — really applicable to India? It seems entirely possible that Feit's hypothesis is correct, but that the empirical indicator he proposed to tap military size is not apt. With this in mind, we retested the hypothesis using the absolute size of a nation's military force (taken from Taylor and Hudson, 1972) rather than the MPR. But here, too, the results were contrary to Feit's prediction. For the 88 nations, the tau correlation between absolute military size and intervention was +.261 (p < .001), barely different from the result obtained using the MPR, and still positive. Again, too, controlling for region decreased the magnitude of the correlation, but failed to reverse the sign (see Table 3).

TABLE 2. DIFFERENCES IN MILITARY INTERVENTION FOR NATIONS WITH SMALL AND LARGE MILITARIES

Nations	MPR	N	Mean MII Score	Pooled Variance Estimate		
				t-value	d.f.	P (2-tailed)
Entire Sample	MPR<1%	70	47.29	1.95	86	.055
	MPR>1%	18	57.63			
Latin America	MPR<1%	19	56.94	0.40	20	.692
	MPR>1%	3	62.33			
Middle East	MPR<1%	4	44.13	1.28	10	.230
	MPR>1%	8	59.79			
Asia	MPR<1%	11	51.16	0.18	16	.858
	MPR>1%	7	53.14			

TABLE 3. THE RELATIONSHIP BETWEEN ABSOLUTE MILITARY SIZE AND INTERVENTION, BY REGION[a]

Nations	N	Correlation	P
Entire Sample	88	+.261	.001
Latin America	22	+.171	.133
Africa	36	+.151	.089
Middle East	12	+.092	.338
Asia	18	+.168	.165

[a]The coefficient is Kendall's tau, an ordinal measure of association.

CONCLUSIONS

The present study, even if it performed no other function, serves as a reminder of the danger involved in generalizing broadly on the basis of a few case studies. Feit tentatively accepted his military size — military intervention hypothesis on the basis of an intensive analysis of six cases. Without disputing the merits of the case study method, it ought to be obvious that hypotheses of broad applicability need to be tested broadly — across a wide array of polities.

Beyond this methodological caveat, however, the findings reported here have substantive implications as well. Samuel Huntington (1968:194) contends that "military explanations do not explain military interventions." In other words:

> The effort to answer the question, 'What characteristics of the military establishment of a new nation facilitate its involvement in domestic pollitics?' is misdirected because the most important causes of military intervention in politics are not military but political and reflect . . . the political and institutional structure of society (Huntington, 1986:194).

Much the same point — that "Weak governments, not strong armies, account for the prevalence of military coups" — is made by Dankwart Rustow (1967:176). Of course, this contention is far broader than any conclusion which could emerge from the present study. It is possible that military dimensions which are not examined here, e.g., internal structure, technological sophistication, or class composition, might prove to be closely related to patterns of intervention. It can be said, however, that this study casts grave doubt on the validity of one particular military explanation of intervention: clearly, there is *not* an inverse relationship between military size and intervention.

REFERENCES

Adelman, Irma and Morris, Cynthia Taft
  1967 Society, Politics, and Economic Development. Baltimore: Johns Hopkins Press.
Banks, Arthur S.
  1971 Cross-Polity Time Series Data. Cambridge: MIT Press.
Banks, Arthur S. and Textor, Robert B.
  1963 A Cross-Polity Survey. Cambridge: MIT Press.
Coleman, James S.
  1960 "The Political Systems of the Developing Areas." Pp. 532-576 in Gabriel Almond and James Coleman (eds.), The Politics of the Developing Areas. Princeton: Princeton University Press.
Feit, Edward
  1973 The Armed Bureaucrats. Boston: Houghton Mifflin.
Finer, Samuel E.
  1970 Comparative Government. New York: Basic Books.
Huntington, Samuel P.
  1968 Political Order in Changing Societies. New Haven: Yale University Press.
Rustow, Dankwart A.
  1967 A World of Nations. Washington, D.C.: Brookings Institution.
Sigelman, Lee
  1974 "Military Intervention: A Methodological Note." Journal of Political and Military Sociology 2 (Fall): 275-281.
Taylor, Charles L. and Hudson, Michael
  1972 World Handbook of Political and Social Indicators, 2d ed. New Haven: Yale University Press.

17

MILITARY INTERVENTION
IN SEARCH OF A DEPENDENT VARIABLE*

R. NEAL TANNAHILL

Rice University

This note is an examination of one of the more unwieldy problems facing researchers studying military intervention into domestic political processes—the operationalization of a dependent variable. The author briefly notes and criticizes some of the more frequently employed indicators of military intervention. Then, he outlines a new operationalization of military intervention. Finally, he presents an example of the application of the new variable in the context of military intervention in South America.

One of the major problems facing researchers studying military role and rule is that of finding a satisfactory indicator of domestic military intervention. There are a considerable number of indices and typologies in the literature (Sigelman, 1974), but here, we will note only some of the better known and more frequently used of these. Putnam (1963) has developed an index ranging numerically from zero to three and conceptually from the apolitical military to the ruling military. Needler (1963) offers a classification scheme whose six categories range from no military involvement to open military rule. Banks and Textor (1968), Finer (1962), and Adelman and Morris (1967) present typologies of three, four, and eight categories respectively. Finally, in their collection of events data indicators, Taylor and Hudson (1972) include an "irregular power transfer" event which, they say, is "close conceptually to what are conventionally thought of as *coups d'etat*" (Taylor and Hudson, 1972:86).

A number of criticisms can be raised against these and other measures of military intervention. First, as Sigelman (1974) argues, these measures lack sensitivity. Scales with few categories mean that levels of intervention that are intuitively distinct must be placed in the same grouping. Also, the lack of variance is a liability in statistical analysis. Sigelman's solution to this and other problems which he notes is to create a composite intervention measure derived by combining five indicators.[1] This ingenious tactic handles the problem of sensitivity, but does little for the researcher who wishes to work with a time period or universe not already coded in terms of the five indicators.[2]

*I wish to express my appreciation to John S. Ambler, John Deegan, Jr., Robert H. Dix, Michael A. Freney, and Fred R. von der Mehden for their kind assistance with this paper. Its faults, of course, remain my own.

1. Those of Adelman and Morris (1967), Banks and Textor (1968), Banks (1971), Finer (1962), and Coleman (1960).

2. It apparently can also be faulted on the basis of points three and four below.

Secondly, all of the scales to a greater or lesser degree have a judgmental quality to them. In the best of all possible worlds, this should be eliminated; with a variable such as military intervention, however, a degree of subjectivity seems inevitable. Nevertheless, the minimization of subjectivity is a desirable goal.

Thirdly, many of the scales are based on broad time spans sometimes as great as five years. Consequently, they do not lend themselves to use by researchers using longitudinal analysis who wish to code their data on a yearly basis.

Fourthly, the indices fail to recognize that there are two aspects to the political phenomenon known as military intervention. The first of these is the actual, overt intervention of the armed forces into the political arena resulting in the overthrow and replacement of the incumbent regime— the *coup d'etat*. The second aspect of military intervention involves the scope and degree of military participation in the political system. Does the military actually govern? Does it enjoy veto power in certain policy areas? or, Does it refrain from acting as more than a pressure group in governmental policies directly affecting the military? The indicators of military intervention most frequently used by social scientists invariably overlook this distinction between the *event* of intervention and intervention as a *continuing process*. The measure of Taylor and Hudson (1972) accounts for the event only. Those of Finer (1962), Banks and Textor (1968), Needler (1963), Adelman and Morris (1967), and Putnam (1963) focus primarily on the continuing process. Since researchers deal with military intervention both as an event and as a continuing process, it is first necessary to operationalize each of these separately. At the same time, however, researchers wish to deal with military intervention in a broader sense combining these two aspects. Thus, a third problem is to operationalize the underlying concept taking account of both the event and the process of intervention. It is to these tasks that we now turn.

MILITARY INTERVENTION AS AN EVENT

The simplest but probably least useful method of classifying the event of intervention is the dichotomous variable of "coup" or "no coup." There are statistical techniques which are applicable to the dichotomous dependent variable (Finney, 1971), but the limitations of a dependent variable with such minimal variance are well-known.

The researcher need not and cannot be content, however, with such an elementary classification. In every case, he has more imformation than just whether or not a military coup has taken place and he can use that information to create a typology of coups which can be employed as an ordinal scale ranking the degree of, or severity of, military intervention. This can be done by asking two questions: (1) Against whom is the coup carried out?, and (2) What type of government is established by the coup? A coup may be staged against three types of regime—the civilian-led government chosen through civilian processes, the civilian-led government established by prior military action, or a military regime. Two types of results may follow a coup—the establishment of a civilian-led government or the investiture of a military regime. Table 1 graphically presents the six possible classifications along with a rank-ordering rating the coups as to degree or severity of military intervention based on the two dimensions of the table—the type of government displaced, and the type of government established by the coup.

TABLE 1. COUP CLASSIFICATION

Coup against whom?	Coup establishes what?	
	Civilian Government	Military Government
Military government	1	2
Civilian government established by military	3	4
Civilian government	5	6

On the first dimension, the most severe form of intervention is that against a civilian regime established through constitutional processes. This is a direct violation of the norms of civilian rule and requires a significant psychological step by military leaders. Although still a coup, intervention against a civilian regime previously established by military action requires much less of a step because the norms of civilian rule have already been transgressed. What the military has created the military can undo. Finally, a coup against a military regime is classified as the least violative of the norms of civilian rule. The second dimension considers the type of government established by the coup. Clearly, a coup resulting in a military junta involves a greater degree of intervention than one establishing a civilian regime.

Now, having justified the ordinality within the dimensions, how is their combination in Table 1 justified? Why is precedence given to the dimension that ranks coups according to whom they are against? Can one not argue that a coup resulting in or maintaining a military government should always be regarded as a more severe form of intervention than the coup that establishes a civilian government regardless of the type of government displaced? Although this may be true concerning the *continuing process* of intervention, it is not true regarding military intervention as an *event*. In this aspect, the determining dimension of severity is the type of regime against which the coup is enacted. Irrespective of the results of the coup, intervention as an *act*, as an *event*, represents as bolder step on the part of the military when taken against a constitutional civilian regime than against a civilian regime formerly installed by military action or a military government. The type of regime resulting from the coup must be regarded as secondary in regards to intervention *as an event*. Thus, we have an ordinal ranking of coups ranging from zero (no coup) to six.[3]

MILITARY INTERVENTION AS A CONTINUING PROCESS

If one desires to explore the other aspect of military intervention, the continuing process of the military's influence in the political system, another

---

3. If he so desired, the researcher on theoretical grounds could convert this ordinal scale into an interval scale following the suggestions offered by Abelson and Tukey (1970). Spearman's rs and Kendall's tau are tests of association suitable for ordinal data (Buchanan, 1974).

index is required. A classification of coups tells nothing about the military's role in years in which no coup occurs and the simple summation of coups occurring over an extended period of time is far from enlightening.

The literature contains a number of typologies which could be useful in constructing an index,[4] but because of its relative sensitivity and simple logic of classification, the decision here is to construct a scale based upon a typology offered by John Lovell (1970). Borrowing from Janowitz (1964), Lovell makes a distinction between three levels of intensity or degree of military influence. In the first of these, the military wield minimal political influence. At the second level, the military are influential but not the ruling group. Finally, at the highest level of influence, the military rule. To Janowitz's ranking of *degree* or *intensity* of influence, Lovell adds a second dimension—scope of influence. Thus, Lovell argues, a distinction can be made between a military which *are* the ruling elite (Burma after the 1962 coup) and one which shares meaningful participation with civilian elites (Korea since 1963); between a military which is somewhat influential, but generally apolitical (Burma before the 1958 coup) and one which is clearly a key political group although not the only political group (Burma 1960-1962); and between a military whose function is essentially symbolic (Ethiopia in the 1920s and 1930s) and one whose influence has expanded (Ethiopia in the 1940s) (Lovell, 1970:4-7).[5]

Table 2 presents Lovell's paradigm along with a rank ordering from least to greatest influence. Clearly, the lowest ranking should be given to what Lovell calls the "palace guard." Although perhaps not apolitical in the strictest sense of the word, the political influence of the military in this case is relatively low and limited to matters directly related to the military itself. The next highest ranking is assigned to Lovell's "praetorian army." Here, also, the degree of the military's influence in policy-making is low, but broader than that of the palace guard perhaps extending to matters usually considered police matters or matters of national development. At the third level is the

TABLE 2.   LOVELL CLASSIFICATION

Degree of Influence	Scope of Influence	
	Relatively extensive	Relatively limited
High	Ruling elite 6	Ruling coalition 5
Medium	Predominant political bloc 4	Competitive political bloc 3
Low	Praetorian army 2	Palace guard 1

4. Some of which are cited above.
5. The examples are his.

"competitive political bloc." The military in this case is one of the chief *political* forces in the nation, but not *the* chief political power. Other forces exist (the Church, parties, unions, etc.) limiting its political influence. At the next level, the military is the "predominant political bloc," overshadowing the interests which act to check the military playing the role of competitive political bloc. At the next level is the "ruling coalition" in which the military actually share in the decision-making process with other groups. Finally, at the highest level is the military as "ruling elite." Thus, this typology provides the researcher with an ordinal level dependent variable of military intervention as a process.[6]

MILITARY INTERVENTION

The Underlying Concept. Having dealt with the separate aspects of military intervention, we now turn to the problem of integrating these into a single scale. Broadly speaking the *coup d'etat* and the ubiquitous Pentagon lobbying for a higher defense budget are both forms of military intervention and can be conceived as the ends of a long continuum. To get at this underlying phenomenon it is necessary to create a composite index reflecting both the event and the process of intervention. To accomplish this, the two indices of the

TABLE 3.   COMPOSITE MI INDEX

Is there a coup?   No.

Degree of influence	Scope of influence	
	extensive	limited
high	7	5
medium	4	3
low	2	1

Is there a coup?   Yes.

Against whom?	Establishes what?	
	Civilian government	Military government
Military gov.	6	8
Civ. gov. estab. by military	9	10
Civilian gov.	11	12

6. Again, the researcher may employ Abelson and Tukey's method (1970) to convert this into an interval scale. Additionally, if other data are available such as the number of military personnel in the cabinet and the bureaucracy or the percent of the budget allocated for defense, and there are theoretical justifications, the researcher may use this classification as a base and supplement it with his other information.

separate aspects are combined into a single scale by asking a single question: does a coup occur in the time period or not? If the answer is no, one scores the observation according to the Lovell classification; if yes, according to the rankings for *coups d'etat.*

In Table 3 the composite index of military intervention is presented. With one notable exception, time periods containing coups are ranked higher than time periods without coups. This is because the coup by its very nature is the most extreme expression of the political power of the military. The sole exception is that of a coup against a military regime establishing a civilian government. Since this is a reflection of an apparent withdrawal of the military from the political arena (at least to a degree), it is ranked below the case of a military maintaining itself (i.e., no coup) as the ruling elite.[7]

An Application. The true test of any classification scheme or index, of course, is how well it works in practice. Can it be applied in actual research? Does it discriminate among cases? Is it overly judgmental? In our research, we have been using the above approach in an empirical examination of military intervention in South America from 1948 to 1967. Thus, it was necessary for us to assign scores to the dependent variable for each of the twenty years in the time period (a universe of 200 nation-years).

Table 4 presents the correlations among the indicators of the event of military intervention—the coup, the indicator of the continuing process of involvement based on Lovell's typology, the composite index (MI), the index developed by Putnam (1963),[8] and another rough indicator of intervention—the proportion of cabinet members who are listed in *Chiefs of State and Cabinet*

TABLE 4. CORRELATIONS

	1	2	3	4	5
1	1.0				
2	.3	1.0			
3	.8	.8	1.0		
4	.28	.89	.72	1.0	
5	.02	.54	.32	.46	1.0

```
1 = Coup classification
2 = Lovell classification
3 = Composite MI index
4 = Putnam classification
5 = Proportion military in the cabinet
```

7. Once again, the researcher may wish to adopt Abelson and Tukey's suggestions (1970).

8. Since Putnam's index only covers the period 1956-1965, it was necessary to complete the data matrix by coding the years 1948-1955 and 1966-1967 for each country using his method.

Ministers of the American Republics with military titles.[9] Of the five indicators, Putnam, Lovell, and the proportion of military men in the cabinet are all measures of the continuing process of intervention. We would expect them to intercorrelate rather highly, and they do. The coup index, however, is a measure of the other aspect of intervention, the event. Our expectation, then, is that it would not correlate well with the three measures of involvement. Again, our expectation is fulfilled. The combined index of military intervention is designed to reflect both aspects; so, we would hope that it would correlate well with measures of both of these aspects of military intervention. It does. Consequently, we feel some justification for its use.

This still leaves unanswered, however, the question of the actual coding process. To illustrate the application of this approach, we will examine the year-by-year codings for Brazil, a country which experienced overt military intervention twice from 1948 to 1967, and Uruguay, a country which witnessed no coups in the period. Table 5 presents the data for Brazil for each of the five indicators whose correlations are presented in Table 4 above. The coup

TABLE 5.   INDEX CODINGS FOR BRAZIL

Year	Putnam	Coup	Lovell	MI	Military in cabinet
1948	2	0	4	4	4/11
1949	2	0	4	4	4/11
1950	2	0	4	4	4/11
1951	2	0	4	4	4/11
1952	2	0	4	4	3/11
1953	2	0	4	4	3/11
1954	2	5	4	11	3/12
1955	2	0	4	4	3/12
1956	2	0	4	4	3/11
1957	2	0	4	4	4/12
1958	2	0	4	4	4/12
1959	2	0	4	4	4/12
1960	2	0	4	4	4/12
1961	2	0	4	4	3/14
1962	2	0	4	4	3/13
1963	2	0	4	4	3/13
1964	3	6	6	12	5/13
1965	3	0	6	7	5/16
1966	3	0	6	7	6/16
1967	3	0	6	7	6/18

9. This is a possible indicator whose advantages have not been explored. In our research, we have experimented with it, but the results have been mixed. Standing alone, we are inclined at this point to believe that the proportion of cabinet posts held by military men is not as useful an indicator of military intervention as some of the more "judgmentally-based" measures. There is the possibility, however, that combined with other indicators this measure may prove highly useful to social scientists.

classification is relatively straightforward. In 1954, the Brazilian military intervened against a constitutional civilian regime allowing another group of civilians to attain power; thus, it was coded with a 5. In 1964, however, the armed forces ousted the constitutionally elected civilian regime of Goulart, assuming power themselves. Thus, the coding of 6 for that year. The coding for the continuing process index (Lovell) is also relatively simple. The coding of 4 for each year from 1948 to 1963 reflects the view of Brazilian specialists regarding the preeminent role of the military during that period (Stepan, 1971; Roett, 1972; Schmitter, 1971). From 1964 to the end of the period, the military ruled and thus a score of 6 was recorded. The combined intervention index shows a continued high level of intervention with peaks occurring in years of coups and then a leveling off at a higher plain after the 1964 take-over.

Table 6 presents similar data for Uruguay. There were no coups in the period; so, the composite index is the same as the Lovell measure. The early years of the period were years of minimal military involvement in domestic politics. In 1958, however, the ranking was raised from "palace guard" (1) to "praetorian army" (2) because in this year Uruguay saw the use of the military to control student strikes and riots at the National University in Montevideo, an action which previously had been contrary to Uruguayan practice. In 1963, the level of military involvement was upped to that of "competitive political bloc" (3). In February and March, troops were called out to operate electric

TABLE 6. INDEX CODINGS FOR URUGUAY

Year	Putnam	Coup	Lovell	MI	Military in cabinet
1948	0	0	1	1	0/9
1949	0	0	1	1	0/9
1950	0	0	1	1	0/9
1951	0	0	1	1	0/9
1952	0	0	1	1	0/9
1953	0	0	1	1	0/9
1954	0	0	1	1	0/9
1955	0	0	1	1	1/9
1956	0	0	1	1	1/9
1957	0	0	1	1	0/9
1958	0	0	2	2	0/9
1959	0	0	2	2	2/9
1960	0	0	2	2	2/9
1961	0	0	2	2	2/9
1962	0	0	2	2	2/9
1963	0	0	3	3	1/9
1964	0	0	3	3	1/9
1965	0	0	3	3	1/9
1966	1	0	3	3	1/9
1967	1	0	3	3	1/14

power stations and telephone centrals during a strike. Later in the year, the country was flooded with rumors about military unrest and the possibility of a coup—something unheard of a decade before (Taylor, 1960; Weil et al, 1971).[10] Undeniably, not all of the criticisms raised by Sigelman (1974) or in this paper (above) are fully satisfied by this approach. Ideally, one would hope for more variance in the indices and a coding system eliminating judgmental decisions. Nevertheless, this approach does meet (to a degree, at least) many of the criticisms. Consequently, we feel it will be of use in empirical analysis of military intervention.[11]

REFERENCES

Abelson, Robert P. and Tukey, John W.
1970   "Efficient Conversion of Non-Metric Information into Metric Information." Pp. 407-417 in Edward Tufte (ed.), The Quantitative Analysis of Social Problems. Reading: Addison-Wesley.

Adelman, Irma and Morris, Cynthia Taft
1967   Society, Politics, and Economic Development. Baltimore: Johns Hopkins Press.

Banks, Arthur S.
1971   Cross-Polity Time Series Data. Cambridge, Mass.: MIT Press.

Banks, Arthur S. and Textor, Robert B.
1968   A Cross-Polity Survey. Cambridge, Mass.: MIT Press.

Buchanan, William
1974   "Nominal and Ordinal Bivariate Statistics: The Practitioner's View." American Journal of Political Science 28 (August):625-646.

Coleman, James S.
1960   "The Political Systems of the Developing Areas." Pp. 532-576 in Gabriel Almond and James Coleman (eds.), The Politics of the Developing Areas. Princeton: Princeton University Press.

Finer, Samuel E.
1962   The Man on Horseback. New York: Praeger.

Finney, D.J.
1971   Probit Analysis. 3rd ed. Cambridge, Eng.: University Press.

Janowitz, Morris
1964   The Military in the Political Development of New Nations. Chicago: University of Chicago Press.

Lovell, John P.
1970   "An Introductory Essay." Pp. 1-14 in John P. Lovell (ed.), The Military and Politics in Five Developing Nations. Kesington, Md.: Center for Research in Social Systems.

Needler, Martin
1963   Latin American Politics in Perspective. Princeton, N.J.: Van Nostrand.

Putnam, Robert D.
1963   "Toward Explaining Military Intervention in Latin American Politics." World Politics 20 (October):83-110.

Roett, Riordan
1972   Brazil: Politics in a Patrimonial Society. Boston: Allyn and Bacon.

Schmitter, Phillippe C.
1971   Interest Conflict and Political Change in Brazil. Stanford, Calif.: Stanford University Press.

---

10. In addition to books by area specialists on each country, a number of year books were consulted in the coding process: The New International Yearbook, The Americana Book of the Year, Collier's Yearbook, and Britannica Book of the Year.

11. We would suggest that researchers using military intervention as a dependent variable seriously consider subsetting the data as to regime type or employing a dummy variable. Hypothetically, at least, those factors leading to intervention against a civilian regime may not be the same factors that would sustain the military once in power. Indeed, the opposite could be the case.

Sigelman, Lee
    1974   "Military Intervention: A Methodological Note." Journal of Political and Military
              Sociology 2(Fall):275-281.
Stepan, Alfred
    1971   The Military in Politics: Changing Patterns in Brazil. Princeton: Princeton
              University Press.
Taylor, Charles L. and Hudson, Michael C.
    1972   World Handbook of Political and Social Indicators. New Haven: Yale University
              Press.
Taylor, Philip B.
    1960   Government and Politics in Uruguay. New Orleans: Tulane University Press.
Weil, Thomas E. et al.
    1971   Area Handbook for Uruguay. Washington, D.C.: U.S. Government Printing Office.

The Contributors

GABRIEL BEN-DOR is Senior Lecturer in Political Science and Director of the Institute of Middle Eastern Studies at the University of Haifa. Recent publications include a book on the Druze minority in Israel and a book on political participation in Turkey (co-editor and co-author), as well as articles on military regimes, political culture, political corruption and political culture in the Middle East. Present research interests include selected aspects of the Arab-Israeli conflict, inter-Arab relations, and the politics and strategy of terrorism.

JOHN D. BLAIR is Assistant Professor of Sociology at the University of Maryland. He recently received his Ph.D. from the University of Michigan.

WILLIAM C. COCKERHAM is Assistant Professor of Sociology and Basic Medical Sciences at the University of Illinois at Urbana-Champaign. He is author of a forthcoming book entitled *Introduction to Medical Sociology.* Recent publications include articles in *Pacific Sociological Review, Journal of Studies on Alcohol, International Journal of the Addictions* and *Sociology of Education.* Current research are in the area of the sociology of mental illness.

BETTY A. DOBRATZ is assistant editor of the *Journal of Political and Military Sociology* and a Ph.D. candidate at the University of Wisconsin, Madison where she has been a social organization trainee in the program sponsored by the National Institute of Mental Health. She has co-authored three articles and a monograph with Dr. Kourvetaris. Her current research interests include ethnic minorities, stratification, election turnout and voting patterns.

BRUCE R. DRURY is Assistant Professor of Government at Lamar University. His research interests include Brazilian politics, civil-military relations, and political corruption. He is currently conducting research on correlates of military rule in South America and the political power of the Italian military.

MAURICE A. GARNIER is Assistant Professor of Sociology at Indiana University. He has recently published a series of articles dealing with a number of aspects of the socialization of British officers. He is presently engaged in an investigation of occupational mobility partially funded by a grant from the National Science Foundation.

DALE R. HERSPRING received his Ph.D. from the University of Southern California and is a Foreign Service Officer with the Department of State. He is the author of *East German Civil-Military Relations: The Impact of Technology, 1949-1972* and several articles dealing with Polish and East German civil-military relations. He is currently working with Ivan Volgyes on a study of the military as agent of political socialization in Eastern Europe.

GEORGE A. KOURVETARIS is Associate Professor of Sociology at Northern Illinois University. He has published numerous articles on the Greek military including ones on professional self-images and political perspectives in the *American Sociological Review* (1971) and recruitment and change in Greek academies in *The Military and the Problem of Legitimacy* (1976). He has written a book on Greek-Americans in Chicago and co-authored a monograph on social origins and politics of various officer corps. He is the founder and editor of the *Journal of Political and Military Sociology* and serves on the editoral boards of half a dozen other journals. His current research interests are on stratification, ethnicity, political conflict, and American foreign policy.

KURT LANG is Professor of Sociology at the S.U.N.Y., Stony Brook. His major publications include *Military Institutions and the Sociology of War* (Sage Publications 1972), *Politics and Television* (co-author, Quadrangle, 1968) and *Collective Dynamics* (co-author, Crowell, 1961). He is currently involved on a computerized bibliography on research on military organization; mass media and politics; and cohort succession within an academic setting.

ARTHUR D. LARSON is a member of the faculty at the University of Wisconsin-Parkside. He was formerly on the faculty of the Departments of Government and Politics at the University of Maryland, and prior to that he was a legislative assistant to Senator Gaylord Nelson. He is the editor of *Civil-Military Relations and Militarism: A Bibliography* and *National Security Affairs: A Guide to Information Sources*. Currently he is a book review editor for the *Journal of Political and Military Sociology*.

W. LUCAS is with Rand Corporation's Washington Domestic Program Center. He is currently directing a social experiment testing new applications of two-way cable television and studying the effects of television news on community knowledge and awareness. His work in civil-military relations has concentrated on the role of military professionalism and on the organization and process of defense policy-making in his *The Organizational Politics of Defense.* (International Studies Association, 1974) with Raymond H. Dawson.

ROBERTA E. McKOWN is Associate Professor and Chairman of the Department of Political Science at the University of Alberta. Current research interests include studies of Economic Nationalism in Black Africa, and Multiculturalism and Political Institutional forms in Black Africa. Recent publications are "Nationalism in Africa: Measurements and Correlates in Ghana and Nigeria," in the *Canadian Review of Studies in Nationalism* and "Ghana's Status Systems," in *Journal of Asian and African Studies.*

FRANK NEWPORT is Assistant Professor of Sociology at the University of Missouri in St. Louis. He obtained his Ph.D. in Sociology from the University of Michigan. His current research interests center around issues related to inequalities in societies, including particularly individual preceptions of distributive justice.

DAVID R. SEGAL is Professor of Sociology and of Government and Politics at the University of Maryland. He is a member of the Executive Council of the Inter-University Seminar on Armed Forces and Society, a member of the editorial board of the *Journal of Political and Military Sociology,* and co-chairman of the Working Group on Human Resource Management of the Military Operations Research Society. His current research deals with the social organization of the volunteer army.

LEE SIGELMAN is Associate Professor of Political Science at Texas Tech University. Professor Sigelman, who holds the Ph.D. degree from Vanderbilt University, is the author of numerous articles concerning comparative politics and administration, having contributed articles to such journals as the *American Political Science Review,* the *Journal of Developing Areas,* and *Comparative Political Studies.* His current research focuses on the linkage between war and public opinion.

SUSAN A. STEPHENS is currently Assistant Professor of Sociology at Indiana University and Training Director, Indianapolis Area Project. She is engaged in research on determinants of conceptions of urban space and participation in neighborhoods.

R. NEAL TANNAHILL is a recent Ph.D. in Political Science from Rice University. He has published articles on military intervention and the comparative performance of military and civilian governments. His current research interests also include the comparative study of communism in Western Europe.

WILLIAM R. THOMPSON is Associate Professor of Government and Director of Graduate Studies. He is author of *The Grievances of Military Coup-Makers* (Beverly Hills: Sage, 1973) and articles in *Journal of Peace Research, International Studies Quarterly, Journal of Political and Military Sociology, Comparative Political Studies, Journal of Conflict Resolution,* and *Comparative Politics.* His current research interests include further work on the military in politics; great power summitry behavior; regional, subsystemic structure; and war, alliance, and interaction processes.

INDEX